Classical Japanese Reader and
Essential Dictionary

Classical Japanese Reader and Essential Dictionary

Haruo Shirane

Columbia University Press
New York

Columbia University Press wishes to express its appreciation for assistance given by the Japan Foundation Japanese-Language Institute, Urawa, toward the cost of publishing this book.

Columbia University Press
Publishers Since 1893
New York   Chichester, West Sussex

Library of Congress Cataloging-in-Publication Data
Shirane, Haruo
    Classical Japanese reader and essential dictionary / Haruo Shirane.
        p. cm.
    ISBN 978-0-231-13990-8 (cloth: alk. paper)
    ISBN 978-0-231-50945-9 (electronic)
    1. Japanese language—Readers—Japanese literature.   2. Japanese language—Grammar, Classical.
    3. Japanese language—Dictionaries.   I. Title.
    PL537.S555 2007
    495.6'82421—dc22   2006023247

Columbia University Press books are printed on permanent and durable acid-free paper.
Printed in the United States of America

Frontispiece: From Namura Jōhaku, *Onna chōhōki* (*Record of Important Treasures for Women*)
This page from the *Onna chōhōki*, an extremely popular educational and encyclopedic guide for women first published in Genroku 5 (1692) by Namura Jōhaku (1674–1748), illustrates some of the pursuits that the author considered appropriate for women: (*clockwise from top*) practicing calligraphy, cutting fabric and sewing clothing, spinning thread, weaving, playing the *koto*, and reading books. The preceding text notes that women should read "*The Tale of Genji*, *The Tales of Ise*, the *Hyakunin isshu*, the *Kokinshū*, and the *Man'yōshū*." (By permission of Nakajima Takashi)

Composition by Komiyama Printing, Tokyo

Contents

Part IV   Edo/Tokugawa Period

Part V   Meiji Period

Part VI   Nara Period

Preface

Classical Japanese—*kobun* or *bungo*, as it is referred to in modern Japanese—is one of the principal keys to understanding Japanese culture and literature. All forms of writing from the seventh century through World War II are based on classical Japanese, and it continues to be an important part of the Japanese language, especially in proverbs, *haiku*, *tanka*, and grammatical forms like *beshi*. Accordingly, classical Japanese is an indispensable tool for those studying Japanese history, literature, religion, art history, and culture through the Meiji period. Equally important, classical Japanese provides an invaluable background to modern Japanese, offering clues to how it is constructed and used and how it acquired its current forms. Because students learn classical Japanese structurally, based on its grammar, they learn the structure of the language better than they would through the proficiency-based approach to modern Japanese that emphasizes speaking.

Together with *Classical Japanese: A Grammar* (Columbia University Press, 2005), the *Classical Japanese Reader and Essential Dictionary* is designed to provide immediate access to the language. The *Classical Japanese Reader and Essential Dictionary* has two parts, texts and a dictionary of essential vocabulary. I chose and edited the texts both to provide a practical and efficient means of acquiring the language and to give readers a historical overview of the language from the Nara through the Meiji periods. Each of the texts is accompanied by a short introduction, a vocabulary list, grammar notes, and a grammatical annotation. Readers should be able to read most of the text using only the vocabulary and grammar notes, and the grammatical annotation should answer most of their grammatical questions. The grammatical terms used here are those found in *Classical Japanese: A Grammar*, which provides extensive explanations of auxiliary verbs, particles, and other grammatical forms.

The "Essential Dictionary" is a classical Japanese–English dictionary of the vocabulary found in the texts supplemented by vocabulary essential to the mastery of classical Japanese and providing a base from which to read almost any text from the Heian through the Meiji period. In contrast to the individual vocabulary lists, which provide only the meaning of the word as used in the text at hand, the "Essential Dictionary" provides multiple definitions and alternative characters (*kanji*) for each word and indicates its textual source. Important high-frequency words are in capital letters. Most of the words that do not appear in the individual vocabulary lists can be found in the "Essential Dictionary." Also, for practical purposes, the "Essential Dictionary" does not list most Nara-period vocabulary. In short, the "Essential Dictionary" is a useful reference for both beginners and advanced readers. Most important, the vocabulary lists, grammar notes, and the "Essential Dictionary" lessen the readers' dependence on modern Japanese to learn classical Japanese.

The texts in the *Classical Japanese Reader* are divided into two types: the base texts (*An Account of a Ten-foot-square Hut* and *The Tale of the Bamboo Cutter*), which are relatively long, and short selections arranged by historical period (Heian, Kamakura, Edo/Tokugawa, and Meiji). The last part contains poems from the *Collection of Ten Thousand Leaves*, dating from the Nara period. Although this period predates the Heian period, its selections come last because they are more difficult to read.

An Account of a Ten-foot-square Hut was chosen as the opening base text because it contains almost every fundamental grammatical construction in classical Japanese in a style that is relatively easy to understand. The other base text, *The Tale of the Bamboo Cutter*, was selected because it also is an excellent introduction to classical grammar as well as to honorific forms, which almost never appear in *An Account of a Ten-foot-square Hut*.

The short selections in parts II through VI can be read in one to three sessions and are intended to be modular, giving the reader or teacher maximum flexibility and choice and drawing on major texts. Those who are looking for an entry-level text without honorifics are advised to start with "Rashōmon," from the *Collection of Tales of Times Now Past*. Those looking for practice with honorific forms should go to "Young Lavender" in *The Tale of Genji* and *Sarashina Diary*. Most of the texts from the Kamakura period (*Collection of Tales of Times Now Past*, *Collection of Tales from Uji*, and *Essays in Idleness*) center on anecdotes, or *setsuwa*, which are short, entertaining, and readily accessible and also were used by modern writers like Akutagawa Ryūnosuke. The selection from *The Tales of the Heike*, which is representative of the emergent samurai culture in the Kamakura period, shows how the new vernacular was incorporated into classical prose. The selections from the Edo/Tokugawa period—a noted travel diary, a famous description of urban merchant thinking, part of a gothic tale, and a literary essay—offer readers an opportunity to see the transition from classical to modern Japanese. The selection from a Meiji-period educational treatise, Fukuzawa Yukichi's *Encouragement of Learning*, reinforces the point that classical Japanese remains essential to reading both literary and nonliterary texts in the modern period. Classical poetry (*waka*), the most important premodern literary genre, is also a good way of learning classical Japanese, since it is short and does not use honorifics. For that reason, poems from *Hundred Poets, Hundred Poems*, still a popular New Year's game, have been included. The poems from the *Collection of Ten Thousand Leaves* should be read along with the Nara-period chapter in *Classical Japanese: A Grammar*.

Students are urged to study at least part I (introduction and inflected forms) of the *Grammar* before beginning the *Reader* and to use the index to the *Grammar*, which provides a more detailed and systematic explanation of grammar forms. Like the *Grammar*, the *Reader* has been designed to be accessible to students with only a minimal background in modern Japanese.

Almost all the texts (except for *Hundred Poets, Hundred Poems* and *Encouragement of Learning*) are based on the Nihon koten bungaku taikei series published by Iwanami Shoten. Although orthographic changes (including the changing of old *kanji*, or characters, to new characters) have been made, and *furigana* readings have been added to the *kanji* to improve accessibility to readers of modern Japanese, the original grammar has not been altered.

Acknowledgments

This book would not have come to fruition without the assistance of a number of friends, students, and colleagues over a number of years. Anne Commons, Torquil Duthie, Jamie Newhard, and Steven Wills did extensive work on the early drafts and provided feedback. My thanks to Sonja Arntzen, Paul Warnick, Timothy Wixted, and Paul Atkins for testing earlier versions of the manuscript. Jenny Guest, David Atherton, Saeko Shibayama, Chie Nozaki, Song Lee, Noriko Kanahara, Machiko Midorikawa, Hiromi Noguchi, and Winifred Olsen were invaluable assistants at various stages. I am especially grateful to Okuda Isao and Okuda Misao for carefully checking the manuscript at the final stages and to Lewis Cook for extensive and invaluable assistance on the "Essential Dictionary." The Shirato Fund for Japanese Language Study and the Nitta Publications Fund provided generous assistance. Thanks to Jennifer Crewe and Irene Pavitt at Columbia University Press for making this book possible. Finally, I would be remiss in not mentioning Tomi Suzuki, who has been a constant source of support and encouragement.

Elements of the Book

Major Historical Periods

Nara	710–784	奈良
Heian	794–1185	平安
Kamakura	1185–1333	鎌倉
Northern and Southern Courts	1336–1392	南北朝
Muromachi	1392–1573	室町
Warring States	1477–1573	戦国
Edo/Tokugawa	1600–1867	江戸, 徳川
Meiji	1868–1912	明治

Romanization

The texts in classical Japanese in this book follow the standard historical *kana* usage (*rekishiteki kanazukai*), and the romanization uses the modern Hepburn system. That is, *h*-stem syllables like *ha*, *hi*, *hu*, *he*, and *ho* become *a*, *i*, *u*, *e*, and *o*, respectively, except when they begin a word, like *hi* (sun, day), in which case they keep their *h*. When *ha* comes in the middle of a sentence, it becomes *wa*, as in *owasu*. The subject marker case particle *ha* is romanized as *wa*. *W*-stem words like *wa*, *wi*, and *wo* are romanized as *a*, *i*, and *o*, respectively. Thus, *wotoko* (をとこ, man) becomes *otoko*; *wonna* (をんな, woman) becomes *onna*; and *mawiru* (まゐる, to go) becomes *mairu*.

The characters in the following list show the text as it appears in the original texts, with the *furigana* representing the historical *kana* usage. The right column gives the romanization based on modern *kana* usage (as found in the *Kōjien*, Iwanami Shoten, 5th ed.), using the macrons found in *Kenkyūsha shin waei daijiten* (Kenkyūsha, 2003).

逢坂 (あふさか)	Ōsaka/Ausaka (place-name)	居る (ゐ)	iru (to sit down)
調度 (てうど)	*chōdo* (furniture)	一生 (いつしやう)	*isshō* (one lifetime)
へ	*e* (case particle)	言ふ (い)	*iu* (to speak)
栄華物語 (えいぐわものがたり)	*Eiga monogatari* (*A Tale of Flowering Fortunes*)	いづ方 (かた)	*izukata* (which direction)
方丈記 (はうぢやうき)	*Hōjōki* (*An Account of a Ten-foot-square Hut*)	蜻蛉 (かげろふ)	*kagerō* (gossamer)
		観音 (くわんおん)	Kan'on (bodhisattva of mercy)

今日	*kyō* (today)		消息	*shōsoku* (letter)
前	*mae* (front)		秀歌	*shūka* (superior poem)
まゐる	*mairu* (to go)		候ふ	*sōrō* (to be in the service of)
申す	*mōsu* (to speak)		草子	*sōshi* (booklet)
催し	*moyōshi* (event, gathering)		給ふ	*tamō/tamau* (to give)
追ひ風	*oikaze* (tailwind)		遠し	*tōshi* (distant)
往生	*ōjō* (rebirth in the Pure Land)		宇治拾遺物語	*Uji shūi monogatari* (*Collection of Tales from Uji*)
大鏡	*Ōkagami* (*Great Mirror*)		は	*wa* (bound particle)
男	*otoko* (man)		やうやう	*yōyō* (gradually)
おはす	*owasu* (to be)		幽玄	*yūgen* (mystery and depth

Grammatical Terms and Abbreviations

English term	Eng. abbrev.	Japanese term	Romanization	Jpse. abbrev.
BASIC GRAMMATICAL FORMS				
Noun	n.	名詞	*meishi*	名
Proper noun	proper n.	固有名詞	*koyū-meishi*	固名
Pronoun	pron.	代名詞	*daimeishi*	代名
Adverb	adv.	副詞	*fukushi*	副
Interjection	interj.	感動詞	*kandōshi*	感動
Conjunction	conj.	接続詞	*setsuzokushi*	接続
Attributive word	attrib.	連体詞	*rentaishi*	連体詞
Particle	p.	助詞	*joshi*	助
Compound word	comp.	連語	*rengo*	連語
Verb	v.	動詞	*dōshi*	動
Transitive verb	tr. v.	他動詞	*tadōshi*	他動
Intransitive verb	intr. v.	自動詞	*jidōshi*	自動
Adjective	adj.	形容詞	*keiyōshi*	形
Adjectival verb	adj. v.	形容動詞	*keiyōdōshi*	形動
Auxiliary verb	aux. v.	助動詞	*jodōshi*	助動
Supplementary verb	suppl. v.	補助動詞	*hojodōshi*	補助動
SIX INFLECTIONS				
Imperfective form	MZ	未然形	*mizenkei*	未
Continuative form	RY	連用形	*ren'yōkei*	用

Final form	SS	終止形	*shūshikei*	終
Attributive form	RT	連体形	*rentaikei*	体
Perfective form	IZ	已然形	*izenkei*	已
Imperative form	MR	命令形	*meireikei*	命

CONJUGATION TYPES

Four-grade conjugation	YD	四段	*yodan*	四
Upper one-grade conjugation	KI	上一段	*kami-ichidan*	上一
Lower one-grade conjugation	SI	下一段	*shimo-ichidan*	下一
Upper two-grade conjugation	KN	上二段	*kami-nidan*	上二
Lower two-grade conjugation	SN	下二段	*shimo-nidan*	下二
k-row irregular conjugation	KH	カ変	*kahen*	カ変
s-row irregular conjugation	SH	サ変	*sahen*	サ変
n-row irregular conjugation	NH	ナ変	*nahen*	ナ変
r-row irregular conjugation	RH	ラ変	*rahen*	ラ変

ADJECTIVES AND ADJECTIVAL VERBS

ku adjective	*ku* adj.	ク形容詞	*ku keiyōshi*	ク形
shiku adjective	*shiku* adj.	シク形容詞	*shiku keiyōshi*	シク形
nari adjectival verb	*nari* adj. v.	ナリ形容動詞	*nari keiyōdōshi*	ナリ形動
tari adjectival verb	*tari* adj. v.	タリ形容動詞	*tari keiyōdōshi*	タリ形動

AUXILIARY AND SUPPLEMENTARY VERB FUNCTIONS

Causative		使役	*shieki*	使
Passive		受身	*ukemi*	受
Potential	pot.	可能	*kanō*	可
Spontaneous	spont.	自発	*jihatsu*	自
Honorific	hon.	尊敬	*sonkei*	尊
Negative	neg.	打消	*uchikeshi*	打
Past tense		過去	*kako*	過
Recollective		回想	*kaisō*	回
Perfective		完了	*kanryō*	完
Resultative		存続	*sonzoku*	存
Continuative, durative	cont.	継続	*keizoku*	継
Self desiderative		希望	*kibō*	希
Other desiderative		願望	*ganbō*	願
Speculative	spec.	推量	*suiryō*	推

Negative speculation	neg. spec.	打消推量	*uchikeshi suiryō*	打推
Intentional	intent.	意志	*ishi*	意
Negative intentional	neg. intent.	打消意志	*uchikeshi ishi*	打意
Hearsay		伝聞	*denbun*	伝
Copula, declarative		断定	*dantei*	断
Emphasis		強調	*kyōchō*	強
Confidence		確信	*kakushin*	確
Doubt, interrogative		疑問	*gimon*	疑
Rhetorical question		反語	*hango*	反
Appropriateness		当然	*tōzen*	当
Advice, recommendation		適当	*tekitō*	適
Hypothetical	hypo.	仮定	*katei*	仮
Circumlocution		婉曲	*enkyoku*	婉
Prohibition		禁止	*kinshi*	禁
Comparative		比況	*hikyō*	比
Exclamatory		詠嘆	*eitan*	詠

HONORIFICS

Honorific	hon.	尊敬	*sonkei*	尊
Humble	hum.	謙遜	*kenson*	謙
Polite		丁寧	*teinei*	丁

PARTICLES

Case particle	case p.	格助詞	*kaku joshi*	格助
Conjunctive particle	conj. p.	接続助詞	*setsuzoku joshi*	接助
Adverbial particle	adv. p.	副助詞	*fuku joshi*	副助
Bound particle	bound p.	係助詞	*kakari joshi*	係助
Binding function		係り	*kakari*	係
Bound ending		係り結び	*kakari musubi*	結
Final particle	final p.	終助詞	*shū joshi*	終助
Interjectory particle	interj. p.	間投助詞	*kantō joshi*	間助

OTHER

Sound change	音便	*onbin*	音
Word stem	語幹	*gokan*	語幹
Prefix	接頭語	*settōgo*	接頭
Suffix	接尾語	*setsubigo*	接尾
Pivot word, pun	掛詞	*kakekotoba*	掛
Pillow word, epithet	枕詞	*makura-kotoba*	枕
Preface-phrase	序詞	*jokotoba*	序
Associated word	縁語	*engo*	縁

Part I

Base Texts

An Account of a Ten-foot-square Hut

Kamo no Chōmei (1155–1216) was born into a family of hereditary Shintō priests who had served for many generations at the prestigious Kamo Shrine, just north of Kyoto. As a child Chōmei lived in comfortable circumstances and studied classical poetry (*waka*) and music, but then his father died young, while Chōmei was still in his teens, leaving him without the means for social advancement. Chōmei did, however, continue to devote himself to the study of poetry and music, two fields in which he excelled. In the spring of 1204, at the age of fifty, Chōmei suddenly took holy vows. It is generally believed that the cause for his sudden retirement was his disappointment in not being able to receive a high position at the Tadasu Shrine, a position for which he had long hoped but that was blocked by the shrine's existing head administrator.

Chōmei wrote *An Account of a Ten-foot-square Hut* (*Hōjōki*) at the end of the Third Month of 1212 while in retirement at Hino, in the hills southeast of Kyoto. The *Account* was influenced by Yoshishige Yasutane's *Chiteiki* (*Record of a Pond Pavilion*), a record of a recluse's life written in 982. The *Account* is written in a mixed Japanese–Chinese style that draws heavily on Chinese and Buddhist words and sources. Probably the style's most prominent rhetorical feature is the extensive use of parallel phrases and metaphors. Chōmei's work is noted for its vivid descriptions of a series of disasters in the capital during a time of turmoil (the war between the Taira and Minamoto at the end of the twelfth century) and for its observations on the impermanence of all things, one of the central tenets of Buddhism, which had a profound impact on Japan at this time.

The text is based on Nishio Minoru, *Hōjōki*, *Tsurezuregusa*, Nihon koten bungaku taikei 30 (Tokyo: Iwanami Shoten, 1957), 23–45, with minor orthographic changes.

『方丈記』

「1」

ゆく河の流れは絶えずして、しかも、もとの水にあらず。淀みに浮ぶうたかたは、かつ消え
かつ結びて、久しくとどまりたる例なし。世中にある人と栖と、またかくのごとし。

たましきの都のうちに、棟を並べ、甍を争へる、高き、いやしき人の住居は、世々を
経て尽きせぬものなれど、これをまことかと尋ぬれば、昔ありし家は稀なり。或は去年焼
けて今年作れり。或は大家亡びて小家となる。住む人もこれに同じ。所も変らず、人も
多かれど、いにしへ見し人は、二、三十人が中に、わづかにひとりふたりなり。朝に死に、
夕に生るるならひ、ただ水の泡にぞ似たりける。不知、生れ死ぬる人、何方より来たり
て、何方へか去る。また不知、仮の宿り、誰が為にか心を悩まし、何によりてか目を喜
ばしむる。その、主と栖と、無常を争ふさま、いはばあさがほの露に異ならず。或は
露落ちて花残れり。残るといへども朝日に枯れぬ。或は花しぼみて露なほ消えず。消え
ずといへども夕を待つ事なし。

「2」

予、ものの心を知れりしより、四十あまりの春秋をおくれるあひだに、世の不思議を見る
事、ややたびたびになりぬ。去安元三年四月廿八日かとよ。風烈しく吹きて、静かなら
ざりし夜、戌の時許、都の東南より火出で来て、西北に至る。はてには朱雀門・大極殿・
大学寮・民部省などまで移りて、一夜のうちに塵灰となりにき。

火もとは、樋口富の小路とかや、舞人を宿せる仮屋より出で来たりけるとなむ。吹き迷
ふ風に、とかく移りゆくほどに、扇を広げたるがごとく末広になりぬ。遠き家は煙に咽
び、近きあたりはひたすら焰を地に吹きつけたり。空には灰を吹き立てたれば、火の光に
映じて、あまねく紅なる中に、風に堪へず、吹き切られたる焰、飛ぶが如くして一二町
を越えつつ移りゆく。その中の人、現し心あらむや。或は煙に咽びて倒れ伏し、或は
焰にまぐれてたちまちに死ぬ。或は身ひとつ、からうじて逃るるも、資財を取り出づる
に及ばず、七珍万宝さながら灰燼となりにき。その費え、いくそばくぞ。そのたび、公卿
の家十六焼けたり。ましてその外、数へ知るに及ばず。惣て都のうち、三分が一に及べ
りとぞ。男女死ぬるもの数十人、馬・牛のたぐひ辺際を不知。

人の営み、皆愚かなるなかに、さしも危ふき京中の家をつくるとて、宝を費し、心
を悩ます事は、すぐれてあぢきなくぞ侍る。

「3」

また、治承四年卯月のころ、中御門京極のほどより大きなる辻風おこりて、六条わたりまで吹ける事侍りき。三、四町を吹きまくる間に、こもれる家ども、大きなるも小さきも、一つとして破れざるはなし。さながら平に倒れたるもあり、桁・柱ばかり残れるもあり。門を吹きはなちて四五町がほかに置き、また、垣を吹きはらひて隣と一つになせり。いはむや、家のうちの資財、数を尽して空にあり、檜皮・葺板のたぐひ、冬の木の葉の風に乱るるが如し。塵を煙の如く吹き立てたれば、すべて目も見えず、おびたたしく鳴りどよむほどに、もの言ふ声も聞えず。かの地獄の業の風なりとも、かばかりにこそはとぞおぼゆる。家の損亡せるのみにあらず、これを取り繕ふ間に、身を損ひ、かたはづける人、数も知らず。この風、未の方に移りゆきて、多くの人の嘆きをなせり。

　辻風は常に吹くものなれど、かゝる事やある、ただ事にあらず、さるべきもののさとしか、などぞ疑ひ侍りし。

「4」

また、治承四年水無月の比、にはかに都遷り侍りき。いと思ひの外なりし事なり。おほかた、この京のはじめを聞ける事は、嵯峨の天皇の御時、都と定まりにけるより後、すでに四百余歳を経たり。ことなるゆゑなくて、たやすく改まるべくもあらねば、これを世の人安からず憂へあへる、実にことわりにも過ぎたり。

　されど、とかくいふかひなくて、帝より始め奉りて、大臣・公卿みな悉く移ろひ給ひぬ。世に仕ふるほどの人、たれか一人ふるさとに残りをらむ。官・位に思ひをかけ、主君のかげを頼むほどの人は、一日なりとも疾く移ろはむとはげみ、時を失ひ世に余されて期する所なきものは、愁へながら止まり居り。軒を争ひし人のすまひ、日を経つつ荒れゆく。家はこぼたれて淀河に浮び、地は目のまへに畠となる。人の心みな改まりて、ただ馬・鞍をのみ重くす。牛・車を用する人なし。西南海の領所を願ひて、東北の庄薗を好まず。

　その時、おのづから事の便りありて、津の国の今の京に至れり。所のありさまを見るに、その地、程狭くて、条理を割るに足らず。北は山にそひて高く、南は海近くて下れり。波の音、常にかまびすしく、塩風殊にはげし。内裏は山の中なれば、かの木の丸殿もかくやと、なかなか様かはりて、優なるかたも侍り。日々にこぼち、川も狭に運び下す家、

いづくに作れるにかあるらむ。なほ空しき地は多く、作れる家は少し。古京はすでに荒れて、新都はいまだ成らず。ありとしある人は皆浮雲の思ひをなせり。もとよりこの所にをるものは、地を失ひて愁ふ。今移れる人は、土木のわづらひある事を嘆く。道のほとりを見れば、車に乗るべきは馬に乗り、衣冠・布衣なるべきは、多く直垂を着たり。都の手振りたちまちに改まりて、ただひなびたる武士に異ならず。世の乱るる瑞相とか聞けるもしるく、日を経つつ世中浮き立ちて、人の心もをさまらず、民の愁へ、つひに空しからざりければ、同じき年の冬、なほこの京に帰り給ひにき。されど、こぼちわたせりし家どもは、いかになりにけるにか、悉くもとの様にしも作らず。

　伝へ聞く、古の賢き御世には、憐みを以て国を治め給ふ。すなはち、殿に茅ふきて、その軒をだにととのへず、煙の乏しきを見給ふ時は、限りある貢物をさへゆるされき。これ、民を恵み、世を助け給ふによりてなり。今の世の中のありさま、昔になぞらへて知りぬべし。

「5」

また、養和のころとか、久しくなりて覚えず、二年があひだ、世中飢渇して、あさましき事侍りき。或は春・夏ひでり、或は秋、大風、洪水など、よからぬ事どもうち続きて、五穀ことごとくならず。むなしく春かへし、夏植うるいとなみありて、秋刈り冬收むるぞめきはなし。

　これによりて、国々の民、或は地を棄てて境を出で、或は家を忘れて山に住む。さまざまの御祈はじまりて、なべてならぬ法ども行はるれど、更にそのしるしなし。京のならひ、何わざにつけても、みなもとは田舎をこそ頼めるに、絶えて上るものなければ、さのみやは操も作りあへむ。念じわびつつ、さまざまの財物、かたはしより捨つるがごとくすれども、更に、目見立つる人なし。たまたま換ふるものは、金を軽くし、粟を重くす。乞食、路のほとりに多く、愁へ悲しむ声耳に満てり。前の年、かくの如く辛うじて暮れぬ。明くる年は立ち直るべきかと思ふほどに、あまりさへ疫癘うちそひて、まさざまに、あとかたなし。世人みなけいしぬれば、日を経つつきはまりゆくさま、少水の魚のたとへにかなへり。はてには、笠打ち着、足引き包み、よろしき姿したるもの、ひたすらに家ごとに乞ひ歩く。かくわびしれたるものどもの、歩くかと見れば、すなはち倒れ伏しぬ。築地のつら、道のほとりに、飢ゑ死ぬるもののたぐひ、数も不知。取り捨つるわざも知らねば、くさき香世界にみち満ちて、変りゆくかたちありさま、目も当てられぬこと多かり。いはむや、

河原などには、馬・車の行き交ふ道だになし。あやしき賤・山がつも力尽きて、薪さへ乏しくなりゆけば、頼むかたなき人は、自らが家をこぼちて、市に出でゝ売る。一人が持ち出でたる価、一日が命にだに不及とぞ。あやしき事は、薪の中に、赤き丹着き、箔など所々に見ゆる木、あひまじはりけるを尋ぬれば、すべきかたなきもの、古寺に至りて仏を盗み、堂の物の具を破り取りて、割り砕けるなりけり。濁悪の世にしも生れ合ひて、かかる心憂きわざをなむ見侍りし。

　また、いとあはれなることも侍りき。さりがたき妻・をとこ持ちたるものは、その思ひまさりて深きもの、必ず先立ちて死ぬ。その故は、わが身を次にして、人をいたはしく思ふあひだに、稀々得たる食ひ物をも、かれに譲るによりてなり。されば、親子あるものは、定まれる事にて、親ぞ先立ちける。また、母の命尽きたるを不知して、いとけなき子の、なほ乳に吸ひつつ臥せるなどもありけり。仁和寺に隆暁法印といふ人、かくしつつ数も不知死ぬる事を悲しみて、その首の見ゆるごとに、額に阿字を書きて、縁を結ばしむるわざをなむせられける。人数を知らむとて、四、五両月を数へたりければ、京のうち、一条より南、九条より北、京極よりは西、朱雀よりは東の、路のほとりなる頭、すべて四万二千三百余りなむありける。いはむや、その前後に死ぬるもの多く、また河原・白河・西の京、もろもろの辺地などを加へていはば、際限もあるべからず。いかにいはむや、七道諸国をや。

　崇徳院の御位の時、長承のころとか、かかる例ありけりと聞けど、その世のありさまは知らず、まのあたりめづらかなりし事なり。 ...

「6」

ここに六十の露消えがたに及びて、更に末葉の宿りを結べる事あり。いはば、旅人の一夜の宿をつくり、老いたる蚕の繭を営むがごとし。これを中比の栖にならぶれば、また百分が一に及ばず。とかくいふほどに、齢は歳々にたかく、栖は折々にせばし。その家のありさま、よのつねにも似ず。広さはわづかに方丈、高さは七尺がうちなり。所を思ひ定めざるがゆゑに、地を占めてつくらず。土居を組み、うちおほひを葺きて、続目ごとにかけがねを掛けたり。若、心にかなはぬ事あらば、やすく外へ移さむがためなり。その、あらため作る事、いくばくのわづらひかある。積むところ、わづかに二両、車の力を報ふほかには、さらに他の用途いらず。 ...

「7」

おほかた、この所に住みはじめし時は、あからさまと思ひしかども、今すでに、五年を経たり。仮りの庵もややふるさととなりて、軒の朽ち葉ふかく、土居に苔むせり。おのづから、ことの便りに都を聞けば、この山にこもり居てのち、やむごとなき人のかくれ給へるもあまた聞こゆ。まして、その数ならぬたぐひ、尽くしてこれを知るべからず。たびたびの炎上にほろびたる家、またいくそばくぞ。ただ仮りの庵のみ、のどけくしておそれなし。ほどせばしといへども、夜臥す床あり、昼居る座あり。一身をやどすに不足なし。かむなは小さき貝を好む。これ身知れるによりてなり。みさごは荒磯に居る。すなはち、人をおそるるがゆゑなり。われまたかくのごとし。身を知り、世を知れれば、願はず、走らず。ただしづかなるを望みとし、憂へ無きをたのしみとす。惣て世の人のすみかをつくるならひ、必ずしも、身のためにせず。或は妻子・眷属の為につくり、或は親昵・朋友の為につくる。或は主君・師匠、および財宝・牛馬の為にさへこれをつくる。われ、今、身の為にむすべり。人の為につくらず。ゆゑいかんとなれば、今の世のならひ、この身のありさま、ともなふべき人もなく、たのむべき奴もなし。縦、ひろくつくれりとも、誰を宿し、誰をか据ゑむ。　...

Vocabulary for Section 1

ゆく （行く） (*intr. v. YD*) to flow by (clouds, water, etc.)

河 (*n.*) river

流れ (*n.*) flow

絶ゆ (*intr. v. SN*) to be exhausted, run out

しかも （然も） (*conj.*) besides, moreover

もと （本・元） (*n.*) origin

淀み (*n.*) still water, still place (in stream or river)

浮かぶ (*intr. v. YD*) to float to the surface, float on water

うたかた （泡沫） (*n.*) froth, bubbles on the surface of the water

かつ （且つ） (*adv.*) indicates two elements occurring at the same time; while

久し (*shiku adj.*) continuous, long-lived

とどまる （留まる・止まる・停まる） (*intr. v. YD*) to stay in one place

例 (*n.*) example, precedent

なし （無し） (*ku adj.*) nonexistent, not present

世中 (*n.*) human society, secular world (this world)

あり （有り・在り） (*intr. v. RH*) to exist, be

栖 (*n.*) dwelling

また （又・復・亦） (*adv.*) in the same way, same fashion

かく （斯く） (*adv.*) in this way, in this manner, in this fashion, thus

ごとし （如し） (*aux. v.*) comparison, similarity; to be like, similar, the same as

たましき （玉敷き） (*n.*) (lit., strewn with jewels) beautiful thing, beautiful place; a *makura-kotoba* (pillow word) or an epithet that modifies the noun that follows; here, *miyako*, "capital"

都 (*n.*) capital, site of the imperial palace

棟 (*n.*) ridge, ridgepole (highest point of a roof)

並ぶ (*tr. v. SN*) to line up, place in a row

甍 (*n.*) roof tile, roof made of tile

争ふ (*intr. v. YD*) to vie, compete

高し (*ku adj.*) high-ranking

いやし （卑し・賤し） (*shiku adj.*) low-ranking, lowly

住居 (*n.*) house, dwelling

世々 (*n.*) generation after generation, many years

経 (*intr. v. SN*) to spend time, pass time

尽きす (*intr. v. SH*) to be exhausted, disappear

尋ぬ (*tr. v. SN*) to investigate

稀 (*nari adj. v.*) rare, scarce, unusual

或は (*attrib.*) (often in *aruiwa . . . aruiwa . . .* pattern; for example, in a certain situation X and in another situation Y) a certain (thing), certain (time), certain (situation)

去年 (*n.*) last year

焼く (*intr. v. SN*) to burn, catch fire

作る (*tr. v. YD*) to construct, build, put together

亡ぶ (*intr. v. KN*) to deteriorate

変る (*intr. v. YD*) to change

多し (*ku adj.*) many, numerous

いにしへ （古） (*n.*) distant past, long ago

わづか （僅か） (*nari adj. v.*) a small number, a little, few

死ぬ (*intr. v. NH*) to die

生る (*intr. v. SN*) to be born

ならひ （慣らひ・習ひ） (*n.*) custom

ただ （唯・只） (*adv.*) only, just

泡 (*n.*) foam

似る (*intr. v. KI*) to resemble

知る　(tr. v. YD) to know, understand

何方　(pron.) which direction, which thing

来たる　(intr. v. YD) (from KH v. ku, "to come," and YD v. itaru, "to reach") to come, arrive

去る　(intr. v. YD) to leave, go away from, to die

仮　(n.) temporary

宿り　(n.) dwelling, lodging

誰　(pron.) personal pron. referring to an unidentified individual: who

悩ます　(tr. v. YD) to trouble, cause to worry

よる (因る・由る・依る)　(intr. v. YD) to be based on, the result of

主　(n.) landowner, head of household, lord

無常　(n.) impermanence

いはば (言はば)　(comp.) (from MZ of YD v. iu, "to say," and conj. p. ba) that is, if one were to give an example

あさがほ (朝顔)　(n.) morning glory

露　(n.) dew

異　(nari adj. v.) different

落つ　(intr. v. KN) to fall

残る　(intr. v. YD) to remain behind

枯る　(intr. v. SN) to dry up, wither

萎む　(intr. v. YD) to shrivel

なほ (尚・猶)　(adv.) as before, as expected, still

Grammar Notes for Section 1

ゆく河の流れ　RT of YD v. yuku (yuka, yuki, yuku, yuku, yuke, yuke), "to go," modifying n. kawa, "river," attrib. case p. no, and n. nagare, "flow"

絶えずして　MZ of SN v. tayu (tae, tae, tayu, tayuru, tayure, taeyo), "to be exhausted," RY of neg. aux. v. zu, and conj. p. shite, indicating coexistence ("at the same time")

水にあらず　n. mizu, "water," RY of copular nari (nara, nari/ni, nari, naru, nare, nare), MZ of RH suppl. v. ari (ara, ari, ari, aru, are, are), and SS of neg. aux. v. zu; copular nari is equivalent to MJ desu or de aru

淀みに浮ぶうたかた　n. yodomi, "still water," locational case p. ni, and RT of YD v. ukabu, "to float," modifying n. utakata, "froth"

かつ消えかつ結びて　adv. katsu, used in the form katsu . . . katsu indicating two simultaneous actions, RY of SN v. kiyu, "to disappear," RY of YD v. musubu, "to form," and conj. p. te

久しく　RY of shiku adj. hisashi, "long," modifying v. todomaru, "to stop"

とどまりたる例なし　RY of YD v. todomaru, "to stop," RT of aux. v. tari, indicating a continuing state, n. tameshi, "example," and SS of ku adj. nashi, "not have"

にある人と栖と　locational case p. ni, RT of v. ari, "to be," modifying both hito, "person," and sumika, "dwelling"; to is case p., meaning "and" and indicating parallel items

かくのごとし　adv. kaku, "in this fashion," case p. no, and SS of aux. v. gotoshi, "like"

争へる　IZ of YD v. arasou, "to compete," and RT of aux. v. ri, which follows IZ and indicates a continuing state; arasoe-ru modifies n. sumai, "dwelling"

高き、いやしき　RT of ku adj. takashi, "superior," and RT of shiku adj. iyashi, "lowly," both modifying n. sumai

尽きせぬものなれど　MZ of SH v. tsukisu, "to exhaust," RT of neg. aux. v. zu, pron. mono, "that," IZ of copular nari, "to be," and concessive conj. p. do, which follows IZ

尋ぬれば　IZ of SN v. tazunu, "to inquire," and conj. p. ba, meaning "when" or "because" when following IZ

ありし   RY of RH v. *ari*, "to be," and RT of past-tense aux. v. *ki* (se, —, ki, *shi*, shika, —), modifying n. *ie*, "house"

作れり   IZ of YD v. *tsukuru*, "to construct," and SS of aux. v. *ri*, indicating a continuing state

亡びて   RY of KN v. *horobu*, "to deteriorate," and cont. conj. p. *te*

となる   case p. *to* and SS of YD v. *naru*, "to become"; do not confuse this *naru* with copular *nari*, "to be"

多かれど   IZ of *ku* adj. *ōshi* (kara, ku/kari, shi/kari, ki/karu, kere/*kare*, kare), "many," and concessive conj. p. *do*, which follows IZ; normally the IZ in the *kari* column is not used, but *ōshi* is an exception

見し   RY of KI v. *miru*, "to see," and RT of past-tense aux. v. *ki* (se, —, ki, *shi*, shika, —), modifying *hito*, "person"

二、三十人が中に   *ga* here is attrib. case p.

わづかに   RY of adj. v. *wazuka-nari*, "few"; RY of adj. v. functions like an adv.

生るる   RT of intr. SN v. *umaru* or *mumaru*, "to be born," modifying n. *narai*, "custom"; do not confuse with tr. YD v. *umu*, "to give birth to"

ぞ似たりける   emphatic bound p. *zo*, with RY of KI v. *niru*, "to resemble," RY of aux. v. *tari*, indicating a continuing state, and RT of past-tense aux. v. *keri*

知らず   MZ of YD v. *shiru*, "to know," and RY of neg. aux. v. *zu*; this and the next sentence are inverted constructions: "We do not know . . ."; "We cannot comprehend . . ."

何方より   pron. *izukata*, "which direction," and case p. *yori*, "from," indicating direction

へか去る   directional case p. *e* (he), interrogative bound p. *ka*, and RT of YD v. *saru*, "to leave," "to die"; *ka* is "bound" at the end by RT of v. *saru*

誰が為にか   pron. *ta*, "who," attrib. case p. *ga*, n. *tame*, "(for) the sake (of)," case p. *ni*, and interrogative bound p. *ka*

心を悩まし   n. *kokoro*, "heart," case p. *o*, indicating a direct object of the v., and RY of YD v. *nayamasu*, "to trouble"

よりてか   RY of intr. YD v. *yoru*, "to use as a means to," conj. p. *te*, and interrogative bound p. *ka*

喜ばしむる   MZ of intr. YD v. *yorokobu*, "to be happy," and aux. v. *shimu*, which is causative, in the RT because of bound p. *ka*; *shimu* is SN conjugation (shime, shime, shimu, *shimuru*, shimure, shimeyo)

その   comp. meaning "that," consisting of pron. *so*, "that," and attrib. case p. *no*

争ふさま   RT of intr. YD v. *arasou*, "to compete with," modifying n. *sama*, "appearance"

異ならず   MZ of adj. v. *koto-nari*, "different," and SS of neg. aux. v. *zu*

落ちて   RY of KN v. *otsu*, "to fall," and conj. p. *te*

残れり   IZ of YD v. *nokoru*, "to remain," and aux. v. *ri*, here having a resultative function: the result of the action (falling) continues or remains

といへども   citational case p. *to*, IZ of YD v. *iu*, "to say," and concessive conj. p. *domo*

枯れぬ   RY of SN v. *karu*, "to wither," and SS of aux. v. *nu*, which is perfective, indicating completed action

Annotated Grammar for Section 1

四/体	名	格助	名	係助	下二/未	助動/打/用	接助	接	名	格助	名	断/用	ラ変補動/未	助動/打/終	名	格助
ゆく	河	の	流れ	は	絶え	ず	して、	しかも、	もと	の	水	に	あら	ず。	淀み	に

四/体	名	係助	副	下二/用	副	四/用	接助	シク形/用	四/用	助動/完/体	名	ク形/終	名	格助	ラ変/体
浮ぶ	うたかた	は、	かつ	消え	かつ	結び	て、	久しく	とどまり	たる	例	なし。	世中	に	ある

名	格助	名	格助	副	副	格助	助動/比/終
人	と	栖	と、	また	かく	の	ごとし。

名	格助	名	格助	名	格助	名	格助	下二/用	名	格助	四/已	存続/体	ク形/体	シク形/体	名	格助	名

たましき の 都 の うち に、棟 を 並べ、甍 を 争へ る 、高き、いやしき、人 の 住居

係助	名	格助	下二/用	接助	サ変/未	打/体	名	助動/断/已	接助	代	格助	名	係助	格助	下二/已	接助	名	ラ変/用

は、世々 を 経 て 尽きせ ぬ もの なれ ど、これ を まこと か と 尋ぬれ ば、昔 あり

助動/過/体	名	係助	ナリ形動/終	連体詞	名	下二/用	接助	名	四/已	助動/完/終	連体詞	名	上二/用	接助	名	格助

し 家 は 稀なり。或は 去年 焼け て 今年 作れ り 。或は 大家 亡び て 小家 と

四/終	四/体	名	係助	代	格助	シク形/終	名	係助	四/未	助動/打/用	名	係助	ク形/已	接助	名	上一/用	助動/過/体

なる。住む 人 も これ に 同じ。所 も 変ら ず 、人 も 多かれ ど、いにしへ 見 し

名	係助	名	格助	名	格助	ナリ形動・用	名	名	助動/断/終	名	格助	ナ変/用	名	格助	下二/体

人 は、二三十人 が 中 に、わづかに ひとり ふたり なり 。朝 に 死に、夕べ に 生るる

名	副	格助	名	格助	係助・係	上一/用	助動/完/用	助動/過/体/結	四/未	助動/打/用	下二/用	ナ変/体	名	代

ならひ、ただ 水 の 泡 に ぞ 似 たり ける 。知ら ず 、生れ 死ぬる 人、何方

格助	四/用	接助	代	格助	係助/係	四/体/結	副	四/未	助動/打/用	名	格助	名	代	格助	名	格助	四/体	名

より 来たり て、何方 へ か 去る。また 知ら ず 、仮 の 宿り、誰 が 為 に か 心 を

四/用	代	格助	四/用	接助	係助/係	名	格助	四/未	助動/使/体/結	代	格助	名	格助	名	格助	名	格助	四/体	名

悩まし、何 に より て か 目 を 喜ば しむる。その、主 と 栖 と、無常 を 争ふ さま、

副	名	格助	名	格助	ナリ形動/未	助動/打/終	連体詞	名	上二/用	接助	名	四/已	助動/存続/終	四/体	格助	四/已

いはば あさがほ の 露 に 異なら ず 或は 露 落ち て 花 残れ り 。残る と いへ

接助	名	格助	下二/用	助動/完/終	連体詞	名	四/用	接助	名	副	下二/未	助動/打/終	下二/未	助動/打/終	格助	四/已

ども 朝日 に 枯れ ぬ 。或は 花 しぼみ て 露 なほ 消え ず 。消え ず と いへ

接助	名	格助	四/体	名	ク形/終

ども 夕 を 待つ 事 なし。

Vocabulary for Section 2

予 (*われ*) (*pron.*) I, myself

ものの 心 (*こころ*) (*comp.*) the true meaning of things

あまり(余り) (*suffix*) (following a number) a little more than

春秋 (*はるあき*) (*n.*) spring and autumn

おくる (送る) (*tr. v. YD*) to send off

やや (*adv.*) gradually, eventually

たびたび (度々) (*nari adj. v.*) frequent, repeated

去 (*いんじ*) (*attrib.*) (from NH v. *inu*, "to go," and past-tense aux. v. *ki*) past

安元 (*あんげん*) (*proper n.*) reign-name (1175–1177)

四月 (*うづき*) (*n.*) Fourth Month (lunar calendar)

烈し (*はげ*) (*shiku adj.*) severe

吹く (*ふ*) (*intr. v. YD*) to blow

静か (*しづ*) (*nari adj. v.*) quiet

戌 (*いぬ*) (*n.*) hour of the dog, the eleventh of the twelve horary signs (7:00–9:00 P.M.)

許 (*ばかり*) (*adv. p.*) approximation with regard to number, place, age, time, length, weight, or size: about, around, vicinity

東南 (*たつみ*) (*n.*) southeast

出で来 (*いでく*) (*intr. v. KH*) to come out, emerge into view

西北 (*いぬゐ*) (*n.*) northwest

至る (*いた*) (*intr. v. YD*) to arrive at

はて (果て) (*n.*) end, limit

朱雀門 (*すざくもん*) (*proper n.*) (also Shujaku) front gate, facing south, of the imperial palace (大内裏) in the capital; Suzaku *ōji* was a large north–south street in the center of the capital leading from Rajōmon (Rashōmon) in the south to Suzakumon in the north

大極殿 (*だいこくでん*) (*proper n.*) (also Daigokuden) central building in the imperial palace where the emperor conducted affairs of state and imperial ceremonies were performed

大学寮 (*だいがくれう*) (*proper n.*) state university where the sons of noble families studied

民部省 (*proper n.*) Ministry of Affairs (responsible for taxation, etc.), one of the eight ministries in the Daijōkan (太政官)

移る (*intr. v. YD*) to move, shift to another place

塵灰 (*n.*) dust and ashes

火もと (*comp.*) (from n. *hi*, "fire," and *moto*, "origin") origin of fire

樋口富の小路 (*proper n.*) Higuchi was a small alley running east to west, south of Gojō; Tomi no kōji was an alley (*kōji*) running north to south, west of Higashi kyōgoku; Higuchi tomi no kōji refers to the intersection of these two alleys

舞人 (*n.*) *bugaku* dancer

宿す (*tr. v. YD*) to lodge, put up

仮屋 (*n.*) temporary lodging

吹き迷ふ (*intr. v. YD*) to blow around aimlessly

とかく (*adv.*) here and there, variously

ほど (*n.*) interval, duration; while

扇 (*n.*) (*ōgi*) fan

広ぐ (*tr. v. SN*) to widen, to spread (something) out

末広 (*n.*) fan shape

咽ぶ (*intr. v. YD*) to choke, suffocate

ひたすら (*adv.*) intensely, without respite, single-mindedly, earnestly

焔ほ (*n.*) flames

吹きつく (吹き付く) (*tr. v. SN*) to blow on something fiercely

吹き立つ (*tr. v. SN*) to blow up into the air

映ず (*intr. v. SH*) to reflect light or shadows

あまねし (遍し・普し) (*ku adj.*) far and wide, widespread

紅 (*n.*) crimson

堪ふ (*intr. v. SN*) to endure, bear

吹き切る (*tr. v. YD*) to blow and tear to pieces

飛ぶ (*intr. v. YD*) to run, jump

町 (*n.*) unit of length equivalent to 109 meters (about one block)

越ゆ (*intr. v. SN*) to cross over

現し心 (*n.*) sense of sanity, feeling of reality (*utsushi*)

倒れ伏す (*intr. v. YD*) to fall and lie flat

まぐる (眩る) (*intr. v. SN*) to faint, lose consciousness

たちまちに (忽ちに) (*adv.*) immediately, instantly

身 (*n.*) body

からうじて (辛うじて) (*adv.*) barely, with difficulty, narrowly

逃る (*intr. v. SN*) to escape from a particular situation, to avoid (danger)

資材 (*n.*) property, possessions

取り出づ (*tr. v. SN*) to take out, select

及ぶ (*intr. v. YD*) (followed by neg.) to be equal to

七珍万宝 (*n.*) seven precious gems (*shitchin*) and myriad treasures (*manpō*), treasures or valuables

さながら (*adv.*) all, everything, in its entirety

灰燼 (*n.*) ashes and embers

費え (*n.*) cost, expense, waste, loss

いくそばく (幾十許) (*adv.*) how much

公卿 (*n.*) (also *kuge*) high-ranking nobles of third rank or above, including *daijōdaijin*, *udaijin*, *sadaijin*, *dainagon*, *chūnagon*, and *sangi*

まして (況して) (*adv.*) needless to say, not to mention

惣て (*adv.*) altogether

たぐひ (類) (*n.*) things of a similar kind

辺際 (へんさい) (*n.*) limit (of something)

営み (いとな) (*n.*) endeavor, activity, work

さしも (然しも) (*adv.*) (from adv. *sa*, "that," and adv. p. *shi*, bound p. *mo*) that much, to that extent

危ふし (あや) (*ku adj.*) dangerous

費す (つひや) (*tr. v. YD*) to spend, use up, squander

すぐれて (*adv.*) especially

あぢきなし (味気無し) (*ku adj.*) meaningless, silly

Grammar Notes for Section 2

知れりしより (し) IZ of YD v. *shiru*, "to understand," RY of aux. v. *ri*, which is perfective, RT of past-tense aux. v. *ki* modifying an implied nominal *toki*, "time," and directional case p. *yori*, "from (the time)"; RT implies a following nominal; *ri* can be resultative, continuative, or perfective

おくれるあひだ IZ of YD v. *okuru*, "to pass time," RT of cont. aux. v. *ri*, and n. *aida*, "while"

たびたびになりぬ RY of *nari* adj. v. *tabitabi-nari*, "repeated," RY of YD v. *naru*, "to become," and SS of perfective aux. v. *nu*

かとよ doubt bound p. *ka*, citational case p. *to*, abbrev. of *to omou*, "to think that," and final p. *yo*, which is exclamatory; here *ka* indicates slight doubt

烈しく吹きて (はげ) (ふ) RY of *shiku* adj. *hageshi*, "severe," RY of YD v. *fuku*, "to blow," and conj. p. *te*; RY makes the adj. function like an adv.

静かならざりし夜 (しづ) (よ) MZ of adj. v. *shizuka-nari*, "quiet," RY of neg. aux. v. *zu*, and RT of past-tense aux. v. *ki*, *yo*, "night"

出で来て (い) (き) comp. v.: RY of SN v. *izu*, "to come out," RY of KH v. *ku*, "to come," and conj. p. *te*

となりにき case p. *to*, RY of YD v. *naru*, RY of perfective aux. v. *nu*, and SS of past-tense aux. v. *ki*

宿せる仮屋 (やど) (かりや) IZ of YD v. *yadosu*, "to lodge," RT of aux. v. *ri*, and n. *kariya*, "temporary lodging"

出で来たりけるとなむ (い) (き) RY of KH v. *ideku*, "to come out," RY of perfective aux. v. *tari*, RT of past-tense aux. v. *keri*, citational case p. *to*, and emphatic bound p. *namu* (*nan*); emphatic bound p. *namu* usually appears in the middle of a sentence, but when it comes at the end of the sentence like this, it implies v. *iu*, "to say," which has been abbreviated

広げたるがごとく (ひろ) RY of SN v. *hirogu*, "to spread," RT of resultative aux. v. *tari*, implying nominal *koto*, attrib. case p. *ga*, and RY of comparative aux. v. *gotoshi*, "similar"

吹き立てたれば (ふ) (た) RY of SN v. *fukitatsu*, "to blow up high," IZ of aux. v. *tari*, which is continuative, and conj. p. *ba*, meaning "since" or "when"; the subject implied here is the fire (*hi*): "Since (the fire) blew the ashes into the sky, (the ashes were reflected in the light of the sky)."

あまねく紅なる中 (くれなゐ) (なか) RY of *ku* adj. *amaneshi*, "far and wide," n. *kurenai*, "crimson," RT of copular *nari*, "to be," and n. *naka*, "middle": "amid the crimson that was (spread) far and wide"

吹き切られたる焔 (ふ) (き) (ほのほ) MZ of YD v. *fuki-kiru*, "to blow and tear to pieces," and RY of aux. v. *ru*, which is passive, RT of aux. v. *tari*, and n. *honō*, "flame"

飛ぶがごとくして (と) RT of YD v. *tobu*, "to fly," with case p. *ga*, RY of comparative aux. v. *gotoshi* (*ku* adj. conjugation), and conj. p. *shite*

越えつつ (こ) RY of SN v. *koyu*, "to cross over," with conj. p. *tsutsu*, which indicates either repetitive or simultaneous action; here, *tsutsu* indicates repetitive action

あらむや   MZ of RH v. *ari*, "to have," with SS of aux. v. *mu*, indicating present speculation, and bound p. *ya*, indicating a rhetorical question: "Did (those people) have a sense of reality? (No, they did not.)"

逃^{のが}るるも   RT of SN v. *nogaru*, "to escape"; RT of the v. followed by the bound p. *mo* expresses a hypothetical situation: "even if it were the case"

取^とり出^いづるに及^{およ}ばず   RT of SN v. *tori-izuru*, "to take out," case p. *ni*, MZ of YD v. *oyobu*, "to reach," meaning "not to be able" when followed by neg., and RY of neg. aux. v. *zu*; RT of *tori-izuru* nominalizes the v. and implies a *koto*: "taking out": "They were unable to take out their possessions."

なりにき   RY of YD v. *naru*, "to become," RY of aux. v. *nu*, which is perfective, and SS of past-tense aux. v. *ki*; combination of *ni* and *ki* indicates completion of action

いくそばくぞ   adv. *ikusobaku*, " how much," and emphatic final p. *zo*

その度^{たび}   pron. (代名詞) *so*, attrib. p. *no*, and n. *tabi*, "time," together meaning "at that time"

焼^やけたり   RY of intr. SN v. *yaku*, "to burn," and SS of aux. v. *tari*, which is perfective. Be careful to distinguish this v. from tr. YD v. *yaku*, "to burn something"

数^{かぞ}へ知^しる   comp. v.: RY of SN v. *kazou*, "to count," and RT of YD v. *shiru*, "to know"

に及^{およ}べりとぞ   case p. *ni*, IZ of YD v. *oyobu*, "to reach," SS of aux. v. *ri*, which is perfective, citational case p. *to*, and emphatic bound p. *zo*; *to zo* implies that v. *iu*, "to say," follows

皆愚^{みなおろ}かなるなかに   adv. *mina*, "all," RT of adj. v. *oroka-nari*, "stupid," n. *naka*, "among," and locational case p. *ni*

つくるとて   SS of YD v. *tsukuru*, "to construct," citational case p. *to*, implying *omou*, "to think," and conj. p. *te*: "thinking to build a house in such a dangerous capital"

宝^{たから}を費^{つひや}し，心^{こころ}を悩^{なや}ます事^{こと}   Both phrases, *takara o tsuiyashi*, "to exhaust treasures," and *kokoro o nayamasu*, "to suffer," modify the impersonal pron. *koto*, a nominalizer

すぐれてあぢきなくぞ侍^{はべ}る   adv. *sugurete*, "especially," RY of *ku* adj. *ajikinashi*, "silly," emphatic bound p. *zo*, and RT of polite v. *haberi*, "to be"

Annotated Grammar for Section 2

（代） 名 格助 名 格助 四/已 助動/完/用 助動/過/体 格助 名 名 格助 名 格助 四/已 助動/存続/体
予、 もの の 心 を 知れ り し より、 四十 あまり の 春秋 を おくれ る

名 格助 名 格助 名 格助 上一/体 名 副 ナリ形動/用 四/用 助動/完/終
あひだ に、 世 の 不思議 を 見る 事、 やや たびたびに なり ぬ。

連体詞 名・ 名・ 名・ 名 係助 格助 終助 名 シク形/用 四/用 接助 ナリ形動/未 助動/打/用 助動/過/体 名
去 安元 三年 四月 廿八日 か と よ。 風 烈しく 吹き て、 静かなら ざり し 夜、

名 格助 名 副助 名 格助 名 格助 名 四/用 接助 名 格助 四/終 名 格助 係助 固名 固名・
戌 の 時 許、 都 の 東南 より 火 出で来 て、 西北 に 至る。 はて に は 朱雀門 大極殿

固名 固名 副助 副助 四/用 接助 名 格助 名 格助 名 格助 四/用 助動/完/用 助動/過/終
大学寮 民部省 など まで 移り て、 一夜 の うち に 塵灰 と なり に き。

名 係助 固名 格助 係助 係助 名 格助 四/已 助動/存続/体 名 格助 カ変/用 助動/完/用
火もと は、 樋口富の小路 と か や、 舞人 を 宿せ る 仮屋 より 出で来 たり

助動/過/体 格助 係助 四/体 名 格助 副 四/体 名 格助 名 格助 下二/用 助動/存続/体 格助 助動/比/用
ける と なむ。 吹き迷ふ 風 に、 とかく 移りゆく ほど に、 扇 を ひろげ たる が ごとく

名 格助 四/用 助動/完/終 ク形/体 名 係助 名 格助 ク形/体 名 係助 副 名 格助 名 格助
末広 に なり ぬ。 遠き 家 は 煙 に 咽び、 近き あたり は ひたすら 焔 を 地に

下二/用 助動/完/終 名 格助 係助 名 格助 下二/用 助動/存続/已 接助 名 格助 名 格助 サ変/用 接助 ク形/用 名
吹きつけ たり。 空 に は 灰 を 吹き立て たれ ば、 火 の 光 に 映じ て、 あまねく 紅

助動/断/体・ 名 格助　名 格助 下二/未・ 助動/打/用　四/未　助動/受/用 助動/完/体 名　四/体 格助 助動/比/用 接助
なる 中 に、 風 に 堪へ ず 、 吹き切ら れ たる 焔、 飛ぶ が 如く して

名　格助 下二/用 接助 四/終　代 格助 名 格助 名　ラ変/未 助動/推/終 係助/反語 連体詞 名 格助
一、二町 を 越え つつ 移りゆく。 その 中 の 人、 現し心 あら む や。 或は 煙 に

四/用 接助 下二/用 四/用 連体詞 名 格助 下二/用 接助 副　ナ変/終 連体詞 名 名 副
咽び て 倒れ 伏し、 或は 焔 に まぐれ て たちまちに 死ぬ。 或は 身 ひとつ、 からうじて

下二/体・ 係助 名 格助 下二/体 格助 四/未然 助動/打/用 名 副 名 格助 四/用 助動/完/用
逃るる も、 資財 を 取り出づる に 及ば ず、 七珍万宝 さながら 灰燼 と なり に

助動/過/終 代 格助 名 副 係助/強 代 格助 名 格助 名 名 下二/用 助動/完/終 副
き。 その 費え、 いくそばく ぞ。 その たび、 公卿 の 家 十六 焼け たり。 まして

代 格助 名 四/体 格助 四/未然・ 助動/打/終 副 名 格助 名 名 格助 名 格助 四/已 助動/完/終 格助 係助
その 外、数へ知る に 及ば ず。 惣て 都 の うち、三分 が 一 に 及べ り とぞ。

名 ナ変/体・ 名 名 名 格助 名 名 格助 四/未・ 助動/打/終
男女 死ぬる もの 数十人、馬・牛 の たぐひ 辺際 を 知ら ず。

名 格助 名・ 副 ナリ形動/体 名 格助 副 ク形/体・ 名 格助 名 格助 四/終 格助 接助 名 格助
人 の 営み、皆 愚かなる なか に、さしも 危ふき 京中 の 家 を つくる とて、宝 を

四/用 名 格助 四/体 名 係助 副 ク形/用・ 係助/係 ラ変/丁寧/体/結
費し、心 を 悩ます 事 は、すぐれて あぢきなく ぞ 侍る。

Vocabulary for Section 3

ちしよう
治承　(*proper n.*) reign-name (1177–1181)

うづき
卯月　(*n.*) Fourth Month (lunar calendar)

なかのみかどきやうごく
中御門京極　(*proper n.*) intersection of two streets, Naka-no-mikado and Kyōgoku, in the northeastern corner of the capital

おほ
大き　(*nari adj. v.*) big, large

つじかぜ
辻風　(*n.*) whirlwind

お
起こる　(*intr. v. YD*) to begin, occur, arise

わたり (辺り)　(*n.*) vicinity, surroundings

ふ
吹きまくる (吹き捲くる)　(*intr. v. YD*) to blow hard

こもる (籠る・隠る)　(*intr. v. YD*) to be enclosed within, be inside

やぶ
破る　(*intr. v. SN*) to break down

さながら(然ながら)　(*adv.*) as is, unchanged

ひら
平　(*nari adj. v.*) flat, level

たふ
倒る　(*intr. v. SN*) to fall over, collapse

けた
桁　(*n.*) beam, crossbeam

はしら
柱　(*n.*) pillar

かど
門　(*n.*) gate, entrance

ふ　はな
吹き放つ　(*comp.*) (YD tr. v. *fuku*, "to blow," and YD tr. v. *hanatsu*, "to let go") to blow away

かき
垣　(*n.*) fence, hedge

ふ　はら
吹き払ふ　(*tr. v. YD*) to blow away

なす (成す・為す)　(*tr. v. YD*) to form, make, carry out, do

いはむや (況むや)　(*adv.*) (sound change of *iwa-mu-ya*) (from YD v. *iu*, "to say," and aux. v. *mu*, bound p. *ya*) needless to say, not to mention

つく
尽す　(*tr. v. YD*) to exhaust, use up

ひはだ
檜皮　(*n.*) bark of the *hinoki*, or Japanese cypress, used to thatch roofs

ふきいた
葺板　(*n.*) wooden shingles used as roofing material

みだ
乱る　(*intr. v. SN*) to be confused, in disorder

おびたたし (夥し)　(*shiku adj.*) (later *obitadashi*) noisy, tumultuous

な
鳴りどよむ　(*comp. v. YD*) to reverberate, resound

か　(*pron.*) that (distant)

ぢごく
地獄　(*n.*) hell

業の風 (*set phrase*) (lit., winds of karma) a violent wind that blows through hell in retribution for bad acts committed in one's previous life

おぼゆ (覚ゆ) (*intr. v. SN*) to come to mind, remember

損亡す (*intr. v. SH*) to break down, be destroyed

のみ (*adv. p.*) indicates limitation, restriction; only

取り繕ふ (*tr. v. YD*) to repair, mend, fix

害ふ (*tr. v. YD*) to injure

かたはづく (*intr. v. YD*) to become disabled, crippled

未 (*n.*) south-southwest

嘆き (*n.*) grief, distress

かかる (斯かる) (*attrib.*) this kind of

ただ事 (*n.*) normal, everyday matter

さるべき (然るべき) (*attrib.*) appropriate, suitable

もののさとし (物の諭し) (*n.*) (*set phrase*) an omen or a sign (*satoshi*) from the gods or buddhas (*mono*)

疑ふ (*tr. v. YD*) to doubt, suspect

Grammar Notes for Section 3

吹ける事侍りき   IZ of YD v. *fuku*, "to blow," plus RT of aux. v. *ri*, which is perfective, modifying nominalizer *koto*, and RY of polite v. *haberi* plus SS of past-tense aux. v. *ki*

こもれる家ども   IZ of YD v. *komoru*, "to be enclosed within," RT of cont. aux. v. *ri*, n. *ie*, "house," and suffix *domo*, a plural marker

一つとして   n. *hitotsu*, "one," RY of copular *tari*, "to be," and conj. p. *shite*: "to be as one"

破れざるはなし   MZ of SN v. *yaburu*, "to break down," RT of neg. aux. v. *zu*, bound p. *wa*, and SS of *ku* adj. *nashi*, "not": "There were none that were not destroyed."

倒れたる   RY of SN v. *taoru* and RT of resultative aux. v. *tari*, modifying an implied nominal

残れる   IZ of YD v. *nokoru* and RT of resultative aux. v. *ri*, modifying an implied nominal

四五町がほか   n. *shigochō*, attrib. case p. *ga*, and n. *hoka*, "elsewhere": "four or five blocks away"

なせり   IZ of YD v. *nasu*, "to form," and SS of aux. v. *ri*, which is perfective-resultative

乱るる   RT of SN v. *midaru*, with the RT nominalizing the phrase

ほどに   set phrase, combining n. *hodo*, "degree," and case p. *ni*, indicating cause or reason

なりとも   SS of copular *nari*, "to be," and hypo. concessive conj. p. *tomo*, which follows SS of v. and RY of adj.

かばかりにこそはとぞおぼゆる   adv. *ka-bakari* (pron. *ka*, "that," and adv. p. *bakari*, "degree"), RY of copular *nari*, emphatic bound p. *koso*, bound p. *wa*, citational case p. *to*, emphatic bound p. *zo*, and RT of SN v. *oboyu* (due to bound p. *zo*): "It would probably be to that degree." There is an omitted v. before the citational *to*, something like *ara-me* (MZ of RH suppl. v. *ari* plus IZ of spec. aux. v. *mu*) or *ara-ji* (MZ of *ari* plus IZ of neg. spec. aux. v. *ji*). In the latter case, the meaning would be "even if it were the wind of karma, [the destruction] would not be to this extent."

損亡せる   MZ of SH v. *sonmō-su*, "to be lost," and RT of aux. v. *ri*, which is resultative; *ri* follows IZ of YD v. and MZ of SH v.

にあらず   RY of copular *nari*, MZ of RH suppl. v. *ari*, and RY of neg. aux. v. *zu*

かたはづける   IZ of YD v. *katawazuku*, "to become crippled," and RT of resultative aux. v. *ri*

嘆^{なげ}きなせり   One variant has *nageki o naseri*, and scholars speculate that the object marker case p. *o* was omitted here. *Nageki* is a n., "grief," and *nasu* is a tr. YD v. meaning "to make" or "to carry out": "Many people grieved."

かかることやある   *kakaru* is an attrib., a fixed modifier meaning "this kind of," followed by n. *koto*, "thing," bound p. *ya*, which creates a rhetorical question, and RT of RH v. *ari*, "to exist": "Was there ever a thing like this? (No.)"

疑^{うたが}ひ侍^{はべ}りし   RY of YD v. *utagau*, "to doubt," RY of polite suppl. v. *haberi*, and RT of past-tense aux. v. *ki* (in RT due to emphatic bound p. *zo*)

Annotated Grammar for Section 3

また、治承 四年 卯月 の ころ、中御門 京極 の ほど より 大きなる 辻風 おこり て、六条

わたり まで 吹け る 事 侍り き。

三四町 を 吹きまくる 間 に、こもれ る 家 ども、大きなる も 小さき も、一つ

と して 破れ ざる は なし。さながら 平に 倒れ たる も あり、桁・柱 ばかり

残れ る も あり。門 を 吹き はなち て 四五町 が ほか に 置き、また、垣 を 吹き

はらひ て 隣 と 一つ に なせ り。いはむや、家 の うち の 資財、数 を 尽して 空

に あり、檜皮 葺板 の たぐひ、冬 の 木 の 葉 の 風 に 乱るる が 如し。塵 を 煙 の

如く 吹き 立て たれ ば、すべて 目 も 見え ず、おびたたしく 鳴り どよむ ほど

に、もの 言ふ 声 も 聞え ず。かの 地獄 の 業 の 風 なり とも、かばかり に

こそ は と ぞ おぼゆる。家 の 損亡せ る のみ に あら ず、これ を

取り繕ふ 間 に、身 を 損ひ、かたはづけ る 人、数 も 知ら ず。この 風、未

の 方 に 移り ゆき て、多く の 人 の 嘆き なせ り。

辻風 は 常に 吹く もの なれ ど、かかる 事 や ある、ただ事 に あら

ず、さるべき もの の さとし か、など ぞ 疑ひ 侍り し。

Vocabulary for Section 4

水無月^{みなづき}   (*n.*) Sixth Month (lunar calendar)

にはか (俄か)   (*nari adj. v.*) sudden

都遷り^{みやこうつり}   (*n.*) moving the capital

いと   (*adv.*) very, to a great extent

思ひの外^{おも　ほか}   (*nari adj. v.*) unexpected, surprising

おほかた (大方)   (*adv.*) generally, on the whole

嵯峨の天皇の御時^{さが　てんわう　おんとき}   (*n.*) reign of Emperor Saga (809–823). Heian-kyō, the new capital, was actually established in present-day Kyoto in

794, during the reign of Saga's father, Kanmu; Kiyomori moved the capital to Fukuhara in 1180.

定まる (*intr. v. YD*) to be determined, be decided

すでに (既に・已に) (*adv.*) already

たやすし (容易し) (*ku adj.*) easy

改まる (*intr. v. YD*) to change, become new

やすし (易し) (*ku adj.*) easy, simple

憂へあふ (*comp.*) (intr. YD v. *ureu*, "to worry," and intr. YD v. *au*, "to do together") to worry or lament together

実に (*adv.*) truly

ことわり (理) (*n.*) reason, logic behind things

過ぐ (*intr. v. KN*) to exceed

されど (然れど) (*conj.*) although, nevertheless, however

かひなし (効なし・甲斐なし) (*ku adj.*) ineffective, fruitless, pointless

帝 (*n.*) emperor

大臣 (*n.*) minister, minister of state

悉く (*adv.*) altogether, entirely, completely

移ろふ (*intr. v. YD*) to move, shift to another place

仕ふ (*intr. v. SN*) to serve by the side of a noble

ふるさと (故郷・古里) (*n.*) (lit., old town) old capital, former capital (now decayed)

官 (*n.*) official rank, position

位 (*n.*) bureaucratic rank

思ひをかく (思ひを懸く) (*set phrase*) from n. *omoi*, "thought," case particle *o*, and tr. v. SN *kaku*, "to set, hang, pin one's hopes on, be obsessed with"

主君 (*n.*) lord, superior

かげ (影・景) (*n.*) backing, favor, support

頼む (*tr. v. YD*) to depend on

疾し (*ku adj.*) fast, quick (speed)

はげむ (励む) (*intr. v. YD*) to make full effort to do something, use all one's energy

余す (*tr. v. YD*) to leave behind, overlook

期す (*tr.* v. SH) to expect a result, anticipate

愁ふ (*tr. v. SN*) to lament, complain, express one's dissatisfaction or distress

軒 (*n.*) eaves

荒れ行く (*intr. v. YD*) to fall into ruin, become dilapidated

こぼつ (毀つ) (*tr. v. YD*) to break up, destroy

畠 (*n.*) cultivated field

淀川 (*proper n.*) river running from Lake Biwa to Osaka Bay

鞍 (*n.*) saddle

重くす (*tr. v. SH*) to place emphasize on, to privilege

車 (*n.*) carriage (ox-drawn in Heian period)

用す (*tr. v. SH*) to use

西南海 (*proper n.*) Kyushu and Shikoku

領所 (*n.*) territory, fief

東北 (*proper n.*) provinces to the northeast; present-day Aomori, Iwate, Akita, Yamagata, Miyagi, and Fukushima prefectures, regions where the court's authority was weak, which is why estates located there were not favored

庄薗 (*n.*) private estates owned by nobility and temples (from Heian period)

好む (*intr. v. YD*) to choose, order what one wants

おのづから (自ら) (*adv.*) spontaneously, naturally, of its own accord

便り (*n.*) (from v. *tayoru*, "to depend") convenience, expedience

津の国 (*proper n.*) Settsu Province (part of modern-day Osaka and Hyōgo prefectures)

狭し ^{せば} (*ku adj.*) narrow, small, confined

条理を割る ^{でうり} ^わ (*set phrase*) (n. *jō*, "east–west streets," *ri*, "north–south streets," tr. YD v. *waru*, "to divide") to divide the city up, lay out in a grid

添ふ ^そ (*intr. v. YD*) to follow a particular shape

かまびすし (喧し・囂し) (*shiku adj.*) noisy

塩風 ^{しほかぜ} (*n.*) sea breeze, briny air

殊に ^{こと} (*adv.*) especially, particularly

内裏 ^{だいり} (*n.*) emperor's residence, imperial palace

木の丸殿 ^こ ^{まるどの} (*comp.*) rough structure (*dono*) built of large round timbers (*ko no maru*); refers to temporary palace that Emperor Saimei (r. 665–661) supposedly built in Kyushu in 661

なかなか (中中) (*adv.*) rather, instead, contrary to expectation

様かはる ^{やう} (*comp. n.*) (from *yō*, "form," and intr. YD v. *kawaru*, "to be different") to be unusual in form

優 ^{いう} (*nari adj. v.*) elegant, refined

かた (方) (*n.*) aspect

狭に ^せ (*comp.*) (stem of ku adj. *seshi*, "narrow," and case p. *ni*) narrowly, in narrow conditions

いづく (何処) (*pron.*) where, which

いまだ (未だ) (*adv.*) (with neg.) (not) yet

浮雲の思ひ ^{うきぐも} ^{おも} (*comp.*) (from *omoi*, "thoughts," and *ukigumo*, "floating clouds") uneasy thoughts

もとより (元より) (*adv.*) from the beginning

土木 ^{どぼく} (*n.*) the act of building with wood or earth and sand

わづらひ (煩ひ) (*n.*) worry, anxiety

衣冠 ^{いくわん} (*n.*) court costume, including hat, worn when in attendance at imperial palace

布衣 ^{ほい} (*n.*) courtiers' casual wear (alternative name for *kariginu*)

直垂 ^{ひたたれ} (*n.*) type of robe originally worn by commoners and later by aristocrats and warriors

手振り ^{てぶ} (*n.*) manners, custom, habit

ひなぶ (鄙ぶ) (*intr. v. KN*) to be rustic, provincial, uncouth

武士 ^{もののふ} (*n.*) warrior

異 ^{こと} (*nari adj. v.*) different

瑞相 ^{ずいさう} (*n.*) omen, portent (either positive or negative)

しるし (著し) (*shiku adj.*) expected, as anticipated

浮き立つ ^う ^た (*intr. v. YD*) to be agitated, restless

をさまる (治まる) (*intr. v. YD*) to become peaceful (the land, etc.)

民 ^{たみ} (*n.*) people, subjects

つひに (終に・遂に) (*adv.*) finally, in the end

伝へ聞く ^{つた} ^き (*tr. v. YD*) to hear (about), learn secondhand

賢し ^{かしこ} (*ku adj.*) wise, sagacious

御世 ^{みよ} (*n.*) imperial reign (hon.)

憐み ^{あはれ} (*n.*) pity, sympathy

以て ^{もつ} (*comp.*) (from *mochi-te*) with, by means of

治む ^{をさ} (*tr. v. SN*) to rule, govern

すなはち (即ち・乃ち・則ち) (*conj.*) that is, in other words

殿 ^{との} (*n.*) residence of person of high rank

茅 ^{かや} (*n.*) grass such as *susuki* (pampas grass), *chigaya*, *suge*, for thatching a house

葺く ^ふ (*tr. v. YD*) to cover a roof with shingles or boards; to thatch

だに (*adv. p.*) analogy: gives a lesser or minimal example in order to suggest something greater or more serious: even X, not to mention Y

ととのふ (整ふ・調ふ・斉ふ) (*tr. v. SN*) to put in order, regulate (here, an allusion to the actions of the legendary Chinese emperor Yao)

貢物 <ruby>貢物<rt>みつぎもの</rt></ruby>   (*n.*) tax, tribute

さへ   (*adv. p.*) analogously offers a lesser example to suggest something comparatively greater: even X, not to mention Y

ゆるす (許す)   (*tr. v. YD*) to pardon (This sentence alludes to incidents in the reign of Emperor Nintoku, described in the *Nihon shoki*. The emperor can tell how greatly the people are suffering and impoverished by how little smoke rises from their cooking fires.)

めぐむ (恵む)   (*tr. v. YD*) to bless, show mercy or kindness to

助く   (*tr. v. SN*) to help

なぞらふ (準ふ・擬ふ・准ふ)   (*tr. v. SN*) to compare, liken

Grammar Notes for Section 4

思ひの外なりし   RY of *nari* adj. v. *omoi-no-hoka-nari*, "unexpected," and RT of past-tense aux. v. *ki*

定まりにける   RY of YD v. *sadamaru*, "to be determined," RY of perfective aux. v. *nu*, and RT of past-tense aux. v. *keri*, modifying an implied *toki*, "time"

経たり   RY of SN v. *fu*, "to pass," and SS of aux. v. *tari*, which is perfective

ことなるゆゑなくて   RT of adj. v. *koto-nari*, "special," modifying n. *yue*, "reason," and RY of *ku* adj. *nashi*, "not having," plus conj. p. *te*

改るべく   SS of YD v. *aratamaru*, "to change," and RY of aux. v. *beshi*, indicating appropriateness ("should")

あらねば   MZ of RH v. *ari*, "to be," IZ of neg. aux. v. *zu*, and conj. p. *ba*, indicating cause or reason

ことわりにも過ぎたり   n. *kotowari*, "reason," case p. *ni*, bound p. *mo*, RY of KN v. *sugu*, "to exceed," and SS of aux. v. *tari*, which is perfective: "It was more than reasonable."

とかくいふかひなくて   adv. *tokaku*, "in any event," RT of v. *iu*, "to say," RY of *ku* adj. *kainashi*, "pointless," and conj. p. *te*: "In any event, there was no point in saying"

始め奉りて   RY of SN v. *hajimu*, "to begin," RY of YD hum. suppl. v. *tatematsuru*, and conj. p. *te*: *tatematsuru* serves to humble the author vis-à-vis the emperor

移ろひ給ひぬ   RY of YD v. *utsurou*, "to move," RY of YD hon. suppl. v. *tamau*, indicating respect for the emperor, ministers, etc., and SS of aux. v. *nu*, which is perfective

世に仕ふる   n. *yo*, "world," referring to the court, case p. *ni*, and RT of SN v. *tsukau*, "to serve"

たれか … 残りをらむ   RY of YD v. *nokoru* "to remain," MZ of RH suppl. v. *ori*, indicating a continuing state, and RT of spec. aux. v. *mu*; the bound p. *ka* indicates a rhetorical question: "Who would stay behind? (No one.)"

なりとも   SS of copular *nari* plus conj. p. *tomo*, indicating hypothetical concession

主君のかげを頼むほどの人   "people of a rank that relied on the favor of their superiors"

疾く移ろはむ   RY of *ku* adj. *toshi*, "quick," MZ of YD v. *utsurou*, "to move," and SS of aux. v. *mu*, indicating intention

時を失ひ世に余されて期する所なきもの   MZ of YD v. *amasu*, "to leave behind," RY of SN aux. v. *ru*, which is passive, conj. p. *te*, RT of SH v. *go-su*, "to anticipate," n. *tokoro*, "place," and RT of *ku* adj. *nashi*, "not": "people (*mono*) who were left behind by society and had nothing to hope for"

こぼたれて   MZ of YD v. *kobotsu*, "to break up," RY of aux. v. *ru*, which is passive, and conj. p. *te*

畠 <ruby>畠<rt>はたけ</rt></ruby> となる   n. *hatake*, "fields," case p. *to*, indicating result of action or change, and SS of YD v. *naru*, "to become"

<ruby>至<rt>いた</rt></ruby>れり   IZ of YD v. *itaru*, "to arrive," and SS of aux. v. *ri*, which is resultative

見るに   RT of KI v. *miru* and conj. p. *ni*, meaning "when"; do not confuse this *ni* with case p. *ni*

<ruby>程<rt>ほど</rt></ruby>狭くて   n. *hodo*, "extent," RY of *ku* adj. *sebashi*, "narrow," and conj. p. *te*

<ruby>下<rt>くだ</rt></ruby>れり   IZ of YD v. *kudaru*, "to descend," and SS of aux. v. *ri*, which is resultative

なれば   IZ of copular *nari* and conj. p. *ba*, meaning "since"

かの木の<ruby>丸<rt>まる</rt></ruby>殿もかくやと   pron. *ka*, "that," attrib. case p. *no*, *ko no marudono*, "palace of round timbers," bound p. *mo*, adv. *kaku*, "thus," doubt bound p. *ya*, and citational case p. *to*; before *to*, there is an implied v. like *ari-kemu* (RY of RH v. *ari*, "to be," and RT of past-spec. aux. v. *kemu*)

<ruby>狭<rt>せ</rt></ruby>に   RY of *nari* adj. v. *se-nari*, "narrow (narrowly)," which appears in this form only here

いづくに<ruby>作<rt>つく</rt></ruby>れるにかあるらむ   pron. *izuku* "where," locative case p. *ni*, IZ of YD v. *tsukuru*, RT of aux. v. *ri*, RY of copular *nari*, doubt bound p. *ka*, RT of suppl. v. *ari*, and spec. aux. v. *ramu*: "Where would they be rebuilt?" (although *ramu* normally follows SS, with RH it follows RT)

ありとしある人   emphatic adv. p. *shi* is added to the set phrase *ari to aru*, "all," a phrase meaning "all people," or "every sort of person"

<ruby>移<rt>うつ</rt></ruby>れる   IZ of YD v. *utsuru* "to move," and RT of aux. v. *ri*, which is resultative, modifying *hito*

<ruby>乗<rt>の</rt></ruby>るべき   SS of YD v. *noru*, "to ride," and RT of aux. v. *beshi*, indicating appropriateness and modifying an implied n. like *hito*

なるべき   RT of copular *nari* plus RT of aux. v. *beshi*, indicating appropriateness; *beshi* follows SS except after RH, when it follows RT

とか<ruby>聞<rt>き</rt></ruby>けるも   citational p. *to*, bound p. *ka*, indicating mild doubt, IZ of YD v. *kiku*, RT of aux. v. *ri*, which is perfective, modifying an implicit n., like *koto*, and bound p. *mo*, indicating addition

<ruby>空<rt>むな</rt></ruby>しからざりければ   MZ of *shiku* adj. *munashi*, RY of neg. aux. v. *zu*, IZ of aux. v. *keri*, and conj. p. *ba*, meaning "since"

<ruby>帰<rt>かへ</rt></ruby>り<ruby>給<rt>たま</rt></ruby>ひにき   RY of YD v. *kaeru*, RY of hon. suppl. v. *tamau* (*tamō*), showing respect to the emperor and nobles, RY of aux. v. *nu*, which is perfective, and SS of past-tense aux. v. *ki*

こぼちわたせりし   RY of YD v. *kobotsu*, "to break up," IZ of tr. YD v. *watasu*, "to transfer (the houses) from one place to another," plus RY of aux. v. *ri*, and RT of past-tense aux. v. *ki*

いかになりにけるにか   adv. *ikani*, "how," RY of YD v. *naru*, "to become," RY of aux. v. *nu*, which is perfective, RT of aux. v. *keri*, which is exclamatory, RY of copular *nari*, interrogative bound p. *ka*, and an implied phrase like *ara-mu* (MZ of RH suppl. v. *ari* and RT of spec. aux. v. *mu*): "How did (the broken-down houses) end up?"

にしも<ruby>作<rt>つく</rt></ruby>らず   case p. *ni* and adv. p. *shimo* (from adv. p. *shi* and bound p. *mo*), a strong emphasis

<ruby>治<rt>をさ</rt></ruby>め<ruby>給<rt>たま</rt></ruby>ふ   RY of SN v. *osamu* "to govern," and SS of hon. suppl. v. *tamau* (*tamō*), honoring the implied emperor

だにととのへず   adv. p. *dani*, "even (lower limit)," MZ of SN v. *totonou*, "to put in order," and SS of neg. aux. v. *zu*

さへゆるされき   adv. p. *sae*, MZ of YD v. *yurusu*, "to pardon," RY of aux. v. *ru*, which is honorific, and SS of past-tense aux. v. *ki*

によりてなり   case p. *ni*, RY of YD v. *yoru*, "to be due to," conj. p. *te*, and SS of copular *nari*

<ruby>知<rt>し</rt></ruby>りぬべし   SS of aux. v. *nu*, indicating confidence, and aux. v. *beshi*, indicating appropriatenes

Annotated Grammar for Section 4

接　　固名　　名　　　名・格助　名　　　ナリ形動/用　名　四/用　ラ変/補動/丁寧/用　助動/過/終　副　　　ナリ形動/用
また、治承　四年　水無月　の　比、にはかに　都　遷り　　侍り　　　き　。いと　思ひの外なり

助動/過/体　名　動/断/終　　　副　　　　　　代　格助　名　格助　　名　　格助　四/已　助動/完/体　名　係助　固名　格助　　格助
　し　事　なり　。おほかた、この　京　の　はじめ　を　聞け　る　　事　は、嵯峨　の　天皇　の

名　　名　格助　四/用　　助動/完/用　助動/過/体　格助　名　　副　　　　四/用　助動/完/終　ナリ形動/体
御時、都　と　定まり　　に　　　ける　より　後、すでに　四百余歳　を　経　たり　。ことなる　ゆゑ

ク形/用　接助　ク形/用　　　四/終　　助動/当然/用　係助　ラ変/未　助動/打/已　接助　代　格助　名　格助　名　ク形/未・助動/打/用
なく　て、たやすく　改まる　べく　も　あら　ね　　ば、これ　を　世　の　人　安から　ず

下二/用・四/已　助動/存続/体　副　　名　　　格助　係助　上二/用　助動/完/終
憂へ　あへ　　る　、実に　ことわり　に　も　過ぎ　たり　。

接　　　副　　　四/体　名　ク形/用　接助　名　格助　下二/用・四/補動/謙譲/用　接助　　名　　　名・　名　　副
　されど、とかく　いふ　かひ　なく　て、帝　より　始め　　奉り　　て、大臣・公卿　みな　悉く

四/用　四/補動/尊敬/用・助動/完/終　名　格助　下二/体　名　格助　名　　代　係助/疑/係　名　　　　格助　四/用・
移ろひ　給ひ　　ぬ　。世　に　仕ふる　ほど　の　人、たれ　か　　一人　ふるさと　に　残り

ラ変/未　助動/推量/体/結　名　名　格助　名・　格助　下二/用　名　格助　名　格助　四/体・名　格助　名　係助　名
をら　　む　。宮位　に　思ひ　を　かけ、主君　の　かげ　を　頼む　ほど　の　人　は、一日

助動/断定/終　接助・ク形/用　四/未・　助動/意/終　格助　四/用　名　格助　四/用・名　四/未・助動/受/用　接助　サ変/体　名
なり　とも　疾く　移ろは　む　とはげみ、時　を　失ひ　世　に　余さ　れ　て　期する　所

ク形/体　名　係助　下二/用　接助　四/用　ラ変/終　名　格助　四/用・助動/過/体　名　格助　名　・　名　格助　下二/用　接助
なき　もの　は、愁へ　ながら　止まり　居り　。軒　を　争ひ　し　人　の　すまひ、日　を　経　つつ

下二/用　四/終　名　係助　四/未　助動/受/用　接助　固名・格助　四/用　名　係助　名　格助　名　格助　名　四/終・名
荒れ　ゆく　。家　は　こぼた　れ　て　淀河　に　浮び、地　は　目　の　まへ　に　畠　と　なる　。人

格助　名　副　四/用　接助　副　名　名　格助　副助　サ変/終・名　名　格助　サ変/体・名　ク形/終　固名　格助
の　心　みな　改まり　て、ただ　馬・鞍　を　のみ　重くす　。生、車　を　用する　人　なし　。西南海　の

名　格助　四/用・接助　名　格助　名　格助　四/未・助動/打/終
領所　を　願ひて、東北　の　庄薗　を　好ま　ず　。

代　格助　名　　　副　　名　格助　名　ラ変/用　接助　固名　格助　名　格助　名　格助　名　格助　四/已　助動/完/終　名
その　時、おのづから　事　の　便り　あり　て、津　の　国　の　今　の　京　に　至れ　り　。所

格助　名　　格助　上一/体　接助　代　格助　名　　名　ク形/用・接助　名　格助　四/体　格助　四/未・助動/打/終　名　係助　名
の　ありさま　を　見る　に、その　地、程　狭く　て、条理　を　割る　に　足ら　ず　。北　は　山

格助　四/用　接助　ク形/用　名　係助　名　ク形/用　接助　四/已　助動/存続/終　名　格助　名　ナリ形動/用　シク形/用　名
に　そひ　て　高く、南　は　海　近く　て　下れ　　り　。波　の　音、常に　かまびすしく、塩風

副　　シク形/終　名　係助　名　格助　名　助動/断/已　接助　代　格助　名　格助　名　係助　副　疑/係　格助　　副
殊に　はげし　。内裏　は　山　の　中　なれ　ば、か　の　木　の　丸殿　も　かく　や　と、なかなか

名　四/用・接助　ナリ形動/体　名　係助　ラ変/丁寧/終　名　格助　四/用　名　係助　連語　四/用　四/体　名　　代
様　かはり　て、優なる　かた　も　侍り　。日々　に　こぼち、川　も　狭に　運び　下す　家、いづく

格助　四/已　助動/完/体　助動/断/用　係助/疑/係　ラ変/体　助動/推/体/結　副　シク形/体　名　係助　ク形/用・　四/已　助動/完/体　名　係助
に　作れ　る　に　か　ある　らむ　。なほ　空しき　地　は　多く、作れ　る　家　は

ク形/終　名　係助　副　下二/用　接助　名　係助　副　四/未・助動/打/終　ラ変/終　格助　副助　ラ変/体　名　係助　副
少し　。古京　は　すでに　荒れ　て、新都　は　いまだ　成ら　ず　。ありと　しある　人　は　皆

名　格助　名・　四/已　助動/存続/終　　副　　代　格助　名　格助　名　ラ変/用　名　係助　名　格助　四/用　接助　下二/終
浮雲　の　思ひ　を　なせ　り　。もとより　この　所に　をる　もの　は、地　を　失ひ　て　愁ふ

今　四/已　助動/完/体　名　係助　名　格助　名　ラ変/体　名　格助　四/終　名　格助　名　格助　上一/已・接助　名
今　移れ　る　人　は、土木　の　わづらひ　ある　事　を　嘆く　。道　の　ほとり　を　見れ　ば、車

格助　四/終・助動/当然/体・係助　名　格助　四/用・名　　名　助動/断/用・助動/当然/体・係助　ク形/用　名　格助　上一/用
に　乗る　べき　は　馬　に　乗り、衣冠　布衣　なる　べき　は、多く　直垂　を　着

助動/存続/終　名　格助　名　副　　　　四/用　接助　副　名　名　格助　上二/用　助動/完/体　名　格助　ナリ形動/未・助動/打/終
たり　。都　の　手振り　たちまちに　改まり　て、ただ　ひなび　たる　武士　に　異なら　ず　。

名　格助　下二/体・名　格助　係助/疑　四/已　助動/存続/体　係助　ク形/用・名　格助　下二/用　接助　名　四/用　四/用　接助
世　の　乱るる　瑞相　と　か　聞け　る　も　しるく、日　を　経　つつ　世中　浮き　立ち　て、

名　格助　名　係助　四/未　助動/打/用　名　格助　名・　副　シク形/未　助動/打/用　助動/過/已　接助　シク形/体　名
人　の　心　も　をさまら　ず、民　の　愁へ、つひに　空しから　ざり　けれ　ば、同じき　年

格助	名	副	代	格助	名	格助	四/用・	補動/四/尊/用	助動/完/用	助動/過/終	接		四/用		四・已	助動/完/用	助動/過/体
の	冬、	なほ	この		京	に	帰り	給ひ	に	き。	されど、	こぼち	わたせ			り	し

名	接尾	係助	副	四/用	助動/完/用	助動/過/体	助動/断/用	係助/疑	副	名	格助	名	格助	副助	係助	四/未
家	ども	は、	いかに	なり	に	ける	に	か、	悉く	もと	の	様	に	しも	作ら

助動/打/終
ず。

下二/用	四/体	名	格助	ク形/体	名	格助	係助	名	格助	格助	名	格助	下二/用	補動/四/尊/終	接	名	格助
伝へ	聞く、	古	の	賢き	御世	に	は、	憐み	を	以て	国	を	治め	給ふ。	すなはち、	殿	に

名	四/用	接助	代	格助	名	格助	副助	下二/未	助動/打/用	名	格助	シク形/体	格助	上一/用	補動/尊/体・	名	係助	名
茅	ふき	て、	その		軒	を	だに	ととのへ	ず、	煙	の	乏しき	を	見	給ふ	時	は、	限り

ラ変/体	名	格助	副助	四/未	助動/尊/用	助動/過/終	代	名	格助	四/用・	名	格助	下二/用	助動/尊/体・格助	四/用	接助
ある	貢物	を	さへ	ゆるさ	れ	き。	これ、	民	を	恵み、	世	を	助け	給ふ	に	よりて

助動/断/終	名	格助	名	格助	名	名	格助	下二/用・	接助	四/用	助動/完/終	助動/推/終
なり。	今	の	世	の	ありさま、	昔	に	なぞらへ	て	知り	ぬ	べし。

Vocabulary for Section 5

養和 (やうわ) (*proper n.*) reign-name (1181–1182)

飢渇す (けかつ) (*intr. v. SH*) to starve, hunger, thirst

あさまし (淺まし) (*shiku adj.*) terrible, awful, unbearable

ひでり (日照り・旱) (*n.*) drought

洪水 (こうずい) (*n.*) flood

五穀 (ごこく) (*n.*) five staple grains: rice, wheat, soybeans, and two kinds of millet (*awa, kibi*); grains in general

ことごとく (悉く) (*adv.*) altogether, completely

かへす (反す) (*tr. v. YD*) to hoe, plow a field, cultivate

植う (う) (*tr. v. SN*) to plant (a seed, seedling)

いとなみ (営み) (*n.*) endeavor, activity, work

刈る (か) (*tr. v. YD*) to reap

収む (をさ) (*tr. v. SN*) to store properly, put away

ぞめき (騒き) (*n.*) merrymaking, bustle, activity

棄つ (す) (*tr. v. SN*) to discard, abandon

境 (さかひ) (*n.*) borders (of villages or provinces, etc.)

御祈 (おんいのり) (*n.*) prayer (hon.)

なべて (並べて) (*adv.*) common, ordinary; *nabete naranu* is a set phrase meaning "not ordinary"

法 (ほふ) (*n.*) (Buddhist) rites, ceremonies (such as prayers)

更に (さら) (*adv.*) (when followed by neg.) not at all

しるし (徴・験) (*n.*) efficacy, effect

わざ (業) (*n.*) action, deed

絶えて (た) (*adv.*) (followed by neg.) (not) at all, (not) a bit

上る (のぼ) (*intr. v. YD*) to come to the capital from the provinces

さのみ (然のみ) (*comp. adv.*) (from adv. *sa* and adv. p. *nomi*) (followed by neg.) (not) that much

操作る (みさをつく) (*set phrase*) to feign indifference

念じわぶ (ねん) (*tr. v. KN*) (usually *nenji-wabiru*) to find difficult to endure

かたはし (片端) (*n.*) part, portion

目見立つ (めみたつ) (*tr. v. SN*) to notice

たまたま (偶・適) (*adv.*) occasionally, once in a while, rarely

換ふ (か) (*tr. v. SN*) to trade, barter

軽くす (かろ) (*comp.*) (from RY of adj. *karoshi*, "light," and SH v. *su*, "to do") to think little of, make light of

粟 (ぞく) (*n.*) grain, provisions, millet

乞食 (こつじき) (*n.*) beggar

満つ (*intr. v. YD*) to become full

暮る (*intr. v. SN*) to have the season come to an end

明く (*intr. v. SN*) to start a new year, month, day

立ち直る (*intr. v. YD*) to recover

あまりさへ (剰へ) (*adv.*) on top of that, as if that weren't enough

疫癘 (*n.*) epidemic

うちそふ (うち添ふ) (*intr. v. YD*) to accompany, go along with

まさざま (増様) (*nari adj. v.*) extreme in appearance, extreme

あとかたなし (跡形無し) (*ku adj.*) without a trace

けいす (*v. SH*) to close the door to protect against epidemic

きはまりゆく(極まり行く) (*intr. v. YD*) to approach the end (i.e., death)

たとへ (譬へ・喩へ) (*n.*) example, illustration, comparison, metaphor

かなふ (適ふ・叶ふ) (*intr. v. YD*) to fit, match

笠 (*n.*) hat to protect against snow, rain, sun

引き包む (*tr. v. YD*) to wrap

よろし (宜し) (*shiku adj.*) relatively good, satisfactory

ひたすら (*adv.*) intensely, without respite, single-mindedly, earnestly

家ごとに (*comp.*) (n. *ie*, "house," and suffix *goto*, "each") each house

乞ひ歩く (*intr. v. YD*) to walk around begging

わびしる (侘び痴る) (*intr. v. SN*) to be at a loss or bewildered as a result of encountering difficulty

築地 (*n.*) earthen wall, tiled roof added later

つら (面) (*n.*) surface

飢ゑ死ぬ (*comp. v.*) (*intr. v. NH*) to starve to death

くさし (臭し) (*ku adj.*) stinking, malodorous

香 (*n.*) fragrance, odor

かたち (形・容貌) (*n.*) countenance, visage

いはむや (況むや) (*adv.*) needless to say

河原 (*n.*) riverbed; here, that of the Kamo River, in Kyoto

行き交ふ (*intr. v. YD*) to come and go

あやし (賤し) (*shiku adj.*) low-ranking, coarse, crude

賤 (*n.*) lowly people

山がつ (山賤) (*n.*) mountain dwellers, such as woodcutters

尽く (*intr. v. KN*) to run out, to be used up

薪 (*n.*) firewood

乏し (*shiku adj.*) insufficient, scarce

市 (*n.*) market, marketplace

価 (*n.*) value

丹 (*n.*) red color, red paint

箔 (*n.*) gilding, gold, silver, or copper leaf used for decoration

あひまじはる(相交はる) (*intr. v. YD*) to be mixed in

仏 (*n.*) statue of the Buddha

盗む (*tr. v. YD*) to steal

堂 (*n.*) Buddhist temple where a statue of a deity is enshrined

物の具 (*n.*) instruments, furniture

割り砕く (*tr. v. YD*) to smash, break up

濁悪の世 (*set phrase*) (this) world (*yo*) of sin and pollution (*joku-aku*)

心憂し (*ku adj.*) painful, pitiful

あはれ (*nari adj. v.*) deeply moving, affecting

妻・をとこ (*n.*) wife and husband

まさる (勝る・優る) (*intr. v. YD*) to be superior to, surpass, outdo

先立つ<ruby>先立<rt>さきだ</rt></ruby>つ　(*intr. v. YD*) to precede, predecease

いたはし（労し）　(*shiku adj.*) to desire to take care of

<ruby>得<rt>う</rt></ruby>　(*tr. v. SN*) to acquire, possess

<ruby>譲<rt>ゆづ</rt></ruby>る　(*tr. v. YD*) to turn over, transfer

いとけなし（幼けなし）　(*ku adj.*) young, innocent, helpless

<ruby>乳<rt>ち</rt></ruby>　(*n.*) breast, nipple, breast milk

<ruby>吸<rt>す</rt></ruby>ふ　(*tr. v. YD*) to suck, suckle

<ruby>臥<rt>ふ</rt></ruby>す　(*intr. v. YD*) to lie down, go to sleep

<ruby>仁和寺<rt>にんなじ</rt></ruby>　(*proper n.*) temple in northern Kyōto

<ruby>隆暁法印<rt>りゆうげうほふいん</rt></ruby>　(*proper n.*) Dharma Seal Ryūgyō; Dharma Seal (*Hōin*) was the highest rank conferred on a Buddhist priest by the court·

<ruby>首<rt>かうべ</rt></ruby>　(*n.*) head

<ruby>額<rt>ひたひ</rt></ruby>　(*n.*) forehead

<ruby>阿字<rt>あじ</rt></ruby>　(*n.*) (Buddhist) the letter "a," the first in the Sanskrit alphabet. In Esoteric Buddhism, the letter "a" represented the unchanging source of all things.

<ruby>縁<rt>えん</rt></ruby>を<ruby>結<rt>むす</rt></ruby>ぶ　(*set phrase*) (n. *en*, "bond," and v.

musubu, "to tie") to forge a bond (with the Buddha)

<ruby>白河<rt>しらかは</rt></ruby>　(*proper n.*) area of northern Kyoto east of the Kamo River

<ruby>西<rt>にし</rt></ruby>の<ruby>京<rt>きやう</rt></ruby>　(*comp. n.*) the undeveloped western part of the capital

もろもろ（諸諸）　(*n.*) many, various

<ruby>辺地<rt>へんぢ</rt></ruby>　(*n.*) (also *henchi*) outlying areas, far from the capital, the country

<ruby>加<rt>くは</rt></ruby>ふ　(*tr. v. SN*) to add, pile up

<ruby>際限<rt>さいげん</rt></ruby>　(*n.*) limit, end

<ruby>七道<rt>しちだう</rt></ruby>　(*proper n.*) seven major thoroughfares (in various provinces)

<ruby>崇徳院<rt>すとくゐん</rt></ruby>　(*proper n.*) Cloistered Emperor (*in*) Sutoku, the seventy-fifth emperor (1119–1164; r. 1123–1141)

<ruby>御位<rt>みくらゐ</rt></ruby>　(*n.*) position of the emperor (hon.)

<ruby>長承<rt>ちやうしよう</rt></ruby>　(*proper n.*) (also Chōjō) reign-name (1132–1135)

まのあたり（目のあたり）　(*n. + adj. v.*) before one's eyes

めづらか　(*nari adj. v.*) unusual, remarkable

Grammar Notes for Section 5

<ruby>久<rt>ひさ</rt></ruby>しくなりて　RY of *shiku* adj. *hisashi*, "long," RY of YD v. *naru*, "to become," and conj. p. *te*

あさましき<ruby>事<rt>ことは</rt></ruby><ruby>侍<rt>べ</rt></ruby>りき　RT of *shiku* adj. *asamashi*, "terrible," modifying n. *koto*, RY of polite v. *haberi*, and SS of past-tense aux. v. *ki*

よからぬ<ruby>事<rt>こと</rt></ruby>　MZ of *ku* adj. *yoshi*, "good," and RT of neg. aux. v. *zu*, modifying n. *koto*

うち<ruby>続<rt>つづ</rt></ruby>きて　Prefix *uchi* strengthens v. *tsuzuku*, meaning "to continue one after another"

<ruby>収<rt>をさ</rt></ruby>むるぞめきはなし　RT of SN v. *osamu*, n. *zomeki*, bound p. *wa*, and SS of *ku* adj. *nashi*

<ruby>行<rt>おこな</rt></ruby>はるれど　MZ of v. *okonau*, "to carry out,"

IZ of aux. v. *ru*, which is passive, and concessive conj. p. *do*

をこそ<ruby>頼<rt>たの</rt></ruby>めるに　case p. *o*, indicating a direct object, emphatic bound p. *koso*, IZ of YD v. *tanomu*, "to rely on," RT of aux. v. *ri*, which is continuative, and conj. p. *ni*, "when"

なければ　IZ of *ku* adj. *nashi* and conj. p. *ba*, meaning "since"

さのみやは<ruby>操<rt>みさを</rt></ruby>も<ruby>作<rt>つく</rt></ruby>りあへむ　adv. *sanomi*, "so much," bound p. *yawa*, indicating a rhetorical question, n. *misao*, bound p. *mo*, RY of YD v. *tsukuru*, MZ of SN v. *au*, "to do completely," and spec. aux. v. *mu* in RT: "How could they so completely feign indifference? (They could not.)"

念じわびつつ RY of KN v. *nenji-wabu* and conj. p. *tsutsu*, indicating simultaneous action

すれども IZ of SH v. *su*, "to do," and concessive conj. p. *domo*

暮れぬ RY of SN v. *kuru*, "to come to an end," and SS of aux. v. *nu*, which is perfective

立ち直るべきかと SS of YD v. *tachi-naoru*, "to recover," RT of aux. v. *beshi*, indicating natural expectation, doubt bound p. *ka*, which follows RT at end of sentence, and citational case p. *to*

けいしぬれば RY of SH v. *kei-su*, "to close door to protect against epidemic," IZ of aux. v. *nu*, which is perfective, and conj. p. *ba*, meaning "since" or "when"

経つつ RY of SN v. *fu*, "to pass," and conj. p. *tsutsu*, indicating repetitive or simultaneous action

わびしれたるものどもの RY of SN v. *wabi-shiru*, "to be saddled with difficulty," RT of aux. v. *tari*, which is continuative, modifying n. *mono*, "people," plural suffix *domo*, and case p. *no*, functioning as a subject marker

倒れ伏しぬ RY of YD comp. v. *taore-fusu*, "to fall down and lie flat," and SS of aux. v. *nu*, which is perfective

知らねば MZ of YD v. *shiru*, "to know," IZ of neg. aux. v. *zu*, and conj. p. *ba*, "since"

当てられぬこと多かり MZ of SN v. *atsu*, "to direct one's eyes toward," MZ of aux. v. *raru*, indicating potential, RT of neg. aux. v. *zu*, modifying n. *koto*, and SS of *ku* adj. *ōshi*, "many"

乏しくなりゆけば RY of adj. *tomoshi*, IZ of YD v. *nariyuku*, "to become," and conj. p. *ba*, "when"

あひまじはりけるを尋ぬれば RY of YD v. *ai-majiwaru* "to be mixed," RT of aux. v. *keri*, modifying an implied nominal, case p. *o*, IZ of SN v. *tazunu*, "to inquire," and conj. p. *ba*, "when"

すべきかたなき SS of SH v. *su*, "to do," RT of aux. v. *beshi*, indicating potential, n. *kata*, and RT of *ku* adj. *nashi*, modifying *mono*; lit., "(people) who had nothing they could do"

割り砕けるなりけり IZ of YD comp. v. *wari-kudaku*, RT of aux. v. *ri*, modifying an implied n. like *koto*, RY of copular *nari*, and SS of past-tense aux. v. *keri*

をなむ見侍りし case p. *o*, emphatic bound p. *nan* (sound change of *namu*), RY of KI v. *miru*, RY of polite suppl. v. *haberi*, and RT of past-tense aux. v. *ki* (in RT because of bound p. *namu*)

さりがたき RY of YD v. *saru*, "to leave behind," and RT of aux. v. *gatashi*, "to be difficult or impossible to do"; *gatashi* conjugates like a *ku* adj. and attaches to RY of inflected words

譲るによりて RT of tr. YD v. *yuzuru*, "to yield," modifying an implied nominal, case p. *ni*, and RY of intr. YD v. *yoru*, "to be due to"

定まれる事にて IZ of YD v. *sadamaru*, RT of aux. v. *ri*, which is resultative, modifying n. *koto*, RY of copular *nari*, and conj. p. *te*: "It is something (*koto*) that is decided."

かくしつつ adv. *kaku*, "thus," RY of SH v. *su* "to do," and conj. p. *tsutsu*, indicating repetitive action

結ばしむるわざをなむせられける MZ of YD v. *musubu* "to tie," RT of SN aux. v. *shimu*, which is causative, n. *waza*, "act," case p. *o*, emphatic bound p. *nan*, MZ of SH v. *su* "to do," RY of aux. v. *raru*, which is honorific, and past-tense aux. v. *keri*, in RT because it is "bound" by *nan* (*namu*)

を知らむとて case p. *o*, MZ of YD v. *shiru*, "to know," SS of aux. v. *mu*, which is intentional, citation case p. *to*, and conj. p. *te*; *to-te* implies "thinking that"

数へたりければ RY of SN v. *kazou*, "to count," RY of aux. v. *tari*, which is perfective, IZ of past-tense aux. v. *keri*, and conj. p. *ba*, meaning "when"

一条より南、九条より北、京極よりは西、朱雀よりは東　the south of Ichijō, the north of Kujō, the west of Kyōgoku, the east of Suzaku; the eastern half of the capital. (Suzaku was the midpoint. The western half remained undeveloped.)

加へていはば　case p. *o*, RY of SN v. *kuwau*, "to add," and conj. p. *te*, followed by MZ of YD v. *iu*, "to say," and hypo. conj. p. *ba*

あるべからず　RT of RH v. *ari*, "to be," MZ of aux. v. *beshi*, indicating potential, and SS of neg. aux. v. *zu*; *beshi* follows SS except after RH

いかにいはむや　set phrase: adv. *ika-ni*, "how," which reinforces adv. *iwamuya*, "needless to say"

をや　comp. p.: interj. p. *o* and bound p. *ya*, together functioning as a strong exclamation

めづらかなりし事なり　RY of *nari* adj. v. *mezuraka*, RT of aux. v. *ki*, n. *koto*, and SS of copular *nari*

Annotated Grammar for Section 5

また、養和のころとか、久しくなりて覚えず、二年があひだ、世中飢渇して、あさましき事侍りき。或は春夏ひでり、或は秋、大風、洪水など、よからぬ事どもうち続きて、五穀ことごとくならず。むなしく春かへし、夏植うるいとなみありて、秋刈り冬収むるぞめきはなし。

これによりて、国々の民、或は地を棄てて境を出で、或は家を忘れて山に住む。さまざまの御祈はじまりて、なべてならぬ法ども行はるれど、更にそのしるしなし。京のならひ、何わざにつけても、みなもとは田舎をこそ頼めるに、絶えて上るものなければ、さのみやは操も作りあへむ。念じわびつつ、さまざまの財物、かたはしより捨つるがごとくすれども、更に、目見立つる人なし。たまたま換ふるものは、金を軽くし、粟を重くす。乞食、路のほとりに多く、愁へ悲しむ声耳に満てり。

前の年、かくの如く辛うじて暮れぬ。明くる年は立ち直るべきかと思ふほどに、あまりさへ疫癘うちそひて、まさざまに、あとかたなし。世人みなけいしぬれば、日を経つつきはまりゆくさま、少水の魚のたとへにかなへり。はてには、笠打ち着、足引き包み、よろしき姿したるもの、ひたすらに家ごとに乞ひ歩く。かくわびしれたるものどもの、歩くかと見れば、すなはち倒れ伏しぬ。築地のつら、道のほとりに、飢ゑ死ぬるもののたぐひ、数も知らず。取り捨つるわざも知らねば、くさき香世界に

四/用　接助　四/用　四/体　名　　名　　名　係助　下二/未　助動/可/未　助動/打/体　名　ク形/カリ活用/終
満ち満ち て、変り ゆく かたち ありさま、目 も 当て られ ぬ こと 多かり 。

　副　　名　副助　格助　係助　名　名　格助　四/用　四/体・名　副助　ク形/終　シク形/体　名　名・　係助　名
いはむや、河原 など に は、馬 車 の 行き 交ふ 道 だに なし。あやしき 賤 山がつ も 力

上二/用　接助　名　副助　シク形/用　四/用　四/已　接助　四/体　名　ク形/体　名　係助　　格助　名　格助　四/用　接助
尽き て、薪 さへ 乏しく なり ゆけ ば、頼む かた なき 人 は、自ら が 家 を こぼち て、

名　格助　下二/用・接助　四/終・　名　格助　四/用　接助　下二/用・助動/存続/体　名　副助　名　格助　名　副助　四/未　助動/打/終
市 に 出で て 売る。一人 が 持ち て 出で たる 価、一日 が 命 に だに 及ば ず

格助　係助　シク形/体　名　係助　名　格助　名　ク形/体　名　四/用・　名　副助　格助　下二/体・名　接頭
と ぞ。あやしき 事 は、薪 の 中 に、赤き 丹 着き、箔 など 所々 に 見ゆる 木、あひ

　四/用・　助動/過去/体　係助　下二/已・接助　サ変/終　助動/可/体　名　ク形/体　名　名　格助　四/用　接助　名　格助　四/用
まじはり ける を 尋ぬれ ば、す べき かた なき もの、古寺 に 至り て 仏 を 盗み、

名　格助　名　格助　名　格助　四/用　四/用　接助　四/用　四/已　助動/完/体　助動/断/用　助動/過去/終　名　格助　名　係助　副助
堂 の 物 の 具 を 破り 取り て、割り 砕け る なり けり。濁悪 の 世 に しも

下二/用・　四/用・接助　連体詞　ク形/体　名　格助　係助/強/係　上一/用　補助動/丁寧/用　助動/過去/体/結
生れ 合ひ て、かかる 心憂き わざ を なむ 見 侍り し 。

　　接　副　ナリ形動/体　名　係助　ラ変/丁寧　助動/過去/終　ク形/体　名・　名・　四/用　助動/完/体
また、いと あはれなる こと も 侍り き。さりがたき 妻・をとこ 持ち たる

名　係助　代　格助　名　四/用　接助　ク形/体　名　副　四/用　接助　ナ変/終　代　格助　名　係助　代　格助　名
もの は、その 思ひ まさり て 深き もの、必ず 先立ち て 死ぬ。その 故 は、わが 身

格助　名　格助　サ変/用　接助　名　格助　シク形/用・　四/体・　名・　副　下二/用　助動/完/体　名　格助　係助　代
を 次 に し て、人 を いたはしく 思ふ あひだ に、稀々 得 たる 食ひ物 を も、かれ

格助　四/体・格助　四/用　接助　助動/断/終　接　名　ラ変/体　名　係助　四/已　助動/完了/体　名　助動/断/用　接助　名
に 譲る により て なり。されば、親子 ある もの は、定まれ る 事 に て、親

係助/係　四/用　助動/過去/体/結　接　名　格助　名　上二/用・助動/完/体　格助　四/未　助動/打/用　接助　ク形/体　名　格助
ぞ 先立ち ける 。また、母 の 命 尽き たる を 知ら ず して、いとけなき 子 の、

副　名　格助　四/用・接助　四/已　助動/存続/体　副助　係助　ラ変/用　助動/過去/終　固名　格助　固名　格助　四/用　名
なほ 乳 を 吸ひ つつ 臥せ る など も あり けり。仁和寺 に 隆暁法印 と いふ 人、

副　サ変/用　接助　名　係助　四/未・　助動/打/用　ナ変/体・　名　格助　四/用　接助　代　格助　名　格助　下二/体・接尾・格助
かく し つつ 数 も 知ら ず 死ぬる 事 を 悲しみ て、その 首 の 見ゆる ごと に、

名　格助　名・　格助　四/用　接助　名　格助　四/未・助動/使役・　名　格助　係助/強/係　サ変/未　助動/尊敬/用　助動/過去/体/結　名
額 に 阿字 を 書き て、縁 を 結ば しむる わざ を なむ せ られ ける 。人数

格助　四/未・助動/意/終　格助　接助　名　格助　下二/用・助動/完/用　助動/過去/已　接助　名　格助　名　格助　名　格助
を 知ら む とて、四・五 両月 を 数へ たり けれ ば、京 の うち、一条 より 南、

名　格助　名　名　格助　係助　名　名　格助　名　助動/断/体　名　副
九条 より 北、京極 より は 西、朱雀 より は 東 の、路 の ほとり なる 頭、すべて

名　接尾　係助/強/係　ラ変/用　助動/過去/体/結　副　代　格助　名　格助　ナ変/体・　名　ク形/用　接
四万二千三百 余り なむ あり ける 。いはむや、その 前後 に 死ぬる もの 多く、また

名　名　名　格助　名　名　格助　副助　格助　下二/用・接助　四/未　接助　係助　ラ変/体　助動/推/未
河原 白河 西 の 京、もろもろ の 辺地 など を 加へ て いは ば、際限 も ある べから

助動/打/終　副　副　名　名　間助　係助
ず 。いかに いはむや、七道 諸国 を や。

固名　格助　名　格助　名　固名　格助　名　格助　係助　連体詞　名　ラ変/用　助動/過去/終　格助　四/已　接助　代　格助
崇徳院 の 御位 の 時、長承 の ころ と か、かかる 例 あり けり と 聞け ど、その

名　格助　名　係助　四/未・助動/打/用　副　ナリ形動/用　助動/過去/体　名　助動/断/終
世 の ありさま は 知ら ず、まのあたり めづらかなり し 事 なり。

Becoming disillusioned with the world, Chōmei retreats to the hills and constructs a small dwelling and then, in the following passage, an even smaller home, a ten-foot-square hut.

Vocabulary for Section 6

末葉 <ruby>すゑば</ruby> (*n.*) leaves at the ends of the branches (Chōmei is alluding to his advancing years and the end of his life)

老ゆ <ruby>お</ruby> (*intr. v. KN*) to grow old, become elderly

蚕 <ruby>かひこ</ruby> (*n.*) silkworm

繭 <ruby>まゆ</ruby> (*n.*) cocoon

中比 <ruby>なかごろ</ruby> (*n.*) recent past

方丈 <ruby>はうぢやう</ruby> (*n.*) one *jō* (3.03 meters, or around 10 feet) square

尺 <ruby>しやく</ruby> (*n.*) unit of length: approximately one foot, 10 *shaku* equals one *jō*

土居 <ruby>つちゐ</ruby> (*n.*) base for pillars of a house

うちおほひ (打ち覆ひ) (*n.*) covering, makeshift roof

継目 <ruby>つぎめ</ruby> (*n.*) joint

かけがね (掛け金) (*n.*) metal door latch

積む <ruby>つ</ruby> (*tr. v. YD*) to load (a ship, a carriage)

両 <ruby>りやう</ruby> (*suffix*) counter for clothing, suits of armor, carriages, etc.

報ふ <ruby>むく</ruby> (*tr. v. YD*) to remunerate, pay for work done

用途 <ruby>ようどう</ruby> (*n.*) necessary expense

Grammar Notes for Section 6

老いたる <ruby>お</ruby>   RY of KN v. *oyu*, "to grow old," and RT of aux. v. *tari*, which is resultative

ならぶれば   IZ of SN v. *narabu*, "to compare," and conj. p. *ba*, which is temporal: "when"

七尺がうちなり <ruby>しちしやく</ruby>   attrib. case p. *ga*, n. *uchi*, "within," and SS of copular *nari*

思ひ定めざるがゆゑ <ruby>おも</ruby><ruby>さだ</ruby>   MZ of SN comp. v. *omoi-sadamu*, "to think and decide," RT of neg. aux. v. *zu*, attrib. case p. *ga*, and n. *yue*, "reason"

かなはぬ事あらば <ruby>こと</ruby>   MZ of YD v. *kanau,* "to be in accord with," RT of neg. aux. v. *zu*, n. *koto*, MZ of RH v. *ari*, "to be," and conj. p. *ba*, which is hypothetical: "If there is something that does not accord [with my wishes]."

移さむがためなり <ruby>うつ</ruby>   MZ of YD v. *utsusu*, "to move," RT of aux. v. *mu*, indicating intention, attrib. case p. *ga*, n. *tame*, "reason," and SS of copular *nari*

Annotated Grammar for Section 6

助動/意志/体	格助	名	助動/断/終	代	格助	下二/用	四/体	名	副	格助	名	係助/疑/係	ラ変/体/結	四/体
む	が	ため	なり。	そ	の、	あらため	作る	事、	いくばく	の	わづらひ	か	ある。	積む

名	ナリ形動/用	名	名	格助	名	格助	四/体・	名	格助	係助	副	名	格助	名	四/未	助動/打/終
ところ、	わづかに	二両、	車	の	力	を	報ふ	ほか	に	は、	さらに	他	の	用途	いら	ず。

Vocabulary for Section 7

あからさま   (*nari adj. v.*) temporary, brief

朽ち葉〔くば〕   (*n.*) rotting leaves

苔むす〔こけ〕   (*intr. v. YD*) (from n. *koke*, "moss," and YD v. *musu*, "to grow") to be covered with moss

やむごとなし   (*ku adj.*) (from v. *yamu*, "to stop," and *koto-nashi*, "without") high-ranking

かくる (隠る)   (*intr. v. YD/SN*) to die, pass away

のどけし (長閑けし)   (*ku adj.*) (emotional state, character) collected, at ease, calm

かむな   (*n.*) (also *kamina*) hermit crab

みさご (鶚・雎鳩)   (*n.*) osprey, fish hawk

荒磯〔あらいそ〕   (*n.*) (same as *ariso*) rocky beach

走る〔わし〕   (*intr. v. YD*) to run, run about

眷属〔けんぞく〕   (*n.*) family, immediate relatives

親昵〔しんじつ〕   (*n.*) intimates

朋友〔ほういう〕   (*n.*) friend

師匠〔ししやう〕   (*n.*) master, teacher

むすぶ (結ぶ)   (*tr. v. YD*) to construct, weave together

財宝〔ざいほう〕   (*n.*) treasure

奴〔やっこ〕   (*n.*) servant

据う〔す〕   (*tr. v. SN*) to set, establish, place

Grammar Notes for Section 7

住みはじめし〔す〕   RY of YD v. *sumu*, "to live," RY of SN suppl. v. *hajimu*, "to begin," and RT of past-tense *ki*, modifying implied n. *toki*, "time"

思ひしかども〔おも〕   RY of YD v. *omou*, "to think," IZ of past-tense aux. v. *ki*, and concessive conj. p. *domo*

かくれ給へる〔たま〕   RY of SN v. *kakuru*, "to die," IZ of YD hon. suppl. v. *tamau* (*tamō*), and RT of aux. v. *ri*

知れれば〔し〕   IZ of YD v. *shiru*, "to know," IZ of aux. v. *ri*, and conj. p. *ba*, meaning "since"

ひろくつくれりとも   RY of *ku* adj. *hiroshi*, "large," IZ of YD v. *tsukuru*, "to build," SS of aux. v. *ri*, and hypo. concessive conj. p. *tomo*

誰をか据ゑむ〔たれ〕〔す〕   pron. *tare*, case p. *o*, interrogative bound p. *ka*, MZ of SN v. *suu*, "to place," and RT of intent. aux. v. *mu* (*n*): "Who would I place here (in this dwelling)? (No one.)"

Annotated Grammar for Section 7

副	代	格助	名	格助	四/用	下二/用	助動/過去/体	名	係助	ナリ形動/語幹	格助	四/用・	助動/過/已・	接助・	名
おほかた、	こ	の	所	に	住み	はじめ	し	時	は、	あからさま	と	思ひ	しか	ども、	今

副・	名	格助	下二/用	助動/完/終	名	格助	名	係助	副	名	格助	四/用	接助	名	格助	名
すでに、	五年	を	経	たり。	仮り	の	庵	も	やや	ふるさと	と	なり	て、	軒	の	朽ち葉

ク形/用	名	格助	四/已	助動/存続/終	副	名	格助	名	格助	四/已	接助	代	格助	名
ふかく、	土居	に	苔むせ	り。	おのづから、	こと	の	便り	に	都	を	聞けば、	こ	の	山

格助	四/用	上一/用	接助	名	ク形/体	名	格助	下二/用	補助動/尊敬/已・	助動/完/体	係助	副	下二/終
に	こもり	居	て	のち、	やむごとなき	人	の	かくれ	給へ	る	も	あまた	聞こゆ。

まして、その 数 なら ぬ たぐひ、尽くし て これ を 知る べから ず。たびたび の 炎上 に ほろび たる 家、また いくそばく ぞ。ただ 仮り の 庵 のみ、のどけく して おそれ なし。ほど せばし と いへ ども、夜 臥す 床 あり、昼 居る 座 あり。一身 を やどす に 不足 なし。かむな は 小さき 貝 を 好む。これ 身 知れ る に よりて なり。みさご は 荒磯 に 居る。すなはち、人 を おそるる が ゆゑ なり。われ また かく の ごとし。身 を 知り、世 を 知れ れ ば、願は ず、走ら ず。ただ しづかなる を 望み と し、憂へ 無き を たのしみ と す。惣て 世 の 人 の すみか を つくる ならひ、必ずしも、身 の ために せ ず。或は 妻子・眷属 の 為 に つくり、或は 親昵・朋友 の 為 に つくる。或は 主君・師匠、および 財宝・牛馬 の 為 に さへ これ を つくる。われ、今、身 の 為 に むすべ り。人 の 為 に つくら ず。ゆゑ いかん と なれ ば、今 の 世 の ならひ、この 身 の ありさま、ともなふ べき 人 も なく、たのむ べき 奴 も なし。縦、ひろく つくれ り とも、誰 を 宿し、誰 を か 据ゑ む。

2

The Tale of the Bamboo Cutter

The *monogatari*, or vernacular tale, emerged in the latter half of the ninth century together with the *kana* syllabary. The earliest extant example of this is *The Tale of the Bamboo Cutter* (*Taketori monogatari*, ca. 909), which *The Tale of Genji* cites as the ancestor of the genre. The dating of *The Tale of the Bamboo Cutter* is uncertain. Some scholars believe that it was completed as early as 810 to 823; others give it a much later date, around 940 to 956. We also do not know much about the author, who was probably a male scholar or intellectual like Minamoto Tōru (822–895), who was familiar with both Chinese and Japanese literary and religious texts.

The Tale of the Bamboo Cutter can be roughly divided into four sections: (1) the story of the poor woodcutter who becomes rich as a result of the miraculous birth of Kaguyahime, the shining princess; (2) the stories of the five suitors, each of whom unsuccessfully courts Kaguyahime; (3) the courtship of the shining princess by the emperor; and (4) the return of the shining princess to the moon. The narrative contrasts the beautiful, clean moon, where immortals live and there are no melancholy thoughts, with the dirty, polluted world where people suffer and die. The moon also suggests the Western Paradise (Jōdo) found in Pure Land Buddhism, an association reinforced by the descent of the "moon" people, resembling the *raigō* (heavenly descent) in Pure Land paintings, in which the spirit of the dead person is met by a group of heavenly beings who descend on clouds.

The text is based on Sakakura Atsuyoshi, Otsu Yūichi, Tsukishima Yutaka, Abe Toshiko, and Imai Genei, eds., *Taketori monogatari, Ise monogatari, Yamato monogatari*, Nihon koten bungaku taikei 9 (Tokyo: Iwanami Shoten, 1957), 29–30, 49–60, 63–67.

『竹取物語』

「かぐや姫の生ひ立ち」

いまは昔、竹取の翁といふもの有りけり。野山にまじりて竹を取りつつ、よろづの事に使ひけり。名をば、さかきの造となむいひける。その竹の中に、もと光る竹なむ一筋ありける。あやしがりて寄りて見るに、筒の中光りたり。それを見れば、三寸ばかりなる人、いとうつくしうてゐたり。翁いふやう、「我あさごと夕ごとに見る竹の中におはするにて、知りぬ。子になり給ふべき人なめり」とて、手にうち入れて家へ持ちて来ぬ。妻の女にあづけて養はす。うつくしき事かぎりなし。いとをさなければ籠に入れて養ふ。

　竹取の翁、竹を取るに、この子を見つけて後に竹とるに、節を隔ててよごとに金ある竹を見つくる事かさなりぬ。かくて翁やうやう豊になり行く。

　この児、養ふ程に、すくすくと大きになりまさる。三月ばかりになる程に、よき程なる人に成りぬれば、髪上げなどさうして、髪上げさせ、裳着す。帳のうちよりも出ださず、いつき養ふ。この児のかたちけうらなる事世になく、屋のうちは暗き所なく光り満ちたり。翁心地あしく、苦しき時も、この子を見れば、苦しき事もやみぬ、腹立たしきことも慰みけり。

「かぐや姫の嘆き」

八月十五日ばかりの月に出で居て、かぐや姫いといたく泣き給ふ。人目もいまはつつみ給はず泣き給ふ。これを見て、親どもも「なに事ぞ」と問ひさわぐ。かぐや姫泣く泣く言ふ、「さきざきも申さむと思ひしかども、かならず心惑ひし給はん物ぞと思ひて、いままで過し侍りつるなり。さのみやはとて、うち出で侍りぬるぞ。おのが身はこの国の人にもあらず。月の都の人なり。それを昔の契ありけるによりなん、この世界にはまうで来りける。いまは帰るべきになりにければ、この月の十五日に、かのもとの国より、迎へに人々まうで来んず。さらずまかりぬべければ、思しなげかんが悲しき事を、この春より思ひなげき侍る也」と言ひて、いみじく泣くを、翁、「こは、なでふ事のたまふぞ。竹の中より見つけきこえたりしかど、菜種の大きさおはせしを、わが丈たち並ぶまで養ひたてまつりたるわが子を、なに人か迎へきこえん。まさに許さんや」と言ひて、「われこそ死なめ」とて、泣きののしる事、いと耐へがたげ也。かぐや姫のいはく、「月の都の人にて、父母あり。

かた時の間とて、かの国よりまうで来しかども、かくこの国にはあまたの年をへぬるになん有りける。かの国の父母の事も覚えず、ここには、かく久しく遊びきこえて、ならひたてまつれり。いみじからむ心地もせず。悲しくのみある。されどおのが心ならず、まかりなむとする」と言ひて、もろともにいみじう泣く。使はるる人々も、年頃ならひて、たち別れなむことを、心ばへなど貴やかにうつくしかりつる事を見ならひて、恋しからむことの耐へがたく、湯水飲まれず、同じ心になげかしがりけり。

「かぐや姫の昇天」

かかる程に、宵うち過ぎて、子の時ばかりに、家のあたり昼の明さにも過ぎて光りわたり、望月の明さを十あはせたるばかりにて、ある人の毛の穴さへ見ゆるほどなり。大空より人、雲に乗りて下り来て、土より五尺ばかり上りたるほどに、立ち列ねたり。これを見て、内外なる人の心ども、物におそはるるやうにて、あひ戦はん心もなかりけり。からうじて思ひ起して、弓矢をとり立てんとすれども、手に力もなくなりて、萎えかかりたり。中に心さかしき者、念じて射んとすれども、外ざまへ行きければ、あれも戦はで、心地ただ痴れに痴れて、まもり合へり。

立てる人どもは、装束の清らなること、物にも似ず。飛車一つ具したり。羅蓋さしたり。その中に王とおぼしき人、家に、「宮つこまろ、まうで来」と言ふに、猛く思ひつる宮つこまろも、物に酔ひたる心地して、うつ伏しに伏せり。いはく、「汝、をさなき人、いささかなる功徳を翁つくりけるによりて、汝が助けにとて、かた時のほどとて下ししを、そこらの年頃、そこらの金給ひて、身をかへたるがごと成りにたり。かぐや姫は、罪をつくり給へりければ、かく賤しきおのれがもとに、しばしおはしつる也。罪の限果てぬれば、かく迎ふるを、翁は泣き嘆く、能はぬ事也。はや出したてまつれ」と言ふ。翁答へて申す、「かぐや姫を養ひたてまつること二十余年に成りぬ。かた時との給ふにあやしく成り侍りぬ。又異所に、かぐや姫と申す人ぞおはすらん」と言ふ。「ここにおはするかぐや姫は、重き病をし給へば、え出でおはしますまじ」と申せば、その返事はなくて、屋の上に飛車を寄せて、「いざ、かぐや姫。穢き所にいかでか久しくおはせん」と言ふ。立て籠めたるところの戸、すなはち、ただ開きに開きぬ。格子どもも、人はなくして開きぬ。女抱きてゐたるかぐや姫、外に出でぬ。え止むまじければ、ただし仰ぎて泣きをり。竹取心惑ひて泣き伏せる所に寄りて、かぐや姫言ふ、「ここにも、心にもあらでかく罷るに、

昇らんをだに見おくり給へ」と言へども、「なにしに、悲しきに見おくりたてまつらん。我をいかにせよとて捨てては昇り給ふぞ。具して出でおはせね」と泣きて伏せれば、心惑ひぬ。「文を書きおきてまからん。恋しからむをりをり、とり出でて見給へ」とて、うち泣きて書く言葉は、

此国にうまれぬるとならば、なげかせたてまつらぬほどまで侍らで、過ぎ別れぬる事、返す返す本意なくこそおぼえ侍れ。脱ぎおく衣を、形見と見給へ。月の出でたらむ夜は、見おこせ給へ。見捨てたてまつりてまかる空よりも、落ちぬべき心地する

と書きおく。
　　天人の中に持たせたる箱あり。天の羽衣入れり。又あるは不死の薬入れり。ひとりの天人言ふ、「壺なる御薬たてまつれ。穢き所の物きこしめしたれば、御心地悪しからむ物ぞ」とてもて寄りたれば、わづか嘗め給ひて、すこし形見とて、脱ぎおく衣に包まんとすれば、ある天人包ませず。御衣をとり出でて着せんとす。その時に、かぐや姫「しばし待て」と言ふ。「衣着つる人は、心異になるなりといふ。物一こと言ひおくべき事ありけり」と言ひて文書く。天人、おそしと心もとながり給ひ、かぐや姫「もの知らぬことなの給ひそ」とて、いみじく静かに、公に御文たてまつり給ふ。あわてぬさま也。...

今はとて天の羽衣きるをりぞ君をあはれと思ひいでける

とて、壺の薬そへて、頭中将呼びよせてたてまつらす。中将に天人とりて伝ふ。中将とりつれば、ふと天の羽衣うち着せたてまつりつれば、翁をいとほしく、かなしと思しつることも失せぬ。此衣着つる人は、物思ひなく成りにければ、車に乗りて、百人ばかり天人具して昇りぬ。

Vocabulary for "Early Years"

いま (今) (*n.*) the present, now

昔 (むかし) (*n.*) long time ago

翁 (おきな) (*n.*) old man

いふ (言ふ) (*tr. v. YD*) to name, call

もの (者) (*n.*) person

有り (在り) (あり) (*intr. v. RH*) to exist, be

野山 (のやま) (*comp. n.*) fields and hills

まじる (交じる) (*tr. v. YD*) to enter into

取る (と) (*tr. v. YD*) to harvest, gather, collect

よろづ (万) (*n.*) counter for numerous things

使ふ (使う) (つか) (*tr. v. YD*) to use

名 (な) (*n.*) name

光る (ひか) (*intr. v. YD*) to shine, sparkle

筋 (すぢ) (*n.*) long narrow object, counter for such objects

あやしがる (怪しがる) (*tr. v. YD*) to find suspicious

寄る (よ) (*intr. v. YD*) to approach

筒 (つつ) (*n.*) tube, cylinder

それ (其れ・夫れ) (*pron.*) that, that thing

寸 (すん) (*n.*) unit of measure: one-tenth of a *shaku*, or approx. 1.193 inches

ばかり (*adv. p.*) about, around

いと (*adv.*) very, to a great extent

うつくし (美し・愛し) (*shiku adj.*) lovable, adorable

ゐる (居る) (*intr. v. KI*) to sit

やう (様) (*n.*) phrase nominalizer, as in "*what* he thinks" or "*what* he says"

我 (われ) (*pron.*) I, myself

あさ (朝) (*n.*) morning

夕 (ゆふ) (*n.*) evening

おはす (御座す) (*intr. v. SH*) to be, exist (hon. of *ari, ori*)

知る (し) (*tr. v. YD*) to know, understand

なる (成る) (*intr. v. YD*) to become

入る (い) (*tr. v. SN*) to put inside

持つ (も) (*tr. v. YD*) to hold

来 (く) (*intr. v. KH*) to come

妻 (め) (*n.*) wife

あづく (預づく) (*tr. v. SN*) to entrust someone with something

養ふ (やしな) (*tr. v. YD*) to raise, care for

かぎりなし (限り無し) (*ku adj.*) unlimited, unsurpassed

をさなし (幼し) (*ku adj.*) young

籠 (こ) (*n.*) bamboo box

見つく (見付く) (み) (*tr. v. SN*) to discover, seek out

節 (ふし) (*n.*) bamboo joint, knot

隔つ (へだ) (*tr. v. SN*) to leave a space between

よ (節) (*n.*) hollow spaces between joints

金 (こがね) (*n.*) gold

かさなる (重なる) (*intr. v. YD*) (for similar things) to happen at the same time or occur repeatedly

かくて (斯くて) (*conj.*) in this way

やうやう (漸う) (*adv.*) (from *yōyaku*) gradually, little by little

豊 (ゆたか) (*nari adj. v.*) wealthy, prosperous

児 (ちご) (*n.*) baby, infant

程 (ほど) (*n.*) interval, duration

すくすくと (*adv.*) (neologism) quickly, without stopping

大き (おほ) (*nari adj. v.*) big, large

なりまさる (増さる) (*intr. v. YD*) to increase in degree (height)

髪上げ (かみあ) *(n.)* (lit., putting up the hair) girl's coming-of-age ceremony

さうす (左右す) *(tr. v. SH)* (*sōsu*) (lit., to do left and right) to make arrangements

上ぐ (あ) *(tr. v. SN)* to raise, lift, move to a higher place

裳 (も) *(n.)* skirt a girl wears upon coming of age

着す (き) *(tr. v. SN)* to cause to wear, put on

帳 (ちやう) *(n.)* curtain surrounding a bedroom or bed

出だす (い) *(tr. v. YD)* to put out, take out

いつく (傅く) *(tr. v. YD)* to raise with great care

かたち (形・容・貌) *(n.)* countenance, visage, looks

けうら (清ら) *(nari adj. v.)* (*kyōra*) pure and beautiful in appearance

世 (よ) *(n.)* world

屋 (や) *(n.)* house, room

暗し (くら) *(ku adj.)* dark

光り (ひか) *(n.)* light

満つ (み) *(intr. v. YD)* to fill up, make full

心地 (ここち) *(n.)* mood, feeling

あし (悪し) *(shiku adj.)* ill, sick

苦し (くる) *(shiku adj.)* painful, hard, trying

やむ (止む) *(intr. v. YD)* to come to an end, to stop

腹立たし (はらだ) *(shiku adj.)* irritated, angry

慰む (なぐさ) *(intr. v. YD)* to become peaceful, settle down

Grammar Notes for "Early Years"

いまは 昔 (むかし)   lit., now is a long time ago; a conventional way to begin *monogatari*

いふもの   citational case p. *to* and RT of YD v. *iu*, modifying pron. *mono*, "person"; "a person who is called Old Man, the Bamboo Cutter"

ありけり   RY of RH v. *ari*, "to be," and SS of past-tense aux. v. *keri*

まじり   RY of YD v. *majiru*, "to enter into," and cont. conj. p. *te*

取りつつ (と)   RY of YD v. *toru*, "to gather," and conj. p. *tsutsu*, indicating repetition of action

よろづの事 (こと)   n. *yorozu*, "many," attrib. case p. *no*, and n. *koto*, "thing"

使ひけり (つか)   RY of YD v. *tsukau* and SS of aux. v. *keri*, indicating past

をば   comp.: object marker case p. *o* and emphatic bound p. *wa*, (sound change to *ba*), emphasizing the *o*

さかきの 造 (みやつこ)   Sakaki (clan name) and Miyatsuko (personal name)

なむいひける   emphatic bound p. *namu*, "tied" at the end by RT, RY of YD v. *iu*, "to call," and RT of past-tense aux. v. *keri*: "They called his name (*na*) Miyatsuko of Sakaki!"

なむ一筋ありける (ひとすじ)   emphatic bound p. *namu*, *hito*, "one," *suji* (a counter for bamboo), RY of RH v. *ari*, "to be," and past-tense aux. v. *keri* in RT because it is "tied" to *namu*

寄りて見るに (よ) (み)   RY of YD v. *yoru*, conj. p. *te*, RT of KI v. *miru*, and conj. p. *ni*, indicating time: "when he approached and looked"

光りたり (ひか)   RY of v. *hikaru*, and SS of aux. v. *tari*; *tari* can function as (1) resultative, revealing the result of an action, (2) continuative or durative, indicating continuous action, or (3) perfective, indicating the end of action; here it is continuative: "was shining"

見れば (み)   IZ of KI v. *miru* and conj. p. *ba*; IZ plus *ba* indicates a causal or temporal relationship to the following clause: "when he saw"

うつくしうて   RY of adj. *utsukushi*, with *u*-sound change from *utsukushiku* to *utsukushiu* (*utsukushū*), and conj. p. *te*

ゐたり　RY of intr. KI v. *iru* and SS of aux. v. *tari*, indicating continuous action (sitting)

言ふやう　RT of YD v. *iu* and n. *yō*, meaning "that" or "what": "what the old man said"

ごと　suffix, "each"

におはするにて　case p. *ni*, indicating place of action, RT of hon. v. *owasu*, "to be," and *nite*, a case p. indicating cause

知りぬ　RY of YD v. *shiru*, "to know," and SS of aux. v. *nu* (na, ni, *nu*, nuru, nure, ne)

子となり給ふべき人なめり　case p. *to*, RY of YD v. *naru*, "to become," SS of hon. suppl. v. *tamau*, showing respect toward the child, RT of aux. v. *beshi*, indicating appropriateness, n. *hito*, "person," RT of copular *nari*, "to be," and SS of spec. aux. v. *meri* (*naru-meri* undergoes a nasalized sound change to *nan-meri* and then to *na-meri*, with *n* unmarked but pronounced); *ko to nari* is a pun meaning both "to become a child (*ko*)" and "to become a basket (*ko*)": "She appears to be (*na-meri*) person for whom it is only appropriate that she become (my) child."

とて　citational case p. *to*, implying "to think that" or "to say that," and conj. p. *te*

うち入れて　prefix *uchi*, RY of SN v. *iru*, "to place in," and conj. p. *te*

来ぬ　RY of KH v. *ku*, "to come," and SS of aux. v. *nu*, which is perfective

妻の女　woman who is a wife, the case p. *no* indicating equivalency

あづけてやしなはす　RY of SN v. *azuku*, conj. p. *te*, MZ of YD v. *yashinau*, and SS of aux. v. *su*, which is causative: "He had her raise (the child)."

をさなければ　IZ of adj. *osanashi* and conj. p. *ba*, indicating a causal or temporal relationship: "since she was very young"

かさなりぬ　RY of YD v. *kasanaru*, "to happen often," and aux. v. *nu*, which is perfective

豊に　RY of adj. v. *yutaka-nari* (nara, nari/*ni*, nari, naru, nare, nare), "wealthy"

なり行く　comp. v. RY of YD v. *naru*, "to become," and SS of YD v. *yuku*, "to go"

やしなふ程に　RT of YD v. *yashinau*, "to raise," n. *hodo*, indicating extent, and case p. *ni*; *hodo ni* is generally treated as a comp. meaning "while"

よき程なる人　RT of adj. *yoshi*, "good," n. *hodo*, "size," RT of copular *nari*, "to be," and *hito*, "person"

髪上げさせ　MZ of SN v. *agu*, "to raise," and RY of aux. v. *sasu*, which is causative

世になく　n. *yo*, "world," locative case p. *ni*, and RY of adj. *nashi*, "not existing": "not existing in this world (peerless)"

満ちたり　RY of KN v. *mitsu*, "to fill," and SS of aux. v. *tari*

あしく　RY of *shiku* adj. *ashi*, "bad"

苦しき　RT of *shiku* adj. *kurushi*, "painful," modifying n. *toki*

やみぬ　RY of YD v. *yamu*, "to stop," and SS of aux. v. *nu*, which is perfective

腹立たしきこと　RT of *shiku* adj. *haradatashi*, "angry"

慰みけり　RY of YD v. *nagusamu*, "to find solace in," and aux. v. *keri*, indicating past tense

Annotated Grammar for "Early Years"

名	係助	名	固名	格助	四/体	名	ラ変/用	助動/過/終	名	格助	四/用	接助	名	格助	四/用	接助
いま	は	昔、	竹取の翁	と	いふ	もの	有り	けり。	野山	に	まじり	て	竹	を	取り	つつ、

名	格助	名	格助	四/用・	助動/過/終	名	格助	係助(濁音)	固名	格助	係/四	四/用	助動/過/結	代名	格助	名
よろづ	の	事	に	使ひ	けり。	名	を	ば	、さかきの造	と	なむ	いひ	ける。	そ	の	竹

格助	名	格助	名	四/体	名	係助/係	名・	ラ変/用	助動/過/結	四/用	接助	四/用	接助	上一/体	接助	名	格助	名
の	中	に、	もと	光る	竹	なむ	一筋	あり	ける。	あやしがり	て	寄り	て	見る	に、	筒	の	中

光り　たり。それ　を　見れ　ば、三寸　ばかり　なる　人、いと　うつくしう　て　ゐ　たり。

翁　いふ　やう、「我　あさ　ごと　夕　ごと　に　見る　竹　の　中　に　おはする　にて、知り　ぬ。子

と　なり　給ふ　べき　人　な　めり」とて、手　に　うち　入れ　て　家　へ　持ち

て　来　ぬ。妻　の　女　に　あづけ　て　養は　す。うつくしき　事　かぎりなし。いと

をさなけれ　ば　籠　に　入れ　て　養ふ。

竹取の翁、竹　を　取る　に、この　子　を　見つけ　て　後　に　竹　とる　に、節　を　隔て　て　よ

ごと　に　金　ある　竹　を　見つくる　事　かさなり　ぬ。かくて　翁　やうやう　豊に　なり

行く。

この　児、養ふ　程　に、すくすくと　大きに　なりまさる。三月　ばかり　に　なる　程　に、よき

程　なる　人　に　成り　ぬれ　ば、髪上げ　など　さうして、髪上げ　させ、裳着す。帳　の

うち　より　も　出ださ　ず、いつき　養ふ。この　児　の　かたち　けうらなる　事　世　に　なく、

屋　の　うち　は　暗き　所　なく　光り　満ち　たり。翁　心地　あしく、苦しき　時　も、この　子　を

見れ　ば、苦しき　事　も　やみ　ぬ、腹立たしき　こと　も　慰み　けり。

Vocabulary for "Princess's Lament"

八月 (葉月) (*n.*) Eighth Month (lunar calendar)

十五日 (望) (*n.*) day of the full moon, fifteenth day of the lunar month

泣く (*intr. v. YD*) to weep

人目 (*n.*) eyes of others

つつむ (慎む) (*tr. v. YD*) to show restraint toward

さわぐ (騒ぐ) (*intr. v. YD*) to make a commotion

さきざき (先先) (*n.*) before, past

心惑ひ (*n.*) emotional confusion

過ごす (*tr. v. YD*) to let time pass

うち出づ (打ち出づ) (*tr. v. SN*) to speak of

都 (*n.*) capital (now Kyoto)

契 (*n.*) karmic bond, fate, pledge, vow

ふる (由る・因る・依る) (*intr. v. YD*) to be the result of

世界 (*n.*) human world, earth

来る (*intr. v. YD*) to come, arrive

迎へ (*n.*) welcome, welcoming party

さる (避る) (*tr. v. YD*) to avoid

なげく (嘆く) (*intr. v. YD*) to grieve, lament

悲し (*shiku adj.*) painful, sad

いみじ (*shiku adj.*) intense, extreme

こ (此・是) (*pron.*) these, this

なでふ (*attrib. word* 連体詞) (*najō*) (from *nani to iu*) expresses doubt: what? what kind of (thing is that)?

菜種 (*n.*) rapeseed (a metaphor for smallness)

丈 (*n.*) height

たち並ぶ (立ち並ぶ) (*intr. v. YD*) to stand even with, to be the same height

なに人 (何人) (*n.*) what person, what kind of person

まさに (正に) (*adv.*) (1) truly, (2) just, (3) why? (rhetorical question); here, the meaning of 3

ののしる (罵る・喧る) (*intr. v. YD*) to make a commotion

耐ふ (*intr. v. SN*) to endure, bear

かた時 (片時) (*n.*) a moment, short time

ならふ (慣らふ) (*intr. v. YD*) to grow accustomed to, become used to

もろともに (諸共に) (*adv.*) acting together

たち別る (立ち別る) (*intr. v. SN*) to part, separate

心ばへ (*n.*) disposition, temperament

貴やか (*nari adj. v.*) refined, elegant

恋し (*shiku adj.*) beloved, dear

湯水 (*n.*) hot water, water

飲む (*tr. v. YD*) to drink

なげかし (嘆かし・歎かし) (*shiku adj.*) sad, wretched

Grammar Notes for "Princess's Lament"

出で居て RY of SN p. *izu*, "to go out," RY of KI p. *iru*, "to sit," and conj. p. *te*

いたく泣き給ふ RY of *ku* adj. *itashi*, RY of YD p. *naku*, and hon. suppl. p. *tamau*, to show respect toward Kaguyahime: "weep intensely"

つつみ給はず泣き給ふ RY of YD p. *tsutsumu*, MZ of YD hon. suppl. p. *tamau*, RY of YD p. *naku*, and SS of hon. suppl. v. *tamau*

なに事ぞ emphatic bound p. *zo*, which functions like a copula at the end of a sentence, here creating a strong question: "What is going on?"

問ひさわぐ comp. v.: RY of YD v. *tou*, "to ask," and SS of YD v. *sawagu*

泣く泣く adv. (from YD v. *naku*, "to weep"), modifying v. *iu*, "to say"

申さむと MZ of hum. YD v. *mōsu*, "to speak," SS of aux. v. *mu*, which is intentional, and citational case p. *to*: "I intended to speak."

心惑ひし給はん物ぞと RY of SH v. *su*, "to do," which makes n. *kokoromadoi* into a v., MZ of hon. suppl. v. *tamau*, respecting the Bamboo Cutter, and RT of spec. aux. v. *mu*

さのみやは adv. *sa*, "in that way," adv. p. *nomi*, "only," and interrogative bound p. *yawa*, creating a rhetorical question: "(Could it be hidden) in that way? (No.)"

とて citational case p. *tote*, from case p. *to*, implied RY of v. *omou*, "to think," and conj. p. *te*: "thinking that . . ."

それを pron. *sore*, "that," and interj. p. *o*

帰るべきになりにければ SS of YD v. *kaeru*, RT of *beshi* (expectation), implied n. *toki*, "time," case p. *ni*, and RY of YD v. *naru*, "to become": "since the time has come when I am expected to return . . ."

迎へに人々まうで来んず n. *mukae*, case p. *ni*, indicating object of the action, RY of hum. SN v. *mōzu*, "to come," MZ of KH v. *ku*, and SS of spec. aux. v. *muzu* (sound change to *nzu*), indicating future action: "They will come to pick me up."

思しなげかんが悲しき事 MZ of hon. v. *oboshinageku*, "to grieve," and RT of spec. aux. v. *mu* (*n*), modifying an implied *koto*: "the sadness that you would probably feel"

こはなでふ事 pron. *ko*, "this," bound p. *wa*, and attrib. *najō*: "This is what kind of thing?"

のたまふぞ RT of hon. v. *notamau*, showing respect to Kaguyahime; the emphatic bound p. *zo*, coming at the end of the sentence, indicates a strong question: "(What in the world) are you talking about?"

養 ひたてまつりたる　RY of YD v. *yashinau*, "to raise," and RY of YD hum. suppl. v. *tatematsuru*, showing respect toward Kaguyahime: "(my child) whom I had raised"

なに人か迎へきこえん　n. *nanibito*, "what person," rhetorical question bound p. *ka*, RY of SN v. *mukau*, MZ of SN hum. suppl. v. *kikoyu*, showing respect toward Kaguyahime, and RT of aux. v. *mu* (sound change to *n*), indicating speculation: "What person would come to pick you up? (No one.)"

まさに許さんや　adv. *masa ni*, "why," MZ of YD v. *yurusu*, "to allow," SS of aux. v. *mu* (*n*), and bound p. *ya*: "Why would I allow (this to happen)? (I would not.)"

われこそ死なめ　MZ of NH v. *shinu* and IZ of aux. v. *mu* (in IZ because of *koso*), indicating intention: "(If you are going to leave,) I would rather die."

耐へがたげ也　RY of SN v. *tau*, "to bear," stem of *ku* adj. *gatashi*, "difficult," and suffix *ge*, "appearance": "(He) appeared to find it difficult to bear."

かぐや姫のいはく　subject marker case p. *no*, MZ of v. *iu*, "to say," and nominalizing suffix *ku*: "What Kaguyahime said was . . ."

来しかども　MZ of *ku*, IZ of past-tense aux. v. *ki*, and concessive conj. p. *domo*; normally, aux. v. *ki* follows RY, but in the case of the KH v. *ku*, it follows MZ

へぬるになん有りける　RY of SN v. *hu*, "to spend (time)," RT of perfective aux. v. *nu*, modifying an implied *koto*, "fact," RY of

copular *nari*, emphatic bound p. *namu* (sound change to *nan*), and RY of suppl. v. *ari*, aux. v. *keri* in RT because of *namu*: "It is a fact that I have spent (many years)."

遊びきこえて　RY of YD v. *asobu*, "to enjoy oneself," and RY of SN hum. suppl. v. *kikoyu*

ならひたてまつれり　RY of YD v. *narau*, "to grow accustomed," IZ of YD hum. suppl. v. *tatematsuru*, and SS of aux. v. *ri*, which is resultative, indicating that the action is continuing: "I have grown accustomed (to this place)."

いみじからむ心地　MZ of adj. *imiji*, "extreme," RT of aux. v. *mu*, and n. *kokochi*, "feeling": "I don't feel extremely (happy). (I just feel sad.)"

おのが心ならず　"Not of my own will"

まかりなむとする　RY of YD hum. v. *makaru*, "to leave," MZ of aux. v. *nu*, SS of aux. v. *mu*, case p. *to*, and RT of SH v. *su*, "to do"; the combination of *nu* and future spec. *mu* expresses conjecture with confidence, and case p. *to* and v. *su* indicate an action that is about to be taken: "I will no doubt end up leaving."

たち別れなむことを　RY of SN v. *tachiwakaru*, "to part ways," MZ of aux. v. *nu*, RT of aux. v. *mu*, n. *koto*, "action," and case p. *o*, indicating object of an implied v.; this nominal phrase is the object of the v. phrase *nagekashigari-keri* at the end of the sentence

同じ心になげかしがりけり　case p. *ni*, "as," SS of *shiku* adj. *nagekashi*, "sad," RY of suffix *garu*, "to appear to be," which follows the SS of *shiku* adj.: "The (attendants) appeared to be sad, with the same heart as (the old man and his wife)."

Annotated Grammar for "Princess's Lament"

名	名	副助	格助	名	格助	下二/用	上一/用	接助	固名	副	ク形/用	四/用	補助動/尊/終	名	係助
八月	十五日	ばかり	の	月	に	出で	居	て、	かぐや姫	いと	いたく	泣き	給ふ。	人目	も

名	係助	四/用	補助動/尊/未	助動/打/用	四/用	補助動/尊/終	代名	格助	上一/用	接助	名	接尾	係助	名	格助
いま	は	つつみ	給は	ず	泣き	給ふ。	これ	を	見	て、	親	ども	も	「なに事	ぞ」と

四/用	四/終	固名	副	四/体	名	係助	四/謙/未	助動/意/終	格助	四/用	助動/過去/已	接助
問ひ	さわぐ。	かぐや姫	泣く泣く	言ふ、	「さきざき	も	申さ	む	と	思ひ	しか	ども、

かならず 心惑ひ し 給は ん 物 ぞ と 思ひ て、いま まで 過し 侍り つる

なり。さ のみ やは とて、うち 出で 侍り ぬる ぞ。おの が 身 は こ の 国 の

人 に も あら ず。月 の 都 の 人 なり。それ を 昔 の 契 あり ける に

より なん、こ の 世界 に は まうで 来り ける 。いま は 帰る べき に なり に

けれ ば、こ の 月 の 十五日 に、か の もと の 国 より、迎へ に 人々 まうで 来

んず。さら ず まかり ぬ べけれ ば、思しなげか ん が 悲しき 事 を、こ の

春 より 思ひなげき 侍る 也」と 言ひ て、いみじく 泣く を、翁、「こ は、なでふ

事 のたまふ ぞ。竹 の 中 より 見つけ きこえ たり しか ど、菜種 の 大き さ

おはせ し を、わ が 丈 たち 並ぶ まで 養ひ たてまつり たる わ が 子 を、

なに人 か 迎へ きこえ ん。まさに 許さ ん や」と 言ひ て、「われ こそ

死な め」とて、泣き ののしる 事、いと 耐へ がた げ 也。かぐや姫 の いはく、

「月 の 都 の 人 に て、父母 あり。かた時 の 間 とて、か の 国 より まうで 来

しか ども、かく こ の 国 に は あまた の 年 を へ ぬる に なん 有り

ける 。か の 国 の 父母 の 事 も 覚え ず、ここ に は、かく 久しく 遊び

きこえ て、ならひ たてまつれ り。いみじから む 心地 も せ ず。悲しく

のみ ある。されど おの が 心 なら ず、まかり な む と する」と 言ひ て、

もろともに いみじう 泣く。使は るる 人々 も、年頃 ならひ て、たち別れ な む

こと を、心ばへ など 貴やかに うつくしかり つる 事 を 見ならひ て、恋しから む

こと の 耐へがたく、湯水 飲ま れ ず、同じ 心 に なげかし がり けり。

Vocabulary for "Heavenly Ascent"

宵 (n.) dusk, early evening (from sundown to midnight)

過ぐ (intr. v. KN) to exceed

子の時 (set phrase) hour of the rat (11:00 P.M.–1:00 A.M.)

明さ (n.) light, brightness

~わたる (suppl. v., intr. v. YD) to extend over a wide area

望月 (n.) full moon, moon of the fifteenth night

毛の穴 (set phrase) (from ke, "hair," and ana, "hole") pore

立ち列ぬ (intr. v. SN) to stand in a line

内外 (n.) inside and outside (of a building)

おそふ (襲ふ) (tr. v. YD) to attack suddenly

戦ふ (intr. v. YD) to fight

思ひ起す〔おもおこ〕 (*tr. v. YD*) to renew one's resolve, arouse oneself to action

とり立つ〔た〕 (取り立つ) (*tr. v. SN*) to take up

萎えかかる〔な〕 (*comp.*) to lose strength (*nayu*, intr. v. SN) and lean on an object (*kakaru*, intr. v. YD)

心さかし〔こころ〕(心賢し) (*shiku adj.*) brave, stout-hearted

念ず〔ねん〕 (*tr. v. SH*) to endure, persevere

射る〔い〕 (*tr. v. KI*) to shoot

外ざま〔ほか〕(外様) (*n.*) another direction, elsewhere

ある (荒る) (*intr. v. SN*) to go wild, behave wildly

痴る〔し〕 (*intr. v. SN*) to be in a daze, lose one's senses

まもりあふ (守り合ふ) (*tr. v. YD*) to stare at each other

装束〔しやうぞく〕 (*n.*) clothing, dress

車〔くるま〕 (*n.*) carriage (usually ox-drawn)

具す〔ぐ〕 (*tr. v. SH*) to bring, take along

羅蓋〔らがい〕 (*n.*) large silk sunshade (for nobility)

王〔わう〕 (*n.*) (*ō*) king

おぼし (思し・覚し) (*shiku adj.*) similar (in appearance to), bearing a resemblance to

猛し〔たけ〕 (*ku adj.*) bold, brave

酔ふ〔ゑ〕 (*intr. v. YD*) to be overcome, intoxicated

うつ伏し〔ぶ〕 (俯し) (*n.*) prone, lying face down

伏す〔ふ〕 (*intr. v. YD*) to face downward

いささか (聊か) (*nari adj. v.*) slight, small

功徳〔くどく〕 (*n.*) good deeds

下す〔くだ〕 (*tr. v. YD*) to send down

かふ (換ふ) (*tr. v. SN*) to trade, barter

罪〔つみ〕 (*n.*) sin, transgression

おのれ (己) (*pron.*) second-person derogatory: the likes of you

しばし (暫し) (*adv.*) for a (little) while

限り〔かぎ〕 (*n.*) limit

能ふ〔あた〕 (*intr. v. YD*) to be able to do (followed by neg.)

異所〔ことどころ〕 (*n.*) another place, somewhere else

いざ (*interj.*) used to summon or address someone: well

穢し〔きたな〕 (*ku adj.*) unclean, defiled

久し〔ひさ〕 (*shiku adj.*) lengthy, appearance that a long time has passed

籠む〔こ〕 (*tr. v. SN*) to place inside, shut up

開く〔ひら〕 (*intr. v. YD*) to open

格子〔かうし〕 (*n.*) (*kōshi*) lattice

抱く〔いだ〕 (*tr v. YD*) to hold, embrace

ここ (此処・此所) (*pron.*) first person: I

仰ぐ〔あふ〕 (*intr. v. YD*) to look up at

昇る〔のぼ〕 (*intr. v. YD*) to climb, ascend

見送る〔みおく〕 (*tr. v. YD*) to send off

いかに (如何に) (*adv.*) how

折々〔をりをり〕 (*n.*) times, moments

本意なし〔ほい〕 (*ku adj.*) (lit., not of one's original intention) regrettable

衣〔きぬ〕 (*n.*) dress, robe

形見〔かたみ〕 (*n.*) keepsake, memento

見おこす〔み〕 (見遣す) (*tr. v. SN*) to look in this direction from afar

見捨つ〔みす〕 (*tr. v. SN*) to abandon, leave behind

天人〔てんにん〕 (*n.*) heavenly beings (creatures)

箱〔はこ〕 (*n.*) box

羽衣〔はごろも〕 (*n.*) feathered robe

不死〔ふし〕 (*n.*) immortality, eternal life

壺〔つぼ〕 (*n.*) jar

薬〔くすり〕 (*n.*) medicine

きこしめす (聞こし召す) *(tr. v. YD)* to eat, drink (hon.)

<ruby>嘗<rt>な</rt></ruby>む *(tr. v. SN)* to lick

すこし (少し) *(adv.)* a little, slightly

<ruby>包<rt>つつ</rt></ruby>む *(tr. v. YD)* to wrap

<ruby>異<rt>こと</rt></ruby> *(nari adj. v.)* different

おそし (遅し) *(ku adj.)* late, tardy

<ruby>心<rt>こころ</rt></ruby>もとながる (心許ながる) *(intr. v. YD)* to feel uneasy, impatient, irritated

<ruby>公<rt>おほやけ</rt></ruby> *(n.)* emperor

あわつ (慌つ) *(intr. v. SN)* to be in a panic

<ruby>思<rt>おも</rt></ruby>ひいづ (思ひ出づ) *(tr. v. SN)* to recall, remember

<ruby>頭<rt>とう</rt></ruby>の<ruby>中将<rt>ちうじゃう</rt></ruby> *(n.)* head (*tō*) of the *kurōdodokoro* (imperial household office) and *chūjō* (middle captain) in the imperial guards

<ruby>伝<rt>つた</rt></ruby>ふ *(tr. v. SN)* to entrust with a message

いとほし *(shiku adj.)* pitiful, pathetic, to feel pity toward

<ruby>物思<rt>ものおも</rt></ruby>ひ *(n.)* troubled thoughts, grief

Grammar Notes for "Heavenly Ascent"

かかる<ruby>程<rt>ほど</rt></ruby>に   attrib. *kakaru*, "this," "this kind of," and n. *hodo*, "time": "during this time"

うち<ruby>過<rt>す</rt></ruby>ぎて   prefix *uchi* (euphony) and RY of KN v. *sugu*, "to pass by"

<ruby>光<rt>ひか</rt></ruby>りわたり   RY of YD v. *hikaru* and suppl. v. *wataru*, "to extend over": "to shine throughout"

あはせたるばかりにて   RY of SN v. *awasu*, "to combine," RT of aux. v. *tari*, indicating an existing state, adv. p. *bakari* (indicating extent), RY of copular *nari*, and conj. p. *te*

<ruby>立<rt>た</rt></ruby>ち<ruby>列<rt>つら</rt></ruby>ねたり   RY of SN v. *tachitsuranu* and SS of aux. v. *tari* (continuative), "to be standing in line"

<ruby>物<rt>もの</rt></ruby>におそはるるやうにて   n. *mono*, "some (terrifying) thing," case p. *ni*, indicating agent of action, MZ of YD v. *osou*, RT of aux. v. *ru* (passive), and aux. v. *yō-nari*, "to resemble": "It was as if they had been attacked by something (possessed by an evil spirit)."

あれも<ruby>戦<rt>たたか</rt></ruby>はで   (text appears to be corrupted here) RY of SN v. *aru*, "to be wild," bound p. *mo*, "even," MZ of YD v. *tatakau*, and neg. conj. p. *de*: "Even when they went wild they could not fight."

<ruby>痴<rt>し</rt></ruby>れに<ruby>痴<rt>し</rt></ruby>れて   Repeating the RY of the v. with case p. *ni* between emphasizes the content of the v.: "to be totally dazed."

まもり<ruby>合<rt>あ</rt></ruby>へり   RY of YD v. *mamoru*, IZ of YD suppl. v. *au*, "to do mutually," and SS of aux. v. *ri*: "They stared at one another."

<ruby>汝<rt>なんぢ</rt></ruby>、をさなき人   The moon person is addressing the old man: "you, an immature person"

<ruby>汝<rt>なんぢ</rt></ruby>が<ruby>助<rt>たす</rt></ruby>けにとて、かた<ruby>時<rt>とき</rt></ruby>のほどとて<ruby>下<rt>くだ</rt></ruby>ししを   citational case p. *tote*, "thinking to," occurs twice here: "(Since the old man [you] did a few good deeds,) thinking (*tote*) to help you, I sent her (Kaguyahime) down, thinking (*tote*) (I would do that) for a short time."

<ruby>金給<rt>こがねたま</rt></ruby>ひて、<ruby>身<rt>み</rt></ruby>をかへたるがごと<ruby>成<rt>な</rt></ruby>りにたり   *tamai-te* is RY of hon. v. *tamau*, "to give," RY of SN tr. v. *kau*, "to change," RT of aux. v. *tari*, modifying an implied person, case p. *ga*, stem of comparative aux. v. *gotoshi*, RY of YD v. *naru*, "to become," RY of aux. v. *nu*, and SS of aux. v. *tari*: "I gave (you) money and you became like a changed person."

<ruby>罪<rt>つみ</rt></ruby>をつくり   Kaguyahime committed a sin before descending to earth and is being sent to live with the bamboo cutter as part of her punishment.

<ruby>罪<rt>つみ</rt></ruby>の<ruby>限<rt>かぎ</rt></ruby>り<ruby>果<rt>は</rt></ruby>てぬれば   RY of SN v. *hatsu*, "to finish," IZ of aux. v. *nu* (perfective), and conj. p. *ba*, indicating cause: "since the punishment has come to its end"

出だしたてまつれ   RY of YD v. *idasu*, "to bring out," and MR of hum. suppl. v. *tatematsuru*, humbling the bamboo cutter with respect to Kaguyahime: "Quickly, bring her out."

養ひたてまつる   The bamboo cutter's use of the hum. suppl. v. *tatematsuru* humbles himself with respect to Kaguyahime.

かた時との給ふにあやしく成り侍りぬ   The polite suppl. v. *haberi* is used here because it is polite dialogue: "When you say 'for a short time,' I end up becoming suspicious."

ぞおはすらん   bound p. *zo*, SS of hon. SH v. *owasu*, "to be," and RT of aux. v. *ramu*, which speculates about what is not visible but exists in the present

え出でおはしますまじ   correlated adv. *e*, "able," RY of SN v. *izu*, "to come out," SS of YD hon. suppl. v. *owashimasu*, and aux. v. *maji*, indicating negative potential

いかでか久しくおはせん   adv. *ikade*, "why," interrogative bound p. *ka*, RY of *ku* adj. *hisashi*, "long (time)," MZ of hon. SH v. *owasu*, "to be," and RT of spec. aux. v. *mu*, creating a rhetorical question: "Why should you (Kaguyahime) be here for a long time? (You should not.)"

ただ開きに開きぬ   adv. *tada*, "simply," emphasizing that nothing is preventing the door from opening; repetition of the v. emphasizes its content

女抱きてゐたるかぐや姫 ... え止むまじければ   Here, "woman" is the old woman, who is holding Kaguyahime in her arms but cannot prevent her from going outside.

さし仰ぎて   RY of YD v. *sashi-aogu*, "to look up," and conj. p. *te*; *sashi* is a prefix adding emphasis; the person who is looking up is the old woman

ここにも心にもあらでかく罷るに   *koko*, first-person pron., "I," *ara-de*, MZ of RH v. *ari*, "to be," neg. aux. v. *de*, adv. *kaku*, "in this way," RT of hum. YD v. *makaru*, "to take leave," and case p. *ni*, indicating reason/cause: "since (*ni*) I, too (*koko ni mo*), take leave

(*makaru*) in this fashion (*kaku*), not of my own accord (*kokoro ni mo ara-de*) . . ."

昇らんをだに   MZ of YD v. *noboru*, RT of aux. v. *mu*, case p. *o*, and adv. p. *dani*, "at least"

なにしに   pron. *nani*, RY of SH v. *su*, and case p. *ni*: "Why? For what purpose (should I send you off in sorrow)? (None.)"

我をいかにせよとて捨てては昇り給ふぞ   adv. *ikani*, "what," MR of SH v. *su*, and citational case p. *tote*: "What are you saying (*tote*) I should do (*seyo*) after you abandon me and ascend? (There's nothing I can do.)"

具して出でおはせね   RY of SH v. *gusu*, conj. p. *te*, RY of SN v. *izu*, "to leave," MZ of hon. suppl. v. *owasu*, and final p. *ne*, a Nara-period final p. that follows MZ and indicates a request: "I wish you would take me along when you leave!"

心惑ひぬ   The subject here is Kaguyahime, who writes the following letter.

恋しからむをりをり   MZ of *shiku* adj. *koishi*, "dear," RT of spec. aux. v. *mu*, and n. *oriori*: "those times when you miss me dearly"

うまれぬるとならば   RY of SN v. *umaru*, "to be born," RT of aux. v. *nu*, case p. *to*, MZ of copular *nari*, and conj. p. *ba*: "If I had been born (into this world)"

なげかせたてまつらぬほどまで侍らで ...   MZ of YD v. *nageku*, "to grieve," RY of aux. v. *su* (causative), MZ of hum. YD suppl. v. *tatematsuru*, RT of neg. aux. v. *zu*, MZ of RH hum. v. *haberi*, "to serve," and neg. conj. p. *de*. The text is unclear here, and a phrase like *haberu-beki-o* 侍るべきを, "I would have served you but," needs to be inserted after *made*: "(I would have served you) so as not to cause you grief, but I was not able to serve you (in that way)."

過ぎ別れぬる事、返す返す本意なくこそおぼえ侍れ   RY of *oboyu*, "to feel," and IZ of polite suppl. v. *haberi*: "Repeatedly I regret that I have had to part with you (without serving you in that way)."

見おこせ給へ RY of SN v. *miokosu* and MR of hon. suppl. v. *tamau*: "look from afar in (my) direction (on the nights when the moon comes out)"

落ちぬべき心地する RY of KN v. *otsu*, "to fall," SS of aux. v. *nu* (confidence), and RT of aux. v. *beshi* (speculation): "(From the sky where I have left you behind) I will no doubt feel as if I am falling."

天人の中に持たせたる箱 MZ of YD *motsu* and RY of *su*, which is causative: "a box (*hako*) that they had one (*naka*) of the heavenly creatures (*tennin*) hold (*mota-se-taru*)"

又あるは conj. *mata*, "in addition," and attrib. (RT) *aru*, "a certain," implying another *hako*

壺なる御薬たてまつれ n. *tsubo*, "jar," RT of copular *nari*, indicating location, and MR of YD hon. v. *tatematsuru*, "to drink"; *tatematsuru* is usually a hum. v., "to give" or "to send (someone)," but here it is an hon. v. meaning "to drink/eat"

物ぞ combination of n. *mono* and emphatic bound p. *zo* make a strong declaration, functioning like a copula at the end of a sentence

すこし形見とて citational case p. *tote*: "thinking that she (Kaguyahime) would (treat the robe) a little as a keepsake"

御衣 (also *mizo*) hon. for clothing of a person of high status; here, the "feathered robe"

着せむとす MZ of tr. SN v. *kisu*, "to put on," and SS of aux. v. *mu*, indicating intention:

"(The heavenly beings) attempted to put the robe (on Kaguyahime)."

異になるなり RY of adj. v. *koto-nari*, RT of YD v. *naru*, "to become," and SS of copular aux. v. *nari*

なの給ひそ prohibition correlative adv. p. *na*, RY of YD hon. v. *notamau*, "to say," and prohibition final p., *so*, which follows RY

公に御文たてまつり給ふ *ōyake* refers to the emperor, who had unsuccessfully courted Kaguyahime earlier; hum. v. *tatematsuru*, "to give," shows respect to the emperor, and hon. suppl. v. *tamau* shows the narrator's respect toward Kaguyahime

今はとて *ima wa* is a phrase indicating the final moments (before death or departure): "now is the time." Kaguyahime sends this poem to the emperor: "Thinking (*tote*) that now is the time (to depart), when I put on the heavenly feathered robe, I recall my lord with deep emotion (*aware to*)."

頭の中将呼び寄せてたてまつらす MZ of hum. YD v. *tatematsuru*, "to give," and SS of causative aux. v. *su*; Kaguyahime calls over (*yobi-yosete*) the *chūjō* and has him give the object to the emperor

とりて伝ふ RY of YD v. *toru*, "to take," conj. p. *te*, and SS of YD v. *tsutau*. The heavenly being takes the poem and the medicine from Kaguyahime and gives them to the *chūjō*.

失せぬ MZ of SN v. *usu*, "to disappear," and SS of perfective *nu*: "(Those feelings) disappeared altogether."

Annotated Grammar for "Heavenly Ascent"

連体詞 名 格助 名 上二/用 接助 名 副助 格助 名 格助 名 格助 名 格助 係助 上二/用 接助
かかる 程 に、宵 うち過ぎ て、子の時 ばかり に、家 の あたり 昼 の 明さ に も 過ぎて

四/用 補助動/四/用 名 格助 名 格助 名 下二/用 動動/存/体 副助 助動/断/用 接助 ラ変/体 名 格助 名 格助 名 副助
光り わたり、望月 の 明さ を 十 あはせ たる ばかり に て、ある 人 の 毛 の 穴 さへ

下二/体 名 助動/断/終 名 格助 名 格助 名 名 格助 四/用 接助 カ変/用 接助 名 格助 名 副助 四/用 助動/存/体
見ゆる ほど なり。大空 より 人、雲 に 乗り て 下り来 て、土 より 五尺 ばかり 上り たる

名 格助 下二/用 助動/存/終 代名 格助 上一/用 接助 名 助動/断/体 名 名 格助 名 接尾 名 格助 四/未 助動/受/体
程 に、立ち列ね たり。これ を 見 て、内外 なる 人 の 心 ども、物 に おそは るる

やうに て、あひ戦は ん 心 も なかり けり。からうじて 思ひ起し て、弓矢 を とり立て

ん と すれ ども、手 に 力 も なく なり て、萎え かかり たり。中 に 心さかしき 者、

念じ て 射 ん と すれ ども、外ざま へ 行き けれ ば、あれ も 戦は で、心地 ただ

痴れ に 痴れ て、まもり合へ り。

立て る 人 ども は、装束 の 清らなる こと、物 に も 似 ず。飛車 一つ 具し

たり。羅蓋 さし たり。その 中 に 王 と おぼしき 人、家 に、「宮つこまろ、まうで来」

と 言ふ に、猛く 思ひ つる 宮つこまろ も、物 に 酔ひ たる 心地し て、うつ伏し に 伏せ

り。いはく、「汝、をさなき 人、いささかなる 功徳 を 翁 つくり ける に よりて、汝

が 助け に とて、かた時 の ほど とて 下し し を、そこら の 年頃、そこら の 金 給ひ

て、身 を かへ たる が ごと 成り に たり。かぐや姫 は、罪 を つくり 給へ

り けれ ば、かく 賤しき をのれ が もと に、しばし おはし つる 也。罪 の 限

果て ぬれ ば かく 迎ふる を、翁 は 泣き嘆く、能は ぬ 事 也。はや 出し

たてまつれ」と 言ふ。翁 答へ て 申す、「かぐや姫 を 養ひ たてまつる 二十余年 に 成り

ぬ。かた時 と の 給ふ に あやしく 成り 侍り ぬ。又 異所 に、かぐや姫 と 申す

人 ぞ おはす らん」と 言ふ。「ここ に おはする かぐや姫 は、重き 病 を し 給へ

ば、え 出で おはします まじ」と 申せ ば、その 返事 は なくて、屋 の 上 に 飛車 を

寄せ て、「いざ、かぐや姫。穢き 所 に いかで か 久しく おはせ ん」と 言ふ。立て籠め

たる ところ の 戸、すなはち、ただ 開き に 開き ぬ。格子 ども も、人 は なく して 開き

ぬ。女 抱き て ゐ たる かぐや姫、外 に 出で ぬ。え 止む まじけれ ば、ただ

さし仰ぎ て 泣き をり。竹取 心 惑ひ て 泣き伏せ る 所 に 寄り て、かぐや姫 言ふ、

「ここ に も 心 に も あら で かく 罷る に、昇ら ん を だに 見おくり 給へ」と

言へ ども、なに し に 悲しき に、見おくり たてまつら ん。我 を いかに せよ とて

捨て て は 昇り 給ふ ぞ。具して 出で おはせ ね」と 泣き て 伏せ れ ば、心

惑ひ ぬ。「文 を 書きおき て まから ん。恋しから む をりをり、とり出で て 見

給へ」とて、うち泣き て 書く 言葉 は、

此 国 に むまれ ぬる と なら ば、なげか せ たてまつら ぬ

ほど まで 侍ら で 過ぎ 別れ ぬる 事、返々 本意なく こそ おぼえ

侍れ。脱ぎおく 衣 を 形見 と 見 給へ。月 の 出で たら

む 夜 は、見おこせ 給へ。見捨て たてまつり て まかる 空 よりも、

落ち ぬ べき 心地 する

と 書きおく。

天人 の 中 に 持た せ たる 箱 あり。天 の 羽衣 入れ り。又 ある は 不死の薬

入れ り。ひとり の 天人 言ふ、「壺 なる 御薬 たてまつれ。穢き 所 の 物 きこしめし

たれ ば、御心地 悪しから む 物 ぞ」とて もて 寄り たれ ば、わづか 嘗め 給ひ

て、すこし 形見 とて、脱ぎおく 衣 に 包ま ん と すれ ば、ある 天人 包ま せ ず。

御衣 を とり出で て 着せ ん と す。その 時 に、かぐや姫「しばし 待て」と 言ふ。

「衣 着せ つる 人 は、心異に なる なり と いふ。物 一こと 言ひおく べき 事 あり

けり」と 言ひ て、文 書く。天人、おそし と 心もとながり 給ひ、かぐや姫「もの 知ら

ぬ ことな の給ひ そ」とて、いみじく 静かに、公 に 御文 たてまつり 給ふ。あはて

ぬ さま 也。…

今 は とて 天の羽衣 きる を り ぞ 君 を あはれ と 思ひいで ける

とて、壺 の 薬 そへ て、頭中将 呼びよせ て たてまつら す。中将 に 天人 とりて

伝ふ。中将 とり つれ ば、ふと 天の羽衣 うち 着せ たてまつり つれ ば、翁 を いとほしく、

かなし と 思し つる 事 も 失せ ぬ。此 衣 着 つる 人 は、物思ひ なく 成り

に けれ ば、車 に 乗り て、百人 ばかり 天人 具して 昇り ぬ。

Part II

Heian Period

3

The Tales of Ise

The Tales of Ise (*Ise monogatari*) is a collection of 125 tales of poems (*uta-gatari*) presented as episodes in the life of Ariwara Narihira (825–880), a nobleman celebrated as the greatest male poet of his time. Within a decade or so of his death, Narihira had become the legendary antihero of early Heian court society, idealized for sacrificing political favor, fortune, and propriety for love and poetry. The legend of Narihira flourished for centuries and ensured *The Tales of Ise* a place among the most-read and -quoted classics of Japanese literature.

Although each of the 125 sections of *The Tales of Ise* is essentially autonomous, they are arranged in a roughly chronological and partially biographical sequence, beginning with the protagonist's youth (sec. 1) and progressing from his transgressions in the capital (sec. 4) to his exile in the East (sec. 9) to his return to the capital, and finally to his death (sec. 125). Significantly, Narihira violates social convention, engaging in forbidden love in unexpected places and transgressing the prerogatives of the throne (sec. 69). The inevitable consequences for himself and his lovers become the impetus for poetry of profound feeling and resignation to separation, disappointment, and sorrow, composed with an elegance of diction and rhetorical subtlety that seem to overcome every form of loss or defeat.

The text is based on Horiuchi Hideaki and Akiyama Ken, eds., *Taketori monogatari, Ise monogatari*, Shin Nihon koten bungaku taikei 17 (Tokyo: Iwanami Shoten, 1997), 87–90, with minor orthographic changes.

『伊勢物語』

「9」

むかし、をとこありけり。そのをとこ、身をえうなきものに思ひなして、京にはあらじ、あづまの方に住むべき国求めにとて行きけり。もとより友とする人ひとりふたりしていきけり。道知れる人もなくて、まどひいきけり。三河の国、八橋といふ所にいたりぬ。そこを八橋といひけるは、水ゆく河の蜘蛛手なれば、橋を八つわたせるによりてなむ八橋といひける。その沢のほとりの木の蔭に下りゐて、乾飯食ひけり。その沢にかきつばたいとおもしろく咲きたり。それを見て、ある人のいはく、「かきつばたといふ五文字を句の上にすゑて、旅の心をよめ」といひければ、よめる。

　　　　から衣きつつなれにしつましあればはるばるきぬる旅をしぞ思ふ

とよめりければ、皆人、乾飯のうへに涙おとしてほとびにけり。

　行き行きて、駿河の国にいたりぬ。宇津の山にいたりて、わが入らむとする道は、いと暗う細きに、つたかへでは茂り、物心ぼそく、すずろなるめを見ることと思ふに、修行者あひたり。「かかる道はいかでかいまする」といふを見れば、見し人なりけり。京に、その人の御もとにとて、文書きてつく。

　　　　駿河なる宇津の山べのうつつにも夢にも人にあはぬなりけり

富士の山を見れば、五月のつごもりに、雪いと白う降れり。

　　　　時知らぬ山は富士の嶺いつとてか鹿の子まだらに雪のふるらん

　その山は、ここにたとへば、比叡の山を二十ばかり重ねあげたらんほどして、なりは塩尻のやうになんありける。

　猶行き行きて、武蔵の国と下総の国との中に、いと大きなる河あり。それをすみだ河といふ。その河のほとりにむれゐて思ひやれば、限りなくとほくも来にけるかなとわびあへるに、渡守、「はや舟に乗れ、日も暮れぬ」といふに、乗りて渡らんとするに、皆人物わびしくて、京に思ふ人なきにしもあらず。さるをりしも、白き鳥の嘴と脚と赤き、鴫の大きさなる、水のうへに遊びつつ魚をくふ。京には見えぬ鳥なれば、皆人見知らず。渡守に問ひければ、「これなん都鳥」といふをききて、

　　　　名にし負はばいざ言とはむ都鳥わが思ふ人はありやなしやと

とよめりければ、舟こぞりて泣きにけり。

Vocabulary

えうなし (要なし)　(*ku adj.*) worthless, unnecessary

思^{おも}ひなす　(*tr. v. YD*) to assume, take for granted

あづま (東)　(*proper n.*) Eastern Provinces (east of Kyoto)

住^すむ　(*intr. v. YD*) to live

求^{もと}む　(*tr. v. SN*) to seek out, look for

もとより (元より・固より)　(*adv.*) from before

知^しる　(*tr. v. YD*) to know, understand

まどふ (惑ふ)　(*intr. v. YD*) to be lost, wander

いたる (至る)^い　(*intr. v. YD*) to arrive at

三河の国^{みかは　くに}　(*proper n.*) province in present-day southern Aichi Prefecture

蜘蛛手^{くもで}　(*n.*) (lit., spider legs) river or road forking in multiple directions

わたす (渡す)　(*tr. v. YD*) to lay down a bridge

沢^{さは}　(*n.*) swamp

ほとり (辺)　(*n.*) edge, side

おる (降る)　(*intr. v. KN*) to get down from a high position

ゐる (居る)　(*intr. v. KI*) to sit

乾飯^{かれいひ}　(*n.*) dried rice (when moistened, it turns soft enough to eat)

食^くふ　(*tr. v. YD*) to eat

かきつばた (杜若)　(*n.*) type of iris, perennial grass that grows in lakes and swamps

おもしろし (面白し)　(*ku adj.*) charming, wonderful, delightful

咲^さく　(*intr. v. YD*) to bloom, blossom

句^く　(*n.*) one of the five phrases of a thirty-one-syllable (5/7/5/7/7) Japanese poem (*waka*)

上^{かみ}　(*n.*) beginning

すう (据う)　(*tr. v. SN*) to place, set

よむ (詠む)　(*tr. v. YD*) to compose a poem

唐衣^{からころも}　(*n.*) Chinese-style robe with long sleeves

きる (着る)　(*tr. v. KI*) to wear

なる (慣る・馴る)　(*intr. v. SN*) to be used to, familiar with

つま (夫・妻)　(*n.*) wife (*tsuma* also means "hem" [of a robe])

はるばる (遥〻)　(*adv.*) from far away

皆人^{みなひと}　(*n.*) everyone

おとす (落す)　(*tr. v. YD*) to drop, let fall

ほとぶ (潤ぶ)　(*intr. v. KN*) to absorb moisture and expand, to swell up

駿河の国^{するが　くに}　(*proper n.*) province in present-day Shizuoka Prefecture

宇津の山^{うつ　やま}　(*proper n.*) mountain in Shizuoka Prefecture

暗^{くら}し　(*ku adj.*) dark

細^{ほそ}し　(*ku adj.*) thin, narrow

つた (蔦)　(*n.*) Japanese ivy

かへで (楓)　(*n.*) maple tree, known for bright leaves in autumn

茂^{しげ}る　(*intr. v. YD*) to grow thick

心^{こころ}ぼそし(心細し)　(*ku adj.*) forlorn, lonely

すゞろ (漫ろ)　(*nari adj. v.*) unexpected

目^めを見^みる　(*set phrase*) to experience, encounter

修行者^{すぎゃうじゃ}　(*n.*) ascetic, wandering monk

かかる (斯かる)　(*attrib.*) this kind of

いかで (如何で)　(*adv.*) question: why, how

います (坐す)　(*intr. v. SH*) to go, come (hon. for *yuku, ku*)

文^{ふみ}　(*n.*) letter

つく (着く)　(*tr. v. SN*) to entrust to someone

山べ^{やま} (山辺)　(*n.*) mountainside

うつつ (現)　(*n.*) reality, awakened state (as opposed to dream)

夢^{ゆめ}　(*n.*) dream

富士の山^{ふじ　やま}　(*proper n.*) Mount Fuji

つごもり (晦日) (*n.*) last part of the month (lunar calendar)

降る (*intr. v. YD*) to fall (snow, rain, etc.)

嶺 (*n.*) peak

鹿 (*n.*) (old reading for *shika*) deer

子 (*n.*) child, fawn

まだら (斑) (*nari adj. v.*) spotted, dappled

比叡の山 (*proper n.*) Mount Hiei (near the capital)

重ぬ (*tr. v. SN*) to pile up

あぐ (上ぐ・挙ぐ・揚ぐ) (*tr. v. SN*) to raise, lift

ほど (程) (*n.*) degree, extent

なり (形・態) (*n.*) shape, figure

塩尻 (*n.*) salt mound (seawater poured on a sand mound and left to dry in the sun to make salt)

やう (様) (*n.*) shape

猶 (*adv.*) all the more, even more so

武蔵の国 (*proper n.*) province in present-day Tokyo, Saitama, and Kanagawa prefectures

下総の国 (*proper n.*) old name for Shimōsa Province, now part of Chiba and Ibaraki prefectures

すみだ河 (*proper n.*) Sumida River, on the east side of modern Tokyo, on the border of Musashi and Shimotsufusa (Shimōsa) provinces

むる (群る) (*intr. v. SN*) to gather in one spot

思ひやる (*tr. v. YD*) to think of something or someone far away, imagine

限りなし (*ku adj.*) unlimited

わぶ (侘ぶ) (*intr. v. KN*) to find difficult to bear

あふ (合ふ) (*intr. v. YD*) to do ~ together (suppl. v.)

渡守 (*n.*) ferryman

乗る (*intr. v. YD*) to board (a boat)

暮る (*intr. v. SN*) to set (sun)

渡る (*intr. v. YD*) to cross to the other side

わびし (侘びし) (*shiku adj.*) painful

思ふ (*tr. v. YD*) to love, cherish

さる (然る) (*attrib.*) that, that kind of

をり (折) (*n.*) moment, occasion, opportunity

嘴 (*n.*) bill, beak

鴫 (*n.*) snipe, longbill

魚 (*n.*) fish

くふ (食ふ・喰ふ) (*tr. v. YD*) to eat

都鳥 (*n.*) (lit., capital bird) type of water bird

負ふ (*tr. v. YD*) to bear as a name (as in 名に負う)

いざ (*interj.*) used to initiate speech, to encourage oneself: well, here we go . . .

問ふ (*tr. v. YD*) to inquire, ask

言問ふ (*intr. v. YD*) to question, ask

こぞる (挙る) (*intr. v. YD*) to gather together, do together

Grammar Notes

あらじ MZ of RH v. *ari*, "to be," plus aux. v. *ji*, which is negative intentional

住むべき SS of YD v. *sumu* and RT of aux. v. *beshi*, indicating appropriateness: "a province where it would be appropriate (or good) to live in"

求めにとて RY of SN v. *motomu*, turning it into a n. that becomes the objective of an implied v., case p. *ni*, which points to the objective and implies after it *yuka-mu*, "to intend to go," and citational case p. *tote*: "thinking to go to seek (*motome*)"

ふたりしていきけり　*shite*, case p. meaning "together with": "he went together with . . ."

知れる人　IZ of YD v. *shiru* and RT of resultative-perfective aux. v. *ri*, modifying *hito*

まどひいきけり　RY of YD v. *madou*, RY of YD v. *iku*, "to go," and SS of past-tense aux. v. *keri*

わたせるによりて　IZ of tr. YD v. *watasu*, RT of aux. v. *ri*, which is resultative, an implied *koto*, case p. *ni*, RY of YD v. *yoru*, "to be the result of," and conj. p. *te*: "as a result of the (bridge) being laid across (in eight places)"

咲きたり　RY of YD v. *saku*, "to bloom," followed by SS of aux. v. *tari*, which is continuative

ある人のいはく　attrib. *aru*, "a certain," n. *hito*, subject marker case p. *no*, MZ of YD v. *iu*, "to say," and nominalizing suffix *ku*: "what a certain person said"

句の上にすゑて　The poet is being asked to compose a *waka* poem in which the five *ku*, or phrases, begin with the syllables *ka*, *ki*, *tsu*, *ba*, and *ta*, respectively.

きつつ　RY of KI v. *kiru*, "to wear," and conj. p. *tsutsu*, indicating repetitive action

なれにし　RY of SN v. *naru*, RY of aux. v. *nu*, which is perfective, and RT of past-tense aux. v. *ki*, referring to both the robe and the poet's wife

しあれば　emphatic adv. p. *shi*, IZ of v. *ari*, and conj. p. *ba*, indicating cause

はるばる　adv. *harubaru*, "from far away," puns on *haru* (張る), "to stretch out," and an associated word (*engo*) of *koromo*, "robe"

きぬる　RY of KH v. *ku*, "to come," which puns on *kiru*, "to wear," and RT of aux. v. *nu*

しぞ思ふ　emphatic adv. p. *shi*, emphatic bound p. *zo*, and RT of YD v. *omou*, "bound" to *zo*

わが入らむとする道　MZ of YD v. *iru*, "to enter," SS of intent. aux. v. *mu*, case p. *to*, indicating the above as the objective of following v. (lit., to do in order to try to enter), and RT of SH v. *su*, "to do," modifying n. *michi*: "the road that they themselves (*waga*) were attempting to enter"

暗う細きに　RY of *ku* adj. *kurashi* (sound change from *kuraku*), RT of *ku* adj. *hososhi*, "narrow," and conj. p. *ni*, indicating "on top of that"

物心ぼそく　prefix *mono* meaning "somehow or another"

かかる道はいかでかいまするといふを見れば　"When the (traveler) looked at (the ascetic) who asked, 'How did you come on this road?'"

京にその人の御もとに　"to the place (*on-moto*) of that person (*sono hito*) (whom one is thinking of) in the capital (*kyō*)"

とて　case p., derived from citational case p. *to*, RY of implied v. such as "to think," and conj. p. *te*: "(What season) does it think it is?"

文書きてつく　"writing a letter and leaving it (with the traveler to take to the capital)"

駿河なる宇津の山べのうつつ　copular *naru* indicating location; first two *ku* (5/7), or phrases, of the poem up to *yamabe no* are a preface-phrase (*jokotoba*) to the main body, which begins with *utsutsu*, with the *utsu* in *utsu no yama* anticipating the word *utsutsu*, "reality"

あはぬなりけり　MZ of YD v. *au*, "to meet," RT of neg. aux. v. *zu*, RY of copular *nari*, and SS of aux. v. *keri*, here exclamatory

降れり　IZ of YD v. *furu*, "to fall," and SS of aux. v. *ri*, which is continuative

時知らぬ山　"a mountain that knows (no) season"

ふるらむ　*ramu* here indicates speculation about cause

重ねあげたらむ　RY of SN comp. v. *kasane-agu*, MZ of aux. v. *tari*, which is perfective or resultative, and RT of aux. v. *mu*, which is speculative

ほどして   n. *hodo*, "extent," plus case p. *shite*, "having"; together they mean "to be to the extent that"

やうになむありける   RY of aux. v. *yō-nari*, "to resemble," and emphatic bound p. *namu*

とほくも来にけるかな   RY of *ku* adj. *tōshi*, "far," bound p. *mo*, RY of KH v. *ku*, "to come," RY of aux. v. *nu*, which is perfective, RT of past-tense aux. v. *keri*, and emphatic final p. *kana*

わびあへるに   IZ of intr. YD v. *wabi-au*, "to commiserate together," RT of aux. v. *ri*, and conj. p. *ni*, which indicates time (when)

暮れぬ   RY of SN v. *kuru*, "to get dark," and SS of aux. v. *nu*, which expresses confidence

渡らんとするに   MZ of YD v. *wataru*, SS of aux. v. *mu* (sound change to *n*), which is intentional, case p. *to*, RT of SH v. *su* (modifying an implied *toki*), and conj. p. *ni*

なきにしもあらず   RT of *ku* adj. *nashi*, "not," RY of copular *nari*, emphatic adv. p. *shimo*, MZ of RH suppl. v. *ari*, and SS of neg. aux. v. *zu*; *shimo* also treated as a combination of adv. p. *shi* and bound p. *mo*, both emphatic

白き鳥の嘴と脚と赤き鴨の大きさなる   first *no*, case p. indicating apposition, that the subject of the preceding phrase and that of the following are the same; *mono* also implied after RT of *akashi*, "red," and RT of *ōki-nari*, "big": "It was a white bird, and its beak and legs were red; (and this bird), which was the size of a snipe, (was eating fish as it played on top of the water)."

負はば   "if you bear (the name of the capital)"

ありやなしやと   "Is (my love) alive or dead?"

Annotated Grammar

むかし、男 ありけり。その 男、身 を えうなき もの に 思ひなし て、京 に は あら

じ、あづま の 方 に 住む べき 国 求め に とて 行き けり。もとより 友 と する

人 ひとり ふたり して いき けり。道 知れ る 人 も なく て、まどひ いき けり。

三河 の 国、八橋 と いふ 所 に いたり ぬ。そこ を 八橋 と いひ ける は、水 ゆく

河 の 蜘蛛手 なれ ば、橋 を 八つ わたせ る に より て なむ 八橋 と いひ

ける。その 沢 の ほとり の 木 の 蔭 に 下り ゐ て、乾飯 食ひ けり。その 沢

に かきつばた いと おもしろく 咲き たり。それ を 見 て、ある 人 の いは く、

「かきつばた と いふ 五文字 を 句 の 上 に すゑ て、旅 の 心 を よめ」 と いひ けれ

ば、よめ る。

から衣 き つつ なれ に し つま し あれ ば

はるばる き ぬる 旅 を し ぞ 思ふ

と よめ り けれ ば、皆人、乾飯 の うへ に 涙 おとし て ほとび に けり。

行き 行き て、駿河 の 国 に いたり ぬ。宇津 の 山 に いたり て、わが 入ら む

と する 道 は、いと 暗う 細き に、つた かへで は 茂り、物心ぼそく、すずろなる め を

上一/体　名　格助　四/体　接助　名　四/用　助動/完/終　連体　名　係助　副・　係助/疑/係　サ変/尊/体/結　格助　四/体
見る こと と 思ふ に、修行者 あひ たり。「かかる 道 は いかで か いまする」と いふ

格助　上一/已　接助　上一/用　助動/過/体　名　助動/断/用　助動/過/終　名　格助　代　格助　名　格助　接頭/尊　名　格助　格助　名
を 見れ ば、見 し 人 なり けり。京 に、その 人 の 御 もと に とて、文

四/用　接助　下二/終
書き て つく。

固名　助動/断/体　固名　格助　名・　格助　名　格助　係助
駿河 なる 宇津 の 山べ の うつつ に も

名　格助　係助　名　格助　四/未　助動/打/体　助動/断/用　助動/詠/終
夢 に も 人 に あは ぬ なり けり

固名　格助　名　格助　上一/已　接助　名　格助　名　格助　名　副　ク形/用　音　四/已　助動/存/終
富士 の 山 を 見れ ば、五月 の つごもり に、雪 いと 白う 降れ り。

名　四/未・助動/打/体　名　係助　固名　格助　名　代　格助　接助　係助/疑/係
時 知ら ぬ 山 は 富士 の 嶺 いつ とて か

名　格助　名　ナリ形動/用・名　格助　四/終　助動/推/体/結
鹿 の 子 まだらに 雪 の ふる らん

代　格助　名　係助　代　格助　下二/未　接助　固名　格助　名　格助　名　副助　下二/用　下二/用　助動/完/未　助動/推/体　名
その 山 は、ここ に たとへ ば、比叡 の 山 を 二十 ばかり 重ね あげ たら ん ほど

格助　名　係助　名　格助　助動/用　係助/係　補助動/ラ変/用　助動/過/体/結
して、なり は 塩尻 の やうに なん あり ける。

副　四/用　四/用　接助　固名　格助　名　格助　固名　格助　名　格助　格助　名　格助　副　ナリ形動/体・名　ラ変/終　代
猶 行き 行き て、武蔵 の 国 と 下総 の 国 と の 中 に、いと 大きなる 河 あり。それ

格助　固名・　格助　四/終　代　格助　名　格助　名　格助　下二/用　上一/用　接助　四/已　接助　ク形/用　ク形/用・
を すみだ河 と いふ。その 河 の ほとり に むれ ゐ て 思ひやれ ば、限りなく とほく

係助　カ変/用　助動/完/用　助動/過/体　終助　格助　上二/用　四/已　助動/存/体　接助　名　副　名　格助　四/命　名　係助　下二/用
も 来 に ける かな と わび あへ る に、渡守、「はや 舟 に 乗れ、日 も 暮れ

助動/完/終　格助　四/体　接助　四/用　接助　四/未・助動/意/終　格助　サ変/体　接助　名　シク形/用　接助　名　格助　四/体　名
ぬ」と いふ に、乗り て 渡ら ん と する に、皆人 物わびしく て、京 に 思ふ 人

ク形/体　助動/断/用　副助　補助動/ラ変/未　助動/打/終　連体　名・　副　ク形/体　名　格助　名　格助　名　格助　ク形/体　名　格助
なき に しも あら ず。さる をり しも、白き 鳥 の 嘴 と 脚 と 赤き、鴫 の

ナリ形動/語幹・接尾　助動/断/体　名　格助　名　格助　四/用　接助　名　格助　四/終　名　格助　係助　下二/未　助動/打/体　名　助動/断/已
大き さ なる、水 の うへ に 遊び つつ 魚 を くふ。京 に は 見え ぬ 鳥 なれ

接助　名　四/未　助動/打/終　名　格助　四/用　助動/過/已　接助　代　係助　名・　格助　四/体　格助　四/用　接助
ば、皆人 見知ら ず。渡守 に 問ひ けれ ば、「これ なん 都鳥」と いふ を きき て、

名　格助　副助　四/未　接助　感　四/未　助動/意/終　名
名 に し 負は ば いざ 言とは む 都鳥

代　格助　四/体・名　係助　ラ変/終　係助　ク形/終　係助　格助
わが 思ふ 人 は あり や なし や と

四/已　助動/完/用　助動/過/已　接助　名　四/用　接助　四/用　助動/完/用　助動/過/終
よめ り けれ ば、舟 こぞり て 泣き に けり。

4

The Pillow Book

Sei Shōnagon was the daughter of Kiyohara Motosuke, a noted *waka* poet and a middle-rank aristocrat. (The Sei in Sei Shōnagon's name comes from the Sino-Japanese reading for the Kiyo in Kiyohara.) In 993, Sei Shōnagon became a lady-in-waiting to Empress Teishi (the daughter of the regent Fujiwara Michitaka), who was a consort to Emperor Ichijō (r. 986–1011). Sei Shōnagon's *Pillow Book* (*Makura no sōshi*), which was completed around 1005, after the demise of Teishi's salon, focuses on the years 993 and 994, when the Michitaka family and Teishi were at the height of their glory, and leaves unmentioned the family's subsequent demise.

The three hundred sections of *The Pillow Book* can be divided into three different types—aesthetic, diary, and essay—which sometimes overlap. The aesthetic sections consist of "noun sections" (*mono wa*), which describe particular categories of things such as "Flowering Trees" and "adjectival sections" (*monozukushi*), which describe a particular state such as "Depressing Things."

Much of *The Pillow Book* is about aristocratic women's education, especially the need for an aesthetic awareness as well as erudition, allusiveness, and extreme refinement in communication. Sei Shōnagon shows a particular concern for delicacy and harmony and for the proper combination of object, sense, and circumstance, usually stressing a fusion of the human and natural worlds. By contrast, incongruity and disharmony become the butt of humor and the target of the author's sharp wit.

The Pillow Book is noted for its distinctive prose style, consisting of rhythmic, compressed, and varied sentences, often set up in alternating couplets.

The text is based on Ikeda Kikan, Kishigami Shinji, and Akiyama Ken, eds., *Makura no sōshi*, *Murasaki Shikibu nikki*, Nihon koten bungaku taikei 19 (Tokyo: Iwanami Shoten, 1958), 43–44, 64–67, with minor orthographic changes.

『枕草子』

「1」

春は曙。やうやうしろくなり行く、山ぎはすこしあかりて、むらさきだちたる雲のほそくたなびきたる。

　夏は夜。月の頃はさらなり、闇もなほ、ほたるの多く飛びちがひたる。又、ただ一つ二つなど、ほのかにうちひかりて行くもをかし。雨など降るもをかし。

　秋は夕暮。夕日のさして山の端いとちかうなりたるに、からすの寝所へ行くとて、三つ四つ、二つ三つなど、とびいそぐさへあはれなり。まいて、雁などのつらねたるが、いと小さく見ゆるはいとをかし。日入りはてて、風の音、虫の音など、はたいふべきにあらず。

　冬はつとめて。雪の降りたるはいふべきにもあらず、霜のいと白きも、またさらでもいと寒きに、火などいそぎおこして、炭もてわたるもいとつきづきし。昼になりて、ぬるくゆるびもていけば、火桶の火もしろき灰がちになりてわろし。

「25」

すさまじきもの。昼ほゆる犬。春の網代。三、四月の紅梅の衣。牛死にたる牛飼。ちご亡くなりたる産屋。火おこさぬ炭櫃、地火炉。博士のうちつづき女子生ませたる。方違へに行きたるに、あるじせぬ所。まいて節分などはいとすさまじ....

　除目に司得ぬ人の家。今年はかならずと聞きて、はやうありし者どものほかほかなりつる、田舎だちたる所に住む者どもなど、みな集まりきて、出で入る車の轅もひまなく見え、物まうでする供に、我も我もとまゐりつかうまつり、もの食ひ、酒飲み、ののしりあへるに、はつる暁まで門たたく音もせず、あやしうなど耳立てて聞けば、前駆追ふ声々などして、上達部などみな出で給ひぬ。もの聞きに、宵より寒がりわななきをりける下衆男、いと物うげにあゆみ来るを、見る者どもはえ問ひにだにも問はず。外より来たる者などぞ、「殿はなににかならせ給ひたる」など問ふに、いらへには、「なにの前司にこそは」などぞかならずいらふる。まことに頼みける者は、いとなげかしと思へり。つとめてになりて、ひまなくをりつる者ども、ひとりふたりすべりいでて往ぬ。ふるき者どもの、さもえ行き離るまじきは、来年の国々、手を折りてうち数へなどして、ゆるぎありきたるも、いとほしうすさまじげなり。

Vocabulary for Section 1 (As for Spring, It Is Dawn)

曙 (あけぼの) (*n.*) first faint light of day, dawn

やうやう (漸う) (*adv.*) gradually, little by little

山ぎは (山際) (やま) (*n.*) mountain edge, where the sky meets the edge of the mountain

あかる (明かる) (*intr. v. YD*) to grow light

むらさきだつ (紫だつ) (*intr. v. YD*) to appear lavender, reddish purple

たなびく (棚引く) (*intr. v. YD*) to trail (clouds, haze, mist)

頃 (ころ) (*n.*) at the time, about

さら (更) (*nari adj. v.*) it goes without saying, needs no repeating

闇 (やみ) (*n.*) darkness, night

なほ (猶・尚) (*adv.*) all the more, even more so

ほたる (蛍) (*n.*) firefly

飛び違ふ (と・ちが) (*intr. v. YD*) to crisscross in flight

ほのか (仄か) (*nari adj. v.*) faint, vague, indistinct (light, color, shape)

をかし (*shiku adj.*) tasteful, charming, interesting

夕暮 (ゆふぐれ) (*n.*) evening, nightfall

夕日 (ゆふひ) (*n.*) evening sun, setting sun

さす (射す・差す・指す) (*intr. v. YD*) to shine

端 (は) (*n.*) edge

ちかし (近し) (*ku adj.*) close, near

からす (烏) (*n.*) crow

寝所 (ねどころ) (*n.*) (lit., sleeping place) bed

まして (況して) (*adv.*) all the more

雁 (かり) (*n.*) wild goose, wild geese

つらぬ (連ぬ・列ぬ) (*intr. v. SN*) to line up

見ゆ (み) (*intr. v. SN*) to appear

はた (将) (*adv.*) again, also

つとめて (*n.*) early morning

霜 (しも) (*n.*) frost

寒し (さむ) (*ku adj.*) cold

起こす (お) (*tr. v. YD*) to light, kindle

炭 (すみ) (*n.*) charcoal

もてわたる (持て渡る) (*intr. v. YD*) to carry, bring

つきづきし (*shiku adj.*) appropriate, harmonious, befitting

昼 (ひる) (*n.*) midday

ぬるし (温し) (*ku adj.*) lukewarm

ゆるぶ (緩ぶ・弛ぶ) (*intr. v. YD*) to loosen up, become gentle, mild

もていく (もて行く) (*intr. v. YD*) to do gradually

火桶 (ひをけ) (*n.*) wooden brazier

灰 (はひ) (*n.*) ashes

〜がち (〜勝ち) (*suffix*) to have a tendency to

わろし (悪し) (*ku adj.*) bad

Grammar Notes for Section 1

たなびきたる Many of the sentences in *Makura* end, as this one does, in RT, creating overtones.

うちひかりて prefix *uchi* emphasizing the brevity of YD v. *hikaru*, "to shine"; together, they mean "to flicker"

ちかう RY of adj. *chikashi*, in sound change from *chikaku* to *chikau*

からすのねどころへ行くとて (ゆ) subject marker case p. *no* indicates that *karasu* is subject of the v.: "The crows (flew hurriedly) with the aim (*to-te*) of going to a resting place."

さへ "Even (that sight—something as lowly as crows—is deeply moving)."

まいて sound change of adv. *mashite*, "all the more," "not to mention"

雁のつらねたる case p. *no* marking *kari*, "wild geese," as subject of v. *tsuranu*, "to line up," in the RY, and RT of aux. v. *tari* (resultative-perfective)

見ゆる RT of SN v. *miyu*, "to appear," implying a nominal, *koto*, "the appearance of . . ."

入りはてて RY of YD v. *iru*, "(the sun) to go down," RY of SN v. *hatsu*, "to do completely,"

and conj. p. *te*: "after the sun had set completely"

いふべきにあらず SS of YD v. *iu*, "to say," RT of aux. v. *beshi*, "should," RY of copular *nari*, MZ of RH suppl. v. *ari*, and SS of neg. aux. v. *zu*: "it is not necessary to say"

さらでも MZ of intr. RH v. *sari*, "to be like this," and neg. conj. p. *de*: "even when not like this"

ゆるびもていけば RY of YD v. *yurubu*, indicating that "(the cold) gets milder," and IZ of YD v. *moteiku*, "to become gradually": "when (the cold) gradually dissipates"

Annotated Grammar for Section 1

名 係助 名 副 ク形/用 四/体 名 副 四/用 接助 四/用 助動/完/体 名 格助
春 は 曙。 やうやう しろく なり行く、 山ぎは すこし あかり て、 むらさきだち たる 雲 の

ク形/用 四/用 助動/存/体
ほそく たなびき たる 。

名 係助 名 名 格助 名 係助 ナリ形動/終 名 係助 副 名 格助 ク形/用 四/用 助動/存/体 接
夏 は よる。 月 の 頃 は さらなり、 闇 も なほ、 ほたる の 多く 飛びちがひ たる 。 又、

副 名 副助 ナリ形動/用 四/用 接助 四/体 係助 シク形/終 名 副助 四/体 係助 シク形/終
ただ 一二 など、 ほのかに うちひかり て 行く も をかし。 雨 など 降る も をかし。

名 係助 名 名 格助 四/用 接助 名 格助 名 副 ク形/用(音) 四/用 助動/存/体 格助 名 格助 名
秋 は 夕暮。 夕日 の さして 山 の 端 いと ちかう なり たる に、 からす の 寝所

格助 四/終 格助 名 名 副助 四/体 副助 ナリ形動/終 副(音) 名 副助 格助 下二/用
へ 行く とて、 二四、 二みつ など、 とびいそぐ さへ あはれなり。 まいて、 雁 など の つらね

助動/存/体 格助 副 ク形/用 下二/体 係助 副 シク形/終 名 下二/用 接助 名 格助 名 名 格助 名
たる が、 いと ちひさく みゆる は いと をかし。 日 入りはて て、 風 の 音 むし の 音

副助 副 四/終 助動/当/体 助動/断/用 補動/ラ変/未 助動/打/終
など、 はた いふ べき に あら ず 。

名 係助 名 名 格助 四/用 助動/完/体 係助 四/終 助動/当/体 助動/断/用 係助 補動/ラ変/未 助動/打/終 名 格助
冬 は つとめて。 雪 の 降り たる は いふ べき に も あら ず 、 霜 の

副 ク形/体 係助 副 ラ変/未 接助 係助 副 ク形/体 格助 名 副助 四/用 四/用 接助 名 四/体
いと しろき も、 また さら で も いと 寒き に、 火 など いそぎ おこし て、 炭 もてわたる

係助 副 シク形/終 名 格助 四/用 接助 ク形/用 四/用 四/已 接助 名 格助 名 係助 ク形/体 名
も いと つきづきし。 昼 に なり て、 ぬるく ゆるび もていけ ば、 火桶 の 火 も しろき 灰

接尾 格助 四/用 接助 ク形/終
がち に なり て わろし。

Vocabulary for Section 25 (Unpleasant Things)

すさまじ (凄じ) (*shiku adj.*) unpleasant, depressing

ほゆ (吠ゆ・吼ゆ) (*intr. v. SN*) to bark, howl

網代 (*n.*) fishing weir (set in rivers in late autumn/winter)

紅梅 (*n.*) color of a *kasane* robe: the outside is

red (*beni*) and the inside is sapang (lavender-tinted red) or lavender, worn in the spring until the Second Month

衣 (*n.*) dress, robe

牛飼 (*n.*) herder, person who takes care of oxen

ちご (稚児・児) (*n.*) baby, infant

産屋 (*n.*) lying-in room, room set aside for childbirth

炭櫃 (*n.*) large brazier

地火炉 (*n.*) hearth, stove

博士 (*n.*) scholar at the university

方違へ (*n.*) avoiding a directional taboo

あるじす (饗す) (*intr. v. SH*) to serve as host, treat, receive guests

節分 (*n.*) time of seasonal change, particularly the day before the beginning of a new season

除目 (*n.*) ceremony announcing official appointments

司 (*n.*) official rank, position

ほかほか (外外) (*nari adj. v.*) separate, scattered

ゐなかだつ (田舎だつ) (*intr. v. YD*) to act or appear provincial, rustic

轅 (*n.*) carriage poles attached to an ox

ひま (隙・暇) (*n.*) gap, space

物まうで (物詣で) (*n.*) visit to a temple or shrine

供 (*n.*) attendance upon a master

まゐる (参る) (*intr. v. YD*) to go to a place of high status (hum.)

つかうまつる (仕うまつる) (*intr. v. RH, YD v.*) to serve (hum.)

はつ (果つ) (*intr. v. SN*) to finish, end

耳立つ (*tr. v. SN*) to listen to carefully

前駆追ふ (*intr. v. YD*) to clear the way (for a person of high station)

上達部 (*n.*) designation for nobles of the third rank and above

ものきき (物聞き) (*n.*) discreet inquiry about affairs, or those who make such inquiries

わななく (戦慄く) (*intr. v. YD*) to shiver, quiver

をり (居り) (*suppl. RH v. following RY*) indicating that the action of the main verb continues

下衆男 (*n.*) low-ranking man, male servant

物うげ (物憂げ) (*nari adj. v.*) miserable-looking, appearing depressed

あゆむ (歩む) (*intr. v. YD*) to walk one step at a time

問ふ (*tr. v. YD*) to inquire, ask

殿 (*n.*) person of high rank

いらへ (答へ・応へ) (*n.*) reply

前司 (*n.*) (also *sen-ji*) former provincial official

かならず (必ず) (*adv.*) for sure, without fail

いらふ (答ふ・応ふ) (*intr. v. SN*) to answer, reply

なげかし (嘆かし・歎かし) (*shiku adj.*) lamentable, deplorable

〜ども (*suffix*) plural marker

すべりいづ (滑り出づ) (*intr. v. SN*) to slip out, slip away

往ぬ (*intr. v. NH*) to leave

さも (然も) (*adv.*) thus, in this way

離る (*intr. v. SN*) to leave

ゆるぐ (揺るぐ) (*intr. v. YD*) to move uncertainly

いとほし (*shiku adj.*) pathetic, pitiful, sorry

すさまじげ (凄じげ) (*nari adj. v.*) depressing-looking, unpleasant-looking

Grammar Notes for Section 25

生ませたる   "when a scholar has one baby girl after another": that is, these academic positions, which were hereditary, could not be inherited by a woman

はやうありしもの   RY of *ku* adj. *hayashi*, "early," with sound change from *hayaku* to *hayau*: "those who had served him earlier (before)"

我も我もとまゐりつかうまつり   citation, "me too, me too," and citational case p. *to*

ののしりあへるに   RY of YD v. *nonoshiru*, "to make a commotion," IZ of YD v. *au*, "to do together," RT of aux. v. *ri*, and concessive conj. p. *ni*

わななきをりける   RY of YD v. *wananaku* and RY of suppl. RH v. *ori*, indicating continued action

え問ひにだにも問はず   neg. pot. correlated adv. *e*, RY of YD v. *tou*, "to ask," and case p. *ni*, which turns the preceding v. into a n.: "They could not even ask the question."

なににかならせ給ひたる   pron. *nani*, "what," case p. *ni*, interrogative bound p. *ka*, MZ of YD v. *naru*, "to become," RY of hon. aux. v. *su*, and RY of hon. suppl. v. *tamau*: "What has (the master) become?" ("What position has the master been appointed to?")

なにの前司にこそは   IZ of suppl. v. *ari* or *haberi* implied after *koso wa*: "(The master) is the former governor of such-and-such a province," a roundabout way of saying the master has not received a new appointment.

さもえいきはなるまじき   adv. *samo*, "that way," neg. pot. adv. *e*, comp. v. *iki-hanaru*, "to go-leave," and RT of neg. pot. aux. v. *maji*: "(The old retainers who) could not leave in that way."

来年の国々   "the provinces (which will be having a change of governor) next year"

手を折りてうちかぞへなどして   "to count on one's fingers and such"

Annotated Grammar for Section 25

すさまじき もの 昼 ほゆる 犬。春 の 網代。三四月 の 紅梅 の 衣。生 死に たる 牛飼。

ちご 亡くなり たる 産屋。火 おこさ ぬ 炭櫃、地火炉。博士 の うちつづき 女子 生ま

せ たる。方違へ に 行き たる に、あるじせ ぬ 所。まいて 節分 など は いと

すさまじ。

（中略）

除目 に 司 得 ぬ 人 の 家。今年 は かならず と 聞き て、はやう あり し 者

ども の ほかほかなり つる、田舎だち たる 所 に 住む 者 ども など、みな 集まり き

て、出で入る 車 の 轅 も ひまなく 見え、物まうで する 供 に、我 も 我 も と まゐり

つかうまつり、もの 食ひ、酒 飲み、ののしり あへ る に、はつる 暁 まで 門 たたく 音

も せ ず、あやしう など 耳立て て 聞け ば、前駆追ふ 声々 など し て、上達部

など みな 出で 給ひ ぬ 。もの聞き に、宵 より 寒がり わななき をり ける 下衆男、

いと 物うげに あゆみ 来る を、見る 者 ども は え 問ひ に だに も 問は ず。外 より 来 たる 者 など ぞ、「殿 は なに に か なら せ 給ひ たる」など とふ に、いらへ に は、「なに の 前司 に こそ は」など ぞ かならず いらふる。まことに 頼み ける 者 は、いと なげかし と 思へ り。つとめて に なり て、ひまなく をり つる 者 ども、ひとり ふたり すべり いで て 往ぬ。ふるき 者 ども の、さも え 行き 離る まじき は、来年 の 国々、手 を 折り て うち 数へ など し て、ゆるぎ ありき たる も、いとほしう すさまじげなり。

5

The Tale of Genji

Murasaki Shikibu (d. ca. 1014) was probably born sometime between 970 and 978, and in 996 she accompanied her father to his new post as provincial governor in Echizen. A year or two later, she returned to the capital to marry Fujiwara no Nobutaka, a mid-level aristocrat who was old enough to be her father. It is generally believed that Murasaki Shikibu started writing *The Tale of Genji* (*Genji monogatari*) after her husband's death, perhaps in response to her grief, and it was probably the reputation of the early chapters that resulted in her being summoned to the imperial court around 1005 or 1006. She became a lady-in-waiting to Empress Shōshi, the chief consort of Emperor Ichijō and the eldest daughter of Fujiwara Michinaga (966–1027), who had become regent.

In the following scene from "Young Lavender" (Wakamurasaki), Genji discovers the child Murasaki, the niece of Fujitsubo, who eventually becomes his great love. Genji is suffering from a bout of *warawayami* (translated as "malaria") and is accompanied by several retainers in the hills to the north of the capital, where he has come to see a reclusive sage (*hijiri*), who will perform services to cure him. From the sage's cave, Genji is able to see a nicely appointed temple below, which he learns is home to a certain high-ranking bishop (*sōzu*). When the sage has finished with him, Genji goes down for a closer look.

In this passage, Genji is referred to by the deferential auxiliary verb *tamau*. Koremitsu is his attendant. The nun (*ama*) is the bishop's sister, who is not in good health. Murasaki, a girl of about ten, is the nun's granddaughter; her mother (the nun's daughter) has died. A female attendant (Shōnagon) serves as the child's nurse. Note the oblique reference to Fujitsubo, the emperor's consort and Genji's stepmother, with whom Genji is hopelessly in love. Fujitsubo is Murasaki's aunt, and Genji notes a resemblance between them, although at this point he does not know that they are related.

The text is based on Yamagishi Tokuhei, ed., *Genji monogatari* 1, Nihon koten bungaku taikei 14 (Tokyo: Iwanami Shoten, 1958), 183–187.

『源氏物語』

「若紫」

「1」

日も、いと長きに、つれづれなれば、夕暮のいたう霞みたるに紛れて、かの小柴垣のもとにたち出で給ふ。人々は、帰し給ひて、惟光の朝臣と、のぞき給へば、ただ、この西おもてにしも、持仏すゑたてまつりて行ふ、尼なりけり。簾垂すこしあげて、花たてまつるめり。中の柱に寄りゐて、脇息のうへに經をおきて、いと、なやましげに読みゐたる尼君、ただ人と見えず。四十余ばかりにて、いとしろうあてに、痩せたれど、つらつきふくらかに、まみの程、髪の美しげにそがれたる末も、「中々、長きよりも、こよなう、いまめかしきものかな」と、あはれに見給ふ。清げなる大人二人ばかり、さては、童べぞ、いでいり遊ぶ。中に、「十ばかりにやあらむ」と見えて、白き衣、山吹などの、なれたる着て、走りきたる女子、あまた見えつる子どもに、似るべうもあらず、いみじく、生ひ先見えて、美しげなるかたちなり。髪は、扇をひろげたるやうに、ゆらゆらとして、顔は、いと赤くすりなして立てり。

　　　尼　「何事ぞや。童べと、腹立ち給へるか」

とて、尼君の、見上げたるに、すこし、おぼえたる所あれば、「子なめり」と、見給ふ。

　　　紫　「雀の子を、犬君が逃がしつる、伏籠の中に、籠めたりつるものを」

とて、「いと口惜し」と思へり。此の、ゐたるおとな、

　　　小納　「例の、心なしの、かかるわざをして、さいなまるるこそ、いと心づきなけれ。
　　　　　　　いづかたへか、まかりぬる。いと、をかしう、やうやうなりつるものを。烏など
　　　　　　　もこそ、見つくれ」

とて、たちて行く。髪ゆるるかにいと長く、めやすき人なめり。少納言の乳母とぞ、人いふめるは、此の子の後見なるべし。尼君、

　　　尼　「いで、あな、をさなや。いふかひなう、ものし給ふかな。おのが、かく、今日・
　　　　　　明日におぼゆる命をば、何ともおぼしたらで、雀したひ給ふほどよ。「罪得るこ
　　　　　　とぞ」と、常に聞ゆるを。心憂く」

とて、

尼 「こちや」

と言へば、ついゐたり。

「2」

つらつき、いとらうたげにて、眉のわたり、うちけぶり、いはけなくかいやりたる額つき、髪ざし、いみじう美し。「ねびゆかむさま、ゆかしき人かな」と、目とまり給ふ。さるは、「限りなう、心を尽くし聞ゆる人に、いとよう似たてまつれるが、まもらるゝなりけり」と、おもふにも、涙ぞ落つる。尼君、髪をかき撫でつつ、

尼 「けづる事をうるさがり給へど、をかしの御髪や。いと、はかなうものし給ふこそ、あはれに、うしろめたけれ。かばかりになれば、いと、かからぬ人もあるものを。故姫君は、十二にて殿に後れ給ひし程、いみじう、ものは、思ひ知り給へりしぞかし。ただ今、おのれ、見すてたてまつらば、いかで、世におはせむとすらむ」

とて、いみじく泣くを、見給ふも、すずろに悲し。幼心地にも、さすがに、うちまもりて、伏目になりてうつぶしたるに、こぼれかかりたる髪、つやつやとめでたう見ゆ。

尼 おひ立たむありかも知らぬ若草をおくらす露ぞ消えむそらなき

又、ゐたる人人、「げに」と、うち泣きて、

大人 はつ草の生ひゆく末も知らぬまにいかでか露の消えむとすらん

と聞ゆる程に、僧都、あなたより来て、

僧都 「こなたは、あらはにや侍らむ。今日しも、端におはしましけるかな。此の、かみの聖の坊に、源氏の中将、わらは病まじなひに、ものし給ひけるを、ただ今なむ、聞きつけ侍る。いみじう、忍び給ひければ、知り侍らで、ここに侍りながら、御とぶらひにもまうでざりけるに」

と、の給へば、

尼 「あな、いみじや。いと、あやしきさまを、人や見つらん」

とて、簾垂おろしつ。

僧都 「この世に、ののしり給ふ光源氏、かかるついでに、見たてまつり給はんや。世

を捨てたる法師の心地にも、いみじう、世の憂へわすれ、齢のぶる、人の御有様なり。いで、御消息聞えむ」

とて、立つ音すれば、かへり給ひぬ。「あはれなる人を見つるかな、かかれば、此のすきものどもは、かかる、ありきをのみして、よく、さるまじき人をも見つくるなりけり。たまさかに、立ち出づるだに、かく、思ひの外なることを見るよ」と、をかしうおぼす。「さても、いと美しかりつる児かな。何人ならん。かの人の御かはりに、明け暮れのなぐさめにも、見ばや」と思ふ心、深うつきぬ。

Vocabulary for Section I

つれづれ (徒然)　(*nari adj. v.*) boredom, free time

いたし (甚し)　(*ku adj.*) extreme

霞む　(*intr. v. YD*) to be misty

紛る　(*intr. v. SN*) to hide in, to go under the cover of

小柴垣　(*n.*) low, woven brushwood fence

たち出づ (立ち出づ)　(*intr. v. SN*) to stand and leave, depart

帰す　(*tr. v. YD*) (also 返す) to make (someone) return

朝臣　(*n.*) honorific placed after the name of a person of the fifth rank or higher

のぞく (覗く)　(*tr. v. YD*) to peep (through a hole or slit)

西面　(*n.*) west side of a building, western room

持仏　(*n.*) personal Buddhist statue kept in one's room

すう (据う)　(*tr. v. SN*) to place, leave as an offering

行ふ　(*intr. v. YD*) to follow the Buddhist path, pray, engage in religious devotions

簾垂　(*n.*) blind

柱　(*n.*) pillar

脇息　(*n.*) armrest

経　(*n.*) sutra

なやましげ (悩ましげ)　(*nari adj. v., suffix ge*) sickly, in poor health

たゞ人 (徒人・直人)　(*n.*) ordinary person

あて (貴)　(*nari adj. v.*) elegant, refined

つらつき (面つき・頬つき)　(*n.*) facial appearance

ふくらか (脹らか)　(*nari adj. v.*) chubby, plump, full

まみ (目見)　(*n.*) eye(s)

うつくしげ (愛しげ・美しげ)　(*nari adj. v.*) adorable-looking, cute-looking

削ぐ　(*tr. v. YD*) to cut or trim (hair)

末　(*n.*) tip, end

こよなし　(*ku adj.*) superior, very good

いまめかし (今めかし)　(*shiku adj.*) up-to-date, fashionable

あはれ　(*nari adj. v.*) deeply moving, affecting

きよげ (清げ)　(*nari adj. v.*) trim and attractive, neat

さては　(*conj. p.*) and then, in addition

童べ　(*n.*) child

衣　(*n.*) dress robe

山吹　(*n.*) color combination of a robe, yellowish brown or russet on the outside and yellow on the inside, worn in the spring

なる (萎る)　(*intr. v. SN*) (for clothing) to become shabby, well-worn (with the starch gone)

女子　(*n.*) young girl (here, Murasaki, Genji's future wife)

生ひ先　(*n.*) future

扇　(*n.*) fan

ゆらゆらと　(*adv.*) waving or moving gently in the air

すりなす (擦りなす)　(*tr. v. YD*) to rub deliberately, vigorously

腹立つ　(*intr. v. YD*) to fight

見上ぐ　(*tr. v. SN*) to look up

覚ゆ　(*intr. v. SN*) to resemble

犬君　(*proper n.*) name of a child

逃がす　(*tr. v. YD*) to release

伏籠　(*n.*) cage-basket placed on top of an

incense burner for scenting clothes (the girl is using it as a makeshift cage)

こむ （籠む・込む） (*tr. v. SN*) to place inside, shut up

心 なし （心無し） (*ku adj.*) thoughtless, careless

さいなむ （苛む・嘖む） (*tr. v. YD*) to scold, criticize

心 づきなし （心付き無し） (*ku adj.*) disagreeable, unpleasant

いづ方 （何方） (*pron.*) which direction

やうやう （漸う） (*adv.*) finally

みつく （見付く） (*tr. v. SN*) to discover

ゆるるか （緩るか） (*nari adj. v.*) loose

めやすし （目安し・目易し） (*ku adj.*) pleasant, agreeable

乳母 (*n.*) wet nurse

いふかひなし （言ふ甲斐なし） (*comp.*) beneath mention, childish, silly

おのが （己が） (*comp.*) I, myself

慕ふ (*tr. v. YD*) to think fondly of, long for

心 憂し (*ku adj.*) unpleasant, distasteful

ついゐる （突い居る） (*intr. v. KI*) to kneel

Grammar Notes for Section 1

日もいと 長きにつれづれなれば   Genji is the implied subject; the days are long because it is spring

かの小柴垣   pron. *ka* (that), referring to the *sōzu* (bishop)

たち出で給ふ   SS of hon. suppl. YD v. *tamau*, indicating that Genji is the subject

人々は、帰し給ひて   Genji "returns the people" (*hitobito*), his assistants.

惟光 の朝臣と   Koremitsu is the son of Genji's wet nurse and serves as his chief retainer.

のぞき給へば   IZ of hon. suppl. v. *tamau*, indicating that Genji is the subject; the object of their gaze is the *sōzu*'s residence

する 奉 りて 行ふ   RY of hum. suppl. v. *tatematsuru*, placing the nun in a humble position with regard to the Buddhist statue

いと白うあてに   RY (sound change from *shiroku*) of *ku* adj. *shiroshi*, "white," and RY of adj. v. *ate-nari*, "elegant"; the implied subject is the nun's face

まみの程   the "area (*hodo*) around the eyes (*mami*)"

髪のうつくしげにそがれたる末   "the ends of (the nun's) hair, which were cut in a seemingly beautiful way"; nuns' hair was trimmed to shoulder length in contrast to the typical Heian noblewoman's hair, which was long and trailed to the floor

あはれに見給ふ   suppl. hon. v. *tamau*, following RY of v. *miru*, "to see," indicating that Genji is seeing this and is "deeply moved" (*aware ni*)

十ばかりにやあらむ   "(Among them) there appeared to be one who was probably around ten."

白き衣、山吹などのなれたる着て   *nare-taru* (to be well worn) ends in RT, implying a nominal (clothing): "wearing a well-worn white underrobe, a *yamabuki* color robe, and such . . ."

走りきたる 女子   This is young Murasaki, Genji's future wife.

似るべうもあらず   "It would not be appropriate to compare her (Murasaki) with the other children."

生ひ先見えて   Genji could imagine "what she would look like in the future (as an adult)."

扇 をひろげたるやうに   n. *yō*, "shape": "(The hair) was the shape of a fan that had been spread out."

何事ぞや   When following nominals, the bound p. *zo* functions as an emphatic copula; *ya* is an interj. p.: "What is going on here!"

わらはべと腹立ち給へるか   IZ of hon. suppl. YD v. *tamau*, deferential toward the young girl Murasaki

尼君の、見上げたるに   *no*, subject marker case p., and *ni*, conj. p. indicating time: "*When* the nun looked up . . ."

すこし、覚えたるところあれば、子なめりと見たまふ   *na-meri*, an abbrev. of RT of copular *nari* and aux. v. *meri*: "Since there were some (*sukoshi*) aspects (of Murasaki) that resembled (*oboe-taru*) the (uplifted face of the nun), she appeared (to Genji) to be the child (of the nun)." The nun is actually the child's grandmother.

籠めたりつるものを   Final p. *mono-o* is exclamatory and has a concessive implication: "even though I had placed it inside (the basket)!"

いと口惜しと思へり   The young Murasaki is the implied subject; she finds it "very regretful."

例の、心なしの、かゝるわざをして、さいなまるゝこそ、いと心づきなけれ   *sainama-ruru* is MZ of YD v., followed by RT of passive aux. v. *ru*: "For a thoughtless (*kokoro-nashi*) person (Inuki) to do this kind of thing (*kakaru waza*), as she always has (*rei no*), and then to

be scolded (by Murasaki) is very unpleasant (*kokorozukinashi*)."

やうやうなりつるものを   The exclamatory final p. *mono-o* has a concessive function, suggesting regret: "Just when it (the sparrow) had finally become very cute!"

鳥などもこそみつくれ   The combination of the bound p. *mo* and *koso* indicate anxiety about the future: "how terrible (*mo koso*) if a crow or something (*nado*) found (the sparrow)."

たちて行く   The female attendant/wet nurse (Shōnagon) speaks here and then gets up to go find the sparrow.

なめり   "she appears to be . . ." ; the use of a spec. aux. v. like *meri* or *beshi* reflects Genji's internal state as he looks in from the outside

少納言の乳母   "the wet nurse (called) Shōnagon"

此の子の後見   "the caretaker (*ushiromi*) of this child (Murasaki)"

命 をば、何とも思ぼしたらで   The honorific here is for Murasaki: "She does not think (at all) (of my, the nun's) life which (may end today or tomorrow)."

罪得ることぞ   To Buddhists, capturing a live animal was a sin.

こちや   pron. *kochi*, "here," and exclamatory p. *ya*: "Come here!"

ついゐたり   SS of aux. v. *tari*, indicating continuing state; the subject here is Murasaki

Annotated Grammar for Section 1

日 も、 いと 長き に、 つれづれなれ ば、 夕暮 の いたう 霞み たる に 紛れ て、 かの

小柴垣 の もと に たち出で 給ふ 。 人々 は、 帰し 給ひ て、 惟光 の 朝臣 と、

のぞき 給へ ば、 ただ、 こ の 西おもて に しも、 持仏 する たてまつり て 行ふ 尼

なり けり。 簾垂 すこし あげ て、 花 たてまつる めり。 中 の 柱 に 寄りゐ て、 脇息

の うへ に 経 を おき て、 いと、 なやましげに 読み ゐ たる 尼君、 ただ人 と 見え

ず。四十余ばかりにて、いとしろうあてに、痩せたれど、つらつき

ふくらかに、まみの程、髪の美しげにそがれたる末も、「中々、長きよりも、

こよなう、いまめかしきものかな」と、あはれに見給ふ。清げなる大人二人ばかり、

さては、童べぞ、いでいり遊ぶ。中に、「十ばかりにやあらむ」と見え

て、白き衣、山吹などの、なれたる着て、走りきたる女子、あまた見えつる

子どもに、似るべうもあらず、いみじく、おひさき見えて、美しげなるかたち

なり。髪は、扇をひろげたるやうに、ゆらゆらとして、顔は、いと赤く

すりなして立てり。

尼　「何事ぞや。童べと、腹立ち給へるか」

とて、尼君の、見上げたるに、すこし、おぼえたる所あれば、「子なめり」

と、見給ふ。

紫　「雀の子を、犬君が逃がしつる、伏籠の中に、籠めたりつるものを」

とて、「いと口惜し」と思へり。此の、ゐたるおとな、

小納　「例の、心なしの、かかるわざをして、さいなまるるこそ、いと

心づきなけれ。いづかたへか、まかりぬる。いと、をかしう、やうやうなり

つるものを。烏などもこそ、見つくれ」

とて、たちて行く。髪ゆるるかにいと長く、めやすき人なめり。少納言の乳母

とぞ、人いふめるは、此の子の後見なるべし。尼君、

尼　「いで、あな、をさなや。いふかひなう、ものし給ふかな。おのが、かく、

今日明日におぼゆる命をば、何ともおぼしたらで、雀したひ

給ふほどよ。「罪得ることぞ」と、常に聞ゆるを。心憂く」

とて、

尼　「こちや」

と言へば、ついゐたり。

Vocabulary for Section 2

らうたげ　(*nari adj. v.*) seemingly adorable, cute

けぶる（煙る・烟る）　(*intr. v. YD*) to appear faintly or softly beautiful

いはけなし（稚けなし）　(*ku adj.*) childish

掻き遣る　(*tr. v. YD*) to brush back with one's hand; here in sound change *kaiyaru*

額つき　(*n.*) shape of the forehead

〜ざし　(*nominal suffix*) form or condition of an object

ねびゆく（ねび行く）　(*intr. v. YD*) to grow up, become an adult

ゆかし　(*shiku adj.*) interesting, attractive

めとまる（目止まる）　(*intr. v. YD*) to catch one's eye

さるは（然るは）　(*conj.*) furthermore

まもる（守る）　(*tr. v. YD*) to stare at

かき撫づ（掻き撫づ）　(*tr. v. SN*) to stroke gently with hand or comb

梳る　(*tr. v. YD*) to comb (hair)

うるさし（煩し）　(*ku adj.*) bothersome, troubling, annoying

はかなし（果無し）　(*ku adj.*) unreliable

うしろめたし（後ろめたし）　(*ku adj.*) worrisome, anxiety-producing

かばかり（斯ばかり）　(*adv.*) this much, so

姫君　(*n.*) daughter of a noble (hon.); here, Murasaki's mother

殿　(*n.*) lord, master; here, the father of Murasaki's deceased mother

おのれ（己れ）　(*pron.*) first-person pron. (hum.)

すずろ（漫ろ）　(*nari adj. v.*) appearance of things happening without reason or aim: somehow or another

さすが　(*nari adj. v.*) even so, nevertheless

うちまもる（打ち守る）　(*tr. v. YD*) to gaze intently at

伏目　(*n.*) looking face down, eyes turned down

うつぶす（俯す）　(*intr. v. YD*) to face down, look down

つやつやと（艶々と）　(*adv.*) glossily, lustrously

生ひ立つ　(*intr. v. YD*) to grow, mature, develop

若草　(*n.*) newly budding grass in spring; metaphor for young girl

ありか（在り処・在り所）　(*n.*) place or location

露　(*n.*) dew

そら（空）　(*n.*) state of mind, emotion (often followed by neg.)

はつ草（初草）　(*n.*) first grass of early spring; metaphor for children

僧都　(*n.*) bishop

あなた（彼方）　(*pron.*) on the far side, other side, over there

こなた（此方）　(*pron.*) here, over here

あらは（顕・露）　(*nari adj. v.*) totally exposed

はし（端）　(*n.*) veranda, porch

坊　(*n.*) monks' living quarters

中将　(*n.*) middle captain

瘧病　(*n.*) malaria

まじなひ（呪ひ）　(*n.*) prayer to the gods for protection from illness and disaster

しのぶ（忍ぶ）　(*intr. v. KN, YD*) to be in hiding, seclusion

とぶらひ（訪ひ）　(*n.*) visit, call

ののしる（罵る）　(*intr. v. YD*) to make a commotion

すき者（好き者）　(*n.*) person of amorous disposition, playboy

聞きつく（聞き付く）　(*tr. v. SN*) to hear, overhear

法師　(*n.*) priest

憂へ （うれ） (*n.*) sorrow, troubles, concerns

齢 （よはひ） (*n.*) lifetime, life span

のぶ（伸ぶ・延ぶ） (*intr. v. KN*) to lengthen

消息 （せうそく） (*n.*) (also *shōsoko*) letter, message

ありき（歩き） (*n.*) going out, walking around

さり（然り） (*intr. v. RH*) to be that way, be thus

たまさか（偶） (*nari adj. v.*) by chance, by happenstance

思ひの外 （おも ほか） (*nari adj. v.*) unexpected, surprising

さても (*adv.*) even so

何人 （なにびと） (*n.*) what person, what kind of person

かはり（代はり） (*n.*) replacement, substitute

心につく（心に付く） (*intr. v. YD*) to take a liking to

Grammar Notes for Section 2

つらつき、いとらうたげにて眉のわたりうちけぶり（まゆ） This passage refers to Murasaki: "Her face (*tsuratsuki*) seemed very (*ito*) adorable (*rautage-nite*), and the area around (*watari*) the eyebrows (*mayu*) was faintly beautiful (*uchi-keburi*)." Since she is a child, her eyebrows have not been shaved or painted over with black makeup as with adult women, so they do not have a sharp outline.

ねびゆかむさま "her appearance (*sama*) as she grows up"

心 を尽くし聞ゆる人 （こころ っ きこ ひと） *hito* refers to Fujitsubo (Genji's stepmother and the emperor's consort, with whom he is secretly in love)

にいとよう似たてまつれるが （に） IZ of hum. suppl. YD v. *tatematsuru*, which humbles Murasaki vis-à-vis Fujitsubo, and RT of aux. v. *ri*, which modifies an implied person (Murasaki): "(the person) who very (*ito*) closely (*yoku*) resembles that person (Fujitsubo) . . ."

まもらるるなりけり MZ of v. *mamoru* and RT of aux. v. *ru*, which is spontaneous: "I find myself staring at (this person who so closely resembles the one whom I have longed for without end)." These are Genji's thoughts and also his tears.

いとはかなうものし給ふこそあはれにうしろめたけれ （たま） "You (Murasaki) act very silly (*hakanaku*), which makes me pity you (*aware ni*) and worry about you (*ushirometakere*)," so says the nun while combing Murasaki's hair.

かばかりになればいとかからぬ人もあるものを （ひと） "When it comes (*nare-ba*) to this (*kabakari*) (age), there are those (children) who are not so (*kakara-nu*) (immature), but (you, Murasaki, are not one of them)." *Mono-o* is an exclamatory final p. that is implicitly concessive.

故姫君 （こ ひめぎみ） *ko-himegimi*, "the late daughter," refers to Murasaki's mother, the nun's daughter

ものは思ひ知り給へりしぞかし （おも し たま）: "She (Murasaki's mother and the nun's daughter) understood things well (when she lost her father)!"

おのれ、見捨て 奉 らば、いかで、世におはせむとすらむ （み す たてまつ よ） MZ of hon. SH v. *owasu*, "to be," shows respect toward Murasaki: "If I (*onore*) were to leave (you) behind (*misute*), how (*ikade*) would you manage (*owasemu to su*) in the world (*yo ni*)?"

見給ふ （み たま） hon. suppl. v. *tamau*, indicating that the subject is Genji

すずろに悲し （かな） "To watch (the nun) weep was (for Genji) somehow sad."

幼 心地にも、さすがに、うちまもりて （をさなごこち） The subject of the v. *uchimamoru*, "to look intently," is Murasaki, and the object is the nun: "Even with her childish heart, nevertheless (*sasuga ni*), she looked intently (at the weeping nun)."

生ひ立たむ ありかも知らぬ 若草を おくらす露
ぞ　*wakakusa* (young grass) and *tsuyu* (dew) represent, respectively, Murasaki and her grandmother, the nun, who is about to die: "The dew that leaves behind (*okurasu*) the young grass that does not know (*shira-nu*) the place (*arika*) where it will grow (*oitata-mu*)."

おくらす露ぞ消えむそらなき　*sora* is "state of mind": "The dew (the nun) does not have (*naki*) the state of mind (*sora*) to disappear (*kie-mu*)"; that is, the dew cannot fade away while the young grass (Murasaki) does not know where to grow

又ゐたる大人　"another adult who was sitting there (other than the Shōnagon)"

はつ草の生ひゆく末も知らぬまにいかでか露
の消えむとすらん　"While (*ma*) the first grass (*hatsugusa*) does not know (*shira-nu*) where (*sue*) it will grow (*oiyuku*), how (*ikade ka*) can the dew (*tsuyu*) attempt to disappear (*kiemu to su ramu*)?"

端におはしましけるかな　The *sōzu* is using an hon. v., *owasu*, "to be," in regard to the nun.

なむ聞きつけ侍る　"I (the *sōzu*) heard it now."

いみじう、忍び給ひければ、知り侍らで　hon. suppl. v. *tamau* used to elevate Genji, and the speaker, the *sōzu*, uses a polite suppl. v., *haberi*, to refer to his own thoughts

御とぶらひにもまうでざりけるに　hon. prefix placed in front of the n., *toburai*, "visit," in

order to show respect to Genji: "I have not paid a visit (to Genji)."

この世にののしり給ふ　"Genji, about whom this world (*ko no yo*) has made a fuss"

見奉り給はんや　*tatematsuru* humbles the nun vis-à-vis Genji, and *tamau* shows the speaker's (*sōzu*'s) respect toward the nun: "Won't you (*mu*) use (this opportunity) to see him (*ya*)?"

御消息聞えむ　hon. prefix for *shōsoku*, "letter," indicating that it is intended for Genji

かへり給ひぬ　hon. suppl. v. *tamau*, indicating that the subject of the verb is Genji

あはれなる人を見つるかな　Genji's thoughts as he looks at Murasaki

ありき　*ariki*, "going out," referring to nocturnal or amorous adventures. Genji is contrasting prowling, amorous types to himself, who goes out rarely.

よくさるまじき人をも見つくるなりけり
"They (prowling types) do a good job (*yoku*) of finding those (attractive women) whom you wouldn't expect to exist in this way (*saru-majiki*)."

かの人の御かけりに、明暮の慰めにも見ば
や　Genji's thoughts; *ka no hito*, "that person," refers to Fujitsubo: "(Genji) wished to see her (Murasaki) as a substitute (*oon-kawari*) for that person and as solace (*nagusame*) night and day (*akekure*)."

Annotated Grammar for Section 2

つらつき、いと らうたげに て、眉の わたり、うち けぶり、いはけなく かいやり たる

額つき、髪ざし、いみじう 美し。「ねびゆか む さま、ゆかしき 人 かな」と、目とまり

給ふ 。さるは、「限りなう、心 を 尽くし 聞ゆる 人 に、いと よう 似

たてまつれ る が、まもら るる なり けり」と、おもふ に も、涙 ぞ 落つる。尼君、

髪 を かき撫で つつ、

尼　「けづる 事 を うるさがり 給へ ど、をかし の 御髪 や。いと、はかなう

_{サ変/用・　補助動/四/尊/体・　係助/係　　ナリ形動/用　　　ク形/已/結　　　　　副　　格助　四/已　接助　　副}
ものし　給ふ　こそ、あはれに、うしろめたけれ。かばかり　に　なれ　ば、いと、

_{ラ変/未　助動/打/体　名　係助　ラ変/体　終助　接頭　名　係助　名　格助　名　格助　下二/用・　補助動/四/尊/用・}
かから　ぬ　人　も　ある　ものを。故　姫君　は、十二　にて　殿　に　後れ　給ひ

_{助動/過/体　名　シク形/用/音　名　係助　四/用　補助動/四/尊/已・　助動/完/用　助動/過/体　係助　終助　副}
し　程、いみじう、もの　は、思ひ知り　給へ　り　し　ぞ　かし。ただ今、

_{代　下二/用　補助動/四/謙/未・　接助　副　名　格助　サ変/尊/未　助動/意/終　格助　サ変/終　助動/推/体}
おのれ、見すて　たてまつら　ば、いかで、世　に　おはせ　む　と　す　らむ」

_{格助　シク形/用　四/体・　格助　上一/用　補助動/四/尊/体　係助　ナリ形動/用　シク形/終・　名　格助　係助　ナリ形動/用}
とて、いみじく　泣く　を、見　給ふ　も、すずろに　悲し。幼心地　に　も、さすがに、

_{四/用　接助　名　格助　四/用　接助　四/用　助動/継/体　接助　下二/用　四/用　助動/完/体　名　副}
うちまもり　て、伏目　に　なり　て　うつぶし　たる　に、こぼれ　かかり　たる　髪、つやつやと

_{ク形/用/音　下二/終}
めでたう　見ゆ。

_{四/未　助動/体　名　係助　四/未・　助動/打/体　名　格助　四/体　名　係助/係　下二/未・　助動/推/体}
尼　　おひ立た　む　ありか　も　知ら　ぬ　若草　を　おくらす　露　ぞ　消え　む

_{名　ク形/体/結}
　　そら　なき

_{副　上一/用　助動/継/体　名　　副　格助　接頭　四/用・　接助}
又、ゐ　たる　大人、「げに」と、うち　泣き　て、

_{名　格助　　四/用　名　係助　四/未・　助動/打/体　名　格助　副　係助/係　名　格助　下二/未・　助動/意/終}
大人　はつ草　の　生ひゆく　末　も　知ら　ぬ　まに　いかで　か　露　の　消え　む

_{格助　サ変/終　助動/推/体/結}
　と　す　らん

_{格助　下二/謙(言ふ)/体・　名　格助　名　代　格助　カ変/用　接助}
と　聞ゆる　程　に、僧都、あなた　より　来　て、

_{代　係助　ナリ形動/用　係助(疑)/係　ラ変/丁/未　助動/推/体/結　　名　副助　係助　名　格助　四/尊/用・}
僧都　「こなた　は、あらはに　や　侍ら　む。今日　しも、端　に　おはしまし

_{助動/過/体　格助　副　係助/係　名　格助　名　格助　名　名　接助}
ける　かな。此　の、かみ　の　聖　の　坊　に、源氏　の　中将、わらは病　まじなひ　に、

_{サ変/用　補助動/尊/四/用　助動/過/体　格助　副　係助/係　下二/用　補助動/丁/ラ変/体/結　シク形/用/音　四/用}
ものし　給ひ　ける　を、ただ今　なむ、聞きつけ　侍る。いみじう、忍び

_{補助動/尊/四/用・　助動/過/已　接助　四/用　補助動/丁/ラ変/未　接助　代　格助　ラ変/丁/用　接助　名　格助}
給ひ　けれ　ば、知り　侍ら　で、ここ　に　侍り　ながら、御とぶらひ　に

_{係助　下二/謙/未　助動/打/用　助動/過/体　接助}
も　まうで　ざり　ける　に」

_{格助　四/尊/已　接助}
と、の給へ　ば、

_{感　シク形/語幹　間投助　副　シク形/体　名　格助　名　係助(疑)/係　上一/用　助動/完/終　助動/推/体/結}
尼　「あな、いみじ　や。いと、あやしき　さま　を、人　や　見　つ　らん」

_{格助　名　四/用　助動/完/終}
とて、簾垂　おろし　つ。

_{代　格助　名　格助　四/用　補助動/尊/四/体・　固名　連語　名　格助　上一/用　補助動/謙/四/用}
僧都　「この　世　に、ののしり　給ふ　光源氏、かかる　ついで　に、見　たてまつり

_{補助動/尊/四/未・　助動/推(誘)/終　係助　名　格助　下二/用・　助動/存/体　名　格助　名　格助　係助　シク形/用/音　名}
給は　ん　や。世　を　捨て　たる　法師　の　心地　に　も、いみじう、世

_{格助　名・　下二/用　名　上二/体　名　格助　名　助動/断/終　感　名　下二/謙/未　助動/意/終}
の　憂へ　わすれ、齢　のぶる、人　の　御有様　なり。いで、御消息　聞え　む」

とて、立つ 音 すれ ば、かへり 給ひ ぬ。「あはれなる 人 を 見 つる かな、

かかれ ば、此 の すきもの ども は、かかる、ありき を のみ し て、よく、さる まじき

人 を も 見つくる なり けり。たまさかに、立ち出づる だに、かく、思ひの外なる こと

を 見る よ」と、をかしう おぼす。「さても、いと 美しかり つる 児 かな。何人 なら

ん。かの 人 の 御かはり に、明け暮れ の なぐさめ に も、見 ばや」と 思ふ 心、

深う つき ぬ。

6

Sarashina Diary

The author of the *Sarashina Diary* (*Sarashina nikki*) was the daughter of Sugawara no Takasue (a provincial governor and a descendant of Sugawara no Michizane) and Tomoyasu, the half sister of the author of the *Kagerō Diary*. In 1017, at the age of about ten, the author accompanied her father to Kazusa Province (in present-day Chiba Prefecture, north of Tokyo), where he had been appointed governor. For the author and her family, who had been accustomed to the aristocratic life and culture in the capital, life in the Eastern Provinces (Azuma) apparently was difficult to bear, and from the age of ten until she was thirteen, the author longed for a copy of *The Tale of Genji*, which had come to embody the romantic world of the capital. In 1020, when the author was thirteen, she returned with her father to the capital. Then in 1039, at the age of thirty-two, the author worked at the imperial court, in the service of Princess Yūshi, but found it difficult to adjust to the new environment and soon left to become the second wife of Tachibana no Toshimichi, a provincial governor who died in 1058. In the 1060s, while in her fifties, she wrote the *Sarashina Diary*, which looks back on her youth and life from the perspective of a woman of advanced age.

The *Sarashina Diary* is known particularly for its vivid descriptions of the author as an avid reader of vernacular tales (*monogatari*), especially *The Tale of Genji*; for its poetic travel narrative (*michiyuki*), which occupies the first part of the narrative; and for the poem-tale (*uta-monogatari*) section at the end, from which the title (a poem on the moon at Sarashina) is derived. The *Sarashina Diary* contains some eighty poems by the author, which probably came from her personal collection of poems.

The text is based on Suzuki Tomotarō, Kawaguchi Hisao, Endō Yoshimoto, and Nishishita Kyōichi, eds., *Tosa, Kagerō, Izumi Shikibu, Sarashina*, Nihon koten bungaku taikei 20 (Tokyo: Iwanami Shoten, 1957), 479–480, 492–493.

『更級日記』

「1」

東路の道の果てよりも、猶奥つ方に生ひいでたる人、いか許かはあやしかりけむを、いかに思ひはじめける事にか、世の中に物語といふ物のあんなるを、いかで見ばやと思ひつつ、つれづれなる昼間、宵居などに、姉、継母などやうの人々の、その物語、かの物語、光源氏のあるやうなど、ところどころ語るを聞くに、いとどゆかしさまされど、わが思ふままに、そらにいかでかおぼえ語らむ。いみじく心もとなきままに、等身に薬師仏を作りて、手洗ひなどして、人間にみそかに入りつつ、京にとくあげ給ひて、物語の多く候ふなる、ある限り見せ給へと、身を捨てて額をつき、祈り申すほどに、十三になる年、上らむとて、九月三日門出して、いまたちといふ所に移る。

　年ごろ遊びなれつる所を、あらはにこぼち散らして、立ち騒ぎて、日の入りぎはの、いとすごく霧りわたりたるに、車に乗るとて、うち見やりたれば、人間には参りつつ、額をつきし薬師仏のたち給へるを、見捨てたてまつる悲しくて、人知れずうち泣かれぬ。. . .

「2」

かくのみ思ひくんじたるを、心も慰めむと、心ぐるしがりて、母、物語など求めて見せ給ふに、げにおのづから慰みゆく。紫のゆかりを見て、つづきの見まほしくおぼゆれど、人語らひなどもえせず。誰もいまだ都なれぬほどにて、え見つけず。いみじく心もとなく、ゆかしくおぼゆるままに、「この源氏の物語、一の巻よりしてみな見せ給へ」と心の内に祈る。親の太秦に籠り給へるにも、異事なく、この事を申して、いでむままにこの物語見果てむと思へど、見えず。いと口惜しく思ひ嘆かるるに、をばなる人の田舎より上りたる所に渡いたれば、「いとうつくしう、生ひなりにけり」など、あはれがり、珍しがりて、帰るに「何をか奉らむ、まめまめしき物は、まさなかりなむ、ゆかしくし給ふなるものを奉らむ」とて、源氏の五十余巻、ひつに入りながら、在中将、とほぎみ、せり河、しらら、あさうづなどいふ物語ども、一袋取り入れて、得て帰る心地の嬉しさぞいみじきや。はしるはしるわづかに見つつ、心も得ず心もとなく思ふ源氏を、一の巻よりして、人も交じらず、几帳の内にうち臥してひき出でつつ見る心地、后の位も何にか

はせむ。昼は日暮らし、夜は目のさめたるかぎり、火を近くともして、これを見るよりほかの事なければ、おのづからなどは、空におぼえ浮かぶを、いみじきことに思ふに、夢にいと清げなる僧の、黄なる地の袈裟着たるが来て、「法華経五巻をとく習へ」といふと見れど、人にも語らず、習はむとも思ひかけず、物語の事をのみ心にしめて、われはこのごろわろきぞかし。盛りにならば、容貌も限りなくよく、髪もいみじく長くなりなむ。光の源氏の夕顔、宇治の大将の浮舟の女君のやうにこそあらめと思ひける心、まづいとはかなくあさまし。

Vocabulary for Section 1 (Early Years)

東路 (あづまぢ) (*proper n.*) Eastern Road (later called Tōkaidō, Eastern Seaboard Highway), leading from the capital to the Eastern Provinces

果て (は) (*n.*) end, limit

猶 (なほ) (*adv.*) even more

奥 (おく) (*n.*) deepest part (of a mountain, region, etc.)

生ひいづ (お) (生ひ出づ) (*intr. v. SN*) to grow, mature, become an adult

いか許 (ばかり) (如何許) (*adv.*) how much, to what extent, to what degree

あやし (*shiku adj.*) shabby, unsophisticated

いかに (如何に) (*adv.*) questions circumstance: how? in what way?

つれづれ (徒然) (*nari adj. v.*) at leisure, with time to spare

宵居 (よひゐ) (*n.*) late at night

継母 (ままはは) (*n.*) stepmother

語る (かた) (*intr. v. YD*) to narrate, tell about an event

いとど (*adv.*) more and more, increasingly

ゆかし (*shiku adj.*) interesting, attractive (causing one to want to see, hear, or know)

ゆかしさ (*n.*) (suffix *sa*) attraction, desire to see, hear, or learn about something

まさる (増さる) (*intr. v. YD*) to increase in number or degree

そら (空・虚) (*nari adj. v.*) from memory

いかでか (如何でか) (*comp.*) (from adv. *ikade* and bound p. *ka*) (rhetorical question) why would I? how could I?

心もとなし (心許なし) (*ku adj.*) impatient, anxious

とうじん (等身) (*n.*) (also *tōshin*) equivalent to human height

薬師仏 (やくしほとけ) (*n.*) Yakushi Buddha, a healing buddha

手洗ひ (てあら) (*n.*) washing of the hands

人間 (ひとま) (*n.*) while no one is looking or is around

みそか (密か) (*nari adj. v.*) secret

とく (疾く) (*adv.*) (from *ku* adj. *toshi*) swiftly, quickly

あぐ (上ぐ) (*tr. v. SN*) to send to the capital

物語 (ものがたり) (*n.*) tale, romance, fictional genre

侯ふ (さぶら) (*intr. v. YD*) (*sōrō*) (polite) to exist, be

額 (ぬか) (*n.*) forehead

上る (のぼ) (*intr. v. YD*) to go to the capital from the provinces

門出 (かどで) (*n.*) (lit., leaving the gate) departure on a journey, including the custom of moving to a nearby location to make the final preparations; here, the noun is turned into a verb with addition of SH v. *su*, "to do"

いまたち (*proper n.*) place-name (location is not clear)

年ごろ (とし) (年頃) (*n.*) many years, interval of many years

あらは (顕・露) (*nari adj. v.*) totally exposed, clearly visible

こほつ (毀つ) (*tr. v. YD*) (from *kobotsu*) to break up, destroy

たちさわぐ (立ち騒ぐ) (*intr. v. YD*) to make a large commotion

すごし (凄し) (*ku adj.*) desolate, frightening

霧りわたる (き) (霧り渡る) (*intr. v. YD*) to be covered in mist

うち見やる (み) (*tr. v. YD*) to look at something from a distance

見捨つ (みす) (*tr. v. SN*) to leave behind the sight of

Grammar Notes for Section 1

東路の道の果てよりもなお奥つ方　n. *oku*, "interior," attrib. case p. *tsu*, and n. *kata*, "direction": "even farther (*nao*) beyond (*yori*) the end (*hate*) of the Eastern Road (*Azumaji*)." Hitachi Province (present-day Ibaraki Prefecture) was considered the end of the Eastern Road. "Even farther" refers to Kazusa Province (present-day Chiba Prefecture), where the author's father was assigned and the author grew up. Kazusa is actually not farther from the capital than Hitachi, but this expresses the author's feelings of being in the provinces.

生ひいでたる人　RY of SN v. *oi-izu*, "to grow up," RT of perfective aux. v. *tari*, and n. *hito*, "person": "someone who had grown up . . ." The author refers to herself in the third person, a form of indirection also found at the beginning of the *Kagerō Diary*.

いかばかりかはあやしかりけむを　doubt bound p. *kawa*, RY of *shiku* adj. *ayashi*, "shabby," RT of past-spec. aux. v. *kemu*, and concessive conj. p. *o*: "How (*ikabakari*) shabby (provincial) I must have been, and yet . . ."

いかに思ひはじめけることにか　adv. *ika-ni*, "how," RY of YD v. *omou*, "to think," RY of SN v. *hajimu*, "to begin," RT of past-tense aux. v. *keri*, n. *koto*, "thing," RY of copular *nari*, and interrogative bound p. *ka*: "How did I begin to think that . . . ?"

世の中に物語といふ物のあんなるを、いかで見ばや　*an-naru* is RT of RH v. *ari*, "to be," with sound change from *aru* to *an*, and RT of hearsay aux. v. *nari*; *nari* is in RT because of case p. *o*, which is preceded by an implied *mono*; *mibaya* is MZ of KI v. *miru*, "to see," plus desiderative final p. *baya*: "They say (hearsay *naru*) that in the world (*yo no naka ni*) there are things called tales (*monogatari to iu*

mono)—how (*ikade*) I would like (*mi-baya*) to see them."

そらにいかでかおぼえ語らむ　RY of adj. v. *sora nari*, adv. *ikadeka*, RY of SN v. *oboyu*, "to remember," MZ of YD v. *kataru*, "to narrate," and RT of spec. aux. v. *mu*: "How could they (my sister and stepmother) recite the text by memory to me? (They couldn't.)"

都にとくあげ給ひて　RY of SN v. *agu*, RY of hon. suppl. v. *tamau*, showing respect to Yakushi Buddha, and conj. p. *te*: "Please send me to the capital (*miyako*) quickly (*toku*)."

物語の多く候ふなる　n. *monogatari*, subject marker case p. *no*, RY of *ku* adj. *ōshi*, "many," SS of polite YD v. *saburau* (*saburō*), "to be," and RT of hearsay aux. v. *nari*, which follows SS

身を捨てて額をつき祈り申すほどに　*mi o sutsu*, "to discard the self/body," is a hyperbolic phrase meaning "to put everything into"; RY of YD v. *tsuku*, "to press," RY of v. *inoru*, "to pray for," and RT of hum. suppl. v. *mousu*: "While (*hodo*) I prayed (*inori-mōsu*), putting everything into it (*mi o sutete*) and pressing my head to the floor (*nuka o tsuki*)."

のぼらむとて　MZ of *noboru*, aux. v. *mu*, indicating intention, and *tote*, expressing reason: "because (her father's term as governor had ended and the family) intended to go to the capital . . ."

見捨てたてまつる　RY of SN v. *misutsu* and RT of hum. suppl. v. *tatematsuru*, showing respect to the Yakushi Buddha, modifying an implied *koto*

うち泣かれぬ　MZ of YD v. *uchinaku*, "to cry," RY of spont. aux. v. *ru*, and perfective aux. v. *nu*: "I ended up finding myself crying."

Annotated Grammar for Section 1

名　格助　名　格助　名　格助　係助　副　名　格助　名　格助　下二/用　助動/完/体　名　副　係助　シク形/用・
東路 の 道 の 果て より も、猶 奥つ 方 に 生ひいで たる 人、いか許 かは あやしかり

助動/過推/体　接助　副　下二/用　助動/過/体　名　助動/断/用　係助　名　格助　名　格助　名　格助　四/体　名　格助
けむ を、いかに 思ひはじめ ける 事 に か、世 の 中 に 物語 といふ 物 の

ラ変/体(音)　助動/伝/体　格助　副　上一/未　終助　格助　四/用　接助　ナリ形動/体　名　名　副助　格助
あん なる を、いかで 見 ばや と 思ひ つつ、つれづれなる。昼間、宵居 など に、

名　名　副助　名・　格助　名　格助　代　格助　名　代　格助　名　固名　格助　ラ変/体　名・　副助
姉、継母 など やう の 人々 の、その 物語、かの 物語、光源氏 の ある やう など、

名　四/体　格助　四/体　格助　副　シク形/語幹　接尾　四/已　接助　代　格助　四/体・　名・　格助　ナリ形容/用
ところどころ 語る を 聞く に、いとど ゆかし さ まされ ど、わ が 思ふ まま に、空に

副・　係助/係　下二/用　四/未・助動/推/体/結　副　ク形/体　名・　名　格助　名　格助　四/用
いかで か おぼえ 語ら む 。いみじく 心もとなき まま に、等身 に 薬師仏 を 作り

接助　名　副助　サ変/用　接助　名　格助　ナリ形動/用　四/用　接助　名　格助　副　下二/用　補助動/尊助・接助　名
て、手洗ひ など し て、人間 に みそかに 入り つつ、京 に とく あげ 給ひ て、物語

格助　ク形/用　四/丁/終・助動/伝/体　ラ変/体　名　下二/用　補助動/尊/命・格助　名　格助　下二/用　接助　名　格助　四/用　四/用
の 多く 候ふ なる、ある 限り 見せ 給へ と、身 を 捨て て 額 を つき、祈り

補助動/謙/体　名　格助　名　格助　四/体　名　四/未　助動/推/終　格助　名　サ変/用・接助　固名　格助　四/体
申す ほど に、十三 に なる 年、上ら む とて、九月三日 門出して、いまたち といふ

名　格助　四/終
所 に 移る。

名　四/用　下二/用　助動/完/体　名　格助　ナリ形動/用　四/用　四/用　接助　四/用　接助　名　格助
年ごろ 遊び なれ つる 所 を、あらはに こぼち 散らし て、立ち騒ぎ て、日 の

名・　格助　副　ク形/用　四/用・　助動/存/体　格助　名　格助　四/終　格助　接頭　四/用　助動/完/已　接助
入りぎは の、いと すごく 霧りわたり たる に、車 に 乗る とて、うち 見やり たれ ば、

名　格助　係助　四/用　接助　名　格助　四/用・・　助動/過/体　名　格助　四/用　補助動/尊/已　助動/存/体　格助　下二/用
人間 に は 参り つつ、額 を つき し 薬師仏 の たち 給へ る を、見捨て

補助動/謙/体　シク形/用　接助　名　下二/未　助動/打/用　接頭　四/未・助動/自/用　助動/完/終
たてまつる 悲しく て、人 知れ ず うち 泣か れ ぬ 。

Vocabulary for Section 2 (Avid Reader of Tales)

かく(斯く)   (*adv.*) in this way, in this manner, in this fashion, thus

思ひくんず (思ひ屈ず)   (*intr. v. SH*) to be depressed

心ぐるし (心苦し)   (*shiku adj.*) worrisome

~がる   (*suffix*) to feel the quality of ~ (here, "to worry about")

巻   (*n.*) book, volume

太秦   (*proper n.*) Shingon temple called Kōryūji in Uzumasa

籠る   (*intr. v. YD*) to stay at a temple/shrine to pray

異事   (*n.*) separate matter, something else

まま (儘)   (*n.*) as soon as, immediately

いづ (出づ)   (*intr. v. SN*) to leave, go out

見果つ   (*tr. v. SN*) to see completely

嘆く   (*intr. v. YD*) to lament, grieve

渡す   (*tr. v. YD*) to hand over

うつくし (愛し)   (*shiku adj.*) lovable, adorable

生ひ成る   (*intr. v. YD*) to grow

あはれがる   (*tr. v. YD*) to feel sympathy toward, be impressed by

めづらし (珍し)   (*shiku adj.*) lovely, adorable, cute (with *-garu*, "to find adorable")

まめまめし   (*shiku adj.*) practical

まさなし (正無し)   (*ku adj.*) inappropriate

ひつ (櫃)   (*n.*) wooden chest with lid

在 中 将 (*proper n.*) abbrev. for *Zaigo chūjō monogatari*, an alternative title for *Ise monogatari*. Zaigo chūjō refers to Ariwara no Narihira.

とほぎみ、せり河、しらら、あさうづ (*proper n.*) titles of nonextant *monogatari*

袋 (*n.*) bag

とり入る (取り入る) (*tr. v. SN*) to place inside

う (得) (*tr. v. SN*) to acquire, possess

几帳 (*n.*) standing curtain, suspended on portable frames (used to partition a room and provide privacy in a Heian residence)

うちふす (うち臥す) (*intr. v. YD*) to lie down, go to sleep

后 (*n.*) empress

ひぐらし (日暮らし) (*adv., n.*) morning to night, all day long

さむ (覚む・醒む) (*intr. v. SN*) to be awake

僧 (*n.*) priest

ともす: (点す・灯す) (*tr. v. YD*) to burn, light (a lantern)

袈裟 (*n.*) surplice, worn by a priest on top of a robe from the left shoulder to the right armpit

法華 経 (*proper n.*) Lotus Sutra

おもひかく (思ひ掛く・思ひ懸く) (*tr. v. SN*) to have on one's mind, think of, take seriously

しむ (染む・浸む) (*tr. v. SN*) to hold deeply in one's heart

わろし (悪し) (*ku adj.*) ugly

盛り (*n.*) prime of life

かたち (形 ・容貌) (*n.*) form, shape, figure, appearance

夕顔、宇治の 大 将 、浮舟 (*proper n.*) characters in *Genji monogatari*

めぎみ (女君) (*n.*) (same as *onnagimi*) wife or lover of noble (hon.)

まづ (先づ) (*adv.*) truly

はかなし (果無し・果敢無し) (*ku adj.*) fruitless, empty, useless

あさまし (*shiku adj.*) disappointing

Grammar Notes for Section 2

かくのみ思ひくんじたるを 心 も 慰 めむと、

　心 ぐるしがりて RY of SH v. *omoi-kunzu*, RT of aux. v. *tari*, indicating a continuing state, and case p. *o*, marking this as the object of v. *nagusami-yuku* at the end of the sentence; MZ of *nagusamu* and SS of aux. v. *mu*, indicating intention (of the mother); *garu* turns adj. *kokorogurushi* into a v., "to worry about": "(My mother) was worried and tried to console my heart, which had become depressed in this way."

見せたまふに RY of tr. SN v. *misu*, "to show," and RT of hon. suppl. v. *tamau*, showing respect to the mother: "When my mother sought out tales and showed them (to me) . . ."

人語らひなどもえせず n. *hitokatarai*, "conferring with someone," pot. adv. *e*, correlated with a neg., and MZ of SH v. *su*, which makes *hitokatarai* into a v.: "I could not confer with anybody."

なれぬほどにて MZ of intr. v. *naru*, "to become familiar," RT of neg. *zu*, RY of copular *nari*, and conj. p. *te*

よりして case p. *yori*, "from," RY of SH v. *su*, "to do," and conj. p. *te*: "starting with the first volume . . ."

籠り給へるにも異事なく、この事を申して IZ of hon. suppl. YD v. *tamau*, which pays respect to the parents: "Even (*mo*) while (my parents) were staying at the temple, I (thought of) nothing else (*kotogoto naku*) and spoke (prayed) for only this (*monogatari*)." The author implicitly goes with her parents to the temple but, instead of praying for her own salvation, prays for *monogatari*.

いでむままに   MZ of SN v. *izu*, "to leave," referring to the parents (and the author) leaving the temple, aux. v. *mu*, which functions as indirection, and comp. *mama ni*, "immediately." As soon as they leave the temple, the author expects to see the rest of this *monogatari* (because of the prayers at the temple), but she does not.

いと口惜しく思ひ嘆かるるに   RY of YD v. *omou*, "to think," MZ of YD v. *nageku*, "to lament," RT of aux. v. *ru*, here spontaneous, and conj. p. *ni*, indicating time: "when I was full of regret and could not help but lament"

渡いたれば   RY of tr. YD v. *watasu* (sound change from *watashi* to *watai*) and RY of perfective aux. v. *tari*: "when (*ba*) (my parents) handed me over (or had me go)"

いとうつくしう生ひなりにけり   RY of adj. *utsukushi* (sound change from *utsukushiku* to *utsukushiu*), RY of intr. YD v. *oi-naru*, RY of perfective aux. v. *nu*, and SS of aux. v. *keri*, which is exclamatory: "You have ended up growing (*oinari-ni-keri*) into (someone) so (*ito*) adorable!"

まさなかりなむ   RY of *ku* adj. *masanashi*, MZ of perfective aux. v. *nu*, and SS of spec. aux. v. *mu*; aux. v. *nu* and *mu* combine (as *na-mu*) to become an emphatic: "would no doubt be inappropriate"

ゆかしくし給ふなるもの   *shi-tamau naru* is RY of SH v. *su*, SS of hon. suppl. v. *tamau*, showing respect to the author when she was a young girl, and RT of hearsay aux. v. *nari*, which follows SS: "something which I hear that you find attractive"

嬉しさぞいみじきや   n. *ureshisa*, from the stem of adj. *ureshi*, "happy," and the nominalizing suffix *sa*, emphatic bound p. *zo*, RT of *ku* adj. *imiji*, and exclamatory p. *ya*: "the joy was immense!"

はしるはしる   *hashiruhashiru*, a neologism that repeats the YD v. *hashiru*, "to run," here functioning as an adv. meaning "excitedly"

心も得ず   MZ of SN v. *u* and RY of neg. aux. v. *zu*: "I was not able to understand."

后の位も何にかはせむ   "What does one do with the rank of an empress? (Nothing. It cannot compare to reading *The Tale of Genji*.)" Achieving the rank of empress was, at the time, considered the ultimate for a woman.

さめたるかぎり   RT of SN v. *samu*, RT of aux. v. *tari*, indicating a continuing state, and n. *kagiri*: "as long as I was awake"

空におぼえ浮かぶをいみじきことに思ふに   RY of adj. v. *sora*, RY of SN v. *oboyu*, "to recall," RT of YD v. *ukabu*, "to float up," and RT of adj. *imiji*, "splendid": "I thought it a splendid thing when (*The Tale of Genji*) floated up (*oboe-ukabu*) in my memory (*sora ni*), but (*ni*) . . ."

われはこのごろわろきぞかし   RT of *ku* adj. *waroshi*, "ugly," emphatic bound p. *zo*, and emphatic final p. *kashi*

髪もいみじく長くなりなむ   n. *kami*, bound p. *mo*, RY of *ku* adj. *imiji*, RY of *ku* adj. *nagashi*, RY of intr. YD v. *naru*, MZ of aux. v. *nu*, and spec. aux. v. *mu*: "My hair (*kami*) will no doubt (*na-mu*) end up becoming (*nari*) extremely long (*nagaku*)." The comp. *na-mu* (*nu* + *mu*) is emphatic, expressing the speaker's certainty about her speculation.

浮舟の女君のやうにこそあらめ   n. *yō*, "likeness," RY of copular *nari*, "to be," emphatic bound p. *koso*, MZ of RH suppl. v. *ari*, and IZ of aux. v. *mu*, which is speculative: "I would no doubt be (*koso ara-me*) like the noble daughter Ukifune . . ."

Annotated Grammar for Section 2

副 副助 サ変/用 助動/存/体 格助 名 係助 下二/未 助動/意/終 格助 シク形/終 接尾・接助 名 名 副助
かく のみ 思ひくんじ たる を、 心 も 慰め む と、心ぐるし がり て、母、物語 など

下二/用 接助 下二/用・補助動/尊/四/体 接助 副 四/用 四/終 名 格助 名 格助 上一/用 接助 名
求めて 見せ 給ふ に、げに おのづから 慰み ゆく。紫 の ゆかり を 見 て、つづき

格助 上一/未 助動/希/用 下二/已・接助 名 副助 係助 副 サ変/未 助動/打/終 代名 係助 副 名 下二/未
の 見 まほしく おぼゆれ ど、人語らひ など も え せ ず。誰 も いまだ 都 なれ

助動/打/体 名・格助 名 断/用 接助 副 下二/未 助動/打/終 シク形/用 ク形/用 シク形/用 下二/体 名・格助
ぬ ほど に て、え 見つけ ず。いみじく 心もとなく、ゆかしく おぼゆる ままに、

代名 格助 固名 格助 名 格助 格助 サ変/用 接助 名 下二/用 補助動/尊/四/命 格助 名 格助 名 格助 四/体
「この 源氏 の 物語、一 の 巻 より し て みな 見せ 給へ」と 心 の 内 に 祈る。

名 格助 固名 格助 四/用 補助動/尊/四/已 助動/存/体 格助 係助 名 下二/用 補助動/尊/四/命 格助 名 格助 名 四/用・接助 下二/未 助動/婉/体
親 の 太秦 に 籠り 給へ る にも、異事 なく、この 事 を 申して、いで む

名・代名 格助 名 下二/未 助動/意/終 格助 四/已 接助 四/未 助動/打/終 副 シク形/用・ 四/用 四/未
ままに この 物語 見果て む と 思へど、見え ず。いと 口惜しく 思ひ 嘆か

助動/自/体 接助 名 断/名 名 格助 四/用 助動/存/体 名 格助 四/用 (音便)・助動/完/已 接助 副
るる に、をば なる 人 の 田舎 より 上り たる 所 に 渡い たれ ば、「いと

シク形/用(音) 四/用 助動/完/用 助動/過/終 副助 四/用 シク形/終 接尾・接助 四/体 格助 代名 係助/係
うつくしう、生ひなり に けり」など、あはれがり、珍し がり て、帰る に「何 を か

四/謙/未・助動/推/未 シク形/体 名 係助 ナリ形動/用 助動/完/未 助動/推/終 シク形/用 サ変/用 補助動/尊/四/終
奉ら む、まめまめしき 物 は、まさなかり な む、ゆかしく し 給ふ

助動/伝/体 名 格助 四/謙/未・助動/意/終 格助 接助 固名 格助 名 格助 四/用・接助 固名
なる もの を 奉ら む」とて、源氏 の 五十余巻、ひつ に 入り ながら、在中将、

固助 固名 固名 固名 副助 四/体 格助 名 下二/用 接助 下二/用 接助 四/体
とほぎみ、せり河、しらら、あさうづ など いふ 物語 ども、一袋 取り入れ て、得 て 帰る

名 格助 シク形/語幹・接尾 係助/係 シク形/体 間助 副 ナリ形動/用 上一/用 接助 名 係助 下二/未
心地 の 嬉し さ ぞ いみじき や。はしるはしる わづかに 見 つつ、心 も 得

助動/打/体・名 四/体 固名 格助 名 格助 名 サ変/未 接助 名 係助 四/未・助動/打/終 名 格助 名
ず 心もとなく 思ふ 源氏 を、一 の 巻 より し て、人 も 交じら ず、几帳 の 内

格助 接頭 四/用・接助 下二/用 接助 上一/体 名 格助 名 係助 代名 格助 上一/体 係助 サ変/未 助動/推/結 係助
に うち 臥して ひき出で つつ 見る 心地、后 の 位 も 何 に かは せ む。昼 は

副 名 係助 名 格助 下二/用 助動/存/体 名 名 格助 四/用 接助 代名 格助 上一/体 名
日暮らし、夜 は 目 の さめ たる かぎり、火 を 近く ともして、これ を 見る より ほか

格助 名 ク形/已 接助 副 副助 係助 ナリ形動/用 下二/未 四/体・格助 シク形/体 名 格助 四/体
の 事 なけれ ば、おのづから など は、空に おぼえ 浮かぶ を、いみじき こと に 思ふ

接助 名 格助 副 ナリ形動/体 名 格助 ナリ形動/体 名 格助 上一/用 助動/存/体 格助 カ変/用 接助 固名
に、夢 に いと 清げなる 僧 の、黄なる 地 の 袈裟 着 たる が 来 て、「法華経五巻

格助 副 四/命 格助 四/終 格助 下二/已 接助 名 格助 係助 四/未・助動/打/終 四/未 助動/意/終 格助 下二/用
を とく 習へ」と いふ と 見れ ど、人 に も 語ら ず、習は む とも 思ひかけ

助動/打/未 接助 名 格助 名 格助 下二/用・接助 名 代名 格助 ク形/体・係助 終助 格助
ず、物語 の 事 を のみ 心 に しめて、われ は この ごろ わろき ぞ かし。盛り に

四/未 接助 名 係助 名 ク形/用 ク形/用 名 係助 シク形/用 ク形/用・四/用 助動/完/未 助動/推/終 固名 格助
なら ば、容貌 も 限りなく よく、髪 も いみじく 長く なり な む。光の源氏 の

固名 名 格助 固名 格助 名 格助 名 格助 ク形/用 係助/係 補助動/ラ変/未 助動/推/已/結 格助 四/用 助動/過/体
夕顔、宇治の大将 の 浮舟 の 女君 の やう に こそ あら め と 思ひ ける

名 副 ク形/用 シク形/終
心、まづ いと はかなく あさまし。

7

Collection of Tales of Times Now Past

The *Collection of Tales of Times Now Past* (*Konjaku monogatari*), a monolithic anthology of 1,039 anecdotes, or *setsuwa*, was compiled in the late Heian period (early twelfth century). It consists of thirty-one volumes, of which three volumes (8, 18, and 21) are missing. The collection is divided into three parts: the first five volumes are on India (Tenjiku); the next five volumes are on China (Shintan); and the remaining twenty-one volumes are on Japan (Honchō). The Japanese section, in turn, is divided into two parts: volumes 11 through 20 are on Japanese Buddhism, and volumes 21 through 31 are on secular topics. It is not clear whether the compiler was a Buddhist monk or an aristocrat, a single author or a group of writers. The compiler traditionally has been thought to be Minamoto Takakuni (1004–1077), but the inclusion of stories dated after Takakuni died makes this improbable. The *Collection of Tales of Times Now Past* is written in a mixed Chinese–Japanese style (*wakan konkō bun*), which simultaneously reflects both the Chinese style of the sources and a strong movement toward vernacular Japanese.

The following story (vol. 29, no. 18), "How a Thief Climbed the Rashōmon Gate and Saw a Corpse," was adapted together with another story, "How a Man Who Was Accompanying His Wife to Tanba Province Got Trussed Up at Oeyama," by the modern author Akutagawa Ryūnosuke (1892–1927) in his short story "Rashōmon," which was then made into a film by Kurosawa Akira (1910–1998).

The text is based on Yamada Yoshio et al., eds., *Konjaku monogatari shū* 5, Nihon koten bungaku taikei 26 (Tokyo: Iwanami Shoten, 1961), 169–170, with minor orthographic changes.

『今昔物語集』

「羅城門の上の層に登りて死にし人を見たる盗人の語」

今は昔、摂津の国のほとりより盗みせむがために京に上りける男の、日のいまだ明かりければ、羅城門のもとに立ち隠れて立てりけるに、朱雀の方に人しげく行きければ、人の静まるまでと思ひて、門のもとに待ち立てりけるに、山城の方より人どものあまた来たりたる音のしければ、其れに見えじと思ひて、門の上の層に、やはらかかづり登りたりけるに、見れば、火ほのかに燃したり。

盗人、「あやし」と思ひて、連子よりのぞきければ、若き女の死にて臥したる有り。其の枕上に火を燃して、年いみじく老いたる嫗の白髪白きが、其の死にし人の枕上に居て、死にし人の髪をかなぐり抜き取る也けり。

盗人此れを見るに、心も得ねば、「此れはもし鬼にや有らむ」と思ひておぢけれども、「もし死にし人にてもぞ有る。おどして試む」と思ひて、やはら戸を開けて、刀を抜きて、「己は己は」と云ひて走り寄りければ、嫗手迷ひをして、手を摺りて迷へば、盗人、「此は何ぞの嫗のかくはし居たるぞ」と問ひければ、嫗、「己が主にておはしましつる人の失せ給ひたるを、あつかふ人の無ければ、かくて置き奉りたる也。其の御髪の長に余りて長ければ、其を抜き取りて鬘にせむとて抜く也。助け給へ」と云ひければ、盗人、死にし人の着たる衣と嫗の着たる衣と抜き取りてある髪とを奪ひ取りて、下り走りて逃げて去りにけり。

然て其の上の層には死にし人の骸骨ぞ多かりける。死にたる人の葬などえせぬをば、此の門の上にぞ置きける。

此の事は其の盗人の人に語りけるを聞き継ぎて、かく語り伝へたるとや。

Vocabulary

羅城門 (*proper n.*) massive gate that stood at the southern entrance to the Heian capital. It remained standing even after that part of the capital had fallen into ruin, and the peculiarity of such an imposing structure gave rise to stories about demons who lived inside.

層 (*n.*) floor of a building

摂津の国 (*proper n.*) province in present-day Hyōgo and Osaka prefectures

ほとり (辺・邊) (*n.*) edge, side, border

いまだ (未だ) (*adv.*) still

朱雀 (*proper n.*) (also Suzaku or Sujaku) The main north–south road in the capital, running from Rashōmon to Suzakumon, the entrance to the imperial palace, and dividing the capital into a western half, called 右京 (Ukyō), and an eastern half, called 左京 (Sakyō)

方 (*n.*) direction

しげし (*ku adj.*) plentiful, abundant

山城 (*proper n.*) province, in southern part of present-day Kyoto Prefecture

~ども (*suffix*) plural marker

あまた (*adv.*) many, in large numbers

やはら (*adv.*) stealthily, slowly, quietly, softly

かかづり登る (*intr. v. YD*) to climb up, scale, scramble up

ほのか (仄か) (*nari adj. v.*) faint, vague, indistinct

燃す (*tr. v. YD*) to burn, set on fire

あやし (奇し・怪し・異し) (*shiku adj.*) strange, incomprehensible

連子 (*n.*) lattice, lattice window

のぞく (覗く) (*tr. v. YD*) to peep at

臥す (*intr. v. YD*) to lie down, go to sleep

枕上 (*n.*) bedside, next to pillow

白髪 (*n.*) white hair

かなぐる (*tr. v. YD*) to grab and pull, yank

抜き取る (*tr. v. YD*) to pull out

もし (*adv.*) if by chance, in case (of), supposing that

おづ (*intr. v. KN*) to be afraid, recoil

おどす (*tr. v. YD*) to frighten, threaten

試みる (*intr. v. KI*) to attempt, try

己 (*pron.*) second-person pron. (derogatory): the likes of you

手迷ひ (*n.*) state of confusion, panic, fear

(手を) 摺る (*tr. v. YD*) to rub (one's hands together)

かく (斯く) (*adv.*) in this way, in this manner, in this fashion, thus

主 (*n.*) owner, head of household, lord

失す (*intr. v. SN*) to die

あつかふ (*tr. v. YD*) to take care of, look after

御髪 (*n.*) hair (hon.)

長 (*n.*) length

鬘 (*n.*) wig

奪ひ取る (*tr. v. YD*) (from *ubai-toru*) to snatch away

然て (*conj.*) then, next, at that point

骸骨 (*n.*) skeleton

葬 (*n.*) burial

聞き継ぐ (*tr. v. YD*) to pass down (a story)

Grammar Notes

盗（ぬす）みせむがために   n. *nusumi*, "stealing," MZ of SH v. *su*, which turns *nusumi* into a v., and RT of intent. aux. v. *mu*

其（そ）れに見（み）えじ   pron. *sore*, referring to the people coming from Yamashiro, MZ of intr. SN v. *miyu*, "to be seen," and SS of neg. intent. aux. v. *ji*

死（し）にて臥（ふ）したる有（あ）り   RT of resultative aux. v. *tari*, modifying an implied body

心（こころ）も得（え）ねば   MZ of SN v. *u*, "to be able," and IZ of neg. aux. v. *zu*: "since he could not make sense of it . . ."

もし鬼（おに）にや有（あ）らむ   RY of copular *nari*, doubt bound p. *ya*, MZ of suppl. v. *ari*, and RT of spec. aux. v. *mu*

己（おのれ）が主（あるじ）にておはしましつる人（ひと）   RY of copular *nari*, conj. p. *te*, RY of hon. suppl. v. *owashimasu*, and RT of perfective aux. v. *tsu*: "the person who was my master"

葬（はうぶり）などえせぬをば   emphatic comp. *woba* (case p. *wo* and bound p. *wa*, vocalized as *ba*), emphasizing object of v.

語（かた）り伝（つた）へたるとや   citational case p. *to*, bound p. *ya*, with an implied *iu*, "to say," at the end. This is a conventional ending in the *Collection of Tales of Times Now Past*: "They say it has been passed on (like this)."

Annotated Grammar

羅城門 の 上 の 層 に 登り て 死に し 人 を 見 たる 盗人 の 語

今 は 昔、摂津 の 国 の ほとり より 盗み せ む が ために 京 に 上り ける

男 の、日 の いまだ 明かり けれ ば、羅城門 の もと に 立ち隠れ て 立て り

ける に、朱雀 の 方 に 人 しげく 行き けれ ば、人 の 静まる まで と 思ひ て、門

の もと に 待ち立て り ける に、山城 の 方 より 人 ども の あまた 来たり

たる 音 の し けれ ば、其れ に 見え じ と 思ひ て、門 の 上 の 層 に

やはら かかづり登り たり ける に、見れ ば、火 ほのかに 燃し たり。

盗人、「あやし」と 思ひ て、連子 より のぞき けれ ば、若き 女 の 死に て 臥し たる

有り。其 の 枕上 に 火 を 燃して、年 いみじく 老い たる 嫗 の 白髪 白き が、其 の

死に し 人 の 枕上 に 居 て、死に し 人 の 髪 を かなぐり 抜き取る 也

けり。

盗人 此れ を 見る に、心 も 得 ね ば、「此れ は もし 鬼 に や 有ら

む」と 思ひ て おぢ けれ ども、「もし 死に し 人 に て も ぞ

有る。おどして 試む」と 思ひ て、やはら 戸 を 開けて、刀 を 抜きて、

「己 は 己 は」と 云ひ て 走り 寄り けれ ば、嫗 手迷ひ を して、手 を 摺りて

四/已・ 接助　名　　代 係助 代 係助/係 格助 名 格助 副 係助 サ変/用 上一/用 助動/存/体/結 係助 格助 四/用・ 助動/過/已
迷へ ば、盗人、「此 は 何 ぞ の 嫗 の かく は し 居 たる ぞ」と 問ひ けれ

接助 名 代 格助 名 助動/断/用 接助 補助動/尊/四/用 助動/完/体 名 格助 下二/用 補助動/尊/四/已・ 助動/完/体 接助 四/体
ば、嫗、「己 が 主 に て おはしまし つる 人 の 失せ 給へ る を、あつかふ

名 格助 ク形/已・ 接助 副 四/用 補助動/謙/四/用 助動/存/体 助動/断/終 代 格助 名 格助 名 格助 四/用・ 接助
人 の なけれ ば、かくて 置き 奉り たる 也。其 の 御髪 の 長 に 余りて

ク形/已・ 接助 代 格助 四/用 接助 名 格助 サ変/未 助動/意/終 格助 接助 四/体 助動/断/終 下二/用 補助動/尊/四/命・ 格助
長けれ ば、其 を 抜き取りて 鬘 に せ む とて 抜く 也。助け 給へ」と

四/用・ 助動/過/已 接助 名 ナ変/用 助動/過/体 名 格助 上一/用 助動/存/体 名 格助 名 格助 上一/用 助動/存/体 名 格助
云ひ けれ ば、盗人、死に し 人 の 着 たる 衣 と 嫗 の 着 たる 衣 と、

四/用 接助 ラ変/体 名 格助 格助 四/用 接助 上二/用 四/用 接助 下二/用 接助 四/用 助動/完/用 助動/過/終
抜き取り て ある 髪 と を 奪ひ取り て、下り 走り て 逃げ て 去り に けり。

接 代 格助 名 格助 名 格助 係助 ナ変/用・ 助動/過/体 名 格助 名 係助/係 ク形/用 助動/過/已/結 ナ変/用 助動/完/体
然て 其 の 上 の 層 に は 死に し 人 の 骸骨 ぞ 多かり ける。死に たる

名 格助 名 副助 副 サ変/未 助動/打/体 格助 係助 代 格助 名 格助 名 格助 係助/係 四/用 助動/過/体/結
人 の 葬 など え せ ぬ をば、此 の 門 の 上 に ぞ 置き ける。

代 格助 名 係助 代 格助 名 格助 名 格助 四/用 助動/過/体 格助 四/用 接助 副 四/用 下二/用・ 助動/存/体
此 の 事 は 其 の 盗人 の 人 に 語り ける を 聞き継ぎ て、かく 語り 伝へ たる

格助 係助
と や。

Part III

Kamakura Period

8

Hundred Poets, Hundred Poems

Hundred Poets, Hundred Poems (*Ogura hyakunin isshu*, better known simply as *Hyakunin isshu*), is a collection of one hundred classical poems (*waka*) whose compilation, around 1235, is attributed to Fujiwara no Teika (1162–1241), the leading poet of his time and one of the editors of the *Shinkokinshū*. *Hundred Poets, Hundred Poems* is the result of a tradition of canonizing outstanding earlier poets and selecting their best poems. Accordingly, all the poems in *Hundred Poets, Hundred Poems* are from imperial poetry collections (*chokusenshū*), beginning with the *Kokinshū*. Earlier poets like Kakinomoto no Hitomarō, who wrote in the ancient period, are represented by poems found in the imperial poetry collections of the Heian and Kamakura periods. *Hundred Poets, Hundred Poems* contains poems by seventy-nine male poets and twenty-one female poets: six spring poems, four summer poems, sixteen autumn poems, six winter poems, forty-three love poems, four travel poems, one parting poem, and twenty miscellaneous poems. The collection begins with poems by two early emperors, Tenchi and Jitō. In the Edo/Tokugawa period, *Hundred Poets, Hundred Poems* became popular as a card game, in which the bottom half of each poem was matched with the top half in a speed contest. The first fifteen poems in the anthology follow.

The text is based on Ariyoshi Tamotsu, Inukai Kiyoshi, and Hashimoto Fumio, eds., *Hyakunin isshu* (*Kensai hitsu*), Eiin kōchū koten sōsho 2 (Tokyo: Shintensha, 1974), 11–23, with minor orthographic changes.

『百人一首』

「1」

秋の田の　仮庵の庵の　苫をあらみ

わが衣手は　露にぬれつつ

天智天皇

「2」

春すぎて　夏来にけらし　白妙の

衣 ほすてふ　天の香具山

持統天皇

「3」

あしびきの　山鳥の尾の　しだり尾の

ながながし夜を　ひとりかも寝む

柿本人麻呂

「4」

田子の浦に　うち出でてみれば　白妙の

富士の高嶺に　雪は降りつつ

山辺赤人

「5」

奥山に　紅葉ふみわけ　鳴く鹿の

声きく時ぞ　秋は悲しき

猿丸大夫

「6」

かささぎの　渡せる橋に　おく霜の

白きをみれば　夜ぞふけにける

中納言家持

「7」

天の原　ふりさけ見れば　春日なる

三笠の山に　出でし月かも

安倍仲麿

「8」

わが庵は　都のたつみ　しかぞすむ

世をうぢ山と　人はいふなり

喜撰法師

「9」

花の色は　うつりにけりな　いたづらに
わが身世にふる　ながめせしまに

小野小町

「10」

これやこの　行くも帰るも　別れては
知るも知らぬも　逢坂の関

蝉丸

「11」

わたの原　八十島かけて　漕ぎ出でぬと
人には告げよ　海人の釣船

参議 篁

「12」

天つ風　雲の通ひ路　吹き閉ぢよ
をとめの姿　しばしとどめむ

僧 正 遍昭

「13」

筑波嶺の　峰より落つる　男女川
恋ぞつもりて　淵となりぬる

陽成院

「14」

陸奥の　しのぶもぢずり　誰ゆゑに
乱れそめにし　われならなくに

河原左大臣

「15」

君がため　春の野に出でて　若菜つむ
わが衣手に　雪は降りつつ

光 孝 天皇

Author of Poem 1

天智天皇 (てんぢてんわう)　Tenji tennō (626–671), Emperor Tenji, also was known as Prince Nakanoōe (中 大 兄 皇子 なかのおほえのわうじ).
He enacted the Taika Reforms and moved the capital to Ōmi (present-day Shiga Prefecture).

Vocabulary for Poem 1

仮庵 (かりほ)　(*n.*) (*kari-o*, also *kari-io*) temporary shelter, hut

苫 (とま)　(*n.*) thatch, woven together from sedge or straw and used for roofing

あらし (粗し)　(*ku adj.*) coarse, rough, full of holes

衣手 (ころもで)　(*n.*) sleeve of a robe

庵 (いほ)　(*n.*) rough hut of sticks and brush

み　(*suffix*) (follows adj. stem) because, since

ぬる (濡る)　(*intr. v. SN*) to get wet

Grammar Notes for Poem 1

苫をあらみ (とま)　n. *toma*, interj. p. *o*, stem of adj. *arashi*, and suffix *mi*, indicating cause. From the late Heian period on, *toma* was associated with images of loneliness and solitude.

ぬれつつ　conj. p. *tsutsu*, indicating both repetition and continuation of the action

Annotated Grammar for Poem 1

名 格助 名 格助 名 格助 名 格助 名 間助 ク形/語幹 接尾 代名 格助 名 係助 名 格助 下二/用 接助
秋 の 田 の 仮庵 の 庵 の 苫 を あら み わ が 衣手 は 露 に ぬれ つつ
(あき)(た)　　(かりこや)　　　(やね)(ふ)(とま)(め)(あめ)(めら)

Modern Japanese: 秋の田のほとりにある仮小屋の、その屋根を葺いた苫の編み目が粗いので、
私(わたし)の袖(そで)は露(つゆ)に濡(ぬ)れていくばかりである。

Author of Poem 2

持統天皇 (ぢとうてんわう)　Empress Jitō (645–702), daughter of Emperor Tenji, became consort to Emperor Tenmu, whom she succeeded. She was one of the most famous female sovereigns in Japanese history.

Vocabulary for Poem 2

白妙の (しろたへ)　(*makura-kotoba*, "pillow word") (from n. *shirotae*, "white fabric") modifying words associated with undyed clothing, such as *koromo* (robe), or images of whiteness like *yuki* (snow)

ほす　(*tr. v. YD*) to dry out

てふ　(*comp.*) (*chō*) (contraction of case p. *to* and YD v. *iu*, "to say") it is said that 〜

天の香具山 (あま)(かぐやま)　(*proper n.*) Kaguyama is a mountain in present-day Nara Prefecture. It is labeled "heavenly" (*ama no*) because it was believed to come from the heavens.

Grammar Notes for Poem 2

夏来にけらし *kerashi*, a comp. that underwent a sound change from *keru-rashi* to *kerashi*; *ke-rashi* expresses speculation about the past based on evidence, which here is the white robes laid out to dry on Mount Kagu, evidence of the arrival of summer

天の香具山 The white robes on the mountain implicitly resemble the *unohana*, or deutzia, which have white flowers. The nominal ending creates overtones, leaving the rest to the reader's imagination.

Annotated Grammar for Poem 2

名 四/用 接助 名 カ変/用 助動/完/用 助動/過/体 助動/推/終 枕 名 四/体 連語 固名/歌枕

春 すぎ て 夏 来 に け (る) らし 白妙の 衣 ほす てふ 天の香具山

Modern Japanese: 春が過ぎて夏が来たらしい。夏になると真っ白な 衣 を干すという天の香具山(にあのように白い 衣 が干してあるよ)。

Author of Poem 3

柿本人麻呂 Kakinomoto no Hitomaro (late seventh c.–early eighth c.), was one of the greatest poets of the *Man'yōshū* era (seventh–eighth c.). He was a low-ranking official serving at the court of Empress Jitō.

Vocabulary for Poem 3

あしびきの *makura-kotoba* modifying *yama* (mountain), *mine* (peak), *iwo* (boulder), and mountains like Mount Kazuraki

山鳥 (*n.*) copper pheasant

しだり尾 (し垂り尾) (*n.*) drooping tail

ながながし(長長し) (*ku adj.*) extremely long

尾 (*n.*) tail

Grammar Notes for Poem 3

山鳥の尾の It was believed that the male and female mountain pheasant spent their days together but separated at night. The bird thus became associated with the melancholy of a lover spending the night alone.

しだり尾の Note the repeated *o* and *no* sounds in the second and third phrases (*ku*). The first three *ku* (5/7/5) function as a *jokotoba*, or preface, which leads into the main body (7/7). The long tail implies a male pheasant longing for its mate. The effect of the *jokotoba* is to associate the length of the pheasant's drooping tail with the length of a lonely night.

ながながし夜 *naganagashi*, which functions as both a SS and a RT, modifying both the droopy tail and the night (*yo*)

ひとりかも寝む interrogative bound p. *ka* and exclamatory bound p. *mo*

Annotated Grammar for Poem 3

枕	名	格助	名	格助	名	格助	ク形/終/体	名	格助	名	係助/係	係助	下二/未	助動/推/体/結
あしびきの	山鳥	の	尾	の	しだり尾	の	ながながし	夜	を	ひとり	か	も	寝	む

あしびきの 山鳥(やまどり) の 尾(お) の しだり尾 の ながながし 夜 を ひとり か も 寝 む

Modern Japanese: 山鳥の尾の、その垂れ下がった尾が長々(ながなが)しいように、秋(あき)の長々(ながなが)しい夜(よる)をひとりで寝(ね)ることになるのだろうか。

Author of Poem 4

山辺赤人(やまべのあかひと)　　Yamabe no Akahito (mid-eighth c.) was a noted poet of the *Man'yōshū* era, active in the early Nara period (710–784). He was probably a low-ranking official serving at court.

Vocabulary for Poem 4

田子の浦(たごうら)　　(*proper n.*) Tago Bay, off the coast of present-day Shizuoka Prefecture

うち出(い)づ　　(*intr. v. SN*) to come out, appear

高嶺(たかね)　　(*n.*) tall, lofty peak

Grammar Notes for Poem 4

うち出(い)でてみれば　　The prefix *uchi* strengthens the v.; IZ plus the conj. p. *ba* indicates that the act of looking results in the following observation.

白妙(しろたへ)の　　*makura-kotoba* associated with whiteness emphasizing the whiteness of Mount Fuji's peak

雪(ゆき)は降(ふ)りつつ　　conj. p. *tsutsu*, indicating that snow "keeps falling"

Annotated Grammar for Poem 4

固名/歌枕	格助	接頭	下二/用	接助	上一/已	接助	枕	固名/歌枕	格助	名	格助	名	係助	四/用	接助
田子の浦	に	うち	出で	て	みれ	ば	白妙の	富士	の	高嶺	に	雪	は	降り	つつ

田子の浦(たごうら) に うち 出(で)で て みれ ば 白妙(ましろ)の 富士(ふじ) の 高嶺(たかね) に 雪(ゆき) は 降(ふ)り つつ

Modern Japanese: 田子の浦に出てみると、真っ白な富士の高嶺にしきりに雪が降っていることだよ。

Author of Poem 5

猿丸大夫(さるまるだいふ)　　Almost nothing is known about Sarumaru Dayū (eighth c.–ninth c.), but he is mentioned in the *mana* (Chinese) preface to the *Kokinshū*.

Vocabulary for Poem 5

奥山(おくやま)　　(*n.*) remote mountain

紅葉(もみぢ)　　(*n.*) bright autumn leaves

ふみわく（踏みわく）　　(*tr. v. SN*) to walk over or make one's way through snow or fallen leaves

Grammar Notes for Poem 5

鳴く鹿の (な し か)　The sound of a male deer crying out to a female in autumn was commonly associated with longing for one's wife or lover.

ぞ秋は悲しき (あき かな)　The bound p. *wa* emphasizes autumn over the other seasons. The *ku* adj. *kanashi*, "sad," is in RT because of the emphatic bound p. *zo*.

Annotated Grammar for Poem 5

名	格助	名	下二/用	四/体	名	格助	名	四/体	名	係助/係	名	係助	シク形/体/結
奥山	に	紅葉	ふみわけ	鳴く	鹿	の	声	きく	時	ぞ	秋	は	悲しき

Modern Japanese: 人里離れた奥山で、散り敷いた紅葉を踏み分けて鳴いている鹿の声を聞く時こそ、いよいよ秋は悲しいものと感じられる。

Author of Poem 6

中納言家持 (ちゅう な ごんやかもち)　Chūnagon (Middle Counselor) Yakamochi (718–785), better known as Ōtomo no Yakamochi (大伴家持 (おほとものやかもち)), was the son of Tabito, one of the major poets of and the main compiler of the *Man'yōshū*.

Vocabulary for Poem 6

かささぎ　(*n.*) magpie (bird with a long tail)

渡す (わた)　(*tr. v. YD*) to move from one place to another, to cross to the opposite shore

霜 (しも)　(*n.*) frost

ふく（更く）　(*intr. v. SN*) to grow late (in the night, season)

Grammar Notes for Poem 6

かささぎの　According to Chinese legend, magpies form a bridge across the Milky Way (Ama no gawa) once a year to allow two constellations, Herdsman (Altair) and Weaver Woman (Vega), to unite. This is celebrated in Japan on the seventh day of the Seventh Month as the Tanabata Festival.

夜ぞふけにける　RY of perfective aux. v. *nu* and RT of aux. v. *keri*, conveying the speaker's exclamatory response to becoming aware of something that has occurred

Annotated Grammar for Poem 6

名	格助	四/已	助動/存/体	名	格助	四/連体	名	格助	ク形/体	格助	上一/已	接助	名	係助/係	下二/連用	助動/完/用
かささぎ	の	渡せ	る	橋	に	おく	霜	の	白き	を	みれ	ば	夜	ぞ	ふけ	に

助動/詠/体/結
ける

Modern Japanese: かささぎが翼 (つばさ)をつらねて渡 (わた)したという橋—宮中 (きゅうちゅう)の御階 (みはし)におりている霜 (しも)が白 (しろ)いのを見 (み)ると、もう夜 (よる)もふけてしまったのだった。

Author of Poem 7

<ruby>安倍 仲麿<rt>あ べのなかまろ</rt></ruby>　Abe no Nakamaro (701–770) was a Nara court official who traveled to China on an official embassy in 716 and, despite several attempts, was never able to return.

Vocabulary for Poem 7

<ruby>天の原<rt>あま はら</rt></ruby>　(*n.*) vast sky

ふりさけ見る (振り放け見る)　(*intr. v. KI*) to look up afar, gaze upward

<ruby>春日<rt>かすが</rt></ruby>　(*proper n.*) area of present-day Nara City

<ruby>三笠の山<rt>みかさ やま</rt></ruby>　(*proper n.*) mountain in the eastern part of present-day Nara City

Grammar Notes for Poem 7

<ruby>春日<rt>かすが</rt></ruby>なる<ruby>三笠<rt>みかさ</rt></ruby>の　RT of copular *nari*, indicating location: "Mikasa Mountain that is in Kasuga"

<ruby>出<rt>い</rt></ruby>でし<ruby>月<rt>つき</rt></ruby>かも　Nara-period final p. *kamo* is emphatic. The poem reflects Nakamaro's nostalgic longing for his homeland.

Annotated Grammar for Poem 7

天の原 ふりさけ 見れ ば 春日 なる 三笠の山 に 出で し 月 かも

Modern Japanese: <ruby>大空<rt>おおぞら</rt></ruby>をふり<ruby>仰<rt>あお</rt></ruby>いではるか<ruby>遠<rt>とお</rt></ruby>くを<ruby>眺<rt>なが</rt></ruby>めると、<ruby>今<rt>いま</rt></ruby><ruby>美<rt>うつく</rt></ruby>しい<ruby>月<rt>つき</rt></ruby>が<ruby>出<rt>で</rt></ruby>ているが、<ruby>見<rt>み</rt></ruby>ているあの<ruby>月<rt>つき</rt></ruby>は、かつて<ruby>奈良<rt>なら</rt></ruby>の<ruby>春日<rt>かすが</rt></ruby>にある<ruby>三笠山<rt>みかさやま</rt></ruby>の<ruby>上<rt>うえ</rt></ruby>に<ruby>出<rt>で</rt></ruby>ていた<ruby>月<rt>つき</rt></ruby>と<ruby>同<rt>おな</rt></ruby>じ<ruby>月<rt>つき</rt></ruby>なのだなあ。

Author of Poem 8

<ruby>喜撰 法師<rt>き せんほふ し</rt></ruby>　Although only one poem can be attributed with certainty to Priest Kisen (early ninth c.), he was regarded as one of the Six Poetic Sages (Rokkasen).

Vocabulary for Poem 8

わが　(*set phrase*) (from pron. *wa* and attrib. case p. *ga*) my

たつみ　(*n.*) southeast

しか　(*adv.*) in this way

うぢ山　(*proper n.*) area to the southeast of the capital (Kyoto)

Grammar Notes for Poem 8

<ruby>うぢ山<rt>やま</rt></ruby>　There is a pun on *u*, which can be taken as both the stem of the *ku* adj. *ushi*, "sorrowful" (憂し), and the first syllable in the place-name Uji.

と<ruby>人<rt>ひと</rt></ruby>はいふなり　SS of hearsay aux. v. *nari*, which follows SS

Annotated Grammar for Poem 8

代名 格助 名 係助 名 格助　名　　　副　係助/係 四/体/結 名 格助 固名/掛/歌枕 格助 名 係助 四/終　助動/伝/終
わ が 庵 は 都 の たつみ しか ぞ 住む 世 を うぢ山 と 人 は いふ なり

Modern Japanese: 私の庵は都の東南にあって、このように心のどかに暮らしている。それなのに、私がこの世をつらいと思って、逃れ住んでいる宇治山だと、世間の人は言っているようだ。

Author of Poem 9

小野小町　Ono no Komachi (early Heian period) was known in legend for her beauty and numerous love affairs, and she is the subject of many popular tales. The *Kokinshū* lists her as one of the Six Poetic Sages.

Vocabulary for Poem 9

うつる (移る) (*intr. v. YD*) to fade (color)

いたづら (*nari adj. v.*) useless, fruitless, empty

ながめ (眺め) (*n.*) gazing off into the distance, lost in melancholy thought

Grammar Notes for Poem 9

花の色は　The flowers also represent a woman's physical beauty.

うつりにけりな　*keri* is exclamatory, indicating that the speaker has noticed something for the first time

いたづらに　RY of adj. v. *itazura-nari* functioning like an adv.: "in vain," "fruitlessly"

わが身　(set phrase) one's body, one's self

世にふる　RT of SN v. *fu*, "to pass through,"

which implies RT of YD v. *furu*, "to fall" (the rain)

ながめ　pun on n. *nagame* or *nagaame*, "long rains," and n. *nagame*, "gazing off"

せしまに　MZ of SH v. *su*, "to do," RT of past-tense aux. v. *ki*, which follows RY except after SH and KH when it follows MZ, and n. *ma*, "period of time." The third, fourth, and fifth phrases, which would normally precede the first two, are shifted to the end for dramatic effect, a rhetorical technique called "grammatical inversion" (倒置法).

Annotated Grammar for Poem 9

名 格助 名 係助　四/用　　助動/完/用 助動/詠/終 終助　　ナリ形/用　　代名 格助 名 名 格助 四/体/掛　　名/掛　サ変/未
花 の 色 は うつり に けり な いたづらに わ が 身 世 に ふる ながめ せ

助動/過/体 名 格助
し ま に

Modern Japanese: 桜の花はむなしく色あせてしまった。春の長雨が降っていた間に。— 私の容姿もすっかり衰えてしまった。生きていることのもの思いをしていた間に。

Author of Poem 10

蝉 丸 せみまる   Semimaru was an early Heian *waka* poet and noted *biwa* (lute) player.

Vocabulary for Poem 10

逢 坂 の 関 あふさか せき (*proper n.*) barrier between Yamashiro Province (present-day Kyoto) and Ōmi Province (present-day Shiga Prefecture). From the middle of the sixth to the end of the eighth century, people entering or returning from the Eastern Provinces passed through this checkpoint. Since it contains the word *au*, "to meet," in its name, Ausaka (Ōsaka) Barrier became associated with meeting friends or loved ones.

Grammar Notes for Poem 10

これやこの *kore ya kono*, "this is that place!" an emphatic phrase used in poems expressing strong emotion at the sight of a place the speaker knows or has heard of in the past

行くも帰るも ゆ かへ Both verbs modify an implied subject, *hito* (people).

別れては わか RY of SN v. *wakaru*, "to part ways." The combination of conj. p. *te* and bound p. *wa* emphasizes the repetition of the acts of separating and meeting.

知るも知らぬも し し RT of v. *shiru* and RT of aux. v. *zu* both modify an implied *hito*: "people you know, and those you do not . . ."

Annotated Grammar for Poem 10

代名　間助　代名　格助　四/連体　係助　四/連体　係助　下二/用　接助　係助　四/体　係助　四/未　助動/打/体　係助　固名/歌枕
これ や こ の 行く も 帰る も 別れ て は 知る も 知ら ぬ も 逢坂の関

Modern Japanese: これがあの、これから旅立つ人も 都 へ帰る人もここで別れ、知っている人も たびだ ひと みやこ かへ ひと わか し ひと
知らない人も、ここでまた逢うという、逢坂の関なのですよ。 し ひと あ あうさか せき

Author of Poem 11

参議 篁 さんぎ たかむら Sangi (Consultant) Takamura (802–852) was better known as Ono no Takamura (小野 篁 をののたかむら), a scholar of Chinese letters. He was selected for a diplomatic mission to China but refused to go and was exiled to Oki Island. Later he was readmitted to the capital and reached the position of *sangi*.

Vocabulary for Poem 11

わたの原 はら (*set phrase*) wide-open sea

八十島 や そ しま (*n.*) (from *yaso*, "eighty," and *shima*, "island") numerous islands

漕ぎ出づ こ い (*intr. v. SN*) to row out to sea

告ぐ つ (*tr. v. SN*) to report, inform

海人 あ ま (*n.*) fisherman, salt maker

釣船 つりぶね (*n.*) fishing boat

Grammar Notes for Poem 11

漕ぎ出でぬと (こ い)　citational case p. *to*, indicating that the first three phrases are the content of the speaker's message

人には告げよ (ひと つ)　Ono no Takamura is said to have written this poem on the occasion of his exile.

Thus *hito* is taken to refer to the people he has left behind in the capital.

海人の釣船 (あま つりぶね)　a form of personification (擬人法) (ぎ じんほう) in which an inanimate object (the fishing boat) is treated as though it were human

Annotated Grammar for Poem 11

名　　　名　　下二/用 接助 下二/用　　助動/完/終 格助 名 格助 係助 下二/命　名　格助　名
わたの原 八十島 かけ て 漕ぎ出で　ぬ　と 人 に は 告げよ 海人 の 釣船

Modern Japanese: 海原をたくさんの島々を目ざして漕ぎ出してしまったと、都にいる人に伝えておくれ。漁師の釣船よ。 (うなばら／しまじま め／こ だ／みやこ／ひと つた／りょうし つりぶね)

Author of Poem 12

僧正遍昭 (そうじょうへんぜう)　Sōjō (Bishop) Henjō (816–890) was a clerical name for Yoshimine no Munesada (良岑宗貞). Henjō became a priest of the Tendai school after the death of Emperor Nin'myō (810–850).

Vocabulary for Poem 12

通ひ路 (かよ ぢ)　(*n.*) commuting road, route

吹き閉づ (ふ と)　(*tr. v. KN*) to blow shut

をとめ (少女・乙女)　(*n.*) (1) maiden, (2) courtly dancer at Gosechi Festival. Here both.

姿 (すがた)　(*n.*) physical appearance, figure, shape

Grammar Notes for Poem 12

天つ風 (あま かぜ)　Nara-period attrib. case p. *tsu*

雲の通ひ路 (くも かよ ぢ)　Legend had it that beautiful women who lived in the heavens and descended onto this road to perform a dance at court then returned to their homes.

をとめの姿 (すがた)　The maidens (*otome*) referred to here are the daughters of court nobles who have been chosen to dance at court. Comparing these maidens with the legendary heavenly beauties is an example of *mitate*, or visual comparison.

Annotated Grammar for Poem 12

名 格助 名 名 格助　名　　上二/命　名　格助 名　副助　下二/未 助動/意/終
天 つ 風 雲 の 通ひ路 吹き閉ぢよ をとめ の 姿 しばし とどめ　む

Modern Japanese: 空吹く風よ、雲の通い路を閉ざしておくれ。天女の舞い姿をしばらくこの地上にとどめておこう。 (そらふ かぜ／くも かよ じ と／てんにょ ま すがた／ち じょう)

Author of Poem 13

陽成院
やうぜいいん
Yōzei-in (868–949), or Cloistered Emperor Yōzei, was the son of Emperor Seiwa. Yōzei abdicated at the age of seventeen because of poor health.

Vocabulary for Poem 13

筑波嶺
つくばね
(*proper n.*) Same as Mount Tsukuba, a well-known mountain in present-day Ibaraki Prefecture. Its twin peaks were thought to resemble a couple, male and female.

峰
みね
(*n.*) mountain peak, summit

男女川
みなのがは
(*proper n.*) river originating at the peak of Mount Tsukuba

恋
こひ
(*n.*) love, longing

つもる (積もる) (*intr. v. YD*) to pile up

淵
ふち
(*n.*) deep, still pool

Grammar Notes for Poem 13

筑波嶺の峰
つくばね　みね
The use in succession of two different words for "peak" (*ne, mine*) emphasizes the height of the mountain.

より落つる男女川
お　みなのがは
Minano-gawa, which uses the characters for man and woman, is narrow at its origin, gradually swelling as it descends the mountain. The first three phrases create a

jokotoba, providing a metaphor for the speaker's feelings of longing.

恋ぞつもりて
こひ
koi carries connotations of deep longing for someone who is either in a distant place or has died and who is implicitly melancholy or depressed.

Annotated Grammar for Poem 13

固名/歌枕	格助	名	格助	上二/体	固名	名	係助/係	四/用	接助	名	格助	四/用	助動/完/結
筑波嶺	の	峰	より	落つる	男女川	恋	ぞ	つもり	て	淵	と	なり	ぬる

Modern Japanese: 筑波の峰から激しく流れ落ちてくる男女川がしだいに水量を増やして深い淵となるように、私の恋心も積もり積もって淵のように深くなってしまった。

Author of Poem 14

河原左大臣
かはらのさだいじん
Riverbank Minister of the Left (822–895) was named after the magnificent estate he built along the riverbank (*kawara*) of the Sixth Ward (Rokujō) of the capital. He is better known as Minamoto no Tōru (源融), the son of Emperor Saga.

Vocabulary for Poem 14

陸奥
みちのく
(*proper n.*) eastern part of present-day Tōhoku (northeastern Honshū)

乱れそむ (乱れ初む) (*intr. v. SN*) to begin to be disturbed, agitated, upset

ならなくに (*set phrase*) (from MZ of copular *nari*, MZ of aux. v. *zu*, nominalizing suffix *ku*, and case p. *ni*) though it is not the case that ～

Grammar Notes for Poem 14

陸奥のしのぶもぢずり   n. *shinobumojizuri*, "a tie-dyed robe with a twisting design," which uses a dye obtained from *shinobugusa*, "longing" ferns. Michinoku evokes a sense of rustic coarseness, and *shinobu* suggests a hidden (*shinobu*) affair and enduring something painful (*shinobu*). The speaker's turbulent emotional state is implicitly compared to the twisted pattern, a *jokotoba* leading to the word *midare*, "wild," "turmoil," in the main body.

誰ゆゑに乱れそめにし   The doubt bound p. *ka* is probably omitted after the case p. *ni*, which explains why the past-tense aux. v. *ki* is in RT. *Some* can be taken to mean both "to begin to do something" (初む) and "to dye" (染む). Both *midare* and *some* are associated words (*engo*) of *shinobumojizuri*: "Who (*dare*) is the cause (*yue*) of the beginning (*some*) of (this) turmoil (*midare*) (which is like a wild Michinoku pattern)?"

われならなくに   "It is not me (my fault). (Instead, it must be you.)"

Annotated Grammar for Poem 14

陸奥 の しのぶもぢずり 誰 ゆゑ に 乱れそめ に し われ なら な く に

Modern Japanese: 陸奥のしのぶもじずりの乱れ模様のように、ほかの誰のせいで乱れはじめてしまったのか、私のせいではないのに…。ほかならぬあなたのせいなのですよ。

Author of Poem 15

光孝天皇   Emperor Kōkō (830–887) was the son of Emperor Nin'myō (810–850).

Vocabulary for Poem 15

若菜   (*n.*) young greens that sprout early in spring and were traditionally consumed to drive away evil spirits, prevent illness, and secure longevity. On the seventh day of the First Month, members of the imperial court participated in this ritual prayer for long life.

つむ (摘む・抓む)   (*tr. v. YD*) to pick

Grammar Note for Poem 15

雪は降りつつ   The green of the *wakana*, symbolizing spring, and the whiteness of the snow, symbolizing winter, suggest the transition between the two seasons.

Annotated Grammar for Poem 15

君 が ため 春 の 野 に 出で て 若菜 つむ わ が 衣手 に 雪 は 降り つつ

Modern Japanese: あなたのために、春の野に出かけていって、若菜を摘んでいる私の袖に、雪が次から次へと降りかかってくることだ。

9

Collection of Tales from Uji

The *Collection of Tales from Uji* (*Uji shūi monogatari*) is the most popular and widely read of the medieval anecdote (*setsuwa*) collections. Although the author is not known, the *Collection* is generally thought to have been written in the early Kamakura period (early thirteenth century). Minamoto no Takakuni, a late-Heian-period aristocrat and senior counselor (*dainagon*) who lived in the twelfth century at the Byōdōin at Uji, south of the capital, is thought to have written a work called *Tales of the Uji Senior Counselor* (*Uji dainagon monogatari*), which was very popular but was lost. The attempt to reconstruct the lost text in the early thirteenth century resulted in the *Collection of Tales from Uji* (*Uji shūi monogatari*). The *Uji* in the title refers to the Byōdōin, and *shūi* (collection of remains) probably refers to collecting the remains of *Tales of the Uji Senior Counselor*.

The modern writer Akutagawa Ryūnosuke (1892–1927) made "The Priest with the Long Nose" (vol. 2, no. 7) into a noted short story, "Nose" (Hana). Akutagawa also used "How Yoshihide, Painter of Buddhist Pictures, Took Pleasure in Seeing His House on Fire" (vol. 3, no. 38) as the basis for his famous short story "Hell Screen" (Jigokuhen).

The text is based on Kobayashi Chishō, ed., *Uji shūi monogatari*, Nihon koten bungaku zenshū 28 (Tokyo: Shōgakukan, 1973), 107–110, 141–142, with minor orthographic changes.

『宇治拾遺物語』

「鼻長僧の事」

昔、池の尾に、善珍内供といふ僧住みける。真言などよく習ひて、年久しく行ひて貴かりければ、世の人々、さまざまの祈をせさせければ、身の徳ゆたかにて、堂も僧坊も少しも荒れたる所なし。仏供、御燈なども絶えず、折節の僧膳、寺の講演、しげく行はせければ、寺中の僧房に、隙なく僧も住み賑ひけり。湯屋には、湯沸さぬ日なく、浴みののしりけり。またそのあたりには、小家ども多く出で来て、里も賑ひけり。

さてこの内供は、鼻長かりけり。五六寸ばかりなりければ、頤より下りてぞ見えける。色は赤紫にて、大柑子の膚のやうに、粒立ちてふくれたり。痒がる事限なし。提に湯をかへらかして、折敷を鼻さし入るばかり彫り通して、火の炎の顔にあたらぬやうにして、その折敷の穴より鼻をさし出でて、提の湯にさし入れて、よくよく茹でて引あげたれば、色は濃き紫色なり。それを側ざまに臥せて、下に物をあてて、人に踏ますれば、粒立ちたる孔ごとに、煙のやうなる物出づ。それをいたく踏めば、白き虫の、孔ごとにさし出づるを、毛抜にて抜けば、四分ばかりなる白き虫を、孔ごとに取り出す。その跡は、孔だにあきて見ゆ。それをまた同じ湯に入れて、さらめかし沸すに、茹づれば、鼻小さくしぼみあがりて、ただの人の鼻のやうになりぬ。また二三日になれば、先のごとくに大きになりぬ。

かくのごとくしつつ、脹れたる日数は多くありければ、物食ける時は、弟子の法師に、平なる板の一尺ばかりなるが、広さ一寸ばかりなるを、鼻の下にさし入て、向ひ居て、上ざまへ持て上げさせて、物食ひ果つるまではありけり。異人して持て上げさする折は、あらく持て上げければ、腹を立てて、物も食はず。さればこの法師一人を定めて、物食ふ度ごとに、持て上げさす。それに心地悪しくて、この法師出でざりける折に、朝粥食はむとするに、鼻を持て上ぐる人なかりければ、「いかにせん」などいふ程に、使ひける童の、「吾はよく持て上げ参らせてん。更にその御房にはよも劣らじ」といふを、弟子の法師聞きて、「この童のかくは申」といへば、中大童子にて、みめもきたなげなくありければ、うへに召し上げてありけるに、この童鼻持て上げの木を取りて、うるはしく向ひ居て、よき程に、高からず低からずもたげて、粥をすすらすれば、この内供、「いみじき上手にてありけり。例の法師にはまさりたり」とて、粥をすする程に、この童鼻をひんとて、側ざまに向きて、鼻をひる程に、手震ひて鼻もたげの木揺ぎて、鼻外れて、粥の中へふたりとう

ち入れつ。内供が顔にも、童の顔にも、粥とばしりて、一物かかりぬ。内供大きに腹立ちて、頭、顔にかかりたる粥を紙にてのごひつつ、「おのれは、まがまがしかりける心持ちたる者かな。心なしの乞児とはおのれがやうなる者をいふぞかし。我ならぬやごとなき人の御鼻にもこそ参れ、それには、かくやはせんずる。うたてなりける、心なしの痴者かな。おのれ立て立て」とて、追ひたてければ、立つままに、「世の人のかかる鼻持ちたるがおはしまさばこそ、鼻もたげにも参らめ。をこの事のたまへる御房かな」といひければ、弟子どもは物の後に逃げ退きてぞ笑ひける。

「絵仏師良秀家の焼くるを見て悦ぶ事」

これも今は昔、絵仏師良秀といふありけり。家の隣より火出で来て、風おし掩ひて迫めければ、逃げ出でて大路へ出でにけり。人の書かする仏もおはしけり。また衣きぬ妻子なども、さながら内に有けり。それも知らず、ただ逃げ出でたるを事にして、向ひのつらに立てり。見れば、すでに我が家に移りて、煙、炎くゆりけるまで、大方向ひのつらに立ちて眺めければ、あさましき事とて、人ども来とぶらひけれど、騒がず。「いかに」と人いひければ、向ひに立ちて、家の焼くるを見て、うち頷きて、時々笑ひけり。「あはれ、しつる所得かな。年比はわろく書きけるものかな」といふ時に、とぶらひに来たる者ども、「こはいかに、かくては立ち給へるぞ。あさましき事かな。物の憑き給へるか」といひければ、「何条物の憑くべきぞ。年比不動尊の火焔を悪しく書きけるなり。今見れば、かうこそ燃えけれと、心得つるなり。これこそ所得よ。この道を立てて世にあらんには、仏だによく書き奉らば、百千の家も出で来なん。わたうたちこそ、させる能もおはせねば、物をも惜み給へ」といひて、あざ笑ひてこそ立てりけれ。

　その後にや、良秀がよぢり不動とて、今に人々愛で合へり。

Vocabulary for "Long Nose" 1

池の尾 (いけ を) (*proper n.*) place-name in the current city of Uji, modern-day Kyoto Prefecture

善珍 (ぜんちん) (*proper n.*) priest's name

内供 (ないぐ) (*n.*) (also 内供奉) title for a priest appointed to serve at court and conduct the yearly ceremony to pray for state prosperity and bountiful harvests

真言 (しんごん) (*n.*) (Buddhist) mantra, incantation of mantra

行ふ (おこな) (*intr. v. YD*) to carry out, perform

貴し (たふと) (*ku adj.*) noble, worthy of respect

徳 (とく) (*n.*) wealth, possessions

堂 (だう) (*n.*) Buddhist hall where a statue of a deity is enshrined

僧坊 (そうばう) (*n.*) monks' quarters (attached to a temple)

荒る (あ) (*intr. v. SN*) to fall into ruin, become desolate

仏供 (ぶつく) (*n.*) offerings set before a Buddhist altar

御燈 (みとう) (*n.*) lamps lit in front of a Buddhist altar

折節 (をりふし) (*n.*) season

僧膳 (そうぜん) (*n.*) meals prepared for Buddhist monks

講演 (かうえん) (*n.*) sermon on sutra or Buddhist teachings

暇なし (ひま) (*ku adj.*) ceaseless, without interruption

湯屋 (ゆや) (*n.*) bathhouse

沸す (わか) (*tr. v. YD*) to boi a *shaku*, or approximately three centimeters 1 water

浴む (あ) (*tr. v. KN*) to bathe, soak in water

寸 (すん) (*n.*) one-tenth of

頤 (おとがひ) (*n.*) jaw, chin

大柑子 (おほかうじ) (*n.*) large orange, citrus fruit similar to a tangerine

粒立つ (つぶ だ) (*intr. v. YD*) to be lumpy, granular

ふくる (脹る) (*intr. v. SN*) to swell up, become puffy

痒がる (かゆ) (*intr. v. YD*) to feel itchy

提 (ひさげ) (*n.*) small metal pot with a handle, often used for heating and serving water or saké

かへらかす (返らかす) (*tr. v. YD*) to bring to a boil

折敷 (をしき) (*n.*) square tray

彫り通す (ゑ とほ) (*comp. v. YD*) to cut a hole

さし出づ (差し出づ) (い) (*intr. v. SN*) to protrude, appcar, cmcrge

茹づ (ゆ) (*tr. v. SN*) to cook in boiling water

側ざま (そば) (*n.*) beside

臥す (ふ) (*tr. v. SN*) to lay (something) down, put to sleep

〜ごと (毎) (*suffix*) every 〜, each 〜

毛抜 (けぬき) (*n.*) tweezer

分 (ぶ) (*n.*) one-hundredth of a *shaku*, or approximately three millimeters

さらめかす (*tr. v. YD*) to make a swishing, rustling sound

しぼむ (萎む・凋む) (*intr. v. YD*) to shrivel, shrink

ただの人 (ひと) (*n. phrase*) ordinary person

Grammar Notes for "Long Nose" 1

しげく 行 (おこな) はせければ   RY of adj. *shigeshi*, "often," MZ of v. *okonau*, and RY of causative aux. v. *su*

浴 (あ) みののしりけり   RY of tr. KN v. *amu*, "to bathe," RY of intr. YD v. *nonoshiru*, "to make a commotion," and SS of past-tense aux. v. *keri*

五六寸 (ごろくすん) ばかり   When adv. p. *bakari* follows a measured unit, it expresses approximation.

<table>
<tr><td>鼻さし入るばかり彫り通して　n. *hana*, RT of intr. YD v. *sashi-iru*, "to fit through," and adv.</td><td>p. *bakari* (indicating degree): "He cut a hole big enough for his nose to fit through."</td></tr>
</table>

Annotated Grammar for "Long Nose" 1

昔、池の尾 に、善珍 内供 と いふ 僧 住み ける。真言 など よく 習ひ て、年 久しく 行ひ

て、貴かり けれ ば、世 の 人々、さまざま の 祈 を せ させ けれ ば、身 の 徳

ゆたかに て、堂 も 僧坊 も、少し も 荒れ たる 所 なし。仏供、御燈 など も 絶え ず、

折節 の 僧膳、寺 の 講演、しげく 行は せ けれ ば、寺中 の 僧房 に、隙なく 僧 も

住み 賑ひ けり。湯屋 に は、湯 沸さ ぬ 日 なく、浴み ののしり けり。また その

あたり に は、小家 ども 多く 出で来 て、里 も 賑ひ けり。

さて この 内供 は、鼻 長かり けり。五六寸 ばかり なり けれ ば、頤 より 下がり

て ぞ 見え ける。色 は 赤紫 に て、大柑子 の 膚 の やうに、粒立ち て ふくれ

たり。痒がる 事 限なし。提 に 湯 を かへらかし て、折敷 を 鼻 さし入る ばかり

彫り通し て、火 の 炎 の 顔 に あたら ぬ やうに し て、その 折敷 の 穴 より 鼻

を さし出で て、提 の 湯 に さし入れ て、よくよく 茹で て 引きあげ たれ ば、色 は

濃き 紫色 なり。それ を、側ざま に 臥せ て、下 に 物 を あて て、人 に 踏ま すれ

ば、粒立ち たる 孔 ごと に、煙 の やう なる 物 出づ。それ を いたく 踏め ば、白き

虫 の、孔 ごと に さし出づる を、毛抜 にて 抜け ば、四分 ばかり なる 白き 虫 を、孔

ごと に 取り出す。その 跡 は、孔 だに あき て 見ゆ。それ を また 同じ 湯 に 入れ て、

さらめかし 沸す に、茹づれ ば、鼻 小さく しぼみ あがり て、ただ の 人 の 鼻 の やう

に なり ぬ。また 二三日 に なれ ば、先 の ごとく に、大きに なり ぬ。

Vocabulary for "Long Nose" 2

脹る (intr. v. SN) to be swollen from infection or other causes (of skin or flesh)

日数 (n.) number of days

弟子 (n.) follower, disciple

向ひ居る (intr. v. KI) to sit facing each other

上ざま (n.) top, upper part

持て上ぐ (tr. v. SN) (from 持ちて上ぐ) to lift up

異人 (n.) other people, a different person

折 (n.) moment, occasion

されば (conj.) therefore, for that reason, that being the case

それに　(*conj.*) on top of that, in addition

心地（ここち）　(*n.*) mood, temper

朝粥（あさがゆ）　(*n.*) morning porridge, gruel

いかに（如何に）　(*adv.*) question about circumstance: how? in what way?

童（わらは）　(*n.*) child serving at a temple

よも　(*adv.*) surely (not), definitely (not) (often followed by neg.)

劣る（おと）　(*intr. v. YD*) to be inferior to another, compare

中大童子（ちゆうだいどうじ）　(*n.*) child serving at a temple

みめ（見目）　(*n.*) appearance, looks

きたなげ（汚げ）　(*n.*) dirty or disagreeable appearance

召し上ぐ（め　あ）　(*tr. v. SN*) to summon, entrust with a position (hon.)

うるはし（麗し・美し・愛し）　(*shiku adj.*) formal, ceremonial, proper

低し（ひき）　(*ku adj.*) low (voice, status, height, etc.)

すする　(*tr. v. YD*) to slurp, sip, suck up

いみじ　(*shiku adj.*) outstanding, superb

まさる（勝る）　(*intr. v. YD*) to be superior, surpass, outdo

ひる（嚏る）　(*tr. v. KI*) to sneeze

ふたりと　(*adv.*) (onomatopoeia): sound of something falling or crashing: splash, kerplunk

とばしる（迸る）　(*intr. v. YD*) to splatter, splash

一物（ひともの）　(*adv.*) substantially, fully, totally

頭（かしら）　(*n.*) (person's) head

のごふ（拭ふ）　(*tr. v. YD*) (*nogou*) to wipe

まがまがし（禍禍し）　(*shiku adj.*) hateful, cursed

乞児（かたゐ）　(*n.*) beggar

かし　(*final p.*) adds strong emphasis

やごとなし　(*ku adj.*) (from やんごとなし) high-ranking, of a noted family

うたて　(*nari adj. v.*) terrible, woeful

痴者（しれもの）　(*n.*) fool, idiot

追ひたつ（お）　(*tr. v. SN*) to drive someone away, chase off

おはします（御座します）　(*intr. v. SH*) to be (hon.)

をこ（痴）　(*n.*) stupidity

のたまふ（の給ふ）　(*tr. v. YD*) to say (hon.)

逃げ退く（に　の）　(*comp. v.*) (from SN v. *nigu*, "to escape," and YD v. *noku*, "to withdraw") to run off, run away

Grammar Notes for "Long Nose" 2

かくのごとくしつつ　conj. p. *tsutsu* has a concessive function: "even though . . ."

異人して持て上げさする折（ことひと　も　あ　をり）　case p. *shite*, marking the object of a causative phrase, MZ of SN v. *mote-agu*, "to lift up," and RT of causative aux. v. *sasu*: "When he had another person lift it up"

いかにせん　adv. *ikani*, "how, in what way," MZ of SH v. *su*, "to do," and SS of spec. aux. v. *mu*

よく持て上げ参らせてん（も　あ　まゐ）　RY of SN hum. suppl. v. *mairasu*, lowering the speaker, and MZ of

perfective aux. v. *tsu*, indicating certainty: "I would no doubt do a good job of holding it up."

更にその御房にはよも劣らじ（さら　ごばう　おと）　adv. *sara-ni*, which combines with a following neg. to mean "(not) at all": "I am not at all an inferior to that priest (who normally holds up the priest's nose)."

上手にてありけり（じやうず）　RY of *nari* adj. v. *jōzu nari*, "skillful," conj. p. *te*, and RY of RH v. *ari*

ふたりとうち入れつ（い）　RY of SN v. *uchiiru*, "to fall into," and SS of perfective aux. v. *tsu*

一物かかりぬ　adv. *hitomono*, RY of YD v. *kakaru*, "to splash onto," and SS of perfective aux. v. *nu*

心なしの乞児とはおのれがやうなる者をいふぞかし　bound p. *zo* and emphatic final p. *kashi* create a strong declaration: "A thoughtless fool (*kokoronashi no katai*) is what a person like you (*onore*) should be called!"

我ならぬやごとなき人　"a person of high rank who was *not* me"

御鼻にもこそ参れ　IZ of hum. YD v. *mairu*, "to attend upon": "(if) you were attending an honorable nose (of a high-ranking person who was not me)"

かくやはせんずる　rhetorical question: "Would you act like this? (Of course you wouldn't.)"

おはしまさばこそ、鼻もたげにも参らめ　RY of SN v. *motagu*, "to lift up," case p. *ni*, bound p. *mo*, and hum. YD v. *mairu*, "to attend." Following MZ, *ba koso* stresses the hypothetical quality in a rhetorical form: "*If* there were other people (with noses like this), would (someone) come to hold it up? (No.)"

Annotated Grammar for "Long Nose" 2

かくの ごとく し つつ、脹れ たる 日数 は 多く あり けれ ば、物 食ひ ける 時

は、弟子 の 法師 に、平なる 板 の 一尺 ばかり なる が、広さ さ 一寸 ばかり なる

を、鼻 の 下 に さし入れ て、向ひ居 て、上ざま へ 持て上げ させ て、物 食ひ 果つる

まで は あり けり。異人 して 持て上げ さする 折 は、あらく 持て上げ けれ ば、腹 を

立て て、物 も 食は ず。されば、この 法師 一人 を 定め て、物 食ふ 度 ごと に、

持て上げ さす。それに、心地 悪しく て、この 法師 出で ざり ける 折 に、朝粥 食は

む と する に、鼻 を 持て上ぐる 人 なかり りれ ば、「いかに せ ん」など いふ

程 に、使ひ ける 童 の、「吾 は よく 持て上げ 参らせ て ん。更に その

御房 に は よも 劣ら じ」と いふ を、弟子 の 法師 聞き て、「この 童 の かく は

申す」と いへ ば、中大童子 に て、みめ も きたなげなく あり けれ ば、うへ に

召し上げ て あり ける に、この 童 鼻 持て上げ の 木 を 取り て、うるはしく 向ひ居

て、よき 程 に、高から ず 低から ず もたげ て、粥 を すすら すれ ば、この

内供、「いみじき 上手にて あり けり。例 の 法師 に は まさり たり」と て、粥

を すする 程 に、この 童 鼻 を ひ ん とて、側ざま に 向き て、鼻 を ひる 程

に、手 震ひ て 鼻 もたげ の 木 揺ぎ て、鼻 外れ て、粥 の 中 へ、ふたりと うち入れ

つ。内供 が 顔 に も、童 の 顔 に も 粥 とばしり て、一物 かかり ぬ。内供

大きに 腹立ち て、頭、顔 に かかり たる 粥 を 紙 にて のごひ つつ、「おのれ は

まがまがしかり ける 心 持ち たる 者 かな。心なし の 乞児 と は おのれ が やうなる

者 を いふ ぞ かし。我 なら ぬ やごとなき 人 の 御鼻 に も こそ 参れ、それ に

は、かく やは せ んずる。うたてなり ける、心なし の 痴者 かな。おのれ 立て

立て」とて、追ひたて けれ ば、立つ まま に、「世 の 人 の、かかる 鼻 持ち たる が

おはしまさ ば こそ、鼻 もたげ に も 参ら ＿＿＿ め 。をこ の 事 のたまへ る 御房

かな」と いひ けれ ば、弟子ども は 物 の 後 に 逃げ退き て ぞ 笑ひ ける 。

Vocabulary for "Yoshihide"

絵仏師 (ゑぶつし) (*n.*) painter specializing in Buddhist religious paintings

おし掩ふ (おほ) (*tr. v. YD*) (usually 押し覆ふ) to engulf, blow over and surround

迫む (せ) (*intr. v. SN*) to approach, draw near

大路 (おほち) (*n.*) (usually *ōji* おほぢ) main street, wide road

仏 (ほとけ) (*n.*) statue of the Buddha

おはす (御座す) (*intr. v. SH*) to be (hon.)

さながら (*adv.*) as is, unchanged

事にす (こと) (*set phrase*) (n. *koto*, case p. *ni*, SH v. *su*) to be satisfied with

つら (面) (*n.*) side, edge (of a street)

くゆる (燻る) (*intr. v. YD*) to smolder, rise up (smoke, fragrance)

あさまし (浅まし) (*shiku adj.*) unexpected, astonishing

とぶらふ (訪ふ) (*tr. v. YD*) to ask about someone's health, pay a visit to an ill person

頷く (うなづ) (*intr. v. YD*) to nod one's head in understanding

あはれ (哀) (*interj.*) expresses a deep emotional response: alas! my!

所得 (せうとく) (*n.*) profit, gain

こは (此は) (*interj.*) (from pron. *ko* and bound p. *wa*) What's this!? Well, this . . . !

憑く (つ) (*intr. v. YD*) to possess (by a god or spirit)

何条 (なんでふ) (*attrib.*) (from *nani to iu*) what? what kind of?

不動尊 (ふどうそん) (*proper n.*) Fudō Myōō, one of the five guardian figures of esoteric Buddhism, usually depicted with a sword in his right hand, a noose in the left, and a raging fire behind him

火焔 (くわえん) (*n.*) flame

悪し (あ) (*shiku adj.*) unskilled

心得 (こころう) (*intr. v. SN*) to understand

奉る (たてまつ) (*tr. v. YD*) suppl. v. (hum.)

百千 (ももち) (*n.*) great number (lit., hundred thousand)

わたう (我党, 和党) (*second-person pron.*) expresses affection, sometimes slight derision: you, the likes of you

させる (*attrib.*) (usually followed by neg.) considerable, notable, noteworthy

能 (のう) (*n.*) skill, ability, artistic talent

惜しむ (を) (*tr. v. YD*) to begrudge, be stingy with

あざ笑ふ (わら) (*tr. v. YD*) to laugh mockingly, laugh out loud

よぢる (捩る) (*intr. v. YD*) to twist

今に (いま) (*adv.*) even now, to this very day

愛づ (め) (*tr. v. SN*) to praise highly, esteem, admire

Grammar Notes for "Yoshihide"

良秀といふありけり   YD v. *iu* ends in RT, modifying an implied subject like *mono* or *otoko*.

書かする仏もおはしけり   MZ of YD v. *kaku*, RT of causative aux. v. *su*, n. *hotoke*, bound p. *mo*, and RY of intr. hon. SH v. *owasu*, "to be," which elevates the religious paintings

衣きぬ妻子   n. *kinu*, "clothing," MZ of tr. KI v. *kiru*, "to wear," RT of neg. aux. v. *zu*, and n. *saishi*, "wife and children," suggesting their poverty

それも知らず   "not caring about them (wife and children)"

ただ逃げ出でたるを事にし   RT of aux. v. *tari*, which modifies an implied subject, "the fact that": "He was satisfied with (the fact that) he had just escaped."

しつるせうとくかな   *shitsuru*, RY of SH v. *su* "to do," RT of perfective aux. v. *tsu*, and exclamatory final p. *kana*: "a profit that I have ended up making!"

こはいかに   comp. *kowa* (from pron. *ko* and case p. *wa*), which expresses surprise at encountering an unexpected matter, "What's this?" and adv. *ikani*, "Why?" The speaker expresses surprise at what he sees and then asks why Yoshihide is standing there like that.

物の憑き給へるか   n. *mono*, "an evil spirit," subject marker case p. *no*, RY of intr. YD v. *tsuku*, "to adhere, to transfer," and IZ of hon. suppl. v. *tamau*: "Had an evil spirit been transferred to him? (Had he been possessed by an evil spirit?)"

かうこそ燃えけれと   attrib. *kaku*, "like this" (sound change to *kou*), bound p. *koso*, RY of intr. SN v. *moyu*, IZ of exclamatory aux. v. *keri*, and citational case p. *to*, indicating Yoshihide's thoughts

この道を立てて   "to devote oneself completely (*tatsu*) to this profession," to the way of the painter of Buddhist images

世にあらんには   MZ of RH v. *ari*, RT of circumlocutory aux. v. *mu*, case p. *ni* , and bound p. *wa*: "(as for devoting oneself to this profession and) making a living in this world"

仏だによく書き奉らば   RY of tr. YD v. *kaku* and MZ of hum. suppl. v. *tatematsuru*, which lowers Yoshihide in relation to the Buddha: "if I at least could paint the Buddha well"

百千の家も出で来なん   MZ of perfective aux. v. *nu* and SS of spec. aux. v. *mu*; the combination of *nu* and *mu* indicates conjecture with certainty: "(If I am able to paint at least the Buddha well,) a hundred or a thousand houses will surely be built."

物をも惜しみ給へ   IZ of hon. suppl. v. *tamau*: "You are stingy with things."

その後にや   pron. *so*, "that," RY of copular *nari*, and bound p. *ya*, implying *ara-mu*: "It must have been sometime after that."

良秀がよぢり不動とて   *Yojiri Fudō* refers to a painting of Fudō in which his halo of flames appear to be flickering: "People called it Yoshihide's Flickering Fudō."

Annotated Grammar for "Yoshihide"

代名	係助	名	係助	名	名	固名	格助	四/体	ラ変/用	助動/過/終	名	格助	名	格助	名	カ変/用	接助	名
これ	も	今	は	昔、	絵仏師	良秀	と	いふ	あり	けり。	家	の	隣	より	火	出で来	て、	風

四/用	接助	下二/用	助動/過/已	接助	下二/用	接助	名	格助	下二/用	助動/完/用	助動/過/終	名	格助	四/未
おし掩ひ	て、	迫め	けれ	ば、	逃げ出で	て	大路	へ	出で	に	けり。	人	の	書か

助動/使/体	名	係助	サ変/尊/用	助動/過/終	接	名	上一/未	助動/打/体	名	副助	係助	副	名	格助	ラ変/用
する	仏	も	おはし	けり。	また	衣	き	ぬ	妻子	など	も、	さながら	内	に	有

助動/過/終	代名	係助	四/未	助動/打/用	副	下二/用	助動/完/体	格助	名	格助	サ変/用	接助	名	格助	名	格助
けり。	それ	も	知ら	ず、	ただ	逃げ出で	たる	を	事	に	し	て、	向ひ	の	つら	に

四/已 助動/存/終 上一/已 接助 副 代名 格助 名 格助 四/用 接助 名 名 四/用 助動/過/体 副助 副
立て り。見れ ば、すでに 我 が 家 に 移り て、煙、炎 くゆり ける まで、大方、

名 格助 名 格助 四/用 接助 下二/用 助動/過/已 接助 シク形/体 名 格助 接助 名 接尾 カ変/用 四/用
向ひ の つら に 立ち て 眺め けれ ば、「あさましき 事」と て、人 ども 来 とぶらひ

助動/過/已 接助 四/未 助動/打/終 副 格助 名 四/用 助動/過/已 接助 名 格助 四/用 接助 名 格助 下二/体
けれ ど、騒が ず。「いかに」と 人 いひ けれ ば、向ひ に 立ち て、家 の 焼くる

格助 上一/用 接助 接頭 四/用 接助 名 四/用 助動/過/終 感動 サ変/用 助動/完/体 名 終助 名 係助
を 見 て、うち 頷き て、時々 笑ひ けり。「あはれ、し つる 所得 かな。年比 は、

ク形/用 四/用 助動/詠/体 名 終助 格助 四/体 名 格助 名 格助 カ変/用 助動/完/体 名 接尾 代名 係助
わろく 書き ける もの かな」と いふ 時 に、とぶらひ に 来 たる 者 ども 「こ は

副・ 副 係助 四/用 補助動/尊/已 助動/存/体 係助 シク形/体 名 終助 名 格助 四/用 補助動/尊/已 助動/完/体
いかに、かくて は 立ち 給へ る ぞ。あさましき 事 かな。物 の 憑き 給へ る

係助 格助 四/用 助動/過/已 接助 連体詞 名 格助 四/終 助動/詠/体 係助 名 名 格助 名 格助 シク形/体 四/用
か」と いひ けれ ば、「何条 物 の 憑く べき ぞ。年比 不動尊 の 火焔 を 悪しく 書き

助動/詠/体 助動/断/終 名 上一/已 接助 副(音) 係助 下二/用 助動/過/已/係 格助 下二/用 助動/完/体 助動/断/終 代名 係助 名
ける なり。今 見れ ば、かう こそ 燃え けれ と、心得 つる なり。これ こそ 所得

終助 代名 格助 名 格助 下二/用 接助 名 格助 ラ変/未 助動/婉/体 格助 係助 名 副助 ク形/用 四/用 補助動/謙/未 接助 名
よ。この 道 を 立て て 世 に あら ん に は、仏 だに よく 書き 奉ら ば、百千

格助 名 係助 カ変/用 助動/完(確)/未 助動/推/終 代名 接尾 係助/係 連体詞 名 係助 サ変/尊/未 助動/打/已 接助 名
の 家 も 出で来 な ん。わたう たち こそ、させる 能 も おはせ ね ば、物

格助 係助 四/用 助動/尊/已/結 格助 四/用 接助 四/用 接助 係助/係 四/已 助動/存/終 助動/過/已/結
を も 惜み 給へ」と いひて、あざ笑ひて こそ 立て り けれ。

代名 格助 名 助動/断/用 係助 名 格助 名・ 格助 接助 副 名 下二/用 四/已 助動/存/終
その 後 に や、良秀 が よぢり不動 と て、今に 人々 愛で 合へ り。

10

The Tales of the Heike

The Tales of the Heike (*Heike monogatari*) is about the Genpei Wars (1180–1185), fought between the Heike (Taira) clan, led by Taira no Kiyomori, and the Genji (Minamoto) clan, led by Minamoto no Yoritomo. The initial, rapid ascent to power by the Taira was followed by a series of defeats, resulting in the clan's abandonment of the capital in 1183 (taking with them Antoku, the child emperor). By 1183 Yoritomo had gained control of the Kantō, or eastern region; Kiso Yoshinaka, another Minamoto leader, had brought Kyoto under his power; and the Taira had fallen back to the Inland Sea. During an interlude of fighting among the Minamoto in 1184, Yoshinaka was defeated and eliminated by Yoritomo and his half brother (Minamoto) Yoshitsune.

In the following passage from book 9, Kiso Yoshinaka, a cousin of Minamoto no Yoritomo, is the commander of the northern Genji forces. After defeating the Heike armies sent to put down the unrest that he had been fomenting in the north, Yoshinaka marches on and takes the capital, forcing the Heike to flee to the west. In his new position as protector of the capital, Yoshinaka quickly grows arrogant and despotic, behaving even more badly than the Heike had before him and eventually waging war on the retired emperor GoShirakawa. Yoritomo sends his brothers Noriyori and Yoshitsune to defeat Yoshinaka, whose army fares badly in the ensuing battle. Yoshinaka escapes with only six men and flees toward Seta (south of Lake Biwa), hoping to find his foster brother Imai Shirō Kanehira in order that the two of them may die together.

The text is based on Takagi Ichinosuke et al., eds., *Heike monogatari ge*, Nihon koten bungaku taikei 33 (Tokyo: Iwanami Shoten, 1960), 176–181, with minor orthographic changes.

『平家物語』

「木曽最期」

鎧踏んばり立ち上がり、大音声をあげて名乗りけるは、「昔は聞きけんものを、木曽の、今は見るらん、左馬頭兼伊予守、朝日の将軍源義仲ぞや。甲斐の一条次郎とこそ聞け。互ひによい敵ぞ。義仲討ッて兵衛佐に見せよや」とて、をめいて駆く。

一条次郎、「只今名乗るは大将軍ぞ。余すな、者ども。漏らすな、若党。討てや」とて、大勢の中に取りこめて、我討ッ取らんとぞ進みける。

木曽三百余騎、六千余騎が中を縦さま・横さま・蜘手・十文字に駆け割って、後ろへつッと出でたれば、五十騎ばかりになりにけり。そこを破って行くほどに、土肥次郎実平二千余騎でささへたり。

其をも破ッて行くほどに、あそこでは四、五百騎、ここでは二、三百騎、百四、五十騎、百騎ばかりが中を駆け割り駆け割りゆくほどに、主従五騎にぞなりにける。五騎が内まで巴は討たれざりけり。

木曽殿「おのれは疾う疾う、女なれば、いづちへも行け。我は討死せんと思ふなり。もし人手にかからずは自害をせんずれば、『木曽殿の最後の軍に、女を具せられたり』なんど言はれん事も然るべからず」と宣ひけれども、猶落ちも行かざりけるが、あまりに言はれ奉りて、「あッぱれ、よからう敵がな。最後の軍して見せ奉らん」とて、控へたるところに、武蔵国に、聞えたる大力、御田八郎師重、三十騎ばかりで出できたり。

巴そのなかへ駆け入り、御田八郎に押し並べ、むずと取って引き落とし、わが乗ッたる鞍の前輪に押しつけて、ちッとも働かさず、首捻ぢ切って捨ててんげり。其の後物の具脱ぎ捨て、東国の方へ落ちぞ行く。手塚太郎討死す。手塚の別當落ちにけり。

今井四郎、木曽殿、只主従二騎になって、宣ひけるは、「日来はなにとも覚えぬ鎧が、今日は重うなッたるぞや」。今井四郎申しけるは、「御身も未疲れさせ給はず、御馬も弱り候はず。何によってか一両の御着背長を重うは思しめし候ふべき。それは御方に御勢が候はねば、臆病でこそさは思しめし候へ。兼平一人候ふとも、余の武者千騎と思しめせ。矢七八候へば、しばらく防ぎ矢仕らん。あれに見え候ふ、粟津の松原と申す。あの松の中で御自害候へ」とて、打って行程に、又新手の武者五十騎ばかり出で来たり。

「君はあの松原へ入らせ給へ。兼平は此敵防ぎ候はん」と申しければ、木曽殿宣ひけるは、「義仲都にていかにもなるべかりつるが、これまで遁れ来るは、汝と一所で死なんと思ふため也。所々で討たれんよりも、一所でこそ討死をもせめ」とて、馬の鼻を並べて駆けんとし給へば、今井四郎馬より飛び降り、主の馬の口に取りついて申しけるは、「弓矢取りは年来日来いかなる高名候へども、最後の時不覚しつれば長き疵にて候ふ也。御身は疲れさせ給ひて候ふ。続く勢は候はず。敵に押し隔てられ、言ふかひなき人の郎等に組み落とされさせ給ひて、討たれさせ給ひなば、「さばかり日本国に聞こえさせ給ひつる木曽殿をば、某が郎等の討ち奉ッたる」なンど申さん事こそ口惜う候へ。ただあの松原へ入らせ給へ」と申しければ、木曽、さらばとて、粟津の松原へぞ駆け給ふ。

今井四郎只一騎、五十騎ばかりが中へ駆け入り、鐙踏ンばり立ち上がり、大音声あげて名乗りけるは、「日来は音にも聞きつらん、今は目にも見給へ、木曽殿の御乳母子、今井四郎兼平、生年三十三にまかりなる。さる者ありとは鎌倉殿までも知ろしめされたるらんぞ。兼平討ッて見参に入れよ」とて、射残したる八筋の矢を、差しつめ引きつめさんざんに射る。死生は知らず、矢庭に敵八騎射落とす。其後打物抜いてあれに馳せ合ひ、これに馳せ合ひ、切ッて回るに、面を合はする者ぞなき。分捕りあまたしたりけり。只「射取れや」とて、中に取りこめ、雨の降る様に射けれども、鎧良ければ裏かかず、開間を射ねば手も負はず。

木曽殿は只一騎、粟津の松原へ駆け給ふが、正月二十一日、入相ばかりの事なるに、薄氷は張ッたりけり、深田ありとも知らずして、馬をザッと打ち入れたれば、馬の首も見えざりけり。あふれどもあふれども、打てども打てども、働かず。今井が行方のおぼつかなさに、振り仰ぎ給へる内甲を、三浦の石田次郎為久、おッかかってよッ引いてひやうふつと射る。痛手なれば、真甲を馬の首に当ててうつ伏し給へる所に、石田が郎等二人落ち合うて、つひに木曽殿の首をば取ッてンげり。太刀の先に貫ぬき、高く差し上げ、大音声をあげて、「この日来日本国に聞こえさせ給ひつる木曽殿を、三浦の石田次郎為久が討ち奉りたるぞや」と名乗りければ、今井四郎軍しけるが、是を聞き、「今はたれを庇はんとてか軍をばすべき。是を見給へ、東国の殿原、日本一の剛の者の自害する手本」とて、太刀の先を口に含み、馬よりさかさまに飛び落ち、貫ぬかッてぞ失せにける。さてこそ粟津の軍はなかりけれ。

Vocabulary for Paragraphs 1–4

鐙 あぶみ (*n.*) stirrups

名乗る なのる (*intr. v. YD*) to announce one's full name

冠者 くわんじや (*n.*) youth who has undergone a coming-of-age ceremony, young man

左馬頭兼伊予守 さまのかみけんいよのかみ (*comp. n.*) chief of the left stables (*sama no kami*) and governor of Iyo Province (present-day Ehime Prefecture); *ken* indicates that Yoshinaka held the two positions concurrently

朝日の将軍 あさひのしやうぐん (*proper n.*) title given to Yoshinaka (lit., General of the Rising Sun)

兵衛佐 ひやうゑのすけ (*n.*) deputy chief (*suke*) of the military guard; refers to Minamoto no Yoritomo, who when he held this position was exiled to Izu Province at the age of thirteen

をめく (喚く, 叫く) (*intr. v. YD*) (*omeku*) to yell, scream, shout

余す あま す (*tr. v. YD*) to leave behind, overlook

漏らす も らす (*tr. v. YD*) to allow to escape

若党 わかたう (*n.*) young samurai

縦さま たて (*n.*) vertical direction

横さま よこ (*n.*) horizontal direction

蜘手 くもで (*n.*) (lit., spider legs) moving in opposite directions

十文字 じふもんじ (*n.*) moving one's body or weapon back and forth in a rapid motion

つつと (*adv.*) swiftly, hurriedly, in a flash

ささふ (支ふ) (*tr. v. SN*) (*sasau, sasou*) to block, guard

Grammar Notes for Paragraphs 1–4

聞きけんものを き RY of tr. YD v. *kiku*, RT of past-spec. aux. v. *kemu*, and conj. p. *mono-o*

見せよや ,,, 討てや み う both commands made more urgent by adding interj. p. *ya*

余すな … 漏らすな あま も both negative commands created by adding final p. *na* to SS of the v.

我討ッ取らん われ う と first-person pron. *ware* and MZ of tr. YD v. *uchitoru* (sound change to *uttoru*), "to strike down." *Ware* indicates that each of the warriors wanted to be the one to kill Yoshinaka.

Annotated Grammar for Paragraphs 1–4

鐙 踏んばり 立ち上がり、大音声 を あげ て 名乗り ける は、「昔 は 聞き けん ものを、

木曽 の 冠者、今 は 見る らん、左馬頭兼伊予守、朝日の将軍 源義仲 ぞ や。甲斐 の

一条次郎 と こそ 聞け。互ひに よい 敵 ぞ。義仲 討ッ て 兵衛佐 に 見せよ や」とて、

をめい て 駆く。

一条次郎、「只今 名乗る は 大将軍 ぞ。余す な、者ども。漏らす な、若党。討て や」とて、

大勢 の 中 に 取りこめ て、我 討ッ取ら ん と ぞ 進み ける 。

木曽 三百余騎、六千余騎 が 中 を 縦さま・横さま・蜘手・十文字 に 駆け割ッ て、後ろ

格助　副　　下二/用　助動/完/已 接助　　名　　　副助　格助 四/用　助動/完/用 助動/過/終　代名 格助 四/用（音）接助 四/体
へ つッと 出で たれ ば、五十騎 ばかり に なり に けり。そこ を 破ッ て 行く

名　　格助　固名　　　固名　　　名　　格助 下二/用 助動/存/終
ほど に、土肥 次郎実平 二千余騎 で ささへ たり。

代名 格助 係助 四/用（音）接助 四/体　名　格助　代名　格助 係助 名　　代名 格助 係助 名　　名
其 を も 破ッ て 行く ほど に、あそこ で は 四、五百騎、ここ で は 二、三百騎

名四　　名　　　名　　副助 格助 名 格助 四/用　四/用　四/体　名　格助　名　　名　　格助 係助/係
百四、五十騎、百騎 ばかり が 中 を 駆け割り 駆け割り ゆく ほど に、主従 五騎 に ぞ

四/用 助動/完/用 助動/過/体/結　名 格助 名　副助 固名 係助 四/未 助動/受/未 助動/打/用 助動/過/終
なり に ける。五騎 が 内 まで 巴 は 討た れ ざり けり。

Vocabulary for Paragraphs 5–7

おのれ（己れ）　（*pron.*）derogatory second-person: the likes of you

疾く疾く（とと）　（*adv.*）（from adj. *toshi*, "quick"）quickly, right away

いづち（何方・何処）　（*pron.*）somewhere

人手にかかる（ひとで）　（*set phrase*）（intr. YD v. *kakaru*, "to be caught by"）to be killed by someone

なんど　（*adv. p.*）（same as *nado*）indicates that the citation is general, not literal: (to say) such things as

あッぱれ　（*interj.*）expresses strong emotion

控ふ（ひか）　（*intr. v. SN*）to wait, stand by

大力（だいぢから）　（*n.*）great strength, incredibly strong person

押し並ぶ（おなら）　（*tr. v. SN*）to force into line

むずと　（*adv.*）with a jerk, swiftly and powerfully

前輪（まへわ）　（*n.*）pommel, raised front of a Japanese saddle

ちッと　（*adv.*）（from ちと, *chito*）a little

捻ぢ切る（ねき）　（*tr. v. YD*）to twist and cut off

物具（もののぐ）　（*n.*）weapons (esp. armor, helmet, etc.)

手塚の別当（てづか べッたう）　（*proper n.*）Superintendent (Bettō) Tezuka, the uncle of Tezuka Tarō

Grammar Notes for Paragraphs 5–7

自害をせんずれば（じがい）　n. *jigai*, "suicide," case p. *o*, MZ of tr. SH v. *su*, "to do," IZ of emphatic intent. aux. v. *muzu*, and conj. p. *ba*: "when I (Yoshinaka) commit suicide . . ."

具せられたり（ぐ）　MZ of SH v. *gusu*, "to take along," RY of hon. aux. v. *raru*, and RY of cont. aux. v. *tari*. Yoshinaka is imagining what others might say about him and uses honorifics for himself.

言はれん事も然るべからず（い こと しか）　MZ of YD v. *iu*, "to say," MZ of passive aux. v. *ru*, RT of spec. aux. v. *mu*, and RT of RH v. *shikari*, "to be that way": "I should not be spoken of in this way."

言はれ奉りて（い たてまつ）　MZ of YD v. *iu*, RY of passive aux. v. *ru*, and RY of hum. suppl. v. *tatematsuru*, indicating that the sentence subject has shifted from Yoshinaka to Tomoe

よからう敵がな（かたき）　MZ of ku adj. *yoshi*, RT of circumlocutory aux. v. *mu*, in sound change to *u*, n. *kataki*, "opponent (in battle)," and desiderative final p. *gana*

捨ててんげり　RY of tr. SN v. *sutsu*, "to discard," RY of perfective aux. v. *tsu*, and SS of past-tense aux. v. *keri*. *Tengeri* is a sound change from and an emphatic form of *te-keri*: "ended up doing."

Annotated Grammar for Paragraphs 5–7

_{固名}木曽殿「_{代名}おのれ _{係助}は _副疾う疾う、_名女 _{助動/断/已}なれ _{接助}ば、_{代名}いづち _{格助}へ _{係助}も _{四/命}行け。_{代名}我 _{係助}は _{サ変/未}討死せ _{助動/意/終}ん _{格助}と

_{四/体}思ふ _{助動/断/終}なり。_副もし _名人手 _{格助}に _{四/未}かから _{助動/打/用}ず _{係助}は _名自害 _{格助}を _{サ変/未}せ _{助動/意/已}んずれ _{接助}ば、『_{固名}木曽 _{接尾}殿 _{格助}の _名最後

_{格助}の _名軍 _{格助}に、_名女 _{格助}を _{サ変/未}具せ _{助動/尊/四/用}られ _{助動/存/終}たり』_{副助}なんど _{四/未}言は _{助動/受/未}れ _{助動/推/体}ん _名事 _{係助}も _{ラ変/体}然る _{助動/当/}べから

_{助動/打/終}ず」_{格助}と _{四/尊/用}宣ひ _{助動/過/已}けれ _{接助}ども、_副猶 _{上二/用}落ち _{係助}も _{四/未}行か _{助動/打/用}ざり _{助動/過/体}ける _{接助}が、_副あまりに _{四/未}言は _{助動/受/用}れ

_{補助動/謙/四/用}奉り _{接助}て、「_{感動}あッぱれ、_{ク形/未}よから _{助動/婉/体}う _名敵 _{終助/願}がな。_名最後 _{格助}の _名軍 _{サ変/用}して _{接助}て _{下二/用}見せ _{補助動/謙/四/未}奉ら

_{助動/意/終}ん」_{格助}とて、_{接助}控へ _{下二/用}たる _{助動/存/体}ところ _名に、_{格助}武蔵国 _{固名}に、_{格助}聞え _{下二/用}たる _{助動/存/体}大力、_名御田八郎師重、_{固名}三十騎 _名

_{副助}ばかり _{格助}で _{下二/用}出で _{カ変/用}き _{助動/完/終}たり。

_{固名}巴 _{代名}その _{格助}なか _名へ _{格助}駆け入り、_{四/用}御田八郎 _{固名}に _{格助}押し並べ、_{下二/用}むずと _副取ッ _{四/用(音)}て _{接助}引き落とし、_{四/用}わ _{代名}

_{格助}が _{四/用(音)}乗ッ _{助動/存/体}たる _名鞍 _{格助}の _名前輪 _{格助}に _{下二/用}押しつけ _{接助}て、_副ちッとも _{係助}も _{四/未}働かさ _{助動/打/用}ず、_名首 _{四/用(音)}捻ぢ切ッ _{接助}て

_{下二/用}捨て _{助動/完/用＋助動/過/終(音)}てんげり。

_{代名}其 _{格助}の _名後 _名物具 _{下二/用}脱ぎ捨て、_{固名}東国 _{格助}の _名方 _{格助}へ _{上二/用}落ち _{係助}ぞ _{四/体}行く。_{固名}手塚太郎 _{サ変/終}討死す。_{固名}手塚 _{格助}の _名別当

_{上二/用}落ち _{助動/完/用}に _{助動/過/終}けり。

Vocabulary for Paragraph 8

殿 (*suffix*) lord, master
【との】

主従 (*n.*) lord and retainer
【しゅじゅう】

騎 (*n.*) horseman
【き】

日来 (*adv.*) usually, normally
【ひごろ】

覚ゆ (*intr. v. SN*) (from *omōyu*, "to think," and
【おぼ】 spont. aux. v. *yu*) to feel naturally

鎧 (*n.*) armor
【よろひ】

重し (*ku adj.*) heavy
【おも】

疲る (*intr. v. SN*) to be tired, exhausted
【つか】

よる (因る・由る・依る) (*intr. v. YD*) to be due
to, the result of

両 (*suffix*) counter for things in pairs and for
【りやう】 carriages, etc.

着背長 (*n.*) formal armor worn by a general
【きせなが】

御方 (*n.*) supporters, comrades, allies, friends
【みかた】

勢 (*n.*) military strength, troops
【せい】

臆病 (*n.*) timidity, nervousness, diffidence
【おくびやう】

余 (*n.*) (following a measurement) somewhat
【よ】 more than

武者 (*n.*) warrior
【むしや】

防ぎ矢 (*n.*) arrows fired in defense
【ふせ や】

粟津 (*proper n.*) place in present-day Ōtsu City,
【あはづ】 Shiga Prefecture

松原 (*n.*) pine forest
【まつばら】

新手 (*n.*) fresh troops
【あらて】

いかに (如何に) (*adv.*) to what extent, how
much

遁る (*intr. v. SN*) to escape, avoid (danger)
【のが】

汝 (*pron.*) you (second person, used for
【なんぢ】 subordinates)

所々 (*n.*) here and there
【ところどころ】

討死 (*n.*) death in battle
【うちじに】

駆く (*intr. v. SN*) to ride swiftly on a horse

飛び降る (*intr. v. KN*) to jump down

取りつく (*intr. v. YD*) to grab hold of, cling to

弓矢取り (*n.*) warrior

年来 (*n.*) for many years

高名 (*n.*) fame, reputation

不覚 (*n.*) carelessness

疵 (*n.*) shame, disgrace

続く (*intr. v. YD*) to follow, line up behind

敵 (*n.*) enemy in war

押し隔つ (*tr. v. SN*) to separate by force

言ふかひなし (言ふ甲斐なし) (*set phrase*) not worth talking about, beneath mention

郎等 (*n.*) retainer, vassal

組み落とす (*comp. v.*) to engage in combat (*kumu*) and strike down (*otosu*)

さばかり (*adv.*) to that extent, that much

某 (*pron.*) vague personal pron.: so-and-so

口惜し (*shiku adj.*) regrettable, disappointing, pitiful

Grammar Notes for Paragraph 8

宣ひけるは hon. v., indicating that the speaker is Yoshinaka

日来はなにとも覚えぬ鎧 "armor that I usually don't feel at all"

今日は重うなったるぞや RY of *ku* adj. *omoshi* (sound change to *omou*): "Today it is heavy!"

申しけるは hum. v., indicating that the speaker is Kanehira, the retainer

疲れさせ給はず RY of hon. aux. v. *sasu* and MZ of hon. suppl. v. *tamau*: "Your body is not yet tired."

何によってか pron. *nani*, "what," case p. *ni*, RY of YD v. *yoru* (with sound change), conj. p. *te*, and interrogative bound p. *ka*: "To what is it due?"

思しめし候ふべき RY of hon. YD v. *oboshimesu*, SS of polite suppl. YD v. *sōrō*, and RT of spec. aux. v. *beshi*: "(For what reason) would you think that (a suit of armor is heavy)?"

御方に御勢が候はねば hon. prefix *on*, indicating that Kanehira is referring to Yoshinaka's forces: "because our side is lacking in military strength"

兼平一人候ふとも、余の武者千騎と思しめせ SS of hum. YD v. *sōrō*, "to be":

"Although (I,) Kanehira, (am) only one man, think of me as (being worth) a thousand other warriors."

防ぎ矢仕らん MZ of hum. YD v. *tsukamatsuru*, "to do," and SS of intent. aux. v. *mu*: "I will shoot some arrows and hold off (the enemy)."

あれに見え候ふ RT of polite suppl. YD v. *sōrō*; "that which is visible over there"

御自害候へ MR of polite YD v. *sōrō*, "to be": "Commit suicide (in the pine woods)!"

打ッて行程に RY of YD v. *utsu* (in sound change form), n. *hodo*, "while," and case p. *ni*: "as (they) were going, whipping their horses"

入らせ給へ RY of hon. aux. v. *su* and MR of hon. suppl. v. *tamau*: "Please enter (the woods)."

義仲都にていかにもなるべかりつるが locative case p. *nite*; *ikani mo naru* is a set phrase meaning "to die": "(I), Yoshinaka, should have died in the capital."

汝と一所で死なんと思ふため也 "because I wanted to die together with you"

馬の鼻を並べて駆けんとし RY of SN v. *narabu*, "to align": "(Yoshinaka), bringing his horse alongside, attempted to gallop on."

としごろ ひごろ / かうみやうさうら

年来日来いかなる 高名 候 へども   "however great (*ika-naru*) a reputation (a man) usually (*higoro*) has over many years (*toshigoro*)"

さいご ときふかく / なが きず なり

最後の時不覚しつれば長き疵にて 候 ふ也
RY of SH v. *fukaku-su*, "to be careless":

"When in his final hour (a warrior is careless), it becomes a lasting shame."

く お たま

組み落とされさせ給ひて   MZ of passive aux. v. *ru* and RY of hon. aux. v. *sasu*: "to be brought down in combat (by the enemy)"

Annotated Grammar for Paragraph 8

今井四郎、木曽殿、只 主従 二騎に なッ て 宣ひ ける は、「日来 は なに とも 覚え

ぬ 鎧が、今日 は 重う なッ たる ぞ や」。今井四郎 申し ける は、「御身 も

未 疲れ させ 給は ず、御馬 も 弱り 候は ず。何 に よッ て か 一両

の 御着背長 を 重う は 思しめし 候ふ べき 。それ は 御方 に 御勢 が

候は ね ば、臆病 で こそ さ は 思しめし 候へ 。兼平 一人 候ふ とも、余 の

武者 千騎 と 思しめせ。矢 七、八 候へ ば、しばらく 防ぎ矢 仕ら ん 。あれ に 見え

候ふ 、粟津 の 松原 と 申す。あの 松 の 中 で 御自害 候へ」 とて、打ッ て 行く

程 に、又 新手 の 武者 五十騎 ばかり 出で 来 たり。「君 は あ の 松原 へ 入ら

せ 給へ 。兼平 は 此 敵 防ぎ 候は ん」 と 申し けれ ば、木曽殿 宣ひ

ける は、「義仲 都 にて いかに も なる べかり つる が、これ まで 遁れ 来る は、

汝 と 一所 で 死な ん と 思ふ ため 也。所々 で 討た れ ん より も、

一所 で こそ 討死 を も せ め」 とて、馬 の 鼻 を 並べ て 駆け ん とし

給へ ば、今井四郎 馬 より 飛び降り、主 の 馬 の 口 に 取りつい て 申し ける は、

「弓矢取り は 年来 日来 いかなる 高名 候へ ども、最後 の 時 不覚し つれ ば 長き 疵

に て 候ふ 也。御身 は 疲れ させ 給ひ て 候ふ。続く 勢 は 候は ず。

敵 に 押し隔て られ、言ふ かひ なき 人 の 郎等 に 組み落とさ れ させ 給ひ

て、討た れ させ 給ひ な ば、「さ ばかり 日本国 に 聞こえ させ 給ひ

つる 木曽殿 を ば、某 が 郎等 の 討ち 奉ッ たる」 なんど 申さ ん 事

こそ 口惜う 候へ。ただ あ の 松原 へ 入ら せ 給へ」 と 申し けれ ば、

木曽 さらば とて、粟津 の 松原 へ ぞ 駆け 給ふ 。

Vocabulary for Paragraph 9

踏んばる (踏ん張る) (*intr. v. YD*) to plant one's feet and press down

立ち上がる (*intr. v. YD*) to stand up

大音声 (*n.*) loud voice

名乗る (*intr. v. YD*) to announce one's full name

音に聞く (*set phrase*) to hear rumors, hear from someone

乳母子 (*n.*) child of wet nurse, foster brother (Kanehira is the son of Yoshinaka's wet nurse)

生年 (*n.*) age (counting from birth)

鎌倉殿 (*proper n.*) lord of Kamakura (shōgun Minamoto no Yoritomo)

知ろしめす (*tr. v. YD*) to know, be aware of (hon.)

見参に入る (*set phrase*) (n. *genzan*, "sight of a person of high rank," tr. v. SN *iru*, "to put in") to show a person or an object to a person of high rank

筋 (*n.*) long, narrow object, counter for such

差しつめ引きつめ (*set phrase*) shooting arrows rapidly one after the other

さんざん (散散) (*nari adj. v.*) violent, fierce

死生 (*n.*) life and death

矢庭に (*adv.*) on the spot, immediately

打物 (*n.*) forged iron weapon, such as a sword or pike

抜く (*tr. v. YD*) to pull out, unsheathe

馳せ合ふ (*intr. v. YD*) to spur on one's horse and engage (the enemy) in combat

面 (*n.*) face

合はす (*tr. v. SN*) to bring together, sum up

分捕り (*n.*) taking an enemy's head and/or weapon on the battlefield

射取る (*tr. v. YD*) to kill with an arrow

取りこむ (*tr. v. SN*) to surround, enclose

裏かく (*tr. v. YD*) to pierce through to the back (arrows, swords, etc.)

開間 (*n.*) chink (in armor), small gaps (between plates of armor)

手を負ふ (*set phrase*) to be wounded

Grammar Notes for Paragraph 9

音にも聞きつらん n. *oto*, "rumor": "You must have heard of me."

まかりなる RY of YD v. *makaru*, normally meaning "to leave," here a prefix to the main YD v. *naru*, "to become," making it polite: "I have reached (thirty-three years of age)."

さる者ありとは鎌倉殿までも知ろしめされたるらんぞ attrib. *saru*, "such": "That such a person (Kanehira) exists is probably known even to the lord of Kamakura!"

死生を知らず "heedless of one's own life"

面を合はする者ぞなき "There was no one who would face (Kanehira)."

射取れや interj. p. *ya*: "(The enemy simply said) Shoot him down!"

開間を射ねば "because they did not shoot (arrows) through the chinks in his armor"

Annotated Grammar for Paragraph 9

<small>固名　副　名　名　副助　格助　名　格助　四/用　名　四/用　四/用　名　下二/用</small>
今井四郎 只 一騎、五十騎 ばかり が 中 へ 駆け入り、鎧 踏んばり 立ち上がり、大音声 あげ

<small>接助　四/用　助動/過/体　係助　名　係助　名　格助　係助　四/用　助動/完/終　助動/推/終　名　係助　名　格助　上一/用</small>
て 名乗り ける は、「日来 は 音 に も 聞き つ らん、今 は 目 に も 見

<small>補助動/尊/四/命　固名　格助　固名　名　名　格助　四/丁/用　連体　名　ラ変/終　格助</small>
給へ、木曽殿 の 御乳母子、今井四郎兼平、生年 三十三 に まかりなる。さる 者 あり と

<small>係助　固名　副助　係助　四/尊/未　助動/尊/用　助動/存/体　助動/推/体　係助　固名　四/用（音）　接助　名　格助　下二/命</small>
は 鎌倉殿 まで も 知ろしめさ れ たる らん ぞ。兼平 討ッ て 見参 に 入れよ」

<small>格助　接助　四/用　助動/存/体　名　格助　名　格助　下二/用　下二/用　ナリ形動/用　上一/終　名　係助　四/未</small>
とて、射残し たる 八筋 の 矢 を、差しつめ 引きつめ さんざんに 射る。死生 は 知ら

<small>助動/打/用　副　名　名　四/終　代名　格助　名　四/用（音）　接助　代名　格助　四/用　代名　格助</small>
ず、矢庭に 敵 八騎 射落とす。其 の 後 打物 抜い て あれ に 馳せ合ひ、これ に

<small>四/用　四/用（音）　接助　四/体　接助　名　格助　下二/体　名　係助/係　ク形/体/結　名　副　サ変/用　助動/完/用</small>
馳せ合ひ、切ッ て 回る に、面 を 合はする 者 ぞ なき。分捕り あまた し たり

<small>助動/過/終　副　四/命　間助　格助　接助　名　格助　下二/用　名　格助　四/体　名　格助　上一/用　助動/過/已　接助　名　ク形/已</small>
けり。只「射取れ や」と て、中 に 取りこめ、雨 の 降る 様 に 射 けれ ども、鎧 良けれ

<small>接助　四/未　助動/打/用　名　格助　上一/未　助動/打/已　接助　名　係助　四/未　助動/打/終</small>
ば 裏かか ず、開間 を 射 ね ば 手 も 負は ず。

Vocabulary for Paragraph 10

<small>しやうぐわつ</small>
正 月　(n.) First Month (lunar calendar)

<small>いりあひ</small>
入相　(n.) sunset, dusk

<small>うすごほり</small>
薄 氷　(n.) thin ice

<small>ふかた</small>
深田　(n.) rice fields where the mud is deep

どっと　(adv.) (onomatopoeia) plunging in suddenly, with a splash

あふる (煽る)　(tr. v. YD) (ao-ru) to spur on a horse using stirrups

<small>ゆくへ</small>
行方　(n.) direction, destination

おぼつかなし　(ku adj.) worrisome, uncertain

<small>ふ あふ</small>
振り仰ぐ　(intr. v. YD) (furi-ao-gu) to turn one's head and look upward

<small>うちかぶと</small>
内 甲　(n.) inside the front of a helmet, part of the forehead that touches that part of the helmet

<small>みうら　いしだのじらうためひさ</small>
三浦の石田次郎為久　(proper n.) warrior from Sagami Province (present-day Kanagawa Prefecture); Miura is the clan-name

<small>いた で</small>
痛手　(n.) serious or severe wound

<small>まつかう</small>
真甲　(n.) front of the helmet

<small>お あ</small>
落ち合ふ　(intr. v. YD) (ochi-a-u, ochi-o-u) to come together, come across one another

つひに　(adv.) finally, in the end

<small>たち</small>
太刀　(n.) large sword

<small>さき</small>
先　(n.) tip, point

<small>つらぬ</small>
貫 く　(tr. v. YD) to pierce, run through

<small>かば</small>
庇ふ　(tr. v. YD) to protect from harm, defend

<small>とのばら</small>
殿原　(n.) (plural suffix bara) used to address a group of high-ranking people: my lords, gentlemen

<small>かう もの</small>
剛の者　(set phrase) exceptionally strong, courageous person

<small>ふく</small>
含む　(tr. v. YD) to place in

さかさま (逆様, 倒様)　(adj. v.) upside down, backward

<small>う</small>
失す　(intr. v. SN) to die

Grammar Notes for Paragraph 10

事^{こと}なるに   n. *koto*, "thing," RT of copular *nari*, and case p. *ni*, "on top of which . . ." (i.e., in addition to its being twilight, there was a layer of ice on the paddy fields)

今井が行方^{いまゐ　ゆくへ}のおぼつかなさに   stem of adj. *obotsukanashi* and noun-forming suffix *sa*: "unsure of Imai's whereabouts"

おッかかッて   RY of YD v. *ou* (追ふ), "to pursue," RY of YD v. *kakaru*, "to come in contact with," and conj. p. *te*: "to catch up with"

よッ引^ぴいて   sound change from *yoku hikite* and conj. p. *te*: "drawing the bowstring well back"

ひょうふつと   sound of an arrow whizzing through the air and striking a target

討ち奉^{う　たてまつ}りたるぞや   RY of hum. YD suppl. v. *tatematsuru*, indicating that the recipient of the action (Yoshinaka) is of higher status than the person carrying out the action (Ishida's retainer)

今^{いま}はたれを庇^{かば}はんとて   "thinking (*tote*), 'Now whom do I have to defend?'"

馬^{むま}よりさかさまに飛び落ち   "leaping headfirst from (his) horse"

Annotated Grammar for Paragraph 10

木曽 殿 は 只 一騎、粟津 の 松原 へ 駆け ＿ 給ふ が、正月廿一日 入相 ばかり の 事

なる に、薄氷 は 張ツ たり けり、深田 あり と も 知ら ず して、馬 を ざツ と

打ち入れ たれ ば、馬 の 首 も 見え ざり けり。あふれ ども あふれ ども、打て ども

打て ども、働か ず。今井 が 行方 の おぼつかな さ に、振り仰ぎ 給へ ＿ る 内甲

を、三浦 の 石田次郎為久、おツかかツ て よツ引い て ひやうふつと 射る。痛手 なれ ば、

真甲 を 馬 の 首 に 当て て うつ伏し 給へ ＿ る 所 に、石田 が 郎等 二人

落ち合う て、つひに 木曽 殿 の 首 を ば 取ツ てん ＿ げり。太刀 の 先 に

貫き、高く 差し上げ、大音声 を あげ て、「こ の 日来 日本国 に 聞こえ させ ＿ 給ひ

つる 木曽 殿 を、三浦 の 石田次郎為久 が 討ち ＿ 奉り ＿ たる ぞ や」と 名乗り

けれ ば、今井四郎 軍し ける が、是 を 聞き、「今 は たれ を 庇は ん とて か

軍 を ば す べき。是 を 見 給へ、東国 の 殿原、日本一 の 剛 の 者 の

自害する 手本」と て、太刀 の 先 を 口 に 含み、馬 より さかさまに 飛び落ち、貫ぬかツ

て ぞ 失せ に ＿ ける。さて こそ 粟津 の 軍 は なかり ＿ けれ。

Essays in Idleness

Essays in Idleness (*Tsurezuregusa*) was written by Priest Kenkō, the name given to the author by later generations. Although Kenkō's birth date is unknown, he is thought to have been born during the Kōan era (1278–1288) and to have died in 1352, during the Northern and Southern Courts period (1336–1392). He was a member of the Urabe family, a noted Shintō family, but he did not become a Shintō priest. Instead, during his teens, he served Emperor GoNijō (r. 1301–1308) and wrote *waka*. In 1313, at around the age of thirty, Kenkō took the tonsure and lived until the age of seventy or eighty. He lived in seclusion at Yokawa, outside Kyoto, while continuing to mingle with the most powerful figures of the time.

Essays in Idleness now consists of a preface and 243 sections (*dan*). The shortest *dan* is only one sentence long, and the longest one, section 137, "Do We View Cherry Blossoms Only at Their Peak?" which is included here and which is often thought to encapsulate medieval aesthetics, is four pages long. Today the dominant view is that Kenkō wrote most of the *Essays* when he was in his late forties, in two or three years during the Gentoku (1329–1331) era.

In contrast to the first part of *Essays in Idleness*, in which Kenkō drew on his rich knowledge of Chinese classics, Japanese poetry, and Heian texts, in the second part he gradually broke away from the earlier value judgments and aesthetic standards and used more medieval anecdotes, or *setsuwa*, as in section 89, "On *Nekomata*."

The text is based on Nishio Minoru, ed., *Hōjōki, Tsurezuregusa*, Nihon koten bungaku taikei 30 (Tokyo: Iwanami Shoten, 1957), 89, 161–162, 201, with minor orthographic changes.

『徒然草』(つれづれぐさ)

「89」

「奥山に、猫またといふものありて、人を食ふなる」と、人のいひけるに、「山ならねども、これらにも、猫の経上りて、猫またに成りて、人とる事はあなるものを」と云ふ者ありけるを、何阿弥陀仏とかや、連歌しける法師の、行願寺の辺にありけるが、聞きて、ひとり歩かん身は、心すべきことにこそと思ひける比しも、ある所にて夜更くるまで連歌して、ただひとり帰りけるに、小川の端にて、音に聞きし猫また、あやまたず足許へふと寄り来て、やがてかきつくままに、首のほどを食はんとす。肝心も失せて、防がんとするに力もなく、足も立たず、小川へ転び入りて、「助けよや、猫また、よやよや」と叫べば、家々より、松どもともして走り寄りて見れば、このわたりに見知れる僧なり。「こは如何に」とて、川の中より抱き起したれば、連歌の賭物取りて、扇・小箱など懐に持ちたりけるも、水に入りぬ。希有にして助かりたるさまにて、這ふ這ふ家に入りにけり。飼ひける犬の、暗けれど主を知りて、飛び付きたりけるとぞ。

「137」

花はさかりに、月は隈無きをのみ見るものかは。雨に向かひて月を恋ひ、垂れ籠めて春の行方知らぬも、なほ哀に情深し。咲きぬべきほどの梢、散り萎れたる庭などこそ見所多けれ。歌の詞書にも、「花見にまかれりけるに、はやく散り過ぎにければ」とも、「障る事ありてまからで」なども書けるは、「花を見て」と言へるに劣れる事かは。花の散り、月の傾くを慕ふならひはさる事なれど、殊にかたくななる人ぞ、「この枝、かの枝散りにけり。今は見所なし」などは言ふめる。

　万の事も、始終こそをかしけれ。男女の情も、ひとへに逢ひ見るをば言ふものかは。逢はで止みにし憂さを思ひ、あだなる契をかこち、長き夜をひとり明し、遠き雲井を思ひやり、浅茅が宿に昔を偲ぶこそ、色好むとは言はめ。

　望月のくまなきを千里の外まで眺めたるよりも、暁ちかくなりて待ち出でたるが、いと心ふかう、青みたるやうにて、深き山の杉の梢に見えたる木の間の影、うちしぐれたる村雲がくれのほど、またなく哀なり。椎柴・白樫などの濡れたるやうなる葉の上にきらめきたるこそ、身にしみて、心あらん友もがなと、都恋しう覚ゆれ。

すべて、月・花をば、さのみ目にて見るものかは。春は家を立ち去らでも、月の夜は閨のうちながらも思へるこそ、いとたのもしう、をかしけれ。

よき人は、ひとへに好けるさまにも見えず、興ずるさまも等閑なり。片田舎の人こそ、色こく万はもて興ずれ。花の本には、捩ぢ寄り立ち寄り、あからめもせずまもりて、酒飲み、連歌して、果ては、大きなる枝、心なく折り取りぬ。泉には手・足差し浸して、雪にはおりたちて跡つけなど、万の物、よそながら見る事なし。

Vocabulary for Section 89 (On *Nekomata*)

猫また (*n.*) cat monsters (It was believed that cats that grew old turned into monsters that would eat people and cause sickness. These cat monsters were called *nekomata* because their tails were supposed to have split into two, or *mata*.)

食ふ (*tr. v. YD*) (*kura-u, kuro-u*) to eat, drink

これら (*pron.*) these (people, things, etc.)

経上る (*intr. v. YD*) to grow older and change

連歌 (*n.*) linked verse

行願寺 (*proper n.*) temple in Kyoto

辺 (*n.*) vicinity, nearby

歩く (*intr. v. YD*) to walk, move, ride a vehicle

心す (*intr. v. SH*) to be careful, pay attention to

更く (*intr. v. SN*) to grow late (night, season)

小川 (*proper n.*) (also Kokawa) small river in Kyoto

ふと (*adv.*) swiftly

やがて (*adv.*) immediately

かきつく（掻き付く） (*intr. v. YD*) to cling to, grab hold of

肝心 (*n.*) (also *kimogokoro*) spirit, heart, life, vitality

防ぐ (*tr. v. YD*) to ward off, defend against, prevent

転び入る (*intr. v. YD*) to fall, roll into

叫ぶ (*intr. v. YD*) to scream, shout

松 (*n.*) pine torch

ともす（点す・灯す） (*tr. v. YD*) to burn, light (a lantern, etc.)

抱き起す (*tr. v. YD*) to lift up in one's arms

賭物 (*n.*) prize offered at a competition

希有 (*n., nari adj. v.*) rare, unusual, strange

這ふ這ふ (*adv.*) as if crawling along, finally, at long last

飼ふ (*tr. v. YD*) to raise, care for (animals)

主 (*pron.*) owner

Grammar Notes for Section 89

食ふなる hearsay aux. v. *nari* ends in RT, even though it is not tied to a bound p., a RT-*dome* technique adding emphasis

あなるものを RT of RH v. *ari*, "to be," RT of hearsay aux. v. *nari* (sound change from *aru-naru* to *a-naru*), and conj. p. *mono o*, functioning as a concessive: "There is a rumor that (there is a *nekomata* around here) but (it is probably safe)."

云ふ者ありけるを RT of aux. v. *keri* turns this into a nominal phrase and the object of the following v. *kiku*: "hearing that there was a person who said . . ."

何阿弥陀仏とかや *to-ka-ya*, citational case p. *to* and bound p. *ka* and *ya* indicates uncertainty about something one has heard: "(The priest)

is said to be called something like Amida Buddha."

心すべきことにこそ n. *koto*, RY of copular *nari*, emphatic bound p. *koso*, with IZ of suppl. v. *ari* implied at the end

比しも *shi-mo*, indicating that it was precisely at that time

音に聞きし猫また n. *oto*, "rumor"

あやまたず set phrase: "without error," "accurately"

防がんとするに力もなく "Although he tried to ward it off, he was powerless . . ."

助けよや、猫また、よやよや interj. *yoya* (from interj. p. *yo* and interj. p. *ya*) is used to call out to another person: "Hey! hey!"

こは如何に　adv. p. *ikani,* "What?" "What in the world is going on here!"

飛び付きたりけるとぞ　*to zo* indicates that the speaker has heard the preceding from others and that YD v. *iu,* "to say," is implied afterward

Annotated Grammar for Section 89

「奥山 に、猫また と いふ もの あり て、人 を 食ふ なる」と、人 の いひ ける に、
「山 なら ね ども、これら に も、猫 の 経上り て、猫また に 成り て、人 とる 事
は あ なる ものを」と 云ふ 者 あり ける を、何阿弥陀仏 と か や、連歌
し ける 法師 の、行願寺 の 辺 に あり ける が、聞き て、ひとり 歩か ん 身 は、
心す べき こと に こそ と 思ひ ける 比 しも、ある 所 にて 夜 更くる まで
連歌し て、ただ ひとり 帰り ける に、小川 の 端 にて、音 に 聞き し 猫また、
あやまた ず 足許 へ ふと 寄り来 て、やがて かきつく ままに、首 の ほど を 食は
ん と す。肝心 も 失せ て、防が ん と する に 力 も なく、足 も 立た ず、
小川 へ 転び入り て、「助けよ や、猫また、よや よや」と 叫べ ば、家々 より、松 ども
ともし て 走り寄り て 見れ ば、こ の わたり に 見知れ る 僧 なり。「こ は
如何に」とて、川 の 中 より 抱き起し たれ ば、連歌 の 賭物 取り て、扇・小箱 など 懐
に 持ち たり ける も、水 に 入り ぬ。希有に し て 助かり たる さま にて、
這ふ這ふ 家 に 入り に けり。飼ひ ける 犬 の、暗けれ ど 主 を 知り て、飛び付き
たり ける とぞ。

Vocabulary for Section 137 (Do We View Cherry Blossoms Only at Their Peak?), Paragraph 1

さかり（盛り）　(*n., nari adj. v.*) full bloom, peak

限無し（*ku adj.*) unshaded, unclouded, undarkened

垂れ籠む　(*intr. v. SN*) to draw the blinds and stay inside

行方　(*n.*) direction, destination

情　(*n.*) human feeling, emotion, especially warmth, sympathy, affection

散り萎る　(*intr. v. SN*) to fall and wither (flowers)

見所　(*n.*) something worth looking at

詞書　(*n.*) headnote (to a poem)

散り過ぐ　(*intr. v. KN*) to end up scattering completely

障る　(*intr. v. YD*) to be blocked, hindered

劣る　(*intr. v. YD*) to be inferior to

傾く　(*intr. v. YD*) to sink, set (sun, moon)

慕ふ　(*tr. v. YD*) to think fondly of, long for

ならひ (慣らひ・習ひ)　(*n.*) custom

さる (然る)　(*attrib.*) appropriate, fitting

殊に　(*adv.*) especially, particularly

かたくな (頑なり)　(*nari adj. v.*) uncultivated, unrefined, boorish

枝　(*n.*) branch

Grammar Notes for Section 137, Paragraph 1

咲きぬべきほど　When *nu* is combined with *beshi*, it stresses confidence in the outcome: "at the time when they will no doubt bloom."

散り萎れたる庭　RT of resultative-perfective aux. v. *tari*: "a yard where (the blossoms) have fallen and withered"

花見にまかれりけるに、はやく散り過ぎにければ　"When I went to see the blossoms, they had already all fallen, so . . ."

障る事ありてまからで　MZ of hum. YD v. *makaru*, "to go," and neg. conj. p. *de*: "There was something that blocked me and I did not go (to see the blossoms)."

劣れる事かは　bound p. *kawa*, indicating a rhetorical question: "Is it inferior? (No.)"

さる事なれど　*koto* refers to the attitude being praised in the previous sentence

Annotated Grammar for Section 137, Paragraph 1

名 係助 ナリ形動/用 名 係助 ク形/体 格助 副助 上一/体 名 係助 名 格助 四/用 接助 名 格助 四/用
花 は さかりに、 月 は 隈無き を のみ 見る もの かは。 雨 に 向かひ て 月 を 恋ひ、

下二/用 接助 名 格助 名 四/未 助動/打/体 係助 副詞 ナリ形動/用 名 ク形/終 四/用 助動/完 (確)/用 助動/推/体 名
垂れ籠め て 春 の 行方 知ら ぬ も、なほ 哀に 情 深し。咲き ぬ べき ほど

格助 名 下二/用 助動/完/体 名 副助 係助/係 名 ク形/已/結 名 格助 名 格助 係助 名 格助 四/丁/已
の 梢、散り萎れ たる 庭 など こそ 見所 多けれ。 歌 の 詞書 に も、「花見 に まかれ

助動/完/用 助動/過/体 接助 副 上二/用 助動/完/用 助動/詠/已 接助 格助 ラ変/用 接助 四/丁/未
り ける に、はやく 散り過ぎ に けれ ば」 とも、「障る 事 あり て まから

接助 (打) 副助 係助 四/已 助動/存/体 係助 名 格助 上一/用 接助 格助 四/已 助動/存/体 四/已 助動/存/体 名 係助
で」 など も 書け る は、「花 を 見 て」 と 言へ る に 劣れ る 事 かは。

名 格助 四/用 名 格助 四/体 格助 四/体 係助 連体 名 助動/断/已 接助 副 ナリ形動/体 名 係助
花 の 散り、月 の 傾く を 慕ふ ならひ は さる 事 なれ ど、殊に かたくななる 人 ぞ、

代名 格助 名 代名 格助 名 四/用 助動/完/用 助動/詠/終 名 係助 名 ク形/終 副助 係助 四/終 助動/推/体/結
「この 枝、かの 枝 散り に けり。今 は 見所 なし」 など は いふ める 。

Vocabulary for Section 137, Paragraphs 2–3

万　(*n.*) all things, everything

始終　(*n.*) beginning and end

をかし　(*shiku adj.*) (*okashi*) tasteful, charming, interesting

ひとへに　(*adv.*) completely, intensely

逢ひ見る　(*tr. v. KI*) to have a romantic relationship

止む　(*intr. v. YD*) to come to an end, stop

憂さ　(*n.*) sorrow, grief, distress

あだ (徒)　(*nari adj. v.*) empty, fleeting

契　(*n.*) pledge, vow

かこつ (託つ)　(*tr. v. YD*) to complain, gripe about

明す　(*tr. v. YD*) to stay up all night

雲井　(*n.*) distant and cloudy sky, distant place

思ひやる　(*tr. v. YD*) to think of something or someone far away

浅茅が宿　(*n.*) dilapidated house, overgrown with reeds

偲ぶ　(*tr. v. YD*) to think fondly of, long for

千里　(*n.*) a thousand leagues, a great distance

外　(*n.*) another place, elsewhere

眺む　(*tr. v. SN*) to gaze out across a distance, look off into the distance

暁　(*n.*) just before dawn

待ち出づ　(*tr. v. SN*) to wait for something (someone) to appear

心 ふかし　(*ku adj.*) profoundly moving, tasteful, elegant

青む　(*intr. v. YD*) to turn green

杉　(*n.*) Japanese cedar

木の間　(*n.*) space between trees

うちしぐる（うち時雨る）　(*intr. v. SN*) to rain suddenly, shower

村雲がくれ　(*comp. n.*) hidden in gathered clouds

またなし（又なし）　(*ku adj.*) incomparable

椎柴　(*n.*) type of oak tree

白樫　(*n.*) white oak

濡る　(*intr. v. SN*) to get wet

きらめく　(*intr. v. YD*) to sparkle, shine, glisten

しむ（染む）　(*intr. v. YD*) to feel deeply, go to one's heart

心 あり　(*intr. v. RH*) to appreciate refinement, have taste

Grammar Notes for Section 137, Paragraphs 2–3

ひとへに逢ひ見るをば言ふものかは　emphatic comp. p. *oba* and bound p. *kawa*, indicating a rhetorical question: "Is (love) to be spoken about as meeting intensely?"

逢はで止みにし憂さを思ひ　"to think of the misery of an affair that ended without a meeting"

遠き雲井を思ひやり　"thinking of a distant place"

眺めたるより　"more than gazing (at the full moon from far away)"

待ち出でたる　moon is implied after *taru*: "the moon for which one has been waiting"

青みたるやう　RT of aux. v. *tari* and n. *yō*, "appearance": "greenish in color"

うちしぐれたる村雲がくれのほど　n. *hodo*, "time": "times when (the moon) is hidden in a cluster of clouds during a shower"

濡れたるやうなる葉　"leaves that appear to be wet" (the shine caused by moonlight)

きらめきたる　n. like *kage*, "(moon)light," implied after *tari*

心 あらん友もがな　circumlocutory aux. v. *mu* and desiderative final p. *mogana*: "If only a friend with a sensitive spirit (were here)."

Annotated Grammar for Section 137, Paragraphs 2–3

万 の 事 も、始終 こそ をかしけれ。男女 の 情 も、ひとへに 逢ひ見る を ば 言ふ もの

かは。逢は で 止み に し 憂さ を 思ひ、あだなる 契 を かこち、長き 夜 を

ひとり 明し、遠き 雲井 を 思ひやり、浅茅 が 宿 に 昔 を 偲ぶ こそ、色好む と は 言は

め。

望月 の くまなき を 千里 の 外 まで 眺め たる より も、暁 ちかく なりて

待ち出で たる が、いと 心ふかう、青み たる やうに て、ふかき 山 の 杉 の 梢 に 見え

たる 木 の 間 の 影、うち しぐれ たる 村雲がくれ の ほど、またなく 哀なり。椎柴・

白樫 など の 濡れ たる やうなる 葉 の 上 に きらめき たる こそ、身 に しみ て、

心あら ん 友 もがな と、都 恋しう 覚ゆれ。

Vocabulary for Section 137, Paragraphs 4–5

さのみ (然のみ)   (*comp.*) in this way only

立ち去る (たちさる)   (*intr. v. YD*) to leave, get up and go

閨 (ねや)   (*n.*) bedroom

うち (内)   (*n.*) inside (a room, building)

たのもしし (頼もしし)   (*shiku adj.*) promising, eagerly anticipated

好く (す)   (*tr. v. YD*) to enjoy, have a taste for, like

興ず (きょう)   (*intr. v. SH*) to be amused by, enjoy

等閑 (なほざり)   (*n., nari adj. v.*) measured, moderate, simple

片田舎 (かたゐなか)   (*n.*) backwoods, countryside, remote village

色こし (色濃し) (いろ)   (*ku adj.*) excessive, gaudy, cloying, showy

花の本 (はな もと)   (*comp.*) base of a tree in bloom

捩ぢ寄る (ねよ)   (*intr. v. YD*) to creep up to, sidle up to

立ち寄る (たさ)   (*intr. v. YD*) to approach, draw near

あからめ (あから目)   (*n.*) looking at something else, glancing aside

まもる (守る)   (*tr. v. YD*) to stare at, fix one's gaze on

心なし (こころ)   (*ku adj.*) unkind, coldhearted

泉 (いづみ)   (*n.*) spring, fountain

差し浸す (さ ひた)   (*comp. v.*) (from prefix *sashi* and tr. YD v. *hitasu*) to thrust into water

おりたつ (下り立つ)   (*intr. v. YD*) to get down and stand on

よそながら (余所ながら)   (*adv.*) while at a distance, at a remove

Grammar Notes for Section 137, Paragraphs 4–5

さのみ目にて見るものかは (め み)   bound p. *kawa*, indicating a rhetorical question: "Are (the moon and blossoms) things to be seen in this way, only with the eyes?"

閨のうちながらも思へる "to think of (the moonlit night) while inside one's bedroom"

よき人 "a person with good taste," "a connoisseur"

ひとへに好けるさまにも見えず "(Connoisseurs) do not appear to pursue pleasure in a single-minded fashion."

色こく万はもて興ずれ n. *yorozu*, "all (things)," and emphatic v. prefix *mote*: "(People from the countryside) enjoy all things excessively."

あからめもせずまもりて "(They) stare (at the blossoms) without looking at anything else."

おりたちて跡つけ n. *ato*, "footprints," and RY of SN v. *tsuku*, "to leave (footprints)": "stepping down onto (the snow) and leaving footprints"

よそながら見る事なし "There is nothing that (boorish country people) look at from a distance (they have to get up close to it, break off branches, make footprints, etc.)."

Annotated Grammar for Section 137, Paragraphs 4–5

すべて、月・花をば、さのみ目にて見るものかは。春は家を立ち去らでも、

月の夜は闇のうちながらも思へるこそ、いとたのもしう、をかしけれ。

よき人は、ひとへに好けるさまにも見えず、興ずるさまも等閑なり。

片田舎の人こそ、色こく万はもて興ずれ。花の本には、捩ぢ寄り立ち寄り、

あからめもせずまもりて、酒飲み、連歌して、果ては、大きなる枝、心なく

折り取りぬ。泉には手・足差し浸して、雪にはおりたちて跡つけなど、万

の物、よそながら見る事なし。

Part IV

Edo/Tokugawa Period

12

Japan's Eternal Storehouse

Ihara Saikaku (1642–1693) was born into a well-to-do merchant family in Osaka. The first of Saikaku's so-called *chōnin* (urban commoner) narratives, *Japan's Eternal Storehouse* (*Nippon eitaigura*, 1688), suggests the techniques for achieving wealth in this new economy. Its subtitle is *Fortune, Gospel of the New Millionaire* (*Daifuku shin chōja kyō*), indicating that it is a sequel to *Gospel of the Millionaire* (*Chōjakyō*), a short book published in 1627 describing how three merchants had become millionaires. The word "millionaire" (*chōja*) means "self-made man," but the term "eternal generations" (*eitai*) also suggests that the objective was to establish a prosperous family line. The book is thus a "storehouse" (*kura*) of such models. As with much of Saikaku's fiction, the appeal of these stories frequently derives from their humorous twists.

The story "Foremost Lodger in the Land" begins with a description of Fuji-ichi, an urban commoner who began with no money but managed to make a fortune through extreme thrift and ingenuity. He also teaches his daughter how to be extremely frugal. Here the neighbors send their children to learn from Fuji-ichi. The following selection is from the last part.

The text is based on Noma Kōshin, ed., *Saikaku shū ge*, Nihon koten bungaku taikei 48 (Tokyo: Iwanami Shoten, 1960), 62–63, with minor orthographic changes.

『日本永代蔵』

「世界の借屋大将」

折ふしは正月七日の夜、近所の男子を、藤市かたへ、長者に成やうの指南を頼むとて遣しける。座敷に灯かかやかせ、娘を付置、「露路の戸の鳴時しらせ」と申置しに、此の娘、しをらしくかしこまり、灯心を一筋にして、物申の声する時、元のごとくにして、勝手に入ける。三人の客、座に着時、台所に摺鉢の音ひびきわたれば、客、耳をよろこばせ、是を推して、「皮鯨の吸物」といへば、「いやいや、はじめてなれば、雑煮なるべし」といふ。又ひとりは、よく考て、「煮麺」とおち付ける。必ずいふ事にして、をかし。

　藤市出でて、三人に、世渡りの大事を、物がたりして聞せける。一人申せしは、「今日の七草といふ謂は、いかなる事ぞ」と尋ねける。「あれは、神代の始末はじめ、雑炊と云ふ事を知らせ給ふ」。又一人、「掛鯛を六月迄、荒神の前に置けるは」と尋ぬ。「あれは、朝夕に肴を喰はずに、是をみて、喰うた心せよと云ふ事也」。又、太箸をとる由来を問ひける。「あれは、穢し時白げて、一膳にて一年中あるやうに、是も神代の二柱を表すなり。よくよく、万事に気を付給へ。扨、宵から今まで、各々咄し給へば、最早夜食の出づべき所なり。出さぬが長者に成心なり。最前の摺鉢の音は、大福帳の上紙に引糊を摺らした」といはれし。

Vocabulary

世界の借屋大将 (*n. phrase*) chief (*daishō, taishō*) of the world's (*sekai*) renters (*kashiya*) (The protagonist, Fuji-ichi, takes pride in being the richest of all the townspeople who rent homes.)

折ふし (*n.*) time, moment

かた (*n.*) direction

長者 (*n.*) wealthy person

指南 (*n.*) guidance, instruction

座敷 (*n.*) room for receiving visitors, waiting room

灯 (*n.*) lamp, lantern

かかやく(輝く，赫く) (*intr. v. YD*) (from Edo-period *kagayaku*) to shine, give off light

露路 (*n.*) garden attached to a tea room or path leading to a tea room (In the Kyoto–Osaka region, people visiting a merchant's home entered through this path rather than the shop entrance, which was used only by customers.)

しをらし (*shiku adj.*) commendable, praiseworthy

かしこまる (畏まる) (*intr. v. YD*) to sit respectfully

灯心 (*n.*) wick (of a lantern)

物申 (*interj.*) (from *mono-mōsu*, "to speak humbly") Excuse me! Hello! (used primarily by men when requesting entry into someone's home)

勝手 (*n.*) kitchen

摺鉢 (*n.*) mortar, used with a pestle for grinding things like sesame seeds

ひびきわたる (響き渡る) (*intr. v. YD*) (from *hibiku* and *wataru*) to ring out or reverberate over a wide space

推す (*tr. v. SH*) to guess, speculate

皮鯨 (*n.*) whale blubber (usually preserved with salt and prepared with miso paste or in soups during the winter, considered a delicacy)

吸物 (*n.*) soup

雑煮 (*n.*) special soup prepared with rice cakes (*mochi*) and vegetables to celebrate the New Year

煮麺 (*n.*) miso or soy soup prepared with fine *sōmen* noodles (similar to vermicelli)

おち付く (*tr. v. SN*) to decide, bring to a conclusion

世渡り (*n.*) living or getting by in the world

大事 (*n.*) key point

今日の七草 (*set phrase*) practice of preparing porridge with the seven spring herbs (*nana-kusa*) as part of the New Year celebrations

謂 (*n.*) origins, history

神代 (*n.*) age of the gods

始末 (*n.*) thrift, frugality

雑炊 (*n.*) porridge made with vegetables (considered to be economical)

掛鯛 (*n.*) pair of salted sea bream (*tai*) tied together with a rope through their mouths and placed over the entrance or the kitchen shrine dedicated to the god Kōjin on the New Year (It was customary to grate and eat them on the first day of the Sixth Month.)

荒神 (*proper n.*) god believed to protect the Three Treasures (Buddha, Buddhist law, and Buddhist clergy), worshiped in Edo period as the kitchen god

朝夕 (*n.*) morning and evening meal

太箸 (*n.*) thick chopsticks, usually made of willow, used to eat *zōni* at the New Year (made thicker than usual because it was considered unlucky if they broke)

白ぐ (*tr. v. SN*) to make white (using rice grains)

一膳 (*n.*) pair of chopsticks

表す (*tr. v. SH*) to represent, stand for, symbolize

宵 (n.) dusk, early evening (from sundown to midnight)

各々 (pron.) everyone, all present (used to address audience)

大福帳の上紙 (n.) title page or cover (*uwagami*) of a merchant's ledger book (*daifukuchō*) (Merchants customarily wrote the characters *daifuku*, "great fortune," on the cover of their ledgers. As a New Year's prayer for good fortune, merchants pasted the cover on each new ledger around the eleventh day of the First Month.)

糊 (n.) paste, glue

摺る (tr. v. YD) to grind in a mortar, mash; here, the grinding of the paste for the ledger cover

Grammar Notes

正月七日の夜 seventh day of the First Month, called *jinjitsu* (人日), the first of the five major seasonal festivals (*sekku*). To ward off illness, people prepared a special porridge using the seven spring herbs.

藤市かた n. *kata*, "direction"; Fujiya Ichibei (nicknamed Fuji-ichi), a merchant who lived in the Muromachi district of Kyoto during the mid-seventeenth century and became wealthy by being frugal

長者に成やうの指南 *yau* (*yō*), a suffix that, after n., means "like" and that, after RY of v., as it is here, means "the way to," as in "the way to become a rich person"

遣し RY of tr. YD v. *tsukawasu*, "to send, dispatch"

灯心を一筋にして lamp wick usually branched off in two or three directions to give off more light, which also causes it to burn more quickly. To save money, Fuji-ichi instructs his daughter to twist the wicks into one until the guests arrive.

元のごとくにして When the guests arrive, Fuji-ichi's daughter untwists the wick to give off more light, returning it to its original state (*moto no gotoku*).

はじめてなれば their first visit of the New Year, which would cause them to expect their host to offer a lavish welcome

申せし MZ of hum. tr. YD (treated as SH) v. *mōsu*, "to say," and RT of past-tense aux. v. *ki*, which usually follows RY, but the MZ of SH and KH v.

神代の始末はじめ、雑炊と云ふ事を知らせ給ふ hon. suppl. v. *tamau*, showing respect toward the gods: "That is the beginning of frugality in the age of the gods, and it makes us know what is called *zōsui* (economical food)."

喰うた心せよ RY of YD v. *kuu*, "to eat" (sound change from *kui* to *kuu*), RT of perfective aux. v. *tari* (abbreviated from *taru* to *ta*), and MR of SH v. *kokoro-su*, "to feel"

穢し時白げて、一膳にて一年中あるやうに "to make do with one set of chopsticks all year around, whitening them when they get dirty"

神代の二柱 *hashira*, a counter for deities and nobility. The two gods (*futahashira*) to whom Fuji-ichi refers are Izanagi and Izanami, who were believed to have created the Japanese archipelago. The thick chopsticks are also implicitly compared to two pillars (*hashira*).

摺らした MZ of YD v. *suru*, "to print," RY of causative aux. v. *su*, and abbrev. of perfective aux. v. *tari*

Annotated Grammar

折ふし は 正月 七日 の 夜、近所 の 男子 を、藤市 かた へ、長者 に 成り やう の 指南 を 頼む とて 遣し ける。座敷 に 灯 かかやか せ、娘 を 付け置き、「露路 の 戸 の 鳴 時 しら せ」と 申し置き し に、此 の 娘、しをらしく かしこまり、灯心 を 一筋 に して、物申 の 声 する 時、元 の ごとく に して、勝手 に 入り ける。三人 の 客、座 に 着く 時、台所 に 摺鉢 の 音 ひびきわたれ ば、客、耳 を よろこば せ、是 を 推して、「皮鯨 の 吸物」と いへ ば、「いやいや、はじめて なれ ば、雑煮 なる べし」と いふ。又 ひとり は、よく 考へ て、「煮麺」と おち付け ける。必ず いふ 事 に して、をかし。

　　藤市 出で て、三人 に、世渡り の 大事 を、物がたりし て 聞か せ ける。一人 申せ し は、「今日 の 七草 といふ 謂 は、いかなる 事 ぞ」と 尋ね ける。「あれ は、神代 の 始末 はじめ、雑炊 と 云ふ 事 を 知ら せ 給ふ」。又 一人、「掛鯛 を 六月 迄、荒神 の 前 に 置き ける は」と 尋ぬ。「あれ は、朝夕 に 肴 を 喰は ず に、是 を みて、喰う た 心 せよと 云ふ 事 也」。又、太箸 を とる 由來 を 問ひ ける。「あれ は、穢れ し 時 白げ て、一膳 にて 一年中 ある やう に、是 も 神代 の 二柱 を 表す なり。よくよく、万事 に 気 を 付け 給へ。扨、宵 から 今 まで、各々 咄し 給へ ば、最早 夜食 の 出づ べき 所 なり。出さ ぬ が 長者 に 成る 心 なり。最前 の 摺鉢 の 音 は、大福帳 の 上紙 に 引く 糊 を 摺ら した」と いは れ し。

1 3

Narrow Road to the Deep North

Matsuo Bashō (1644–1694) was born in the castle town of Ueno, in Iga Province (present-day Mie Prefecture), approximately thirty miles southeast of Kyoto. Although his grandfather and great-grandfather had belonged to the samurai class, they were disenfranchised, for reasons that are unclear. By Bashō's generation, the family had fallen so low that they had become farmers with only tenuous ties to the samurai class. In the spring of 1689, Bashō departed with his disciple Sora for Michinoku, in the northeast, in an expedition later commemorated in *Narrow Road to the Deep North* (*Oku no hosomichi*). The arduous journey started in Fukagawa in mid-May 1689 and ended a little more than five months and almost fifteen hundred miles later at Ōgaki in Mino.

Although often read as a travel account, *Narrow Road to the Deep North* is best regarded as a kind of fiction loosely based on the actual journey. The text consists of fifty or so separate sections strung together like a *haikai* linked-verse sequence. These sections describe a series of interrelated journeys: a search for *utamakura*, or noted poetic places, especially the traces of ancient poets like Saigyō, the medieval *waka* poet-priest to whom this account pays special homage; a journey into the past to such historical places as the old battlefield at Hiraizumi; an ascetic journey and pilgrimage to sacred places; and interesting encounters with individuals and poetic partners, with whom Bashō composes or exchanges poetic greetings.

A typical passage begins with a description of the place and a history of the shrine or temple, usually giving some detail about the founder or the name. The climactic *hokku*, which may be a poetic greeting to the divine spirit or head of the temple/shrine, usually conveys a sense of the place's sacred quality or efficacy. Of particular interest is the close fusion between the prose and the poetry, a salient characteristic of *haibun*, in which the prose creates a dramatic context for many of Bashō's best *hokku*.

The text is based on Sugiura Shōichirō et al., eds., *Bashō bunshū*, Nihon koten bungaku taikei 46 (Tokyo: Iwanami Shoten, 1959), 70, 84–87, with minor orthographic changes.

『おくのほそ道』

「序」

月日は百代の過客にして、行きかふ年も又旅人也。舟の上に生涯をうかべ、馬の口とら
へて老いを迎ふる者は、日々旅にして旅を栖とす。古人も多く旅に死せるあり。予もい
づれの年よりか、片雲の風にさそはれて、漂泊の思ひやまず、海浜にさすらへ、去年の秋、
江上の破屋に蜘の古巣をはらひて、やや年も暮れ、春立てる霞の空に白川の関越えんと、
そぞろ神の物につきて心をくるはせ、道祖神のまねきにあひて取るもの手につかず、もも
引の破れをつづり笠の緒付けかへて、三里に灸すうるより、松嶋の月先づ心にかかりて、
住める方は人に譲り杉風が別墅に移るに、

　　　　　草の戸も住み替はる代ぞひなの家

面八句を庵の柱に懸け置く。

「平泉」

三代の栄耀一睡の中にして、大門の跡は一里こなたに有り。秀衡が跡は田野に成りて、金
鶏山のみ形を残す。先づ高舘にのぼれば、北上川南部より流るる大河也。衣川は和泉が
城をめぐりて、高舘の下にて大河に落ち入る。泰衡等が旧跡は、衣が関を隔てて南部口
をさし堅め、夷をふせぐとみえたり。さても義臣すぐつて此の城にこもり、功名一時の
叢となる。「国破れて山河あり、城春にして草青みたり」と笠うち敷きて、時のうつる
まで泪を落し侍りぬ。

　　　　　夏草や兵どもが夢の跡
　　　　　卯の花に兼房みゆる白毛かな　　　　　曽良

兼ねて耳驚かしたる二堂開帳す。経堂は三将の像をのこし、光堂は三代の棺を納
め、三尊の仏を安置す。七宝散りうせて、珠の扉風にやぶれ、金の柱霜雪に朽ちて、
既に頽廃空虚の叢と成るべきを、四面新に囲みて、甍を覆ひて風雨を凌ぐ。暫時千歳
の記念とはなれり。

　　　　　五月雨の降り残してや光堂

「立石寺」

山形領に立石寺と云ふ山寺あり。慈覚大師の開基にして、殊に清閑の地也。一見すべきよし、人々のすすむるに依つて尾花沢よりとつて返し、其の間七里ばかり也。日いまだ暮れず。麓の坊に宿借り置きて、山上の堂にのぼる。岩に巌を重ねて山とし、松柏年旧り、土石老いて苔滑かに、岩上の院々扉を閉ぢて物の音きこえず。岸をめぐり岩を這ひて仏閣を拝し、佳景寂寞として心すみ行くのみおぼゆ。

　　　閑かさや岩にしみ入る蝉の声

Vocabulary for Introduction

百代 (*n.*) (also *hyakudai*) eternity, all time to come

過客 (*n.*) traveler(s), people who come and go

生涯 (*n.*) life, lifetime

古人 (*n.*) ancients (Bashō is referring to great poets of the past like Saigyō [1118–1190], Sōgi [1421–1502], and the Chinese poet Du Fu [712–770], all of whom died while traveling.)

予 (*pron.*) first-person singular, used by men

片雲の風 (*n.*) wind that blows scattered clouds across the sky

漂泊の思ひ (*n.*) wanderlust, desire (*omoi*) to drift aimlessly (*hyōhaku*)

海浜 (*n.*) seashore

さすらふ (*intr. v. SN, YD*) to drift along, wander aimlessly

江上の破屋 (*n.*) broken-down hut (*haoku*) by the (Sumida) river (*kōshō*) (The character 上 here means "vicinity." Bashō's hut was east of the Sumida River, just outside Edo.)

白川の関 (*proper n.*) Shirakawa Barrier (now in Fukushima Prefecture), one of the three checkpoints (*seki*) located in the northeast

そぞろ神 (漫ろ神) (*n.*) god who somehow causes one to wander (Bashō appears to have coined this word.)

道祖神 (*n.*) god who protect travelers (at mountain passes, crossroads, etc.)

もも引 (*n.*) leggings, wrapped around the thigh

笠の緒 (*n.*) strap (*o*) on a sedge hat (*kasa*) (*Kasa* were worn to keep off rain or snow or to protect against the sun.)

三里 (*n.*) depression at the base of one's kneecap, where moxa was burned to prevent illness and ensure strong legs for traveling

灸 (*n.*) moxa (placed on various locations on the body and burned, in the belief that the heat would cure sickness and improve health)

松嶋 (*proper n.*) area around Matsushima Bay, in present-day Miyagi Prefecture; considered one of the three famous views of the Japanese peninsula

杉風が別墅 (*n.*) Sanpū's villa (Sanpū was the *haikai* name of one of Bashō's ten most prominent disciples and an important patron.)

草の戸 (*set phrase*) thatched hut

ひな (雛) (*n.*) paper doll, set out during the Hina or Doll Festival to pray for the health and good fortune of one's daughters

面八句 (*n.*) first front eight verses of a hundred-verse linked-verse sequence (These poems were usually written on four sheets of paper, each of which was folded in half so that verses could be written on the front [*omote*] and back [*ura*].)

Grammar Notes for Introduction

百代の過客にして reference to a poem by the Tang poet Li Bai (Li Po, 701–762), in which time is compared to travelers on an endless voyage

舟の上に生涯をうかべ combination of *fune* and *ukabu*, an example of *engo* (associated words), and the successive images of boatsmen and porters function like poetic couplets

(*tsuiku*), a common feature of classical Chinese poetry

死せるあり MZ of intr. SH v. *shisu*, "to die," and RT of perfective aux. v. *ri*. Note that *ri* follows MZ (not IZ) of SH.

よりか case p. *yori* and doubt bound p. *ka*, with a phrase like *kaku ari-kemu* implying "Which year was it *that I began to feel this way*?"

春立てる 霞　*tate-ru* modifies both *haru* and *kasumi*: "spring has come" and the "mist has risen"

白川の関越えんと　citational case p. *to*, indicating the content of his thoughts: "*Thinking that* I would like to go beyond the Shirakawa Barrier . . ."

心 にかかりて　RY of intr. YD v. set phrase *kokoro ni kakaru*, "to have one's mind set on"

移るに　*ni* can be interpreted as either a conj. p. (concessive) or, as it has been here, a case p., meaning "when (Sanpū) moved"

草の戸も住み替はる代ぞひなの家　RT of intr. YD v. *sumi-kawaru*, "to move into a new place," and n. *yo*, "time." Bashō imagines how the reclusive hut might change when the next residents move in, speculating that it might become a family home where dolls are set out on Doll Festival day (third day of the Third Month)—a striking change in atmosphere.

Annotated Grammar for Introduction

月日 は 百代 の 過客 に して、行きかふ 年 も 又 旅人 也。舟 の 上 に 生涯 を

うかべ、馬 の 口 とらへ て 老い を 迎ふる 者 は、日々 旅 に して 旅 を 栖 と す。

古人 も 多く 旅 に 死せ る あり。予 も いづれ の 年 より か 、片雲 の 風 に

さそは れ て、漂泊 の 思ひ やま ず 、海浜 に さすらへ、去年 の 秋、江上 の 破屋

に 蜘 の 古巣 を はらひ て、やや 年 も 暮れ、春 立て る 霞 の 空 に 白川 の 関

越え ん と、そぞろ神 の 物 に つき て 心 を くるは せ、道祖神 の まねき に

あひ て 取る もの 手 に つか ず 、もも引 の 破れ を つづり 笠 の 緒 付けかへ て、

三里 に 灸 すうる より、松嶋 の 月 先づ 心 にかかり て、住め る 方 は 人 に 譲り

杉風 が 別墅 に 移る に、

　　　草 の 戸 も 住み替はる 代 ぞ ひな の 家

面八句 を 庵 の 柱 に 懸け置く。

Vocabulary for "Hiraizumi"

平泉　(*proper n.*) area in the south of present-day Iwate Prefecture (Hiraizumi is where the northern Fujiwara—Kiyohira, Motohira, and Hidehira—built opulent mansions at the end of the eleventh century and prospered for nearly a hundred years.)

秀衡　(*proper n.*) Fujiwara no Hidehira (d. 1187), son of Motohira and grandson of Kiyohira, succeeded his father as governor of Mutsu Province and the military commander over-seeing Dewa Province. During his time, the Fujiwara enjoyed their greatest level of affluence. Near the end of his life, Hidehira took in Minamoto no Yoshitsune and gave him asylum, which brought the Fujiwara into conflict with Yoshitsune's older brother Yoritomo because the brothers were engaged in a feud at the time. This led Yoritomo to attack Hiraizumi, bringing about the end of the Fujiwaras' prosperity.

金鶏山 (*proper n.*) small hill that Hidehira had built in the shape of Mount Fuji, to the northwest of his residence (Two statues, a rooster and a hen made of gold [*kinkei*], were buried at its base to protect Hiraizumi; hence the name.)

高舘 (*proper n.*) one of the residences that Hidehira built near the Kitakami River, the place where Yoshitsune stayed and later committed suicide.

北上川 (*proper n.*) river that runs through present-day Iwate and Miyagi prefectures

衣川 (*proper n.*) river that empties into the Kitakami River north of Takadachi

和泉が城 (*proper n.*) residence of Hidehira's third son, Tadahira, next to the Koromo River

泰衡等が旧跡 (*n.*) ruins (*kyūseki*) of Yasuhira and the others (plural suffix *ra*)

衣が関 (*proper n.*) checkpoint in Mutsu Province, located to the northwest of Chūsonji, the temple built by Fujiwara no Kiyohira in 1105

さし堅む (*tr. v. SN*) to guard very carefully

夷 (*proper n.*) native inhabitants of northern Japan (also called Emishi or Ebisu)

曽良 (*proper n.*) *haikai* pen name of Kawai Sōgorō, one of Bashō's disciples

開帳す (*tr. v. SH*) to open up (treasures, etc.) for public viewing (at Buddhist temples)

経堂 (*n.*) sutra hall

三将 (*proper n.*) three military commanders (Kiyohira, Motohira, and Hidehira)

光堂 (*n.*) hall decorated with gold leaf

三尊 (*n.*) triad of three Buddhist statues in a temple: here Amida Buddha and two bodhisattvas, Kannon and Seishi

七宝 (*n.*) (also *shippō*) (Buddhist) seven jewels: usually gold, silver, lapis lazuli, crystal, *shako* (giant clam), agate, and coral

散りうす (散り失す) (*intr. v. SN*) to scatter and become lost

珠の扉 (*n.*) door (*tobira*) decorated with pearls (*tama*)

金の柱 (*n.*) pillar (*hashira*) decorated with gold leaf (*kogane*)

頽廃 (*n.*) deterioration, decline

空虚 (*n.*) emptiness, fruitlessness

甍 (*n.*) roof tile, roof made of tile (implying that a shelter with a tiled roof had been built around the hall)

凌ぐ (*tr. v. YD*) to endure or overcome hardship

Grammar Notes for "Hiraizumi"

三代の栄耀一睡の中にして   This is a reference to the famous Chinese story about a young man named Lu Sheng who falls asleep on a pillow in a tea house and has a vivid dream in which he sees himself achieving great success. When he wakes up, he realizes that the millet that had been cooking when he fell asleep is still not done. *Issui* also can be written 一炊, meaning the time it takes to cook a bowl of rice or millet.

義臣すぐつて   n. *gishin*, "loyal retainers," RY of tr. YD v. *suguru*, "to select the best from a group," and conj. p. *te. Sugutte* is a compressed sound change from *sugurite*.

国破れて山河あり、城春にして草青みたり These lines are from a noted poem by Du Fu (712–770) on the contrast between the cycle of nature and the impermanence of civilization.

夏草や兵どもが夢の跡   interj. p. *ya* serves as a *kireji*, or cutting word, splitting the *hokku* in two; plural suffix *domo*; n. *ato*, "remains, traces" (of the soldiers' dreams of glory); *natsukusa* is a seasonal word (*kigo*) for summer, suggesting thick green grass.

卯の花に兼房みゆる白毛かな   n. *u no hana*, "deutzia" (a white flower), a summer *kigo*, echoing the white hair of Kanefusa (an elder retainer of Yoshitsune) who fought by his master's side to the very end

五月雨の降り残してや光堂   *furi-nokosu* is a comp. v. describing the *samidare* (long summer rains) that falls everywhere except on this Hall of Light (Hikari-dō); *ya* expresses the poet's speculation and a sense of admiration that the hall has withstood the elements for so many centuries.

Annotated Grammar for "Hiraizumi"

名 格助 名 名 格助 名 助動/断/用 接助 名 格助 名 係助 名 代 格助 ラ変/終 固名 格助 名 係助
三代 の 栄耀 一睡 の 中 に して、大門 の 跡 は 一里 こなた に 有り。秀衡 が 跡 は

名 格助 四/用 接助 固名 副助 名 格助 四/終 副 固名 四/已 接助 固名 名 格助
田野 に 成り て、金鶏山 のみ 形 を 残す。先づ 高舘 に のぼれ ば、北上川 南部 より

下二/体 名 助動/断/終 固名 係助 固名 格助 四/用 接助 固名 格助 名 格助 名 格助 四/終
流るる 大河 也。衣川 は 和泉が城 を めぐり て、高舘 の 下 にて 大河 に 落ち入る。

固名 接尾 格助 名 係助 固名 格助 下二/用 接助 名・格助 下二/用 名 格助 四/終 格助 下二/用 助動/存/終
泰衡 等 が 旧跡 は、衣が関 を 隔て て 南部口 を さし堅め、夷 を ふせぐ と みえ たり。

接 名・四/用(音) 接助 代 格助 名 格助 四/用 名 名 格助 名 格助 四/体 名 下二/用 接助 名
さても 義臣 すぐつ て 此の 城 に こもり、功名 一時 の 叢 と なる。「国 破れ て 山河

ラ変/終 名 名 助動/断/用 接助 名 四/用 助動/存/終 格助 名 四/用 接助 名 の 四/体 副助 名 格助 四/用
あり、城 春 に して 草 青み たり」と 笠 打ち敷き て、時 の うつる まで 泪 を 落し

補助動/丁/ラ変/用 助動/完/終
侍り ぬ。

名 間助 名 接尾 格助 名 格助 名
夏草 や 兵 ども が 夢 の 跡

名 格助 固名 下二/体 名・ 終助   固名
卯の花 に 兼房 みゆる 白毛 かな   曽良

副 名 四/用 助動/完/体 名 サ変/終 名 係助 名 格助 名 格助 四/用 名 係助 名 格助 名
兼ねて 耳 驚かし たる 二堂 開帳す。経堂 は 二将 の 像 を のこし、光室 は 二代 の 棺

格助 下二/用 名 格助 名 格助 サ変/終 名 下二/用 接助 名 格助 名 名 格助 下二/用 名 格助 名 名
を 納め、三尊 の 仏 を 安置す。七宝 散りうせ て、珠 の 扉 風 に やぶれ、金 の 柱 霜雪

格助 上二/用 接助 副 名 名 格助 名 格助 四/終 助動/当/体 接助 ナリ形動/用 四/用 名 格助 四/用
に 朽ち て、既に 頽廃 空虚 の 叢 と 成る べき を、四面 新に 囲み て、甍 を 覆ひ

接助 名・格助 四/終 副 名 格助 名 格助 係助 四/已 助動/完/終
て 風雨 を 凌ぐ。暫時 千歳 の 記念 と は なれ り。

名 格助 四/用 接助 係助(疑) 名
五月雨 の 降り残し て や 光堂

Vocabulary for "Ryūshakuji"

山形領 (*proper n.*) Yamagata Province

立石寺 (*proper n.*) Tendai Buddhist temple established by the priest Jikaku (Ennin) in 860, twelve miles northeast of present-day Yamagata City

清閑 (*n.*) purity, stillness, removed from mundane, worldly affairs

よし (由) (*n.*) main point

尾花沢 (*proper n.*) area in the north of Yamagata, famous in the Edo period for the cultivation of *benibana* (safflower)

とつて返^{かへ}す (*intr. v. YD*) to turn back immediately upon arrival at a destination

里^り (*n.*) league (roughly equivalent to 3.9 kilometers, or 2.5 miles)

梺^{ふもと} の坊^{ばう} (*comp.*) guesthouse (*bō*) at the foot of a mountain (*fumoto*) (*Bō* refers to either the monks' living quarters or the monks themselves, but here it refers to the temple guesthouse.)

松柏^{しょうはく} (*n.*) evergreen trees, such as pine and oak

旧^ふる (*intr. v. KN*) to grow old, age

苔^{こけ} (*n.*) moss

滑^{なめら}か (*nari adj. v.*) smooth, sleek

岩上^{がんじやう} (*n.*) on top of the rock

院^{ゐんゐん}々 (*n.*) various temple halls

佳景^{かけい} (*n.*) scenic view, beautiful scene

寂寞^{じやくまく} (*tari adj. v.*) solitary, still, hushed

Grammar Notes for "Ryūshakuji"

慈覚大師^{じかくだいし}の開基^{かいき}にして proper n. Master Jikaku (794–864, also known as Ennin) and n. *kaiki*, "founding (of a temple)": "Master Jikaku founded the temple and . . ."

一見^{いつけん}すべきよし SS of tr. SH v. *ikken-su*, "to take a look at," RT of recommendation aux. v. *beshi*, and n. *yoshi*, "main point": "since people recommended that we take one look . . ."

心^{こころ}すみ行^ゆくのみおぼゆ RT of intr. YD v. *sumi-yuku*, "to become clear," adv. v. *nomi*, which here is emphatic, and SS of intr. SN v. *oboyu*, "to feel"

閑^{しづ}かさや岩^{いは}にしみ入^いる蝉^{せみ}の声^{こゑ} stem of adj. v. *shizuka nari*, "still, hushed," nominalizing suffix *sa*, interj. p. *ya*, serving as a *kireji*, RT of intr. YD v. *shimi-iru*, "to sink into," and n. *koe*, "voice" (here, the piercing sound of the cicada)

Annotated Grammar for "Ryūshakuji"

固名 格助 固名 格助 四/体 名 ラ変/終 固名 格助 名 助動/断/用 接助 副 名 格助 名
山形領 に 立石寺 と 云ふ 山寺 あり。慈覚大師 の 開基 に して、殊に 清閑 の 地

助動/断/終 サ変/終 助動/勧誘/体 名 名 格助 下二/体 格助 四/用(音) 接助 固名 格助 四/用 代
也。一見す べき よし、人々 の すすむる に 依つ て 尾花沢 より とつて返し、其

格助 名 名 副助 助動/断/終 名 副 下二/未 助動/打/終 名 名 格助 四/用 接助 名 格助
の 間 七里 ばかり 也。日 いまだ 暮れ ず。梺 の 坊 に 宿 借り置き て、山上 の

名 格助 四/終 名 格助 名 格助 下二/用 接助 名 格助 サ変/用 名 名 上二/用 名 上二/用 接助 名 ナリ形動/用
堂 に のぼる。岩 に 巌 を 重ね て 山 と し、松柏 年 旧り、土石 老い て 苔 滑かに、

名 格助 名 名 格助 上二/用 接助 名 格助 名 下二/未 助動/打/終 名 格助 四/用 名 格助 四/用 接助 名
岩上 の 院々 扉 を 閉ぢ て 物 の 音 きこえ ず。岸 を めぐり 岩 を 這ひ て 仏閣

格助 サ変/用 名 タリ形動/用 接助 名 四/体 副助 下二/終
を 拝し、佳景 寂寞と して 心 すみ行く のみ おぼゆ。

ナリ形動/語幹 接尾 間助 名 格助 四/体 名 格助 名
閑か さや 岩 に しみ入る 蝉 の 声

14

Tales of Moonlight and Rain

Ueda Akinari (1734–1809), a *waka* and *haikai* poet, *kokugaku* scholar, novelist, and practitioner of the tea ceremony, was born in Osaka. An illegitimate child, he was abandoned by his mother when he was four and adopted by Ueda Mosuke, a merchant. At an early age, Akinari contracted polio, which crippled both his hands. In 1771, having lost his property and home in a fire, he decided to become a doctor. Five years later, at the age of forty-three, he returned to Osaka, established a medical practice, and published *Tales of Moonlight and Rain* (*Ugetsu monogatari*), which became his most noted work.

Tales of Moonlight and Rain, which was published under the pseudonym Senshi Kijin, consists of nine stories, each of which draws from Chinese and Japanese sources, particularly *New Tales of Lamplight* (*Jiandeng xinhua*, J. *Sentō shinwa*, ca. 1378), a Ming collection of classical short stories of the supernatural, and *San yan* (J. *Sangen*), three late Ming (early seventeenth century) anthologies of Chinese vernacular short stories.

In the following short story, "Cauldron of Kibitsu" (Kibitsu no kama), Shōtarō, the profligate son of the Izawa family, marries the virtuous Kasada Isora, daughter of a priest of the Kibitsu Shrine. Shōtarō's parents arrange the wedding in the hope that Isora will reform him, but instead he leaves her for another woman (Sode) and runs off to live in the capital, settling in a room next to Sode's cousin, Hikoroku. Shōtarō also tricks Isora into giving Sode money. Sode suddenly becomes ill and dies, and Isora's angry spirit appears before Shōtarō. Terrified, Shōtarō consults with Hikoroku, who advises him to visit an *on'yōji* (yin-yang) priest, who tells Shōtarō that Isora died seven days earlier and that he will have to endure forty-two days of ritual abstinence (*mono-imi*), staying in a room protected by the priest's amulets and spells. Although Shōtarō's name is not mentioned until later in this excerpt, he is the subject of many of the sentences in the first passage.

The text is based on Nakamura Yukihiko, ed., *Ueda Akinari shū*, Nihon koten bungaku taikei 56 (Tokyo: Iwanami Shoten, 1959), 95–97, with minor orthographic changes.

『雨月物語』

「吉備津の釜」

「1」

其の夜三更の比おそろしき声して「あな憎や。ここに尊き符文を設けつるよ」とつぶやきて復び声なし。おそろしさのあまりに長き夜をかこつ。程なく夜明けぬるに生き出でて、急ぎ彦六が方の壁を敲きて昨夜の事をかたる。彦六もはじめて陰陽師が詞を奇なりとして、おのれも其の夜は寝ずして三更の比を待ち暮れける。松ふく風物を倒すがごとく、雨さへふりて常ならぬ夜のさまに、壁を隔てて声をかけあひ、既に四更に至る。下屋の窓の紙にさと赤き光さして、「あな悪やここにも貼しつるよ」と言ふ声、深き夜にはいとど凄しく、髪も生毛もことごとく聳立ちて、しばらくは死に入りたり。明くれば夜のさまをかたり、暮るれば明くるを慕ひて、此の月日頃千歳を過ぐるよりも久し。かの鬼も夜ごとに家を繞り或は屋の棟に叫びて、忿れる声夜ましにすさまし。

「2」

かくして四十二日といふ其の夜に至りぬ。今は一夜にみたしぬれば、殊に慎みて、やや五更の天も白々と明けわたりぬ。長き夢のさめたる如く、やがて彦六をよぶに、壁によりて「いかに」と答ふ。「おもき物忌みも既に満てぬ。絶えて兄長の面を見ず。なつかしさに、かつ此の月頃の憂さ怕ろしさを心のかぎり言ひ和さまん。眠さまし給へ。我も外の方に出でん」と言ふ。彦六用意なき男なれば、「今は何かあらん。いざこなたへわたり給へ」と、戸を明くる事半ばならず、となりの軒に「あなや」と叫ぶ声耳を貫きて、思はず尻居に座す。こは正太郎が身のうへにこそと、斧引き提げて大路に出づれば、明けたると言ひし夜はいまだくらく、月は中天ながら影朧々として、風冷やかに、さて正太郎が戸は明けはなして其の人は見えず。内にや逃げ入りつらんと走り入りて見れども、いづくに竄るべき住居にもあらねば、大路にや倒れけんと求むれども、其のわたりには物もなし。いかになりつるやと、あるいは異しみ、或は恐る恐る、ともし火を挑げてここかしこを見廻るに、明けたる戸腋の壁に腥々しき血灌ぎ流れて地につたふ。されど屍も骨も見えず。月あかりに見れば、軒の端にものあり。ともし火を捧げて照し見るに、男の髪の髻ばかりか

かりて、外には露ばかりのものもなし。浅ましくもおそろしさは筆につくすべうもあらず
なん。夜も明けてちかき野山を探し求むれども、つひに其の跡さへなくてやみぬ。

　此の事井沢が家へも言ひおくりぬれば、涙ながらに香央にも告げしらせぬ。されば
陰陽師が占のいちじるき、御釜の凶しき祥もはたたがはざりけるぞ、いともたふとかりける
とかたり伝へけり。

Vocabulary for Section 1

吉備津の釜 (きびつのかま) (*proper n.*) area in present-day Okayama City. Kibitsu is the site of a shrine famous for a divination ritual, involving a *kama* (cauldron). At the beginning of this story, when the two families that have arranged for their children to be wed conduct this ritual, the cauldron silently comes to a boil, a bad omen.

三更 (さんかう) (*n.*) third watch, hour of the rat (11:00 P.M.–1:00 A.M.) (The night is divided into five *kō*, or watches: first watch [*shokō*], hour of the dog [7:00–9:00 P.M.]; second watch [*nikō*], hour of the boar [9:00–11:00 P.M.]; third watch [*sankō*], hour of the rat [11:00 P.M.–1:00 A.M.]; fourth watch [*shikō*], hour of the ox [1:00–3:00 A.M.]; and fifth watch [*gokō*], hour of the tiger [3:00–5:00 A.M.].)

符文 (ふもん) (*n.*) charm written on an amulet (*o-fuda*) (Shōtarō receives a number of these charms from the *on'yōji* to protect him from Isora's angry spirit.)

つぶやく (呟く) (*tr. v. YD*) to mutter, murmur, grumble

かこつ (託つ) (*tr. v. YD*) to complain, gripe about

程なし (ほど) (*ku adj.*) (time) brief

生き出づ (いい) (*intr. v. SN*) to come back to life, recover consciousness

昨夜 (よべ) (*n.*) last night, night before

陰陽師 (おんやうじ) (*n.*) (also *onmyōji*) yin-yang priest, diviner (He issues protective amulets and tells Shōtarō how to avoid punishment by evil spirits.)

詞 (ことば) (*n.*) words (the *on'yōji*'s predictions that Isora's spirit would come to haunt Shōtarō and that the amulets would protect him if he put them on the walls)

奇 (き) (*nari adj. v.*) unusual, rare

待ち暮る (まく) (*comp. v.*) to wait for, spend the day waiting for

隔つ (へだ) (*tr. v. SN*) to place something in between in order to separate or cut off

かけあふ (掛け合ふ) (*tr. v. YD*) to do mutually (here, to call to each other)

下屋 (しもや) (*n.*) room off the main living quarters (*moya*), usually used by people of low status (This is Shōtarō's shabby room.)

さと (*adv.*) suddenly, quickly

いとど (*adv.*) more and more, increasingly

凄し (すさま) (*shiku adj.*) (usually *susamaji*) desolate, bleak

生毛 (うぶげ) (*n.*) downy hair (on one's cheek, back of one's neck, etc.)

ことごとく (事事く, 悉く) (*adv.*) altogether, entirely, completely

聳立つ (そばた) (*intr. v. YD*) (hair) to stand up (out of fear)

死に入る (しいい) (*intr. v. YD*) to faint, lose consciousness

かの (*attrib.*) refers to people and things at a distance

～ごと (毎) (*suffix*) each ～, every ～

棟 (むね) (*n.*) ridge, ridgepole (highest part of a roof)

叫ぶ (さけ) (*intr. v. YD*) to scream, shout

まし (増し) (*n.*) increase

Grammar Notes for Section 1

其の夜 (そよ) first night of the forty-two days of ritual abstinence

あな憎や (にく) voice of Isora's ghost, infuriated by the protective amulets placed on the walls

彦六が方 (ひころくかた) "Hikoroku's place (*kata*)": Hikoroku is the cousin of Shōtarō's mistress, Sode. Now Hikoroku and Shōtarō are neighbors, living in rooms separated by a wall.

おのれも其の夜は寝ずして　hum. first-person pron. *onore* (used by Hikoroku to refer to himself)

雨さへふりて　adv. p. *sae*, indicating that on top of everything, something else happened

貼しつるよ　RY of tr. YD v. *osu*, "to attach," RT of perfective aux. v. *tsu*, and interj. p. *yo*

暮るれば明くるを慕ひて　"*When* it grew dark, he longed for it to grow light."

怨れる声夜ましにすさまし　here *yo mashi ni* is a comp. adv., meaning "increasing with each passing night"

Annotated Grammar for Section 1

其 の 夜 三更 の 比 おそろしき 声 して 「あな 憎 や。ここ に 尊き 符文 を 設け

つる よ」 と つぶやき て 復び 声 なし。おそろし さ の あまりに 長き 夜 を かこつ。

程なく 夜 明け ぬる に 生き出で て、急ぎ 彦六 が 方 の 壁 を 敲き て 昨夜 の 事 を

かたる。彦六 も はじめて 陰陽師 が 詞 を 奇なり と して、おのれ も 其 の 夜 は

寝 ず して 三更 の 比 を 待ち暮れ ける。松 ふく 風物 を 倒す が ごとく、雨

さへ ふり て 常なら ぬ 夜 の さまに、壁 を 隔て て 声 を かけあひ、既に 四更 に

至る。下屋 の 窓 の 紙 に さと 赤き 光 さして、「あな 悪 や ここ に も 貼し つる

よ」 と 言ふ 声、深き 夜 に は いとど 凄しく、髪 も 生毛 も ことごとく 聳立ち て、

しばらく は 死に入り たり。明くれ ば 夜 の さま を かたり、暮るれ ば 明くる を 慕ひ

て、此 の 月日 頃 千歳 を 過ぐる より も 久し。かの 鬼 も 夜ごと に 家 を 繞り

或は 屋 の 棟 に 叫び て、怨れ る 声 夜ましに すさまし。

Vocabulary for Section 2

かく（斯く）　(*adv.*) in this way

四十二日　(*n.*) forty-two days (The *on'yōji* tells Shōtarō that Isora died seven days earlier, which leaves a total of forty-two days before her spirit will be reborn. According to Buddhist belief, the spirits of the deceased remain on earth for forty-nine days, during which time they are appeased every seven days with Buddhist rituals, such as the reading of sutras.)

みたす　(*tr. v. YD*) to complete, make full

慎む　(*tr. v. YD*) to be very cautious, be abstinent or restrained

やや　(*adv.*) gradually, eventually

さむ（覚む・醒む）　(*intr. v. SN*) to wake up, revive

やがて　(*adv.*) immediately, soon after

物忌み　(*n.*) voluntary confinement

満つ　(*intr. v. SN*) to become full

絶えて (*adv.*) (followed by neg.) (not) at all, (not) a bit

兄長 (*n.*) eldest son, older brother or sister

面 (*n.*) face

かつ (且つ) (*conj.*) as well as, furthermore, in addition

憂さ (*n.*) sorrow, grief, distress

怕ろし (*shiku adj.*) frightening

言ひ和さむ (*intr. v. YD*) to talk about something until one feels better

用意 (*n.*) care, concern, attention

いざ (*interj.*) used when inviting someone to do something: How about . . . ?

貫く (*tr. v. YD*) to pierce, run through

尻居 (*n.*) falling back on one's buttocks

こは (此は) (*interj.*) What's this!?

身の上 (*n.*) one's life, fate, fortune, circumstances

影 (影・景) (*n.*) light (of sun, moon, fire, etc.)

朧々 (*tari adj. v.*) hazy, blurred, dim, misty

さて (*conj.*) then, next, as a result

明けはなす (*tr. v. YD*) to leave open

求む (*tr. v. SN*) to seek out, look for

わたり (辺り) (*n.*) vicinity, surroundings

あるいは (或は) (*attrib.*) (usually in the pattern *aruiwa . . . aruiwa . . .*) certain (thing), certain (time), certain (situation)

異しむ (*tr. v. YD*) to find something odd, strange, to doubt or mistrust

ともし火 (灯し火) (*n.*) lamp, lantern

挑ぐ (*tr. v. SN*) to lift up high

ここかしこ (此処彼処) (*pron.*) here and there, all over

戸腋 (*n.*) part of the wall next to the door

腥々し (*shiku adj.*) fresh, vivid, raw

灌ぎ流る (*intr. v. SN*) to flow, drip, run

つたふ (伝ふ) (*intr. v. YD*) to pass from one place to another

されど (*conj.*) although, nevertheless, however

軒の端 (*set phrase*) edge (*tsuma*) of the eaves (*noki*)

髻 (*n.*) topknot

浅まし (*shiku adj.*) unexpected, astonishing

井沢 (*proper n.*) Shōtarō was the only son of the Izawa family, from Kibi Province, in present-day Okayama.

言ひおくる (言ひ送る) (*tr. v. YD*) to report, transmit a message personally

香央 (*proper n.*) Shōtarō's wife, Isora, came from the Kasada family, who lived at the shrine at Kibitsu.

占 (*n.*) augury, divination, omen

いちじるし (著し) (*shiku adj.*) (from *ichishirushi*) striking, marked, conspicuous (the implication being that the omens turned out to be accurate)

凶し (*shiku adj.*) bad, evil

祥 (*n.*) sign of future occurrence, omen

はた (将) (*adv.*) definitely, no doubt

いとも (*adv.*) truly, completely, absolutely

Grammar Notes for Section 2

一夜にみたしぬれば   RY of tr. YD v. *mitasu*, "to complete." The subject of *mitasu* is *monoimi*, "ritual abstinence."

「いかに」と答ふ   interj. *ikani* (used when calling to someone), "hey there," case p. *to*, and SS of intr. SN v. *kotau*, "to reply"

心のかぎり言ひ和さまん   *kokoro no kagiri*, meaning "to one's heart's content"

何かあらん   rhetorical question: "What could be out there?! (Nothing.)"

半ばならず   "before the door was even halfway open . . ."

正太郎が身のうへにこそと   *mi-no-ue*, "person's situation, status," and case p. *ni*; *koso* at the end of the quotation implies that the rest of the sentence—something like *nani ka arame*, "something must have happened!"—has been abbreviated; citational *to* indicates that these are Hikoroku's thoughts: "Something must have happened to Shōtarō, he thought."

明けたると言ひし夜   RY of intr. SN v. *aku*, "to grow light," and RT of perfective aux. v. *tari*

中天ながら   n. *nakazora*, "sky, overhead," and concessive conj. p. *nagara*, "although"

内にや逃げ入りつらん   RY of intr. YD v. *nige-iru*, "to escape into"

いづくに竄るべき住居にもあらねば   pron. *izuku*, "somewhere," SS of intr. SN v. *kakuru*, "to hide," RT of pot. aux. v. *beshi*, RY of copular *nari*, bound p. *mo*, and MZ of RH suppl. v. *ari*

大路にや倒れけん   n. *ōji*, "street," case p. *ni*, doubt case p. *ya*, RY of intr. SN v. *taoru*, "to fall," and RT of past-spec. aux. v. *kemu*, tied to *ya*

いかになりつるや   adv. *ikani*, "what sort of thing," RY of intr. YD v. *naru*, "to become," RT of perfective aux. v. *tsu*, and interj. p. *ya*

露ばかりのものもなし   comp. *tsuyu-bakari* "a little." When *tsuyu*, literally "dew" but meaning a small amount, is followed by a neg., it means "not at all." *Bakari* is an adv. p. of extent.

筆につくすべうもあらずなん   SS of tr. YD v. *tsukusu*, "to do something fully," RY of pot. aux. v. *beshi* (*u*-sound change from *beku* to *beu*, pronounced *byō*), MZ of confidence aux. v. *nu*, and SS of spec. aux. v. *mu*. The author says that there is no way he could fully express the terror of this scene in words.

Annotated Grammar for Section 2

かくして 四十二日 と いふ 其 の 夜 に 至り ぬ 。今 は 一夜 に みたし ぬれ ば、

殊に 慎み て、やや 五更 の 天 も 白々と 明け わたり ぬ 。長き 夢 の さめ たる

如く、やがて 彦六 を よぶ に、壁 に よりて 「いかに」と 答ふ。「おもき 物忌み も 既に

満て ぬ。絶えて 兄長 の 面 を 見 ず。なつかし さ に、かつ 此 の 月頃 の

憂 さ 怕ろし さ を 心 の かぎり 言ひ和さ ん。眠 さまし 給へ。我 も 外 の

方 に 出で ん」と 言ふ。彦六 用意 なき 男 なれ ば、「今 は 何 か あら

ん。いざ こなた へ わたり 給へ」と、戸 を 明くる 事 半ば なら ず、となり

の 軒 に 「あな や」と 叫ぶ 声耳 を 貫き て、思は ず 尻居 に 座す。こは 正太郎

が 身 の うへ に こそ と、斧 引き提げ て 大路 に 出づれ ば、明け たる と 言ひ
し 夜 は いまだ くらく、月 は 中天 ながら 影 朧々と して、風 冷やかに、さて 正太郎
が 戸 は 明けはなし て 其の 人 は 見え ず。内 に や 逃げ入り つ
らん と 走り入り て 見れ ども、いづく に 竄る べき 住居 に も あら ね
ば、大路 に や 倒れ けん と 求むれ ども、其の わたり に は 物 も なし。
いかに なり つる や と、或は 異しみ、或は 恐る恐る、ともし火 を 挑げ て ここかしこ
を 見廻る に、明け たる 戸腋 の 壁 に 腥々しき 血 灌ぎ流れ て 地 に つたふ。されど
屍 も 骨 も 見え ず。月あかり に 見れ ば、軒 の 端 に もの あり。ともし火 を 捧げ
て 照し見る に、男 の 髪 の 髻 ばかり かかり て、外 に は 露ばかり の もの も なし。
浅ましく も おそろし さ は 筆 に つくす べう も あら ず なん。夜 も 明け て
ちかき 野山 を 探し求むれ ども、つひに 其の 跡 さへ なくて やみ ぬ。
此 の 事 井沢 が 家 へ も 言ひおくり ぬれ ば、涙 ながら に 香央 に も
告げしらせ ぬ。されば 陰陽師 が 占 の いちじるき、御釜 の 凶しき 祥 も はた たがは
ざり ける ぞ、いとも たふとかり ける と かたり 伝へ けり。

15

The Tale of Genji, a Small Jeweled Comb

Motoori Norinaga (1730–1801) was born in Matsusaka in Ise Province (present-day Mie Prefecture), the second son of Ozu Sadatoshi, a wholesale cotton-goods merchant. Norinaga found that he was not suited to be a merchant, and in 1752 he went to Kyoto to study medicine. At that time he changed his surname to Motoori. In Kyoto he read the Chinese classics under Hori Keizan (1688–1757), a Confucian scholar and a friend of Ogyū Sorai (1666–1728), the founder of the Ancient Rhetoric School. Keizan then introduced Norinaga to the commentaries of Keichū (1640–1701), whose philological methodology was a cornerstone of much of Norinaga's own work.

In 1757 Norinaga returned to Matsusaka to practice medicine, and around this time he produced his first treatise, "A Small Boat Punting Through the Reeds" (Ashiwake obune), an essay on *waka*. In the following year, he began giving lectures on *The Tale of Genji* and wrote "Defense of Awaré" (Aware ben), a short piece in which he introduced his theory that *aware* (often translated as "pathos") is the underlying theme of Japanese literature and transcends differences of genre. In 1796 Norinaga wrote *The Tale of Genji, a Small Jeweled Comb* (*Genji monogatari tama no ogushi*), a revision of an earlier work on *The Tale of Genji* entitled *Shibun yōryō*. In the passage included here, Norinaga famously argues that *monogatari* should operate according to a value system different from that of Confucian and Buddhist views of morality, and he supports his theory by citing Murasaki Shikibu's own views on the *monogatari* as presented in the "Fireflies" (Hotaru) chapter of *The Tale of Genji*.

The text is based on Nakamura Yukihiko, ed., *Kinsei bungaku ronshū*, Nihon koten bungaku taikei 94 (Tokyo: Iwanami Shoten, 1966), 93, 101–102, 106–107, with minor orthographic changes.

『源氏物語玉の小櫛』

「大むね」

此の物語のおほむね、むかしより説どもあれども、みな物語といふもののこころばへをたづねずして、ただよのつねの儒仏などの書のおもむきをもて、論ぜられたるは、作りぬしの本意にあらず。たまたまかの儒仏などの書と、おのづからは似たるこころ、合へる趣もあれども、そをとらへてすべてをいふべきにはあらず。大かたの趣は、かのたぐひとは、いたく異なるものにて、すべて物語は、又別に物がたりの一つの趣のあることにして、はじめにもいささかいへるがごとし。…

　然らば物語にて、人の心しわざのよきあしきは、いかなるぞといふに、大かた物のあはれをしり、なさけ有て、よの中の人の情にかなへるを、よしとし、物のあはれをしらず、なさけなくて、よの人のこころにかなはざるをわろしとはせり。かくいへば、儒仏などの道の善悪と、いとしも異なるけぢめなきがごとくなれども、こまかにいはむには、世の人の情にかなふとかなはざるとの中にも、儒仏の善悪とは、合はざることもおほく、又すべてよしあしを論むることも、ただなだらかにやはらびて、儒者などの議論のやうに、ひたぶるにせまりたることはなし。

　さて物語は、物のあはれをしるをむねとはしたるに、そのすぢにいたりては、儒仏の教へには、そむける事もおほきぞかし。そはまづ人の情の、物に感ずる事には、善悪邪正さまざまある中に、ことわりにたがへる事には、感ずまじきわざなれども、情は、我ながらわが心にもまかせぬことありて、おのづからしのびがたきふし有て、感ずることあるもの也。

　源氏の君のうへにていはば、空蝉の君・朧月夜の君・藤つぼの中宮などに心をかけて、逢ひ給へるは、儒仏などの道にていはむには、よにうへもなき、いみじき不義悪行なれば、ほかにいかばかりのよき事あらむにても、よき人とはいひがたかるべきに、その不義悪行なるよしをば、さしもたててはいはずして、ただそのあひだの、もののあはれのふかきかたを、かへすがへす書きのべて、源氏の君をば、むねとよき人の本として、よき事のかぎりを、此の君のうへに、とりあつめたる、これ物語の大むねにして、そのよきあしきは、儒仏などの書の善悪と、かはりあるけぢめ也。

　さりとて、かのたぐひの不義を、よしとするにはあらず。そのあしきことは、今さらい

はでもしるく、さるたぐひの罪(つみ)を論(ろん)ずることは、おのづからそのかたの書(ふみ)どもの、よにここらあれば、物(もの)どほき物語(ものがたり)をまつべきにあらず。

物語(ものがたり)は、儒仏(じゆぶつ)などの、したたかなる道(みち)のやうに、まよひをはなれて、さとりに入(い)るべきのりにもあらず。又国(またくに)をも家(いへ)をも身(み)をも、をさむべきをしへにもあらず。ただよの中(なか)のものがたりなるがゆゑに、さるすぢの善悪(ぜんあく)の論(あげつらひ)は、しばらくさしおきて、さしもかかはらず、ただ物(もの)のあはれをしれるかたのよきを、とりたててよしとはしたる也(なり)。此(こ)のこころばへを、物(もの)にたとへていはば、蓮(はす)をうゑてめでむとする人(ひと)の、濁(にご)りてきたなくはあれども、泥水(ひぢみづ)をたくはふるがごとし。物語(ものがたり)に不義(ふぎ)なる恋(こひ)を書(か)けるも、そのにごれる泥(ひぢ)を、めでてにはあらず、物(もの)のあはれの花(はな)をさかせん料(れう)ぞかし。

Vocabulary for Paragraph 1

玉の小櫛 (*proper n.*) lit., "small jeweled comb." Norinaga's commentary on *The Tale of Genji* takes its name from a *waka* in which he compares his commentary to a comb that will untangle the essence of the past (*sono kami no kokoro*) from mistaken interpretations (*midaretaru suji*).

大むね (*n.*) main point

説 (*n.*) interpretation, view, teaching

こころばへ (心ばへ) (*n.*) meaning, gist, purport

儒仏 (*n.*) Confucianism and Buddhism

おもむき (趣) (*n.*) meaning, purport, point

作りぬし (作り主) (*n.*) creator, author

おのづから (自ら) (*adv.*) by coincidence, accidentally

たぐひ (類) (*n.*) things of a similar kind, sort, type

いささか (聊か) (*adv.*) slightly, just a little, somewhat

Grammar Notes for Paragraph 1

おもむきをもて *mote*, a sound change from *mochi* (RY of tr. YD v. *motsu*, "to use") and conj. p. *te*; following case p. *o*, *mote* functions like a case p. expressing means or method

かの pron. *ka*, "that, those," and attrib. case p. *no*

そをとらへて pron. *so*, "that, those," referring to what happens to resemble or accord with the spirit of Buddhist and Confucian texts

はじめにも This last line refers to the fact that Norinaga makes a similar point in the opening lines of *Tama no ogushi*, not in this excerpt.

Annotated Grammar for Paragraph 1

此 の 物語 の おほむね、むかし より 説 ども あれ ども、みな 物語 と いふ もの の こころばへ を たづね ず して、ただ よ の つね の 儒仏 など の 書 の おもむき を もて 論ぜ られ たる は、作りぬし の 本意 に あら ず。たまたま か の 儒仏 など の 書 と、おのづから は 似 たる こころ、合へ る 趣 も あれ ども、そ を とらへ て、すべて を いふ べき に は あら ず。大かた の 趣 は、か の たぐひ と は、いたく 異なる もの に て、すべて 物語 は、又 別に 物がたり の 一つ の 趣 の ある こと に して、はじめ に も いささか いへ る が ごとし。

Modern Japanese for Paragraph 1

この（源氏）物語 のおよその趣旨については、昔から、いろいろな説があるけれども、皆物語 というものの趣意を探らないで、ただ世間一般の儒教・仏教などの書物の趣意によって、論 じておられるのは、（物語の）作者の本来の意思（に副うもの）ではない。たまにそうした儒

仏などの書物と、偶然に似た精神、合っている趣意もあるけれども、それを取り上げて、（物語の）全般を（かれこれ）いうべきではない。大体の趣意は、そういう（儒仏の）類とは、ひどく違うものであって、総じて物語は、また別に物語（特有）の一つの趣意があるのであって、（そのことは）初めにも、少し述べたとおりである。

Vocabulary for Paragraphs 2–6

物のあはれ (comp.) deeply moving (aware) aspect of things and events in the human and natural worlds

かなふ (適ふ・叶ふ) (intr. v. YD) to be appropriate, suitable, fitting

いとしも (comp.) (followed by neg.) (not) that much

けぢめ (n.) distinction, difference

なだらか (nari adj. v.) calm, gentle

やはらぶ (和らぶ・柔らぶ) (intr. v. YD) to relax, be calm

ひたぶる (頓・一向) (nari adj. v.) single-minded

せまる (迫る) (intr. v. YD) to approach

そむく (背く) (intr. v. YD) to turn one's back on

邪正 (じやしやう) (n.) evil and good, wrong and right

しのぶ (忍ぶ) (tr. v. KN, YD) to bear, endure, repress (an emotion)

ふし (節) (n.) (1) occasion, moment, (2) item, point, reason

源氏の君 (げんじきみ) (proper n.) Lord Genji, hero of Genji monogatari

空蝉の君・朧月夜の君・藤つぼの中宮 (うつせみきみ・おぼろづきよきみ・ふぢつぼのちゆうぐう) (proper n.) Utsusemi, Oborozukiyo, and Empress Fujitsubo, all female characters and Genji's love interests in the tale

いかばかり (如何許) (adv.) how much, to what extent, to what degree

たつ (立つ) (tr. v. SN) to make stand (here, meaning "to point out")

むね (宗) (n.) main point

本 (ほん) (n.) base, essence, foundation

さりとて (conj.) be that as it may, even so, nevertheless

ここら (幾許) (adv.) a lot, often, to a great degree, extremely (here, meaning "there are a lot of writings in the world that deal with such things")

物どほし (もの) (shiku adj.) distant, remote

したたか (nari adj. v.) serious, solemn-looking, dependable

のり (法) (n.) teaching, doctrine

論 (あげつらひ) (n.) critical examination, treatise

さしも (adv.) (followed by neg.) (not even) that much, that far

蓮 (はす) (n.) lotus

うう (植う) (tr. v. SN) to plant (a seed, seedling)

めづ (愛づ) (tr. v. SN) to praise highly

泥 (ひぢ) (n.) mud, dirt, sludge

たくはふ (蓄ふ) (tr. v. SN) to store up, keep

料 (れう) (n.) objective, purpose, reason

Grammar Notes for Paragraphs 2–6

いかなるぞといふに　Here, conj. p. *ni* simply links v. *iu* to what follows: "When speaking about what kind . . ."

わろしとはせり　SS of *shiku* adj. *waroshi*, "bad," case p. *to*, bound p. *wa*, MZ of SH v. *su*, "to consider," and SS of cont. aux. v. *ri*

さしもたててはいはずして　"without taking it up (*tate-te*) that much (*sa-shi-mo*) and mentioning it (*iwa-zu*)"

むねとはしたるに　"although they have made it their main concern . . ."

我ながらわが心にもまかせぬことありて　Here, *ware nagara* means "despite oneself" or "though one knows better."

今さらいはでもしるく　adv. *imasara*, "again, afresh, anew," MZ of YD v. *iu*, "to say," neg. conj. p. *de*, bound p. *mo*, and RY of *ku* adj. *shirushi*, "to be quite clear"

Annotated Grammar for Paragraphs 2–6

接　　名　　格助　名　格助　名　名　格助　ク形/体　シク形/体　係助　ナリ形動/体　係助　格助　四/体　接助　　副
然らば 物語 にて、人 の 心 しわざ の よき あしき は、いかなる ぞ と いふ に、大かた

名　格助　名　格助　四/用　接助　名　ラ変/用 接助　名 格助 名 格助 名 格助 名 格助 四/已 助動/存/体 格助 ク形/終
物 の あはれ を しり、なさけ 有り て、よ の 中 の 人 の 情 に かなへ る を、よし

格助　サ変/用 名　格助　名・格助　四/未　助動/打/用　名　ク形/用 接助 名 格助 名 格助 名 格助 四/未
と し、物 の あはれ を しら ず、なさけ なく て、よ の 人 の こころ に かなは

助動/打/体 格助　ク形/終 格助 係助 サ変/未 助動/存/終　副　四/已 接助 名　副助　格助 名 格助 名 格助　副
ざる を、わろし と は せ り。かく いへ ば、儒仏 など の 道 の 善悪 と、いと

副助　ナリ形動/体　名　ク形/体 格助 助動/比/用 助動/断/已 接助　ナリ形動/用 四/未 助動/仮/用 格助 係助 名 格助 名 格助
しも 異なる けぢめ なき が ごとく なれ ども、こまかに いは む に は、世 の 人 の

名 格助 四/体 格助 四/未 助動/打/体 格助 格助 名 格助 係助 名 格助 名 格助 係助 四/未 助動/打/体 名
情 に かなふ と かなは ざる と の 中 に も、儒仏 の 善悪 と は、合は ざる こと

係助 ク形/用 副　副　名・格助 下二/体 名 係助 副 ナリ形動/用 四/用 接助 名 副助
も おほく、又 すべて よしあし を 論むる こと も、ただ なだらかに やはらび て、儒者 など

格助 名　格助　名・助動/断/用　ナリ形動/用 四/用 助動/存/体 名 係助 ク形/終
の 議論 の やう に、ひたぶるに せまり たる こと は なし。

接　　名　係助　名 格助　名・格助 四/体 格助 名 格助 係助 サ変/用 助動/存/体 接助 代 格助 名 格助
さて 物語 は、物 の あはれ を しる を、むね と は し たる に、その すぢ に

四/用 接助 係助 名 格助 名・格助 係助 四/已 助動/存続/体 名 係助 ク形/体 係助 終助 代 係助 副 名
いたり て は、儒仏 の 教へ に は、そむけ る 事 も おほき ぞ かし。そ は まづ 人

格助 名 格助 名 格助 サ変/体 名 格助 係助　名　　名　　ラ変/体 名 格助　名　格助 四/已
の 情 の、物 に 感ずる 事 には、善悪邪正 さまざま ある 中 に、ことわり に たがへ

助動/存/体 名 格助 サ変/終 助動/打当/体 名 助動/断/已 接助 名 係助 代 接助 代 格助 名 格助 係助 下二/未
る 事 には、感ず まじき わざ なれ ども、情 は、我 ながら わ が 心 に も まかせ

助動/打/体 名 ラ変/用 接助 副 四/用 ク形/体 名 ラ変/用 接助 サ変/体 名 ラ変/体 名
ぬ こと あり て、おのづから しのび がたき ふし 有り て、感ずる こと ある もの

助動/断/終
也。

固名　格助 名 格助 四/未 接助 固名　　固名　　固名　　副助 格助 名 格助 下二/用
源氏の君 の うへ にて いは ば、空蝉の君・朧月夜の君・藤つぼの中宮 など に 心 を かけ

接助 四/用 補助/尊/已 助動/完/体 係助 名 副助 格助 名 格助 四/未 助動/婉/体 格助 係助 副 名 係助 ク形/体
て、逢ひ 給へ る は、儒仏 など の 道 にて いは む に は、よに うへ も なき、

シク形/体　名・　助動/断/已 接助 名 格助 副 格助 ク形/体 名 ラ変/未 助動/仮/体 格助 係助 ク形/体
いみじき 不義悪行 なれ ば、ほか に いかばかり の よき 事 あら む にて も、よき

名 格助 係助 四/用 ク形/体 助動/当/体 接助 代 格助 名 助動/断/体 名 格助 係助（は）　副　下二/用 接助
人 と は いひ がたかる べき に、その 不義悪行 なる よし を ば、さしも たてて

は いは ず して、ただ その あひだ の、もの の あはれ の ふかき かた を、

かへすがへす 書き のべ て、源氏の君 を ば、むねと よき 人 の 本 と して、よき

事 の かぎり を、此 の 君 の うへ に、とりあつめ たる、これ 物語 の 大むね に

して、その よき あしき は、儒仏 など の 書 の 善悪 と、かはり ある けぢめ 也。

さりとて、か の たぐひ の 不義 を、よし と する に は あら ず。その

あしき こと は、今さら いは で も しるく、さる たぐひ の 罪 を 論ずる こと は、

おのづから その かた の 書 ども の、よに ここら あれ ば、物どほき 物語 を まつ

べき に あら ず。

物語 は、儒仏 など の、したたかなる 道 の やう に、まよひ を はなれ て、さとり

に 入る べき のり に も あら ず。又 国 を も 家 を も 身 を も、をさむ

べき をしへ に も あら ず。ただ よ の 中 の ものがたり なる が ゆゑ に、

さる すぢ の 善悪 の 論 は、しばらく さしおき て、さしも かかはら ず、ただ 物 の

あはれ を しれ る かた の よき を、とりたて て よし と は し たる 也。此

の こころばへ を、物 に たとへ て いは ば、蓮 を うゑ て めで む と する 人 の、

濁り て きたなく は あれ ども、泥水 を たくはふる が ごとし。物語 に 不義 なる 恋

を 書け る も、その にごれ る 泥 を めで て に は あら ず、物 の

あはれ の 花 を さか せ ん 料 ぞ かし。

Modern Japanese for Paragraphs 2–6

それでは物語（ものがたり）において、人（ひと）の心（こころ）や行為（こうい）のよいわるいは、どんなものかというと、だいたい「もののあはれ」を知（し）り、情味（じょうみ）があって、世間（せけん）の人々（ひとびと）の人情（にんじょう）にあてはまっているのをよいとし、「もののあはれ」を知（し）らず、情味（じょうみ）がなくて、世間（せけん）の人々（ひとびと）の人情（にんじょう）にあてはまっていないのを、よくないとしている。このようにいうと（物語（ものがたり）における善悪（ぜんあく）は）儒仏（じゅぶつ）などの教えにいう善（ぜん）と、あまりはっきりした区別（くべつ）がないようであるが、（私（わたくし）宣長（のりなが）が）くわしく説明（せつめい）するならば、（物語（ものがたり）の善悪（ぜんあく）は）世間（せけん）の人々（ひとびと）の人情（にんじょう）に当（あ）てはまる場合（ばあい）（善（ぜん））と当（あ）てはまらない場合（ばあい）（悪（あく））が、儒仏（じゅぶつ）の善悪（ぜんあく）とは、一致（いっち）しないことも多（おお）く、またすべてよいわるいを論（ろん）ずるのでも、ただ、四角（しかく）ばらずに和（やわ）らいで、儒者（じゅしゃ）などの議論（ぎろん）のように、性急（せいきゅう）に（善（ぜん）か悪（あく）かの結論（けつろん）に）迫（せま）るということはないのである。

　さて、物語は「もののあはれ」を理解することを主旨とはしているが、その（物語の細部の）筋書きに至っては、儒教や仏教の教えには反していることも多くあるのだよ。それは、まず、人の心の働きが、物に（対して）反応する内容としては、善悪邪正などいろいろある中で、道理に反していることには、共感するはずのないことであるけれども、人の心の働きというものは、自分でも思い通りにならないところがあって、自然と押さえることができない場合があって、道理に反したことにも心を動かされることがあるものである。

　源氏の君に関して言えば、空蝉の君・朧月夜の君・藤壺の中宮などに、思いをかけてお会いになったのは、儒教や仏教などの教えから言ってみれば、まったくこの上もない、ひどい不義悪行であるから、ほかにどれほどのよいことがあったとしても、立派な人とは言いにくいはずであるが、不義悪行である事柄については、それほど取り立てて言及しないで、ただ、人間関係の「もののあはれ」の深い方面のことを繰り返し繰り返し書き記して、源氏の君を専ら立派な人のお手本としてよいことのすべてをこの君の上に取り集めてあるのが（すなわち）この源氏物語の本旨であって、その善し悪しは、儒教や仏教などの書物の善悪とは違って区別しているのである。

　そうかといって、あのような種類の不義をよいとするわけではない。その悪いことは今さら（改めて）言わなくてもはっきりしていて、そのような種類の罪を論ずることは、自然とその方面の書物などがたいそうたくさんあるので、あまり関係のない物語を待つ必要もない。物語は儒教や仏教などのいかめしい道のように、迷いを離れて悟りの境地に入るための教えでもない。また、国をも家をも身をも治めるための教えでもない。ただ、世の中のことを描いた物語であるから、儒教や仏教といった方面からの善悪についての議論はしばらくそのままにしておいて、そんなにこだわることなく、ただ「もののあはれ」を理解している方面のことがすぐれているのを、取り立ててよいことだとしているのである。このような考え方を物に例えて言うならば、蓮を植えて観賞しようとする人が、濁ってきたなくても、泥の水をためておくようなものである。物語に不義である恋のことを書いているのも、その濁った泥を観賞しようとするためではなく、「もののあはれ」という花を咲かせようとするためのものなのであるよ。

Part V

Meiji Period

16

The Encouragement of Learning

Fukuzawa Yukichi (1834–1901), the founder of Keiō University, was one of the most famous intellectuals in the Meiji period. He introduced various aspects of Western thought to Japan and advocated the abolishment of what he viewed as feudalistic aspects of Japan. Fukuzawa's major writings are *Conditions of the West* (*Seiyō jijō*), *The Encouragement of Learning* (*Gakumon no susume*), *An Outline of a Theory of Civilization* (*Bunmeiron no gairyaku*), and *Autobiography of Fukuzawa Yukichi* (*Fukuō jiden*), with much of his thought based on English utilitarianism. *The Encouragement of Learning,* which he wrote between 1872 and 1876 and which was published as a single volume in 1880, encapsulates Fukuzawa's thinking and had a large impact on early Meiji Japan. The classical Japanese is typical of Meiji writing and provides a fascinating view of various aspects of learning and knowledge at this time. The following text is from the famous opening to this book.

The text is based on Fukuzawa Yukichi, *Gakumon no susume*, rev. ed., Iwanami bunko (Tokyo: Iwanami Shoten, 1974), 11–13, with minor orthographic changes.

『学問のすすめ』

天は人の上に人を造らず人の下に人を造らずと言へり。されば天より人を生ずるには、万人は万人皆同じ位にして、生れながら貴賤上下の差別なく、万物の霊たる身と心との働きをもつて天地の間にあるよろづの物を資り、もつて衣食住の用を達し、自由自在、互ひに人の妨げをなさずして各々安楽にこの世を渡らしめ給ふの趣意なり。されども今広くこの人間世界を見渡すに、かしこき人あり、おろかなる人あり、貧しきもあり、富めるもあり、貴人もあり、下人もありて、その有様雲と泥との相違あるに似たるは何ぞや。その次第甚だ明らかなり。実語教に、人学ばざれば智なし、智なき者は愚人なりとあり。されば賢人と愚人との別は、学ぶと学ばざるとに由つて出来るものなり。また世の中にむつかしき仕事もあり、やすき仕事もあり。そのむつかしき仕事をする者を身分重き人と名づけ、やすき仕事をする者を身分軽き人といふ。すべて心を用ゐ心配する仕事はむつかしくして、手足を用ゐる力役はやすし。故に、医者、学者、政府の役人、または大なる商売をする町人、夥多の奉公人を召使ふ大百姓などは、身分重くして貴き者といふべし。身分重くして貴ければ自づからその家も富んで、下々の者より見れば及ぶべからざるやうなれども、その本を尋ぬればただその人に学問の力あるとなきとに由つてその相違も出来たるのみにて、天より定めたる約束にあらず。諺に云く、天は富貴を人に与へずしてこれをその人の働きに与ふるものなりと。されば前にも言へる通り、人は生れながらにして貴賤貧富の別なし。ただ学問を勤めて物事をよく知る者は貴人となり富人となり、無学なる者は貧人となり下人となるなり。

　学問とは、ただむつかしき字を知り、解し難き古文を読み、和歌を楽しみ、詩を作るなど、世上に実のなき文学を言ふにあらず。これらの文学も自づから人の心を悦ばしめ随分調法なるものなれども、古来世間の儒者和学者などの申すやう、さまであがめ貴むべきものにあらず。古来漢学者に世帯持の上手なる者も少なく、和歌をよくして商売に巧者なる町人も稀なり。これがため心ある町人百姓は、その子の学問に出精するを見て、やがて身代を持ち崩すならんとて親心に心配する者あり。無理ならぬことなり。畢竟その学問の実に遠くして日用の間に合はぬ証拠なり。されば今かかる実なき学問は先づ次にし、専ら勤むべきは人間普通日用に近き実学なり。譬へば、いろは四十七文字を習ひ、手紙の文言、帳合の仕方、算盤の稽古、天秤の取扱ひ等を心得、なほまた進んで学ぶべき箇条は甚だ多し。地理学とは日本国中は勿論世界万国の風土道案内なり。究理学とは天地

万物の性質を見てその働きを知る学問なり。歴史とは年代記のくはしきものにて万国古今の有様を詮索する書物なり。経済学とは一身一家の世帯より天下の世帯を説きたるものなり。修身学とは身の行ひを修め人に交はりこの世を渡るべき天然の道理を述べたるものなり。これらの学問をするに、いづれも西洋の翻訳書を取調べ、大抵の事は日本の仮名にて用を便じ、或ひは年少にして文才ある者へは横文字をも読ませ、一科一学も実事を押へ、その事に就きその物に従ひ、近く物事の道理を求めて今日の用を達すべきなり。右は人間普通の実学にて、人たる者は貴賤上下の区別なく皆悉くたしなむべき心得なれば、この心得ありて後に士農工商各々その分を尽し銘々の家業を営み、身も独立し家も独立し天下国家も独立すべきなり。

Vocabulary

天 (n.) heaven. It carries Confucian connotations of a divine principle that gives order to the universe, as well as sometimes standing in for both Chinese and Western concepts of a creator.

されば (然れば) (conj.) therefore, for that reason

生ず (tr. v. SH) to create, bring into being

万人 (n.) all people, the multitude

貴賤 (n.) high and low, noble and vulgar

上下 (n.) up and down, high and low

差別 (n.) distinction, difference

衣食住 (n.) clothing, food, and shelter

用 (n.) need, use

達す (tr. v. SH) to achieve, meet expectations

自由自在 (comp. n.) freedom, liberty

妨げ (n.) obstacle

趣意 (n.) reason, purpose, objective

貴人 (n.) (also kijin) people of high status

下人 (n.) people of low status

相違 (n.) difference, disparity

次第 (n.) reason, circumstances behind something

甚だ (adv.) extremely, very

実語教 (proper n.) children's primer based on selections from the Confucian classics and compiled in the late Heian period. It was widely used to teach children the virtues of scholarship and ethical behavior from the Kamakura through the early Meiji period.

力役 (n.) manual labor, heavy physical work

故に (n.) reason, cause, circumstances

奉公人 (n.) servants

大百姓 (n.) prominent farmer

自づから (adv.) naturally, of its own accord

下々 (n.) people of low status, hoi polloi

諺 (n.) proverb

富貴 (n.) wealth and honor

解す (tr. v. SH) to understand, interpret

古文 (n.) old texts, ancient writings

世上 (n.) world, society

実 (n.) practical value

随分 (adv.) quite, very

調法 (adj. v.) useful, handy

儒者和学者 (n.) scholars of Confucian and Japanese learning.

あがむ (崇む) (tr. v. SN) to respect, admire

世帯持 (n.) management of one's household affairs

出精す (intr. v. SH) to devote oneself to, concentrate energy on

やがて (adv.) soon

身代 (n.) one's fortune

持ち崩す (tr. v. YD) to squander, to use up

畢竟 (adv.) after all, in the end

日用 (n.) daily use

証拠 (n.) proof, evidence

専ら (adv.) devotedly, intently

いろは四十七文字 (n.) forty-seven-character syllabary, called the iroha after the poem (attributed to Priest Kūkai) using each character without repeating it

文言 (n.) phrases, wording

帳合 (n.) balancing a ledger, keeping financial records

算盤 (n.) abacus

稽古 (n.) training, lessons

天秤 (n.) scales

箇条 (*n.*) items, subjects

風土 (*n.*) climate, natural features of a region

道案内 (*n.*) guide

究理学 (*n.*) Western science in general, physics in particular

年代記 (*n.*) chronicles, annals

詮索する (*tr. v. SH*) to inquire into, examine

修身学 (*n.*) ethics, moral training

年少 (*n.*) young person

横文字 (*n.*) Western languages

一科一学 (*n.*) each academic discipline

悉く (*adv.*) all, without exception

たしなむ (嗜む) (*tr. v. YD*) to devote oneself to

心得 (*n.*) understanding

士農工商 (*n.*) four classes: warriors, farmers, artisans, and merchants

銘々の (*adv.*) individually, respectively

Grammar Notes

天より人を生ずるには "when people are brought into being by heaven . . ."

同じ位にして SS of *shiku* adj. *onaji*, "same." Note that SS of *onaji* is sometimes used to modify nominals instead of the RT *onajiki*.

生れながら貴賤上下の差別なく Here *nagara* emphasizes that there are no distinctions between people *at the moment of birth*.

万物の霊たる身 n. *banbutsu*, "all living beings," n. *rei*, "spirit," RT of copular *tari*, and n. *mi*, "body"

身と心との働きをもつて *motte,* comp. formed by RY of YD v. *motsu*, "to hold," and conj. p. *te*, functions like a case p. meaning "by means of." The pattern X *o motte* Y *o su,* can be read as "to use X to do Y" or "to do Y by means of X."

妨げをなさず n. *samatage*, "obstacle," and MZ of tr. YD v. *nasu*, "to create"

この世を渡らしめ給ふ pron. *ko*, MZ of intr. YD v. *wataru*, "to pass through," RY of hon. aux. v. *shimu*, and SS of hon. suppl. v. *tamau*

見渡すに RT of tr. YD v. *mi-watasu*, "to look afar, have an overview"

富めるもあり IZ of intr. YD v. *tomu*, "to grow wealthy," RT of aux. v. *ri*, and bound p. *mo*

何ぞや interrogative pron. *nan*, "what," emphatic bound p. *zo*, and interrogative bound p. *ya*: "Why is it?"

次第甚だ明らかなり SS of *nari* adj. v. *akiraka*, "apparent"

なりとあり citational case p. *to*: "It is written that . . ."

身分重き人と名づけ n. *mibun*, "status," RT of *ku* adj. *omoshi*, "important," citational case p. *to*, and RY of tr. SN v. *nazuku*, "to call"

むつかしくして RY of *shiku* adj. *mutsukashi*, "difficult," and conj. p. *shite*, "and"

夥多の奉公人を召使ふ大百姓 n. *amata*, "many," and RT of tr. YD v. *meshitsukau*, "to keep in one's service"

貴き者といふべし RT of *ku* adj. *tōtoshi*, "of high status," and SS of aux. v. *beshi*, indicating appropriateness

のみにて adv. p. *nomi*, "only," and comp. *ni-te*, consisting of RY of copular *nari* and conj. p. *te*

働きに与ふるものなりと n. *hataraki*, "labor," case p. *ni*, indicating object of action, RT of SN v. *atau*, "to provide," and citational case p. *to*. Beginning a quotation with *iwaku* and ending it with *to* is a convention of *kanbun*-style writing.

言へる通り "just as I said (earlier)"

にして　*ni-shite*, comp. derived from RY of copular *nari* and conj. p. *shite*, meaning "while being"

にあらず　RY of copular *nari*, MZ of RH suppl. v. *ari*, and SS of neg. aux. v. *zu*

悦(よろこ)ばしめ　MZ of tr. YD intr. v. *yorokobu*, "to delight," and RY of causative aux. v. *shimu*

さまであがめ貴(たふと)むべきもの　adv. *sa*, "that much," adv. p. *made*, "to that extent," RY of SN v. *agamu*, SS of tr. YD v. *tōtomu*, "to hold in high esteem," and RT of aux. v. *beshi*, indicating appropriateness

身代(しんだい)を持(も)ち崩(くず)すならんとて　MZ of copular *nari* and SS of spec. aux. v. *mu*. *To-te* is citational case p. *to*, RY of implied v. *omou*, "to think," and conj. p. *te*.

日用(にちよう)の間(ま)に合(あ)わぬ証拠(しようこ)なり　MZ of set phrase YD v. *ma ni au*, "to serve a purpose"

学(まな)ぶべき箇条(かでう)　RT of aux. v. *beshi*, indicating appropriateness, and n. *kajō*, "subjects"

世帯(せたい)を説(と)きたる　RY of tr. YD v. *toku*, "to explain," and RT of cont. aux. v. *tari*

仮名(かな)にて用(よう)を便(べん)じ　case p. *nite*, "by means of," and RY of tr. SH v. *ben-zu*, "to make do with"

実事(じつじ)を押(おさ)へ　n. *jitsuji*, "facts," and RY of tr. SN v. *osau*, "to gain a firm grasp of ~"

悉(ことごと)くたしなむべき心得(こころえ)なれば　SS of intr. YD v. *tashinamu*, "to practice diligently"

分(ぶん)を尽(つく)し　n. *bun*, "one's lot in life," case p. *o*, and RY of tr. YD v. *tsukusu*, "to do one's best"

Part VI

Nara Period

17

Collection of Ten Thousand Leaves

The *Collection of Ten Thousand Leaves* (*Man'yōshū*) is Japan's oldest anthology of poetry. It is made up of twenty volumes and 4,516 poems (*uta*), most of which were composed from the mid-seventh to the mid-eighth century. Although the details of how the *Man'yōshū* came to be compiled are largely unknown, it appears to have been edited in several stages over a span of seventy or eighty years by different people according to a variety of organizational principles. The twenty-volume collection was perhaps completed sometime between 770 and 785.

The text is based on Takagi Ichinosuke et al., eds., *Man'yōshū 1*, Nihon koten bungaku taikei 4 (Tokyo: Iwanami Shoten, 1957), 155, 169, 177; and Takagi Ichinosuke et al., eds., *Man'yōshū 2*, Nihon koten bungaku taikei 5 (Tokyo: Iwanami Shoten, 1959), 63, 139, with minor orthographic changes.

『万葉集』

「柿本朝臣人麻呂の歌一首」

　　　近江の海　夕波千鳥　汝が鳴けば　心もしのに　古　思ほゆ

（巻三・二六六）

山部宿禰赤人

「富士の山を望む歌一首」

　　　天地の　分れし時ゆ　神さびて　高く貴き　駿河なる　富士の高嶺を　天の原　振り放

け見れば　渡る日の　影も隠らひ　照る月の　光も見えず　白雲も　い行きはばかり　時

じくぞ　雪は降りける　語り継ぎ　言ひ継ぎ行かむ　富士の高嶺は

（巻三・三一七）

反歌

　　　田子の浦ゆ　うち出でて見れば　ま白にぞ　富士の高嶺に　雪は降りける

（巻三・三一八）

「山部宿禰赤人の作る歌一首」

　　　み吉野の　象山のまの　木末には　ここだも騒く　鳥の声かも

（巻六・九二四）

山上憶良臣

「宴を罷る歌一首」

　　　憶良らは　今はまからむ　子泣くらむ　それその母も　我を待つらむぞ

（巻三・三三七）

山上億良臣

「子等を思ふ歌一首」

　　　瓜食めば　子ども思ほゆ　栗食めば　ましてしのはゆ　いづくより　来りしものぞ　まな

かひに　もとなかかりて　安寝し寝さぬ

（巻五・八〇二）

反歌

　　　銀も　金も玉も　何せむに　まされる宝　子にしかめやも

（巻五・八〇三）

Kakinomoto no Hitomaro, vol. 3, no. 266

Vocabulary

近江の海 (*proper n.*) Lake Biwa, in the middle of present-day Shiga Prefecture

夕波 千鳥 (*n.*) plovers that fly about between the waves (*nami*) in the evening (*yū*)

しのに (*adv.*) somberly, dejectedly

Grammar Notes

汝が鳴けば second-person pron. *na*, "you," addressing the plovers

思ほゆ SS of intr. SN v. *omohoyu*, "to find oneself thinking" (from MZ of intr. YD v. *omohu* plus spont. aux. v. *yu*). Here, the author is thinking of when Emperor Tenchi (Tenji, r. 668–671) had the capital in Ōmi.

Annotated Grammar

固名 名・ 代 格助 四/已・ 接助 名 係助 副 名 下二/終
近江の海 夕波千鳥 汝 が 鳴け ば 心 も しのに 古 思ほゆ

Yamabe no Akahito, vol. 3, nos. 317–318

Vocabulary

天地 (*n.*) heaven and earth

神さぶ (*intr. v. KN*) to act like a god, appear awe-inspiring

反歌 (*n.*) envoy, thirty-one-syllable *waka* that follows a *chōka* (long poem), usually summarizing or supplementing the main poem

Grammar Notes

分れし時ゆ RY of intr. SN v. *wakaru*, "to separate," "to divide," RT of past-tense aux. v. *ki*, n. *toki*, "time," and Nara-period case p. *yu*, meaning "from"

駿河なる富士 proper n. Suruga, a province now part of Shizuoka Prefecture, and RT of copular *nari*, indicating location

振り放け見れば IZ of KI v. *furisake-miru*, "to look up and afar," and conj. p. *ba*, indicating "when"

隠らひ MZ of intr. YD v. *kakuru*, "to hide," and RY of Nara-period aux. v. *hu*, indicating continuous action over a period of time

い行きはばかり prefix *i*, which adds euphony and gives emphasis to the v., RY of intr. YD v. *yuku*, "to go," and RY of intr. YD v. *habakaru*, "to hesitate due to obstacles." This expression implies being awed by the power of the mountain.

時じく RY of Nara-period *shiku* adj. *tokiji*, "unceasing"

語り継ぎ言ひ継ぎ行かむ RY of YD comp. v. *katari-tsugu*, from *kataru*, "to narrate," and *tsugu*, "to pass on," RY of YD v. *ii-tsugu*, "to pass on," MZ of intr. YD suppl. v. *yuku*, "to carry on," and SS of intent. aux. v. *mu*

田子の浦ゆ   The Bay of Tago sits at the base of Mount Fuji on the coast of present-day Shizuoka Prefecture. Nara-period case p. *yu*, which indicates "passage through," refers to going out into the bay.

うち出でて見れば   RY of intr. SN v. *uchi-izu*, "to go out"

Annotated Grammar

名　格助　下二/用・　助動/過/体　名　格助(起点)　上二/用　接助　ク形/用・　ク形/体　固名　助動/断/体　固名　格助　名　格助
天地　の　分れ　し　時　ゆ　神さび　て　高く　貴き　駿河　なる　富士　の　高嶺　を

名　上一/已　接助　四/体・　名　格助　名　係助　四/未・　助動/継/用　四/体・　名　格助　名　係助　下二/未・
天の原　振り放け見れ　ば　渡る　日　の　影　も　隠ら　ひ　照る　月　の　光　も　見え

助動/打/用　名　係助　接頭　四/用・　四/用　シク形/用・　係助/係　名　係助　四/用・　助動/詠/体/結　四/用
ず　白雲　も　い　行き　はばかり　時じく　ぞ　雪　は　降り　ける　語り継ぎ

四/用　四/未・　助動/意/終　固名　格助　名　係助
言ひ継ぎ　行か　む　富士　の　高嶺　は

名
反歌

固名　格助(経過点)　接頭　下二/用・　接助　上一/已・　接助　ナリ形動/用　係助/係　固名　格助　名　格助　名　係助　四/用・
田子の浦　ゆ　うち　出で　て　見れ　ば　ま白に　ぞ　富士　の　高嶺　に　雪　は　降り

助動/詠/体/結
ける

Yamabe no Akahito, vol. 6, no. 924

Vocabulary

木末 (こぬれ) (*n.*) tip of tree, tip of branch

ここだ (幾許) (*adv.*) many, this many

騒く (さわ) (*intr. v. YD*) (later *sawagu*) to be noisy, make a commotion

かも (*final p.*) exclamatory final particle

Grammar Notes

み吉野 (よしの) prefix *mi*, "beautiful." Yoshino is the area around the Yoshino River in Yamato Province (present-day Nara Prefecture).

象山のま (きさやま) Kisayama, a mountain in Yoshino, attrib. case p. *no*, and n. *ma*, "between"

Annotated Grammar

接頭　固名　格助　固名　格助　名　格助　名　格助　係助　副・　係助　四/体・　名　格助　名　終助(感動)
み　吉野　の　象山　のま　の　木末　に　は　ここだ　も　騒く　鳥　の　声　かも

Yamanoue no Okura, vol. 3, no. 337

Vocabulary

今 (いま) (*n.*) present, now (here indicating that the action of trying to leave has been repeated a number of times)

それ (*conj.*) used at beginning of sentence to introduce new topic: "well"

Grammar Notes

憶良ら (おくら) proper n. Okura and suffix *ra*, which can be either a plural or a humble form. Here it is humble, for the author is referring to himself.

まからむ MZ of hum. YD v. *makaru*, "to leave the place of a person of high status"

子泣くらむ (こな) SS of YD v. *naku*, "to weep," and SS of present-spec. aux. v. *ramu*

その pron. *so*, "that," and attrib. case p. *no*, referring to the mother of the child

待つらむぞ (ま) RT of present-spec. aux. v. *ramu* and bound p. *zo*. At the end of a sentence, bound p. *zo* follows nominals or RT and is a strong declaration.

Annotated Grammar

固名	接尾	係助	名	係助	四/謙/未	助動/意/終	名	四/終・	助動/推/終・	感	代	格助	名	係助	代	格助	四/終・
憶良	ら	は	今	は	まから	む	子	泣く	らむ	それ	そ	の	母	も	我	を	待つ

助動/推/体・	係助
らむ	ぞ

Yamanoue no Okura, vol. 5, nos. 802–803

Vocabulary

瓜 (うり) (*n.*) melon

食む (は) (*tr. v. YD*) to eat

しのふ (偲ふ) (*tr. v. YD*) (later *shinobu*) to long for

まなかひ (目交ひ・眼間) (*n.*) before one's eyes

もとな (*adv.*) constantly

安い (やす) (安寝・安眠) (*n.*) (from adj. stem *yasu*, "easy," and n. *i*, "sleep") sound sleep

思ほゆ (おも) (*intr. v. SN*) to think of naturally

Grammar Notes

子ども (こ) plural suffix *domo*

ましてしのはゆ adv. *mashite*, "all the more," MZ of YD v. *shinou*, "to long for," and SS of spont. aux. v. *yu*

いづくより interrogative pron. *izuku*, "where"

来りしものぞ (きた) RY of YD v. *kitaru*, "to come," and final p. *zo*, which creates a strong question

もとなかかりて adv. *motona*, "constantly," RY of YD v. *kakaru*, "to weigh on," and conj. p. *te*. The subject of this sentence is generally assumed to be the poet's image of his children.

安寝し寝さぬ (やすい・な)　n. *yasui*, adv. p. *shi*, MZ of tr. YD v. *nasu*, "to put to sleep," and RT of neg. aux. v. *zu*: "(the image) does not allow me to sleep well."

何せむに (なに)　set phrase: interrogative pron. *nani*, "what," MZ of SH v. *su*, "to do," RT of intent. aux. v. *mu*, and case p. *ni*. "What can we do with these (treasures)? (Nothing.)"

まされる宝 (たから)　IZ of YD v. *masaru*, "to be superior," and RT of aux. v. *ri*

しかめやも　MZ of YD v. *shiku*, "to be equal to," and IZ of spec. aux. v. *mu*. This is a rhetorical question: "Can superior treasures be equal to (children)? (No, they cannot.)"

Annotated Grammar

名	四/已	接助	名	接尾	下二/終	名	四/已	接助	副	四/未・	助動/自発/終	代	格助	四/用
瓜	食め	ば	子	ども	思ほゆ	栗	食め	ば	まして	しのは	ゆ	いづく	より	来り

助動/過/体	名	係助/係	名	格助	副・	四/用	接助	名	副助	四/未・	助動/打/体/結
し	もの	ぞ	まなかひ	に	もとな	かかり	て	安寝	し	寝さ	ぬ

名
反歌

名	係助	名	係助	名	係助	代	サ変/未	助動/意/体	格助	四/已	助動/完/体	名	名	格助	四/未	助動/推/已	係助/反語
銀	も	金	も	玉	も	何	せ	む	に	まされ	る	宝	子	に	しか	め	や

終助（感動）
も

Essential Dictionary

This dictionary provides the fundamental vocabulary needed for reading classical Japanese, based on words that appear in the texts of this *Reader*, with additional entries for essential items that do not occur in these readings. Whereas the vocabulary lists in the *Reader* supply only the meaning or usage relevant to the text in question, the entries in this dictionary give most or all of the primary meanings for the words included. Entries in the dictionary that appear in the *Reader* are indicated by abbreviations of the titles, shown in the following list, in parentheses at the end of the entry. In addition, a number of commonly used words that do not appear in the *Reader* have been included in the dictionary. The six hundred most essential words of classical Japanese are in boldface capital letters preceded by an asterisk, and the next three hundred most frequently encountered words are in boldface capital letters without an asterisk. The remaining words are those appearing in the *Reader*'s texts.

The dictionary uses the same grammatical abbreviations and conventions of romanization used in the *Reader*. For more information about grammatical conventions, see *Classical Japanese: A Grammar* (Columbia University Press, 2005). Note that all supplementary verbs (*hojo-dōshi*) follow the *ren'yōkei*, or continuative form, of the main verb. Entries for adjectival verbs (such as *honoka-nari*, "faint") list the noun or stem form (as in *honoka*), since many of them can be interpreted as a noun followed by the copular auxiliary verb *nari* rather than as an adjectival verb. Explanations of usage have replaced definitions for grammatical particles, interjections, and some mimetic words that do not have near equivalents in modern English. The historical period in which the word came into wide usage is indicated when such information may be helpful. For example, for the Nara period, "Nara" at the beginning of the entry implies that the entry word became obsolete during the following Heian period. With two exceptions ("fr." for "from" and "rhet." for "rhetorical") the abbreviations used for grammatical terms are the same as those found at the beginning of the *Reader*.

GM	*Genji monogatari*	*OH*	*Oku no hosomichi*
HI	*Hyakunin isshu*	*SN*	*Sarashina nikki*
HJ	*Hōjōki*	*TM*	*Taketori monogatari*
HM	*Heike monogatari*	*TN*	*Tosa nikki*
IM	*Ise monogatari*	*TO*	*Genji monogatari tama no ogushi*
KM	*Konjaku monogatari*	*TZ*	*Tsurezuregusa*
MS	*Makura no sōshi*	*UM*	*Ugetsu monogatari*
MY	*Man'yōshū*	*US*	*Uji shūi monogatari*
NE	*Nippon eitaigura*		

abumi あぶみ (鐙)   *n.* stirrups. (*HM*)

*ADA あだ (徒)   *nari adj. v.* **1.** fleeting, transient. **2.** untrue, inconstant. **3.** empty, pointless, unprofitable. (*HJ, TZ*)

AE-NASHI あへなし (敢へ無し)   *ku adj.* **1.** deflating. **2.** hopeless.

*AGA-RU あがる (上がる・揚がる)   *intr. v. YD* **1.** to go to a higher place. **2.** to be promoted, achieve a high rank. **3.** to improve in technique, learning. **4.** to return to the past. **5.** (of a horse) to buck, rear suddenly.

agata あがた (県)   *n.* **1.** province under state control. **2.** official post in such a province. (*TN*)

age-te あげて (挙げて)   *adv.* **1.** taking up one by one. **2.** every, all. (*HJ*)

agetsurai あげつらひ (論)   *n.* critical examination, treatise. (*TO*)

*A-GU あぐ (上ぐ・挙ぐ・揚ぐ)   *tr. v. SN* **1.** to raise, lift, move to a higher place. **2.** to raise one's voice. **3.** to tie up one's hair. **4.** to donate, offer. **5.** to mention, cite, enumerate. **6.** to send to the capital. **7.** to promote, raise in status or value. **8.** to make an offering. **9.** *suppl. v.* to do (something) completely, carry out to the end. (*HJ, IM*)

agura あぐら (胡床・呉床)   *n.* [fr. n. *a*, "foot," and n. *kura*, "seat"] **1.** high seat with legs. **2.** sitting cross-legged. **3.** wooden footholds for climbing to a high place. (*TM*)

*AIDA あひだ (間)   *n.* **1.** limited period of time or space. **2.** time or space between two points: between, while. **3.** relationship (between one person and another). **4.** indicating a reason, cause: therefore, since. (*HJ, TM*)

*AIGYŌ あいぎやう (愛敬)   *n.* **1.** showing both adoration and reverence, piety. **2.** attractive, adorable appearance. **3.** sympathy, gentleness.

AIGYŌ-ZUKU あいぎやうづく (愛敬づく)   *intr. v. YD* to be attractive, adorable.

ai-majiwa-ru あひまじはる (相交はる)   *intr. v. YD* to be mixed in, mixed together. (*HJ*)

ai-miru あひみる (逢ひ見る・相見る)   *tr. v. KI*

1. to meet someone, interview. **2.** to have a romantic relationship. (*TM, TZ*)

*AI-NA-SHI あいなし   *ku adj.* [fr. n. *ai*, 合ひ, "harmony," and adj. *nashi*, "without"] **1.** unreasonable, illogical, inappropriate. **2.** wasteful, hopeless. **3.** uninteresting, boring. **4.** (*RY*) rashly, recklessly.

a-ji あじ (阿字)   *n.* (Buddhist) first letter in the Sanskrit alphabet. (*HJ*)

*AJIKI-NA-SHI あぢきなし (味気無し)   *ku adj.* **1.** abnormal, unreasonable. **2.** meaningless, silly. **3.** unpleasant, woeful, unsatisfactory. (*HJ*)

aji-ro あじろ (網代)   *n.* fishing weirs (set in rivers in late autumn and winter). (*MS*)

aka-dana あかだな (閼伽棚)   *n.* shelf for offerings of flowers or water to the Buddha. (*HJ*)

akara-me あからめ (あから目)   *n.* **1.** glancing aside. **2.** infidelity. (*TZ*)

*AKARA-SAMA あからさま   *nari adj. v.* **1.** sudden, immediate. **2.** temporary, brief. **3.** (Edo) exposed to view, made public. (*HJ*)

aka-ru あかる (明かる)   *intr. v. YD* to grow light. (*MS*)

aka-ru あかる (赤る)   *intr. v. YD* to turn red.

aka-sa あかさ (明さ)   *n.* [fr. adj. *akashi*, "bright," and nominalizing suffix *sa*] light, brightness. (*TM*)

aka-shi あかし (明し)   *ku adj.* bright. (*TN*)

aka-shi あかし (赤し)   *ku adj.* red. (*GM*)

*AKA-SU あかす (明す)   *tr. v. YD* **1.** to brighten. **2.** to clarify, explain. **3.** to reveal a secret, confess. **4.** to stay up all night. **5.** *suppl. v.* to spend the whole night engaged in (some activity). (*TM, TZ*)

*AKATSUKI あかつき (暁)   *n.* [fr. n. *aka-toki*, "time of light"] just before the dawn. (*HJ, TZ*)

AKEBONO あけぼの (曙)   *n.* first faint light of day, dawn. (*MS*)

akehana-su あけはなす (明けはなす)   *tr. v. YD* to leave open. (*UM*)

aki-ma あきま（開間） *n.* chink (in armor), small gaps (between plates of armor). (*HM*)

a-ku あく（明く） *intr. v. SN* **1.** (for night) to dawn, grow light (of the day). **2.** (of a new year, month, day) to begin. (*HJ*)

a-ku あく（開く・空く） *intr. v. YD* **1.** to open, crack open. **2.** (of a fast, period of abstinence) to end. **3.** (of an official post) to be left open, unfilled.

*A-KU あく（飽く） *intr. v. YD* **1.** to be satisfied with. **2.** to become tired of, bored with, weary of. **3.** *suppl. v.* to grow weary of doing (something). (*HJ, TM, TN*)

*AKUGA-RU あくがる（憧る） *intr. v. SN* **1.** (of the soul) to depart from the body and wander. **2.** to leave home and wander about. **3.** to fall madly in love and become distracted. **4.** to grow distant from someone one has been close to.

akusho-otoshi あくしよおとし（悪所落とし） *n.* **1.** charging down a steep hill while mounted on a horse. **2.** person skilled at this. (*HM*)

AMA あま（尼） *n.* nun. (*GM*)

*AMA あま（海人） *n.* **1.** fisherman, salt maker. **2.** female sea diver who gathers abalone, seaweed, etc. (*III*)

amane-shi あまねし（遍し・普し） *ku adj.* far and wide, widespread. (*HJ*)

ama-no-hara あまのはら（天の原） *n.* **1.** vast sky. **2.** heavenly plain (Takama-no-hara) in Japanese myths. (*HI*)

*AMARI あまり（余り） *n.* **1.** left over, surplus. **2.** excess, result of excess (often in the form . . . *no amari ni*). *suffix* (following a number) **1.** a little more than . . . **2.** indicating anything from 1 to 10 for numbers in excess of 10. *adv.* **1.** excessively, rashly, recklessly. **2.** (followed by neg.) (not) that much. (*HJ*)

amari-sae あまりさへ（剰へ） (also *amatsusae* あまつさへ) *adv.* on top of that, as if that weren't enough. (*HJ*)

ama-su あます（余す） *tr. v. YD* **1.** to leave behind, overlook. **2.** to spill, fill beyond capacity. **3.** to have too much to handle, have difficulty taking care of (something). (*HJ, HM*)

*AMATA あまた（数多） *adv.* **1.** many, in large numbers. **2.** very, extremely. (*KM, TM*)

ame-tsuchi あめつち（天地） *n.* heaven and earth. (*MY*)

amu あむ（浴む） *tr. v. KN* to bathe, soak in water. (*US*)

*ANA あな *interj.* expresses surprise, disappointment or other sudden feeling: oh! my! alas! (*GM, TM*)

ana あな（穴・孔） *n.* **1.** （穴）hole. **2.** （孔）pore. (*TM*)

*ANAGACHI あながち（強ち） *nari adj. v.* [original meaning: imposing one's will] **1.** forceful, willful, impetuous. **2.** earnest, single-minded. **3.** excessive, imprudent.

*A-NAI あない（案内） (also *annai*) *n.* **1.** draft, content (of a text). **2.** circumstance, situation, condition. *n., tr. v. SH* **1.** announcement of a guest's arrival. **2.** inquiry about the situation or circumstances. **3.** guiding (someone) to a destination.

ananai あななひ（麻柱） *n.* scaffold, perch. (*TM*)

*ANATA あなた *pron.* （彼方）**1.** on the far side, other side, over there. **2.** before. （貴方）**3.** that person. **4.** you (*hon.*). (*GM*)

ANAZURAWASHI あなづらはし（侮らはし） *shiku adj.* **1.** contemptuous, scornful. **2.** familiar, on close terms (with).

an-chi あんち（安置） *n., tr. v. SH* installation of a Buddhist statue, sutra, etc., for worship. (*HJ*)

ao-gu あふぐ（仰ぐ） *intr. v. YD* **1.** to look up at. **2.** to respect, hold in esteem. (*TM*)

ao-mu あをむ（青む） *intr. v. YD* **1.** to turn green. **2.** to turn pale. (*TZ*)

ao-ru あふる（煽る） *tr. v. YD* **1.** to spur on a horse using stirrups. **2.** (Edo) to entice, lure. (*HM*)

appare あつぱれ *interj.* **1.** expresses strong emotion: alas! **2.** used when praising another, especially for a performance or an accomplishment: well done! good work! etc. (*HM*)

ara-iso あらいそ (荒磯) *n.* (same as *ariso*) rocky beach or shore. (*HJ*)

arako あらこ (粗籠) *n.* roughly woven basket. (*TM*)

arashi あらし (嵐) *n.* fierce wind, gale, storm. (*HI, HJ*)

ara-shi あらし (荒し・粗し) *ku adj.* **1.** coarse, rough. **2.** coarsely woven or thatched. (*HI*)

araso-u あらそふ (争ふ) *intr. v. YD* **1.** to resist, oppose. **2.** to vie, compete. **3.** to dispute, argue. **4.** to battle, engage in combat. (*HJ*)

aratama-ru あらたまる (改る) *intr. v. YD* to change, be renewed. (*HJ*)

ara-te あらて (新手) *n.* fresh troops. (*HM*)

*ARAWA あらは (顕・露) *nari adj. v.* **1.** exposed to view, clearly visible. **2.** clear, distinct. **3.** publicly known. **4.** blunt, rude. (*GM, SN*)

are あれ (彼) *pron.* **1.** that (person, place, thing) over there. **2.** you. (*HM*)

are-yu-ku あれゆく (荒れ行く) *intr. v. YD* to fall into ruin, become dilapidated. (*HJ*)

*A-RI あり (有り・在り) *intr. v. RH* **1.** to exist, be. **2.** to live in this world, live safely. **3.** to be in a given place. **4.** to pass time. **5.** to flourish, prosper. **6.** *suppl. v.* continuing state or condition (as indicated by the main *v.*). **7.** (following RY of copular *nari*) declarative statement. (*HJ, TM*)

ARIAKE ありあけ (有明) *n.* **1.** period from the sixteenth to the end of the lunar month, when the moon lingers in the sky at dawn. **2.** moon during this period. (*HI*)

*ARI-GATA-SHI ありがたし (有り難し) *ku adj.* **1.** rare, unusual. **2.** superior, of high quality. **3.** difficult to live or survive. **4.** difficult (to do). **5.** honorable, venerable.

ari-ka ありか (在り処・在り所) *n.* place or location (of someone or something). (*GM*)

ariki ありき (歩き) *n.* going out, walking around. (*GM*)

*ARI-KU ありく (歩く) *intr. v. YD* **1.** (of humans) to walk, ride a horse or boat. **2.** (of nonhumans) to move about. **3.** *suppl. v.* to do (something) here and there. (*MS, TZ*)

ari-niku-shi ありにくし (在りにくし) *ku adj.* [fr. v. *ari*, "to exist," and adj. *nikushi*, "difficult"] unlivable, uninhabitable. (*HJ*)

ariso ありそ (荒磯) *n.* [fr. n. *ara-iso*, "rocky shore"] rocky shore struck by rough waves.

a-ru ある (荒る) *intr. v. SN* **1.** to fall into ruin, become desolate. **2.** to go wild, behave wildly. **3.** to grow tired of, lose interest in. (*TM, TN, US*)

a-ru ある (散る) *intr. v. SN* to disperse, separate, grow distant. (*TM*)

aru-i-wa あるいは (或は) *attrib., adv.* (often in *aruiwa . . . aruiwa . . .* pattern; e.g., in a certain situation X and in another situation Y) certain (thing), certain (time), certain (situation). *conj.* (X *aruiwa* Y pattern) or. (*HJ, TM, UM*)

*ARUJI あるじ (主) *n.* **1.** household head, lord. **2.** landowner. (*HJ, KM*)

aruji-su あるじす (饗す) *intr. v. SH* to serve as host, receive guests. (*MS, TM*)

asa あさ (朝) *n.* morning. (*TM*)

asa あさ (麻) *n.* hemp. (*HJ*)

asa-gao あさがほ (朝顔) *n.* **1.** appearance of one's face immediately upon waking in the morning. **2.** flowers that bloom in the morning. **3.** morning glory. (*HJ*)

asa-gayu あさがゆ (朝粥) *n.* morning porridge, gruel. (*US*)

asaji-ga-yado あさぢがやど (浅茅が宿) *n.* dilapidated house overgrown with reeds. (*TZ*)

*ASAMA-SHI あさまし (浅まし) *shiku adj.* **1.** unexpected, astonishing. **2.** disappointing. **3.** heartless, deplorable, lamentable. **4.** terrible, awful, unbearable. **5.** (Edo) shabby, poor, mean, base. (*HJ, TM, UM, US*)

*ASA-SHI あさし (浅し) *ku adj.* **1.** shallow (water, etc.). **2.** light (in color, fragrance). **3.** shallow in taste, uncultivated. **4.** weak (connection, bond). **5.** minor (sin). **6.** (of a season, usually spring, only recently arrived) new, young. **7.** low (in status, name).

*A-SHI あし (悪し・凶し) *shiku adj.* **1.** bad, evil. **2.** unpleasant (situation, person). **3.** sick, ill. **4.** rough, inclement (weather, character, etc.). **5.** unskilled, clumsy. **6.** ugly, unsightly. **7.** poor (economically), lowly (social status). (*TM, UM, US*)

ashi あし (芦) *n.* reed. (*HI*)

*ASHI あし (足・脚) *n.* **1.** leg, foot of human or animal. **2.** walking. **3.** foundation, base. **4.** speed. (*HJ, IM*)

ashibiki-no あしびきの (足引きの) *pillow word* modifying *yama* (mountains), *mine* (peak), *iwa* (boulder), *ki* (trees), *arashi* (storm), and *no* (fields, moors). (*HI*)

*ASHITA あした (朝) *n.* **1.** morning. **2.** following morning, tomorrow morning.

*ASOBA-SU あそばす (遊ばす) *tr. v. YD* [fr. v. *asobu*, "to play," and hon. v. *su*] **1.** to compose poetry, play music, have a banquet, go hunting, etc. (*hon.*). **2.** (of a wide range of action) to do (*hon.*). **3.** (frequently preceded by hon. prefix *o* or *go*) *hon. suppl. v.*

*ASOBI あそび (遊び) *n.* **1.** dance and music performed for the gods. **2.** drinking, hunting in the fields and mountains. **3.** taking pleasure in composing music, playing music, dancing. **4.** entertainment.

*ASO-BU あそぶ (遊ぶ) *intr. v. YD* **1.** to play music. **2.** to do something enjoyable (banqueting, boating, etc.). **3.** to hunt. **4.** to play innocently with children.

*ASON あそん (朝臣) [fr. *asomi*] *n.* **1.** hon. placed after the name of a person of the fifth rank or higher. **2.** used by courtiers to refer to each other in a familiar way. (*GM*)

atai あたひ (価・値) *n.* **1.** price. **2.** value, worth. (*HJ*)

ATARA あたら (惜・可惜) *attrib.* precious, valuable. *adv.* regrettably, regretfully. (*HJ*)

*ATARA-SHI あたらし (惜し) *shiku adj.* (regretting the loss of something excellent) re-

grettable, so outstanding (it would be a waste to leave it as it is): what a waste!

ATARA-SHI あたらし (新し) *shiku adj.* new, fresh.

*ATARI あたり (辺り) *n.* **1.** immediate area, vicinity. **2.** people around one, especially relatives. **3.** circumlocution for person's name or place. (*TM*)

*ATA-RU あたる (当たる) *intr. v. YD* **1.** to run into, bump into, touch. **2.** to face (a certain situation). **3.** to hit the mark or target. **4.** to fit, correspond, be equivalent to. **5.** to make contact with a person.

ata-u あたふ (能ふ) *intr. v. YD* **1.** to be able to do something. **2.** to be appropriate, reasonable. (*HJ, TM*)

*ATE あて (貴) *nari adj. v.* **1.** high-ranking, high-class. **2.** elegant, refined. (*GM, TM*)

ate-yaka あてやか (貴やか) *nari adj. v.* [fr. adj. v. *ate*, "elegant," and suffix *yaka*, "feeling of"] refined, elegant. (*TM*)

*ATO あと (跡) *n.* **1.** footprint. **2.** leg, foot. **3.** signs of a person's coming or going. **4.** one's destination. **5.** keepsake, remains, vestige. **6.** handwriting, style of writing. **7.** heir, heiress. (*TZ*)

*ATO あと (後) *n.* **1.** back, behind, rear. **2.** later on. **3.** earlier, before. **4.** after one's death. (*HJ*)

ato-kata-na-shi あとかたなし (跡形無し) *ku adj.* traceless. (*HJ*)

ato-to-mu あととむ (跡留む) *intr. v. SN* to remain in the world (society), continue to live. (*HJ*)

*A-TSU あつ (当つ) *tr. v. SN* **1.** to hit, strike, touch. **2.** to distribute, divide up (things). **3.** to assign, allot (positions, responsibilities). **4.** to expose (to light, wind, rain, etc.). **5.** to make one face (a certain situation). **6.** to make (one) hit the target, reach the goal. **7.** to look at directly, glare.

atsuka-u あつかふ *tr. v. YD* **1.** to take care of, look after, nurse. **2.** to spread rumors about.

3. to have more of something than one can handle. **4**. to use, know how to handle. (*KM*)

atsuma-ru あつまる (集まる) *intr. v. YD* to gather, assemble. (*TM*)

*A-U あふ (会ふ・逢ふ・遭ふ) *intr. v. YD* **1**. to meet, face. **2**. to be suitable, fitting (for the occasion, season). **3**. (of a man and woman) to have a relationship, be married. **4**. to oppose, fight each other. (*IM, MS*)

*A-U あふ (合ふ) *intr. v. YD* **1**. to come together, become one, do together. **2**. to harmonize. **3**. *supp. v.* to do (something) together. (*IM*)

awa あわ (泡) *n.* foam. (*HJ*)

*AWARE あはれ *nari adj. v.* **1**. deeply moving, affecting. **2**. touching (scene). **3**. lonesome, sad. **4**. pitiful. **5**. cute, beloved, dear. **6**. emotionally sensitive. **7**. outstanding, superior. *n.* **1**. quiet mood. **2**. sadness, loneliness. **3**. love, pity, sympathy. *interj.* expresses a deep emotional response: alas! (*HJ, TN, US*)

aware-bu あはれぶ (哀れぶ・憐れぶ) (also *awaremu*) *tr. v. YD* **1**. to perceive the nature or meaning of something keenly. **2**. to love, adore. **3**. to pity, feel sorry for. (*HJ*)

aware-garu あはれがる *tr. v. YD* [fr. *n. aware* and suffix *garu*] **1**. to be impressed by, admire. **2**. to feel sympathetic toward, to feel sorry for. **3**. to lament. (*SN*)

aware-mi あはれみ (憐み) *n.* pity, sympathy. (*HJ*)

*AWA-SU あはす (合はす) *tr. v. SN* **1**. to bring together, sum up. **2**. to wed, marry. **3**. to make suitable. **4**. to tune an instrument. **5**. to interpret a dream. **6**. to compare, make compete. **7**. to release a falcon for hunting. **8**. to mix, prepare (incense, medicine, etc.). **9**. *suppl. v.* to do (something) together, mutually. (*HM, TM*)

awa-tsu あわつ (慌つ) *intr. v. SN* to panic, be disconcerted. (*TM*)

*AYA-NASHI あやなし (文無し) *ku adj.* [fr. *n. aya*, "logic/design," and *adj. nashi*, "without"] **1**. incomprehensible, illogical. **2**. meaningless, ineffective.

*AYA-SHI あやし (奇し・怪し・異し・賤し) *shiku adj.* (奇し・怪し・異し) **1**. strange, ethereal, mysterious. **2**. unusual, odd. **3**. suspicious, worrisome. **4**. disturbing, unseemly. (賤し) **5**. low-ranking (*hum.*). **6**. shabby, unsophisticated. (*HJ, KM, SN, TN*)

ayashi-ga-ru あやしがる (怪しがる) *tr. v. YD* to find suspicious. (*TM*)

ayashi-mu あやしむ (異しむ) *tr. v. YD* to find something odd, strange, to doubt or mistrust. (*UM*)

ayatsu-ru あやつる (操る) *tr. v. YD* to have command of, use skillfully, play with (words, etc.). (*HJ*)

ayau-shi あやふし (危ふし) *ku adj.* **1**. dangerous. **2**. worrisome, uncertain. (*HJ, TM*)

ayu-mu あゆむ (歩む) *intr. v. YD* to walk one step at a time. (*MS*)

aza-wara-u あざわらふ (あざ笑ふ) *tr. v. YD* to laugh mockingly, laugh out loud. (*US*)

azu-ku あづく (預く) *tr. v. SN* **1**. to entrust someone with something. **2**. to arrange a marriage. (*TM, TN*)

*AZUMA あづま (東) *proper n.* **1**. Eastern Provinces (east of Kyoto). **2**. Kamakura bakufu (military government). (*IM*)

Azuma-ji あづまぢ (東路) *proper n.* Eastern Road (later called Tōkaidō, Eastern Seaboard Highway), leading from the capital to the Eastern Provinces. (*SN*)

*BA ば *conj. p.* indicates **1**. (following MZ) logical connection between preceding and following clauses based on a hypothetical situation: if . . . then. **2**. (following IZ) logical connection between preceding and following clauses based on an existing situation: causal, temporal, or general rule: as a result, when, whenever.

*BAKARI ばかり *adv. p.* indicates **1**. approximation, rough estimate with regard to number, place, age, time, length, weight, or size: about, around, vicinity. **2**. (mainly following SS) extent, degree of an action: to the extent that, to the degree that. **3**. limitation, restriction: only, no more than. **4**. (Kamakura) intense repetition: (do) nothing but. (*HJ, TM*)

*BAYA ばや *final p.* (follows MZ) desiderative: if only I could (do something).

*BESHI べし *aux. v.* (follows SS except after RH, when it follows RT) indicates **1**. conjecture with confidence: for sure, no doubt. **2**. strong intention, resolve, with regard to the speaker's action: I will, I intend to. **3**. appropriateness, natural expectation, obligation based on circumstance or reason: it is only appropriate that, should. **4**. advice, recommendation: you should, it is best that. **5**. imperative, often one which cannot be refused, often in neg. form: you must (not), **6**. potential, often in neg. form: can (not). **7**. something that is already decided or arranged: to be expected, scheduled.

bin-jo びんぢよ (便女・美女) *n.* beautiful female retainer, beautiful woman. (*HM*)

BIN-NASHI びんなし (便無し) *ku adj.* [fr. n. *bin*, "convenience," and adj. *nashi*, "without"] **1**. inconvenient. **2**. unsuitable, unwarranted, reprehensible. **3**. pitiful, pathetic.

biwa びは (琵琶) *n.* lute. (*HJ*)

bō ばう (坊) *n.* **1**. unit of area in the capital: one-sixteenth of a *chō*. **2**. crown prince. **3**. monks' living quarters. **4**. monks. (*GM, OH*)

bu ぶ (分・歩) *n.* **1**. unit of length: one-hundredth of a *shaku*, or approx. 3 millimeters. **2**. unit of weight: one-tenth of a *monme*, or approx. 0.375 grams. **3**. unit of area: approx. 3.3 square meters (approx. 35.5 square feet). **4**. unit of currency: one-fourth of a *ryō*. **5**. ratio, percentage. (*US*)

bun-dori ぶんどり (分捕り) *n.* taking an enemy's head and/or weapon on the battlefield. (*HM*)

chaku-su ちやくす (著す・着す) *intr. v. SH* **1**. to arrive. **2**. to cling to. *tr. v. SH* to wear, put on, possess. (*HJ*)

chi ち (乳) *n.* breast, nipple, breast milk. (*HJ*)

*CHIGIRI ちぎり (契) *n.* **1**. pledge, vow, agreement. **2**. karmic bond (from a previous life), fate. **3**. connection, relationship (between husband and wife, lovers, etc.). (*HM, TM, TZ*)

*CHIGI-RU ちぎる (契る) *tr. v. YD* to vow, pledge. (*HJ*)

chigo ちご (稚児・児) *n.* **1**. baby, infant. **2**. youth working at a temple or warrior house. (*MS, TM*)

chihayaburu ちはやぶる (千早振る) *pillow word* modifying *kami* (god). (*HI*)

chi-ji ちぢ (千々) *nari adj. v.* **1**. many. **2**. various, myriad. (*HI*)

CHIKA-SHI ちかし (近し) *ku adj.* **1**. close, near (temporal, spatial, numerical, emotional). **2**. closely related by blood. **3**. similar. (*MS, TM*)

chiri-hai ちりはひ (塵灰) *n.* dust and ashes. (*HJ*)

chiri-shio-ru ちりしをる (散り萎る) *intr. v. SN* (of flowers) to fall and wither. (*TZ*)

chiri-su-gu ちりすぐ (散り過ぐ) *intr. v. KN* to end up scattering completely. (*TZ*)

chiri-usu ちりうす (散り失す) *intr. v. SN* to scatter and become lost. (*OH*)

CHI-RU ちる (散る) *intr. v. YD* **1**. (of flowers, leaves) to scatter, fall. **2**. to become separated. **3**. (of rumors) to spread, leak out. **4**. to be unsettled (psychologically). (*TZ*)

chi-sato ちさと (千里) *n.* **1**. thousand leagues, great distance. **2**. many villages, communities. (*TZ*)

chitto ちつと (also *chito*) *adv.* **1**. to a small degree. **2**. for a little while. (*HM*)

chokushi ちよくし (勅使) *n.* imperial messenger. (*TM*)

chō ちやう (帳) *n.* curtain surrounding a sleeping place. (*TM*)

chō ちやう (張) *n.* counter for items with strings (stringed instruments, tents, mosquito nets, etc.). (*HJ*)

chō ちやう (町) *n.* unit of length: approx. 109 meters (about one city block). (*HJ*)

chō てふ *comp.* [fr. case p. *to* and v. *iu*, "to say"] it is said that, so they say. (*HI*)

CHŌDO てうど (調度) *n.* **1.** (everyday) furnishings, interior accessories. **2.** bow, arrow.

chō-ja ちゃうじや (長者) *n.* **1.** wealthy person. **2.** head of a family. **3.** master of a post station (*umaya*). **4.** (Edo) brothel owner. **5.** imperially appointed head of a temple in Kyoto known as Tōji (東寺). (*NE*)

chōseki てうせき (朝夕) *n.* **1.** morning and night. **2.** every day, all the time. **3.** morning and evening meal. (*NE*)

chōzu てうず (調ず) *tr. v. SH* **1.** to make, procure. **2.** to cook, prepare. **3.** to exorcise, overcome through prayer. **4.** to punish.

chū-jō ちゆうじやう (中将) *n.* middle captain. (*GM*)

chū-nagon ちゆうなごん (中納言) *n.* middle counselor. (*TM*)

daifuku-chō だいふくちやう (大福帳) *n.* merchant's ledger book. (*NE*)

daigaku-ryō だいがくれう (大学寮) *n.* the state university. (*HJ*)

*DAI-JI だいじ (大事) *n.* **1.** major event, unusual occurrence. **2.** taking holy vows and achieving enlightenment. *n., nari adj. v.* **1.** dangerous, difficult situation. **2.** main, essential, important point. (*NE*)

dai-jikara だいぢから (大力) *n.* incredible strength, person with such strength. (*HM*)

dai-jin だいじん (大臣) *n.* minister, minister of state. (*HJ, TM*)

daikoku-den だいこくでん (大極殿) (also *daigokuden*) *proper n.* central building in imperial palace where the emperor conducted affairs of state. (*HJ*)

dai-onjō だいおんじやう (大音声) *n.* loud voice. (*HM*)

dai-ri だいり (内裏) *n.* emperor's residence, imperial palace. (*HJ*)

DANI だに *adv. p.* indicates **1.** minimum demand, wish or need, expressing a desire for no less if not for more: at the very least. **2.** lesser or minimal example to suggest something greater or more serious: even X, not to mention Y, even X, how much more so Y. (*HJ, US*)

*DATSU だつ *suffix* (after nominal, adj., adj. v.) to have the qualities of . . . (*MS*)

*DE で *conj. p.* [fr. neg. aux. v. *zu* and conj. p. *te*] (follows MZ) neg. conj.: not.

deshi でし (弟子) *n.* follower, disciple, pupil, apprentice. (*US*)

*DO ど *conj. p.* (follows IZ) direct concessive: but, though, although.

dō だう (堂) *n.* Buddhist hall where a statue of a deity is enshrined. (*HJ, US*)

do-boku どぼく (土木) *n.* act of building with wood or earth and sand. (*HJ*)

dō-boku どうぼく (童僕) *n.* servants. (*HJ*)

do-do どど (度々) *adv.* often, frequently. (*HM*)

dōji どうじ (童子) *n.* **1.** child. **2.** child studying to become a priest at a temple or working as a servant at a temple. **3.** (Buddhist) bodhisattva. (*US*)

do-kyō どきやう (読経) *n.* reading aloud of sutras. (*HJ*)

domo ども *suffix* indicates **1.** plural. **2.** (following a first-person word) humility. **3.** (following a nominal denoting two or more people) disdain or familiarity. (*KM, MS*)

*DOMO ども *conj. p.* (follows IZ) direct concessive: but, though, although.

DONO どの (殿) *suffix* lord, master. (*HM*)

dō-sha-tō-myō だうしやたふめう (堂舎塔廟) *n.* shrine and temple buildings. (*HJ*)

dōso-jin だうそじん (道祖神) *n.* gods who protect travelers (at village borders, mountain passes, crossroads, the foot of bridges, etc.). (*OH*)

DOYO-MU どよむ (響む・動む) (also *toyomu*) *intr. v. YD* **1.** to reverberate, resound. **2.** to make a commotion. *tr. v. SN* to cause to ring out. (*HJ*)

e え (得)   *See* **u**.

E え   *adv.* [fr. RY of v. *u*, "to be able"] **1.** (followed by neg.) (not) able. **2.** do well, be able.

e へ   *case p.* indicates direction: to, toward.

ebutsushi ゑぶつし (絵仏師)   *n.* painter specializing in Buddhist religious painting. (*US*)

eda えだ (枝)   *n.* **1.** branch of tree or plant. **2.** legs and arms (of humans, animals). **3.** family, descendants. (*TZ*)

ei-zu えいず (映ず)   *intr. v. SH* to reflect light or shadows. (*HJ*)

ei-zu えいず (詠ず)   *tr. v. SH* to compose or recite poetry. (*HJ*)

eki-rei えきれい (疫癘)   *n.* epidemic. (*HJ*)

EMU ゑむ (笑む)   *intr. v. YD* to smile.

*EN えん (艶)   *nari adj. v.* **1.** elegant, tasteful. **2.** fashionable, stylish. **3.** sensuous, enticing.

EN えん (縁)   *n.* **1.** (Buddhist) karmic causality. **2.** connection, relationship. **3.** blood relations, parent/child, husband/wife, etc. (*HJ*)

en-jō えんじやう (炎上) (also *enshō*)   *n.* (destructive) fire, conflagration. (*HJ*)

eri-tōsu ゑりとほす (ゑり通す)   *comp. v.* [fr. v. *eru*, "to poke a hole," and v. *tōsu*, "to push through"] to cut a hole through. (*US*)

e-u ゑふ (酔ふ)   *intr. v. YD* **1.** to become intoxicated from drink. **2.** to be entranced, captivated by. (*TM*)

Ezo えぞ (夷)   *n.* **1.** native inhabitants of northern Japan (also called Emishi or Ebisu). **2.** old name for Hokkaidō. (*OH*)

e-zō ゑざう (絵像)   *n.* portrait. (*HJ*)

*FU (HU) ふ   *aux. v.* (YD) (Nara) indicates continuous action. (*MY*)

FU ふ (経)   *intr. v. SN* **1.** to spend time, pass time. **2.** to pass by a place. **3.** to experience. (*HJ, TM*)

*FU-BIN ふびん (不便・不憫)   *n., nari adj. v.* [fr. aux. v. *fu*, "without," and n. *bin*, "convenience"] **1.** poor state or condition. **2.** pitiable, sorry, pathetic. **3.** beloved, dear, cherished.

fuchi ふち (淵)   *n.* deep, still pool. (*HI*)

Fudōson ふどうそん (不動尊)   *proper n.* Fudō Myōō (不動明王), one of five guardian figures in esoteric Buddhism, usually depicted with a sword in his right hand, a noose in the left, and a raging fire behind. (*US*)

Fu-gen ふげん (普賢)   *proper n.* (abbrev. for Fugen bosatsu) Fugen (Skt. Samantabhadra), a bodhisattva depicted riding a white elephant. (*HJ*)

fuji-nami ふぢなみ (藤波)   *n.* long, trailing boughs of wisteria blossoms. (*HJ*)

fu-kaku ふかく (不覚)   *n., nari adj. v.* **1.** carelessness. **2.** lack of resolve, lack of psychological preparation. **3.** cowardice, timidity. **4.** unconsciousness. **5.** thoughtlessness, stupidity. (*HM*)

*FUKA-SHI ふかし (深し)   *ku adj.* **1.** deep (water, etc.). **2.** remote interior, depths (of a mountain, etc.). **3.** profound (knowledge, understanding). **4.** late (in the season, year), deep (in the night). **5.** strong, deep (color, scent). **6.** close, intimate (relationship). **7.** many. **8.** extreme, intense. (*GM, TZ*)

fuka-ta ふかた (深田)   *n.* rice paddies where the mud is deep. (*HM*)

fuki-hara-u ふきはらふ (吹き払ふ)   *tr. v. YD* to blow away. (*HJ*)

fuki-ita ふきいた (葺き板)   *n.* wooden shingles used as roofing material. (*HJ*)

fuki-ki-ru ふききる (吹き切る)   *tr. v. YD* to blow and tear to pieces. (*HJ*)

fuki-maku-ru ふきまくる (吹き捲くる)   *intr. v. YD* (of the wind) to blow hard. (*HJ*)

fuki-mayo-u ふきまよふ (吹き迷ふ)   *intr. v. YD* to blow around aimlessly. (*HJ*)

fuki-ta-tsu ふきたつ (吹き立つ)   *tr. v. SN* to

blow up into the air. *intr. v. YD* to start to blow. (*HJ*)

fuki-to-zu ふきとづ (吹き閉づ) *tr. v. KN* to blow shut. (*HI*)

fuki-tsu-ku ふきつく (吹き付く) *tr. v. SN* **1.** to blow (objects) together. **2.** to blow on something fiercely. **3.** to cause a fire to burn stronger by blowing on it. (*HJ*)

FU-KU ふく (更く) *intr. v. SN* **1.** (of the night, a season) to grow late. **2.** to grow old. (*HI, TN, TZ*)

fu-ku ふく (葺く) *tr. v. YD* to cover a roof with shingles or boards, thatch. (*HJ*)

FU-KU ふく (吹く) *intr. v. YD* (of the wind) to blow. *tr. v. YD* **1.** to blow (air or water from the mouth). **2.** to blow (a musical instrument), play a flute, etc. **3.** to blow hard. (*HJ, TN*)

fuku-ka ふくか (福家) *n.* prosperous household. (*HJ*)

fuku-mu ふくむ (含む) *intr. v. YD* to swell, bulge. *tr. v. YD* **1.** to put in one's mouth, place inside and carry. **2.** to keep in one's heart. (*HM*)

fuku-raka ふくらか (脹らか) *nari adj. v.* chubby, plump, full. (*GM*)

fukuro ふくろ (袋) *n.* bag. (*SN*)

fukurō ふくろふ (梟) *n.* owl. (*HJ*)

fuku-ru ふくる (脹る) *intr. v. SN* to swell up, puff up. (*US*)

*FUMI ふみ (文) *n.* **1.** book, text. **2.** letter. **3.** learning, scholarship. **4.** Chinese poetry. (*IM*)

fumi-wa-ku ふみわく (踏みわく) *tr. v. SN* to walk over, make one's way through snow or fallen leaves. (*HI*)

fumon ふもん (符文) *n.* charm written on an amulet (*o-fuda*). (*UM*)

fu-moto ふもと (麓) *n.* foot of a mountain, foothill. (*HJ*)

funa-ji ふなぢ (船路) *n.* sea-lane or, by extension, boat trip. (*TN*)

fun-ba-ru ふんばる (踏ん張る) *intr. v. YD* [fr. ふみはる] to plant one's feet and press down. (*HM*)

furi-ao-gu ふりあふぐ (振り仰ぐ) *intr. v. YD* to raise one's head and look upward. (*HM*)

furisake-miru ふりさけみる (振り放け見る) *intr. v. KI* to look up afar, gaze upward. (*HI*)

fu-ru ふる (震る) *intr. v. YD* to shake. (*HJ*)

fu-ru ふる (降る) *intr. v. YD* (of snow, rain, etc.) to fall. (*IM*)

fu-ru ふる (触る) *intr. v. YD* to touch. *intr. v. SN* **1.** to touch, come into contact with. **2.** to be in relationship to (as in *koto ni furete*). **3.** to eat a little, use chopsticks to eat. **4.** (in the phrase *mimi ni ~*) to hear a little of (a rumor, etc.). *tr. v. SN* to make widely known, inform.

FURU ふる (旧る) *intr. v. KN* to grow old, age. (*OH*)

furu-kuso ふるくそ (古糞) *comp. n.* old droppings. (*TM*)

*FURU-SATO ふるさと (故郷・古里) *n.* **1.** old capital, former capital (now decayed). **2.** birthplace. **3.** former hometown. (*HJ*)

fusegi-ya ふせぎや (防ぎ矢) *n.* arrows fired in defense. (*HM*)

fuse-go ふせご (伏籠) *n.* basket placed over an incense burner or brazier for scenting or drying clothes. (*GM*)

fuse-gu ふせぐ (防ぐ) *tr. v. YD* to ward off, defend against, prevent. (*TZ*)

FUSHI ふし (節) *n.* **1.** joint in a bamboo stalk. **2.** clump, knot. **3.** point, motif, reason, basis (of an argument, a statement, etc.). **4.** occasion, moment. **5.** cadence of a poem. **6.** measure or line from a song. (*HI, TM, TO*)

fushi ふし (不死) *n.* immortality, eternal life. (*TM*)

fushi-me ふしめ (伏目) *n.* looking face down, eyes turned down. (*GM*)

fu-shō ふしやう (不請) *n.* (Buddhist) not of one's own initiative, agreeing to or accepting halfheartedly, reluctantly. (*HJ*)

*FU-SU ふす (伏す・臥す)   *tr. v. SN* **1**. to lay or place (something) face down. **2**. to put to sleep. **3**. to turn one's face downward, prostrate one-self. **4**. to push over. **5**. to hide something. *intr. v. YD* **1**. to lie down, go to sleep. **2**. to look downward. **3**. to go into hiding. (*HJ, KM, TM, US*)

FUSUMA ふすま (衾)   *n*. bedding cover. (*HJ*)

futa ふた (蓋)   *n*. lid. (*TM*)

futa-gu ふたぐ (塞ぐ)   *tr. v. YD* to block, obstruct, fill up. (*TM*)

futari-to ふたりと   *adv*. (onomatopoeia) sound of something falling or crashing: splash, ker-plunk, plop, etc. (*US*)

futo ふと   *adv*. **1**. easily, right away. **2**. swiftly. **3**. suddenly, abruptly, unexpectedly. (*TZ*)

futo-bashi ふとばし (太箸)   *n*. thick chopsticks, usually made of willow. (*NE*)

*FUTSUTSUKA ふつつか   *nari adj. v.* [*futsu*: fr. *futo*, "thick"] **1**. thick (voice, physical shape). **2**. (thick and) shapeless, ugly. **3**. shallow, foolish (lacking judgment, discretion).

FU-ZEI ふぜい (風情)   *n*. **1**. elegant atmosphere, mood. **2**. appearance. **3**. movement in nō drama. (*HJ*)

GA が   *case p*. (follows nominals, RT) indicates **1**. subject marker. **2**. attributive modifier, modifying the following nominal: of. **3**. modification of an implied nominal: that of, pertaining or belonging to. **4**. apposition, indicating that the subject of the preceding phrase is the same as that of the following phrase.

*GA が   *conj. P.* (follows RT) indicates **1**. concessive, contrary to expectation, based on an existing or actual situation: but, though. **2**. simple temporal/sequential connection: and, when.

gachi ~がち (~勝ち)   *suffix* to have a tendency to, to occur often. (*MS*)

gai がい (害)   *n*. harm, damage, ill effects. (*HJ*)

gai-kotsu がいこつ (骸骨)   *n*. skeleton. (*KM*)

gan ぐわん (願)   *n*. prayer. (*TN*)

gan-jō がんじやう (岩上)   *n*. peak or surface of a boulder, crag, rock. (*OH*)

*GARI ~がり (許)   *suffix* (preceded by a n. or pron. representing a person and followed by a v. such as *yuku*) place (of a person) that one is going to.

ga-ru ~がる   *suffix* (creates YD v.) to feel the quality of, act in the fashion of. (*GM, SN, TM*)

gatashi ~がたし (~難し)   *suffix* (follows RY, *ku* adj., conj.) indicates that an action is difficult to pursue, complete, etc. (*TM, TN*)

*GE ~げ (気)   *suffix* (follows adj. stem) giving the appearance of (some state or quality), having an air or aspect of (being in some state). (*GM, TM*)

*GE-NI げに (実に)   *adv*. **1**. truly. **2**. expresses agreement: yes, indeed. (*HJ*)

gen-zan げんざん (見参)   *n., intr. v. SH* **1**. audience with a superior. **2**. audience with a person of lower status. **3**. recording the names of guests in attendance at a banquet or ceremony, or such a list. (*HM*)

gesu-otoko げすをとこ (下衆男)   *n*. low-ranking man, male servant. (*MS*)

gō がふ (合)   *n* counter for objects with covers (baskets, boxes, etc.). (*HJ*)

gō ごふ (業)   *n*. **1**. (Buddhist) actions of mind, body, and speech. **2**. reward or retribution for acts in a previous life, karma. (*HJ*)

go-jō ごぢやう (御諚)   *n*. command or words of a superior (*hon.*). (*HM*)

go-koku ごこく (五穀)   *n*. five staple grains (rice, wheat, soybeans, and two kinds of millet: *awa* and *kibi*), grains in general. (*HJ*)

*GO-RAN-ZU ごらんず (ご覧ず)   *tr. v. SH* to view, see (*hon.*). (*TM*)

goro ごろ (頃)   *n*. time, period. (*SN*)

go-su ごす (期す)   *tr. v. SH* **1**. to expect a result, anticipate. **2**. to resolve to do.

goto ~ごと (毎)   *suffix* each time, every ~, each ~. (*TM, TN, UM, US*)

*GOTOSHI ごとし (如し) *aux. v.* indicates **1**. comparison, similarity: to be like, similar to. **2**. exemplification, representation of a set or category, often by mention of a particular instance: such as. (*HJ*)

*GU-SU ぐす (具す) *tr. v. SH* **1**. to bring something or someone. **2**. to prepare, outfit oneself. **3**. to attach, add. *intr. v. SN* **1**. to go with someone, follow. **2**. to be included, provided. **3**. to accompany, become a wife to. (*TM*)

ha   *See* **wa**.

ha は (端) *n.* edge, tip, rim. (*MS*)

ha は (葉) *n.* leaf, leaves. (*TZ*)

HABAKA-RU はばかる (憚る) *intr. v. YD* **1**. to have trouble moving forward. **2**. to overflow, become rampant. *tr. v. YD* to show deference, avoid (out of concern for taboos), yield. (*MY*)

*HABE-RI はべり (侍り) *intr. v. RH* **1**. to serve a superior, serve by the side of a superior, be in attendance on (*hum.*). **2**. to exist, have, be. **3**. *hum. suppl. v.*

hage-mu はげむ (励む) *intr. v. YD* to make one's fullest effort to do something, strive, endeavor. (*HJ*)

hage-shi はげし (激し・烈し) *shiku adj.* severe, intense. (*HJ*)

hagoromo はごろも (羽衣) *n.* feathered robe. (*TM*)

HA-GUKU-MU はぐくむ (育む) *tr. v. YD* **1**. to raise, bring up, rear, foster. **2**. to look after. (*HJ*)

hai はひ (灰) *n.* ashes. (*MS*)

hajime-owari はじめをはり (始終) *n.* beginning and end. (*TZ*)

haji-mu はじむ (始む・初む) *tr. v. SN* **1**. to begin, start something new. **2**. to begin with, start with. (*SN*)

*HAKABAKA-SHI はかばかし (果々し) *shiku adj.* [fr. n. *haka*, "progress with work"] **1**. moving forward with vigor, alacrity. **2**. reliable, trustworthy. **3**. prominent, clear. (*HJ*)

*HAKA-NA-SHI はかなし (果無し・果敢無し) *ku adj.* [fr. n. *haka*, "progress with work," and adj. *nashi*, "without"] **1**. unreliable. **2**. fruitless, empty, useless. **3**. minor, beneath mention, trivial. **4**. childish, immature, lacking in judgment. (*GM, HJ, SN, TM*)

haka-se はかせ (博士) *n.* scholar at the academy or *daigaku*. (*MS*)

hako はこ (箱) *n.* box. (*TM*)

haku はく (箔) *n.* gilt, gold, silver, or copper leaf used for decoration. (*HJ*)

haku-tai はくたい (百代) (also *hyakudai*) *n.* eternity, countless ages (generations). (*OH*)

ha-mu はむ (食む) *tr. v. YD* to eat. (*MY*)

HANA はな (花) *n.* **1**. plant or tree flower. **2**. plum flower. **3**. cherry blossom. **4**. flower offering to the Buddha. **5**. glory, beauty. **6**. essence of an art or artistic practice. (*GM*)

hanahada はなはだ (甚だ) *adv.* extremely. (*HJ*)

hana-mi はなみ (花見) *n.* flower viewing. (*TZ*)

hana-no-moto はなのもと (花の本) *comp.* **1**. (at the) base of a tree in bloom, especially beneath blossoming cherry trees. **2**. master of *renga* (classical linked verse) or *haikai* (popular linked verse). (*TZ*)

HANA-RU はなる (離る) *intr. v. SN* **1**. to leave, separate. **2**. to lose a connection. **3**. to escape. **4**. to retire from a post. (*MS*)

HANA-TSU はなつ (放つ) *tr. v. YD* **1**. to let go. **2**. to free. **3**. to open (a door, etc.). **4**. to hand over, sell. **5**. to give off light. **6**. to release (an arrow, etc.). **7**. to set (a fire). **8**. to leave aside, leave out. (*HJ, HM, TM*)

hane はね (羽) *n.* wing. (*HJ*)

han-ka はんか (反歌) *n.* envoy, or a thirty-one-syllable *waka* following a *chōka* (long poem), usually summarizing or supplementing the *chōka*. (*MY*)

hara はら (原) *n.* field, plain.

hara-data-shi はらだたし（腹立たし）*shiku adj.* [fr. v. *haradatsu*, "to become angry"] irritable, angry. (*TM*)

hara-da-tsu はらだつ（腹立つ）*intr. v. YD* **1.** to become angry, irritated. **2.** to quarrel, fight. (*GM*)

HA-RU はる（張る）*intr. v. YD* **1.** to form on the surface (as ice on a pond). **2.** to sprout, bud. **3.** to be glued tightly. *tr. v. YD* **1.** to stretch out (a string, rope). **2.** to tape paper or cloth with glue. **3.** to beat, hit. **4.** to set up a military line or front. **5.** to bet money. (*IM*)

haru はる（腫る・張る）*intr. v. SN* (of the skin, flesh) to become swollen (from infection, etc.).

HARU はる（春）*n.* spring (the season). (*TZ*)

HARU-AKI はるあき（春秋）*n.* **1.** spring and autumn. **2.** years, age. (*HJ*)

haru-baru はるばる（遥々）*adv.* from far away. (*IM*)

***HARUKA** はるか（遥か）*nari adj. v.* **1.** distant (in space). **2.** distant (in time). **3.** emotionally distant, reluctant, unwilling.

hase-au はせあふ（馳せ合ふ）*intr. v. YD* to spur on one's horse and engage (the enemy) in combat. (*HM*)

hase-chi-ru はせちる（馳せ散る）*intr. v. YD* to rush off and scatter. (*HM*)

hashi はし（嘴）*n.* bill, beak (of a bird). (*IM*)

***HASHI** はし（端）*n.* **1.** edge, tip. **2.** veranda, porch. **3.** starting point. **4.** part, bit, fragment. **5.** halfway, odds and ends. (*GM*)

hashi はし（階・梯）*n.* **1.** front staircase. **2.** ladder. **3.** status, rank. (*HJ*)

HASHI はし（橋）*n.* **1.** bridge (across a river, etc.). **2.** walkway (connecting buildings).

hashira はしら（柱）*n.* pillar. (*GM, HJ*)

***HASHI-RU** はしる（走る）*intr. v. YD* **1.** to move quickly, run. **2.** to escape. **3.** to scatter. **4.** to become excited. **5.** to roll fiercely. (*GM*)

hashiru-hashiru はしるはしる *adv.* **1.** here and there, off and on. **2.** excitedly, in fits and starts. (*SN*)

***HASHITA-NASHI** はしたなし（端なし）*ku adj.* **1.** unsuitable, ill-suited. **2.** shameful, embarrassing (appearance, behavior). **3.** insensitive, thoughtless, inconsiderate. **4.** extreme, intense (rain, wind). (*IM, MS*)

hasu はす（蓮）*n.* lotus. (*TO*)

ha-su はす（馳す）*intr. v. SN* to hurry, run about. *tr. v. SN* **1.** to make (a horse) run, gallop. **2.** to direct one's thoughts toward. (*HJ*)

HATA はた（将）*adv.* **1.** by chance, perhaps, possibly. **2.** but, despite that, even so. **3.** again, also. **4.** definitely, no doubt. (*HI, MS, UM*)

hatake はたけ（畠・畑）*n.* cultivated (plowed) field. (*HJ*)

hata-mata はたまた（将又）*conj.* used to form a question: (is it X) or (is it Y)? (*HJ*)

***HATE** はて（果て）*n.* **1.** end, limit. **2.** faraway place. **3.** end of a period of mourning. **4.** decline, reduced circumstances. (*HJ, SN*)

hate-wa はては（果ては）*comp.* [fr. n. *hate*, "end," and bound p. *wa*] in the end, finally, eventually. (*TZ*)

***HA-TSU** はつ（果つ）*intr. v. SN* **1.** to finish, end. **2.** to die. **3.** *suppl. v.* to finish doing (something) completely. (*MS, TM, TN*)

hatsu-kusa はつくさ（初草）*n.* **1.** first grasses of early spring. **2.** (metaphor) child. (*GM*)

ha-u はふ（這ふ）*intr., v. YD* **1.** to creep, crawl. **2.** to become overgrown. (*TM*)

hau-hau はふはふ（這ふ這ふ）*adv.* **1.** as if crawling along, just barely, finally, at long last. **2.** in a fluster, panicky. (*TZ*)

haya はや（早）*adv.* quickly. (*IM, TM*)

HAYA-SHI はやし（早し・速し）*ku adj.* **1.** fast. **2.** early. **3.** strong, rapid (current of a stream, river). **4.** intense, powerful (scent). (*MS*)

***HAZU** はづ（恥づ）*intr. v. KN* **1.** (to reflect on one's past actions, deficiencies, sins and) to be ashamed. **2.** to be embarrassed (by the attention of others).

***HAZUKA-SHI** はづかし（恥づかし）*shiku adj.* **1.** embarrassing, causing one to feel inferior, insignificant, out of place. **2.** causing one to feel diffident, shy, inept. **3**. impressive, dauntingly superior (so that one feels worthless, inadequate by comparison). (*TM*)

HA-ZUKI はづき (八月・葉月)   *n.* Eighth Month (lunar calendar). (*TM*)

he   *See* **e**.

heda-tsu へだつ (隔つ)   *tr. v. SN* **1**. to place something in between, shut off, isolate. **2**. to leave a space between (two things, oneself and another, etc.). **3**. to keep at a distance, stay away from. *intr. v. YD* to be separated, stand apart. (*TM, UM*)

hen へん (変)   *n.* **1**. disturbance, uprising, (political) incident. **2**. unusual event. (*HJ*)

hen-ji へんぢ (辺地) (also *henchi*)   *n.* outlying areas remote from the capital, countryside. (*HJ*)

hen-sai へんさい (辺際) (also *henzai*)   *n.* limit. (*HJ*)

hen-un へんうん (片雲)   *n.* scattered clouds. (*OH*)

hetsura-u へつらふ (諂ふ)   *intr. v. YD* to flatter, curry favor with, play up to. (*HJ*)

HI ひ (日)   *n.* **1**. sun, sunshine. **2**. daytime, noon. **3**. day, days. **4**. time elapsed. **5**. weather. **6**. Sun Goddess, Amaterasu oomikami, or her imperial descendants. (*GM*)

hibiki-wata-ru ひびきわたる (響き渡る)   *intr. v. YD* to ring out, reverberate. (*NE*)

hi-deri ひでり (日照り・旱)   *n.* drought. (*HJ*)

*HIGAHIGA-SHI ひがひがし (僻々し)   *shiku adj.* **1**. crooked, twisted, perverse, uncouth. **2**. unsightly, peculiar, unreasonable.

*HIGA-KOTO ひがこと (僻事)   *n.* **1**. mistake, error. **2**. wrongful or immoral act, evil deed.

*HI-GORO ひごろ (日来)   *adv.* **1**. usually, normally. **2**. recently. *n.* (for) a number of days, many days. (*HM*)

hi-gurashi ひぐらし (蜩)   *n.* evening cicada (*Tanna japonensis*). (*HJ*)

HI-GURA-SHI ひぐらし (日暮らし)   *n., adv.* [fr. *hikurashi*] all day long, from morning to evening. (*SN, TZ*)

hi-hada ひはだ (檜皮) (also *hi-wada*)   *n.* bark of *hinoki* tree (Japanese cypress), used for thatching roofs. (*HJ*)

hiji ひぢ (泥)   *n.* mud, dirt. (*TO*)

HIJIRI ひじり (聖)   *n.* **1**. person of great virtue, saint, sage. **2**. ruler, emperor. **3**. admired master of a way or profession (such as the poet Hitomaro). **4**. eminent or virtuous priest. **5**. mountain ascetic. (*HJ*)

hikari ひかり (光り)   *n.* **1**. light, radiance, effulgence. **2**. luster, lustrous or awesome appearance. **3**. glory, celebrity. (*TM*)

hikari-dō ひかりだう (光堂)   *n.* hall decorated with gold leaf. (*OH*)

hika-ru ひかる (光る)   *intr. v. YD* **1**. to shine, sparkle. **2**. to appear exceptional, outstanding. (*MS, TM*)

hika-u ひかふ (控ふ)   *intr. v. SN* **1**. to wait, stand by. **2**. to serve at one's side, attend. *tr. v. SN* **1**. to restrain, hold back. **2**. to put off, postpone. (*HM*)

hikazu ひかず (日数)   *n.* number of days. (*US*)

hiki-a-gu ひきあぐ (引き上ぐ)   *tr. v. SN* **1**. to pull up. **2**. to move (a planned event) up, schedule earlier. (*TM*)

hiki-gu-su ひきぐす (引き具す)   *tr. v. SH* **1**. to take along. **2**. to acquire (a skill, etc.). (*TM*)

hiki-tsutsu-mu ひきつつむ (引き包む)   *tr. v. YD* [fr. intensifier prefix *hiki* and v. *tsutsumu*] to wrap. (*HJ*)

*HI-KU ひく (引く)   *tr. v. YD* **1**. to draw in toward oneself. **2**. to draw (a sword, bowstring, etc.). **3**. to take out, remove. **4**. to lead, guide. **5**. to drag along. **6**. to draw a line. **7**. to stretch out, spread. **8**. to shoot an arrow. **9**. to quote, cite as an example. **10**. to invite, tempt. **11**. to give as a gift. **12**. to bathe, shower with (hot) water. (*HM*)

*HIMA ひま (隙・暇)   *n.* **1**. gap, space. **2**. break, interval, pause. **3**. leisure time. (*MS*)

hima-na-shi ひまなし (隙・暇なし)   *ku adj.* [fr. n. *hima*, "space," and adj. *nashi*, "without"]

1. crowded together with no space between. **2.** ceaseless, without interruption. **3.** extremely cautious. (*MS, TM, US*)

hime-gimi ひめぎみ (姫君) *n.* daughter or older sister of a noble (*hon.*). (*GM*)

hina ひな (雛) (also *hihina*) *n.* **1.** chick, immature bird. **2.** paper doll set out during the Hina or Doll Festival to pray for the health and good fortune of daughters. (*OH*)

HINA-BU ひなぶ (鄙ぶ) *intr. v. KN* to be rustic, provincial, uncouth. (*HJ*)

HINEMOSU ひねもす (終日) *adv.* from morning to evening, all day long.

hi-oke ひをけ (火桶) *n.* wooden brazier. (*MS*)

hira ひら (平) *nari adj. v.* flat, level, even. (*HJ*)

HIRA-KU ひらく (開く) *intr. v. YD* **1.** to open up, spread out. **2.** to flee. *tr. v. YD* **1.** to open. **2.** to make clear. **3.** to cause to flourish. *intr. v. SN* **1.** to blossom. **2.** to emerge. (*TM*)

hira-mu ひらむ (平む) *intr. v. YD* to become flat. (*TM*)

hiro-gu ひろぐ (広ぐ) *tr. v. SN* **1.** to widen, spread out. **2.** to scatter. **3.** to cause to prosper. (*GM, HJ, TM*)

HIRO-U ひろふ (拾ふ) *tr. v. YD* to gather, pick up, collect. (*HJ*)

HIRU ひる (昼) *n.* midday. (*MS*)

hi-ru ひる (嚔る) *tr. v. KI* to sneeze. (*US*)

hisage ひさげ (提) *n.* small metal pot with a handle, often used for heating and serving water or saké. (*US*)

*HISA-SHI ひさし (久し) *shiku adj.* **1.** lengthy. **2.** continuous (over a long period of time). **3.** long time since last meeting. (*HJ, TM*)

hisashi ひさし (庇) *n.* canopy, overhanging part of a roof. (*HJ*)

hishi-gu ひしぐ (拉ぐ) *intr. v. SN* to be crushed, smashed, squashed. *tr. v. YD* **1.** to smash, crush. **2.** to dominate, hold sway over. (*HJ*)

HITA-BURU ひたぶる (頓・一向) *nari adj. v.* (lit., to lean strongly in one direction) **1.** ear-

nest, single-minded. **2.** absolutely, completely. **3.** reckless. **4.** violent. (*TO*)

hitai ひたひ (額) *n.* forehead. (*GM, HJ, TM*)

hitai-tsuki ひたひつき (額つき) *n.* shape of the forehead. (*GM*)

hita-su ひたす (浸す・漬す) *tr. v. YD* to immerse, soak. (*HJ*)

hita-sura ひたすら *adv., nari adj. v.* **1.** intensely, without respite, single-mindedly, earnestly. **2.** completely. (*HJ*)

hita-tare ひたたれ (直垂) *n.* type of robe originally worn by commoners and later by aristocrats and warriors. (*HJ*)

*HITO ひと (人) *n.* **1.** human being. **2.** member of society. **3.** someone else (other than oneself). **4.** adult, mature person. **5.** great, magnificent person. **6.** that person (who is on one's mind). **7.** status, lineage. **8.** character, personality. *pron.* you (between husband and wife, etc.). (*HJ, IM, TM*)

hito-bito ひとびと (人々) *n.* people, assistants. (*GM, TM*)

hitoe-ni ひとへに (偏に) *adv.* completely, intensely. (*TZ*)

hito-giki ひとぎき (人聞き) *n.* reputation. (*TM*)

hito-katarai ひとかたらひ (人語らひ) *n.* conferring with someone, speaking about something to someone. (*SN*)

hito-koto ひとこと (一言) *n.* word or two. (*TM*)

HITO-MA ひとま (人間) *n.* **1.** time when no one is looking or around. **2.** infrequency of visits. (*SN*)

HITO-ME ひとめ (人目) *n.* **1.** eyes of others who might be watching. **2.** visit by a person (friend, lover, etc.). (*HI, TM*)

hito-mono ひともの (一物) *adv.* substantially, fully, totally. (*US*)

hitori-mi ひとりみ (独身) *n.* **1.** single person. **2.** person without dependents. (*HJ*)

hitori-zumi ひとりずみ (独り住み) *n.* living alone. (*TM*)

hitsu ひつ (櫃) *n.* large wooden chest with lid. (*SN*)

hitsuji ひつじ (未) *n.* **1.** south-southwest. **2.** hour of the ram (1:00–3:00 P.M.). (*HJ*)

hō ほふ (法) *n.* (Buddhist) **1.** the truth of all things. **2.** law, dharma: teachings of the Buddha. **3.** rites, ceremonies. (*HJ*)

hōburi はうぶり (葬) *n.* burial. (*KM*)

*HODASHI ほだし (絆) *n.* **1.** handcuff, footcuff. **2.** horse restrainer (placed on legs to prevent movement). **3.** obstruction, restriction.

*HODO ほど (程) *n.* indicates **1.** degree, extent. **2.** time, duration, interval: while. **3.** distance, length, height, depth, width. **4.** vicinity, area. **5.** position, age, status. (*GM, HJ, HM, IM, SN*)

HODO-NASHI ほどなし (程なし) *ku adj.* **1.** narrow, cramped, small. **2.** lowly, low-ranking. **3.** brief, fleeting, young. (*UM*)

hodo-ni ほどに (程に) *conj. p.* **1.** interval, duration: while. **2.** cause: as a result. (*TM*)

hodoro ほどろ *n.* overgrown ears of bracken. (*HJ*)

ho-gumi ほぐみ (穂組) *n.* rice ears bundled for drying. (*HJ*)

ho-i ほい (布衣) *n.* courtiers' casual wear (alternative for *kariginu*). (*HJ*)

HOI ほい (本意) *n.* original intention, original objective, original wish.

HOI-NASHI ほいなし (本意なし) *ku adj.* [fr. n. *hoi*, "intention," and adj. *nashi*, "without"] unintentional, regrettable. (*TM*)

hō-jō はふぢやう (方丈) *n.* unit of area: one *jō* (3.03 meters) square (approx. 10 feet square). (*HJ*)

hoka ほか (外) *n.* **1.** outside world. **2.** outside. **3.** another place, elsewhere. **4.** everything excluding (some set or portion). (*TZ*)

hoka-hoka ほかほか (外々) *n.* separate place. *adj. v.* separate, scattered. (*MS*)

hoka-zama ほかざま (外様・外方) *n.* another direction, elsewhere. (*TM*)

ho-moto ほもと (火元) *n.* origin of a fire. (*HJ*)

hon ほん (本) *n.* **1.** model, guide. **2.** book. **3.** base, origin, essence.

honō ほのほ (焔・炎) *n.* **1.** flames. **2.** (metaphor) passionate, turbulent emotions. (*HJ*)

HONO-KA ほのか (仄か) *nari adj. v.* **1.** faint, vague, indistinct (light, color, shape). **2.** slight. (*KM, MS*)

horo-bu ほろぶ (亡ぶ) *intr. v. KN* **1.** to collapse, disappear. **2.** to deteriorate. (*HJ*)

horo-horo ほろほろ *adv.* **1.** scattering of leaves. **2.** scattering of people. **3.** tearing, rending. **4.** dropping of tears. **5.** (onomatopoeia) call of pheasants, *yamadori*, etc. (*HJ*)

HŌ-SHI ほふし (法師) *n.* priest. (*GM*)

hoso-shi ほそし (細し) *ku adj.* **1.** thin, narrow. **2.** poor, scarce. (*IM*)

ho-su ほす (干す・乾す) *tr. v. YD* to dry (something). (*HI*)

hotaru ほたる (蛍) *n.* firefly. (*MS*)

hoto-bu ほとぶ (潤ぶ) *intr. v. KN* to absorb moisture and expand, swell up. (*IM*)

HOTOKE ほとけ (仏) *n.* **1.** one who has attained enlightenment. **2.** Shakyamuni, the historical Buddha. **3.** statue of the Buddha. **4.** the dead. (*HJ*)

hotori ほとり (辺・邊) *n.* **1.** vicinity, environs. **2.** relative, near kin. **3.** edge, side, border. (*IM, KM, TZ*)

hototogisu ほととぎす (時鳥・杜鵑・子規・不如帰) *n.* mountain cuckoo, associated with summer in Japanese poetry. (*HJ*)

ho-yu ほゆ (吠ゆ・吼ゆ) *intr. v. SN* to bark, howl. (*MS*)

hō-yū ほういう (朋友) *n.* friend. (*HJ*)

hyaku-kan ひやくくわん (百官) *n.* many government officials. (*TM*)

hyō-haku へうはく (漂泊) *n.* wandering, drifting aimlessly as a vagabond. (*OH*)

hyō-su へうす (表す) *tr. v. SH* to represent, stand for, symbolize. (*NE*)

i い (寝) *n.* sleep. (*MY*)

*IBUKA-SHI いぶかし *shiku adj.* **1**. worrisome. **2**. suspicious. **3**. intriguing (making one want to see, hear, or know more).

*IBUSE-SHI いぶせし *ku adj.* **1**. dreary, dismal. **2**. worrisome, anxious. **3**. unpleasant, discomforting. **4**. eerie.

ichi いち (市) *n.* market, marketplace. (*HJ*)

ichi いち (一) *n.* **1**. the numeral one. **2**. first. **3**. the best (of). (*SN*)

ichi-go いちご (一期) *n.* life span, person's whole life. (*HJ*)

ichijiru-shi いちじるし (著し) *ku adj.* [fr. prefix *ichi*, "extreme," and adj. *shirushi*, "clear"] striking, marked, conspicuous. (*UM*)

idaki-oko-su いだきおこす (抱き起す) *tr. v. YD* to lift up in one's arms. (*TZ*)

ida-ku いだく (抱く) *tr. v. YD* to hold, embrace. (*TM*)

idashi-ta-tsu いだしたつ (出し立つ) *tr. v. SN* to send out. (*TM*)

*IDA-SU いだす (出だす) *tr. v. YD* **1**. to move (something) from inside to outside. **2**. to vocalize, express, sing. **3**. to represent in drawing, painting, etc. **4**. to show (feelings) in one's face or demeanor. (*TM*)

*IDE いで *interj.* used to summon someone: well, then, how about . . . (*GM*)

ide-ku いでく (出で来) *intr. v. KH* [fr. v. *izu* and v. *ku*] **1**. to come out, emerge into view. **2**. (of children) to be born, (of an incident) occur. **3**. to meet, encounter. (*HJ*)

IE いへ (家) *n.* **1**. house, home. **2**. household, family, wife. **3**. bloodline, lineage. **4**. secular world. (*TM*)

ie-zuto いへづと (家苞) *n.* souvenir, keepsake. (*HJ*)

ii いひ (飯) *n.* steamed or boiled rice. (*TM*)

ii-kaka-ru いひかかる (言ひかかる) *intr. v. YD* to urge, make advances toward.

ii-nagusa-mu いひなぐさむ (言ひ慰む) *tr. v. SN* to console (a person) with words. *intr. v. YD* to talk until one is consoled. (*UM*)

ii-oku-ru いひおくる (言ひ送る) *tr. v. YD* to report, transmit a message personally. (*UM*)

ii-tsu-gu いひつぐ (言ひ継ぐ) *tr. v. YD* to pass on (a story). (*MY*)

ii-tsuta-u いひつたふ (言ひ伝ふ) *tr. v. SN* **1**. to pass on by word of mouth. **2**. to take a message for someone. (*TM*)

*IKA いか (如何) *nari adj. v.* interrogative: used to form a question **1**. about conditions, means: how? **2**. with regard to reason, cause: why? **3**. with regard to degree: how much? (*TM*)

IKA-BAKARI いかばかり (如何許) *adv.* [fr. adj. v. *ikanari* and adv. p. *bakari*] how much, to what extent, to what degree? (*SN, TM, TO*)

*IKA-DE いかで (如何で) *adv.* **1**. interrogative: why, how? **2**. ironic or rhet. question: why would, how could (such be the case, etc.)? **3**. desiderative: somehow, if only . . . (*IM*)

IKA-DE-KA いかでか (如何でか) *comp.* [fr. adv. *ikade* and bound p. *ka*] indicates **1**. dubious: why? **2**. desiderative: if only I could, how I would like to . . . **3**. ironic or rhet. question: why would I? how could I? (*SN*)

*IKA-GA いかが (如何) *adv.* **1**. interrogative or dubitive: how, in what way? **2**. ironic or rhet. question: why would (such a thing happen, etc.)? **3**. expresses uncertainty, sense of danger. (*TM, TN*)

ikame-shi いかめし *shiku adj.* **1**. solemn, grave. **2**. grand, opulent, magnificent. **3**. awesome, overwhelmingly powerful. (*TM*)

i-kan いくわん (衣冠) *n.* court costume, including hat, worn when in attendance at imperial palace. (*HJ*)

*IKA-NI いかに (如何に) *adv.* **1**. interrogative: how, in what way? to what extent, how much? why? **2**. exclamatory, emphasizing degree: how much (so) . . . ! (*HM, SN, US*)

ikani-iwamu-ya いかにいはむや (如何に況むや) *set phrase* needless to say, of course.

ikazuchi いかづち (雷) *n.* thunder. (*HJ*)

iki いき (息) *n.* breath. (*TM*)

iki-i-zu いきいづ (生き出づ) *intr. v. SN* to come back to life, recover consciousness. (*UM*)

iki-oi いきほひ (勢ひ) *n.* **1.** vitality, strength. **2.** power, authority. **3.** condition, state of affairs. (*HJ, TM*)

*I-KU いく (生く) *intr. v. YD, KN* to live, be alive. *tr. v. SN* to cause to live, bring life to, save a life.

ikusa いくさ (軍) *n.* **1.** troop, military force. **2.** battle, war. **3.** archery. (*HM*)

ikuso-baku いくそばく (幾十許) *adv.* **1.** how many, how much. **2.** a great many, countless numbers (of). (*HJ*)

ikuwan *See* **ikan**.

IMA いま (今) *n.* **1.** the present, now. **2.** that which is new: modern trends, styles, events. *adv.* **1.** soon, right away. **2.** in a moment, after a short while. **3.** even more. **4.** anew, this time. (*HJ, MY, TM*)

IMA-DA いまだ (未だ) *adv.* **1.** (with neg.) (not) yet. **2.** still. (*HJ, HM, KM, TM*)

*IMAIMA-SHI いまいまし (忌々し) *shiku adj.* [fr. v. *imu*, "to avoid pollution"] **1.** inauspicious. **2.** unfortunate, cursed.

*IMA-MEKA-SHI いまめかし (今めかし) *shiku adj.* up-to-date, fashionable. (*GM*)

ima-ni いまに (今に) *adv.* even now, even to this day.

*I-MA-SU います (坐す・在す) *intr. v. YD, SH* **1.** to be (*hon.* for *ari*). **2.** to go, come (*hon.* for *yuku, ku*). *tr. v. SN* **1.** to cause to go. **2.** *hon. suppl. v.* (*IM, TM*)

ima wa mukashi いまはむかし (今は昔) *set phrase* (used at the beginning of *monogatari* and *setsuwa*) in the past (seen from the present), now (it was) a long time ago . . . (*TM*)

*IMI-JI いみじ *shiku adj.* [fr. v. *imu*, "to avoid pollution"] **1.** intense, extreme, immense, great. **2.** outstanding, superb. **3.** terrible, painful, frightening. (*HJ, SN, TM, US*)

*IN ゐん (院) *n.* **1.** residence of a retired or cloistered emperor or empress. **2.** retired or cloistered emperor or empress (*hon.*).

inaka-datsu ゐなかだつ (田舎だつ) *intr. v. YD* [fr. n. *inaka* and suffix *datsu*] to act or appear provincial, rustic. (*MS*)

in-in ゐんゐん (院々) *n.* (collectively) various temple halls. (*OH*)

INISHIE いにしへ (古) *n.* distant past, long ago. (*HJ, TZ*)

inji いんじ (往んじ) *attrib.* [fr. v. *inu*, "to leave," and aux. v. *ki*] past. *n.* the past, long ago. (*HJ*)

*I-NU いぬ (往ぬ) *intr. v. NH* **1.** to leave. **2.** to have time pass. **3.** to pass away, die. (*MS*)

inu いぬ (戌) *n.* **1.** hour of the dog (7:00–9:00 P.M.). **2.** west-northwest. (*HJ, TN*)

inu-i いぬゐ (戌亥・西北) *n.* northwest. (*HJ*)

io いほ (庵) *n.* (same as いほり) rough hut made of sticks and brush. (*HI*)

io いを (魚) *n.* fish. (*IM*)

irae いらへ (答へ・応へ) *n.* [fr. v. *irahu*, "to reply"] reply. (*MS*)

iraka いらか (甍) *n.* **1.** roof tiles, tiled roof. **2.** peak of a roof. (*HJ, OH*)

IRA-U いらふ (答ふ・応ふ) *intr. v. SN* to answer, reply. (*MS, TM*)

iri-ai いりあひ (入相) *n.* **1.** sunset, dusk. **2.** vespers, temple bells rung at dusk, the sound of those bells. (*HM*)

iri-ta-tsu いりたつ (入りたつ) *intr. v. YD* **1.** to enter deeply into. **2.** to have an intimate relationship. **3.** to be deeply knowledgeable about. (*TN*)

*IRO いろ (色) *n.* **1.** color, coloration. **2.** colors that signify social status, rank. **3.** colors reserved for the imperial family. **4.** colors associated with mourning. **5.** complexion. **6.** appearance, atmosphere, aura. **7.** circumstances. **8.** gentleness, sensitivity. **9.** superficial display, flamboyance. **10.** romance, love, affair. **11.** lover. *nari adj. v.* **1.** beautiful, lustrous. **2.** amorous, unfaithful. (*HI*)

iro-kono-mu いろこのむ (色好む) *intr. v. YD* **1**. to understand love. **2**. to seek love or an erotic liaison. (*TZ*)

iro-ko-shi いろこし (色濃し) *ku adj.* **1**. excessive, gaudy, cloying, showy. **2**. rich in hue, deeply colored. (*TZ*)

I-RU いる (入る) *intr. v. YD* **1**. to enter, go into. **2**. (of the sun, moon) to set, become hidden from view. **3**. to go to court, join a Buddhist order. **4**. to need, be in need of. **5**. to reach a certain state, condition. **6**. to sink in deeply, touch one's heart. **7**. to come, go (*hon.* for *ku, yuku*). **8**. *suppl. v.* to do (something) thoroughly, completely. *tr. v. SN* **1**. to put inside, place in. **2**. to put one's heart into, try one's best. **3**. *suppl. v.* to take in, accept ～ (*HM, MS, SN, TM*)

i-ru いる (射る) *tr. v. KI* to shoot. (*TM*)

I-RU ゐる (率る) *tr. v. KI* **1**. to lead, take along. **2**. to carry, wear. (*TM*)

I-RU ゐる (居る) *intr. v. KI* **1**. to stay in one place, remain. **2**. to sit. **3**. to live in, dwell. **4**. to grow. (*IM, TM*)

ISA いさ *interj.* expresses perplexity in the face of a difficult question: well, I wonder. *adv.* (followed by *shira-zu*) well, I don't know.

isasa-ka いささか (聊か・些か) *nari adj. v.* slight, small. *adv.* **1**. slightly, somewhat. **2**. (followed by neg.) (not) at all, absolutely (not). (*HJ, TM, TN, TO*)

ISO-GU いそぐ (急ぐ) *intr. v. YD* to hurry. *tr. v. YD* to prepare.

i-ssho いつしょ (一所) *n.* **1**. same place. **2**. counter for high-ranking people: one person. (*HM*)

itadaki いただき (頂) *n.* summit, top of a mountain. (*TM*)

ita-de いたで (痛手) *n.* serious or severe wound. (*HM*)

ita-ru いたる (至る) *intr. v. YD* **1**. to arrive at. **2**. to think of, take into consideration. **3**. to reach the full extent. (*HJ, IM*)

ITA-SHI いたし (甚し・痛し) *ku adj.* (甚し) **1**. extreme, intense. **2**. very good, superb. (痛し) **1**. physically painful. **2**. mentally painful. **3**. pitiful. (*GM, TM*)

ITA-SU いたす (致す) *tr. v YD* **1**. to deliver, cause to arrive or reach. **2**. to carry out with utmost effort. **3**. to give up one's life to do (e.g., *inochi o itasu*). **4**. to bring about, bring to fruition.

itawari いたはり (労り) *n.* [fr. v. *itawaru*, "to have sympathy for"] **1**. protection, support. **2**. labor, effort. **3**. consideration, care. **4**. illness, exhaustion. (*HM*)

ITAWA-SHI いたはし (労し) *shiku adj.* **1**. painful (due to illness, etc.). **2**. pitiful. **3**. desiring to take care of. (*HJ*)

ITAZURA いたづら (徒ら) *nari adj. v.* **1**. useless, fruitless, empty, in vain. **2**. open or abandoned (space). **3**. bored, having time on one's hands. (*HI, HJ*)

ITO いと *adv.* **1**. very, greatly, extremely, much. **2**. (followed by neg.) (not) that much. (*GM, HJ, TM, TN, TZ*)

ITODO いとど *adv.* more and more, increasingly. (*SN*)

ITOKE-NA-SHI いとけなし (幼けなし) (also *itokinashi*) *ku adj.* young, innocent, helpless. (*IIJ*)

ITOMA いとま (暇) *n.* **1**. leisure. **2**. rest. **3**. retirement. **4**. parting. **5**. words of farewell.

itomo いとも *adv.* [fr. adv. *ito* and bound p. *mo*] **1**. truly, completely, absolutely. **2**. (followed by neg.) hardly, (not) at all. (*UM*)

itonami いとなみ (営み) *n.* endeavor, activity, work. (*HJ*)

i-to-ru いとる (射取る) *tr. v. YD* **1**. to kill with bow and arrow. **2**. to win a prize in an archery competition. (*HM*)

ITŌ-SHI いとほし *shiku adj.* **1**. pathetic, pitiful, sorry. **2**. troubled, unpleasant. **3**. cute, adorable. (*MS, TM*)

ito-shimo いとしも *comp.* [fr. adv. *ito* and adv. p. *shimo*] **1**. sufficiently, especially. **2**. (followed by neg.) (not) that much. (*TO*)

ITO-U いとふ (厭ふ) *tr. v. YD* **1**. to dislike,

hate, find distasteful. **2.** to avoid or flee from society, take religious vows. (*TZ*)

itsu-ku いつく (傅く)   *tr. v. YD* to raise with great care. (*TM*)

*ITSU-SHI-KA いつしか (何時しか)   *adv.* [fr. pron. *itsu*, adv. p. *shi*, and bound p. *ka*] **1.** (often spec.) expresses doubt about a future event: when (might something take place, come about)? **2.** before one knows it, unexpectedly soon. **3.** (followed by desiderative): if only (something might happen, become possible, etc.) soon. *nari adj. v.* all too soon, prematurely.

*I-U いふ (言ふ)   *tr. v. YD* **1.** to speak, express in words. **2.** to name, call. **3.** to gossip about, start rumors. **4.** to recite poetry. *intr. v. YD* **1.** to court, propose to. **2.** (of animals) to cry out. (*HJ, TM, TN*)

*IU-KAI-NA-SHI いふかひなし (言ふ甲斐なし)   *comp.* [fr. v. *iu*, n. *kai*, "effect," and adj. *nashi*] **1.** beyond expression or description in words. **2.** beneath mention, childish, lowly. **3.** pitiful, pathetic. **4.** to die (*iukai-naku naru*). (*GM, HM*)

iwa-ba いはば (言はば)   *comp.* [fr. v. *iu* and conj. p. *ba*] that is, if one were to give an example. (*HJ*)

IWAKE-NA-SHI いはけなし (稚けなし)   *ku adj.* immature, childish. (*GM*)

iwamu-ya いはむや (況むや) (also *iwanya*) *adv.* [fr. v. *iu*, aux. v. *mu*, and bound p. *ya*] needless to say, not to mention. (*HJ*)

iwa-nashi いはなし (岩梨)   *n.* cowberry, kind of azalea. (*HJ*)

iwa-o いはほ (巌)   *n.* large rock, boulder. (*HJ*)

iware いはれ (謂)   *n.* [fr. MZ of YD v. *iu* and passive aux. v. *ru*] legend of origins, history. (*NE*)

i-ya ゐや (居屋)   *n.* dwelling, residence. (*HJ*)

*IYA-SHI いやし (卑し・賤し)   *shiku adj.* **1.** low-ranking, lowly. **2.** vulgar, shabby. **3.** poor, impoverished. **4.** insignificant. **5.** mean-spirited, tight-fisted. (*HJ*)

*IZA いざ   *interj.* used **1.** to summon or address someone: well, then. **2.** to encourage or urge oneself when starting something: well, then (let me get started). (*IM, TM, UM*)

*I-ZU いづ (出づ)   *intr. v. SN* **1.** to leave, go out, come out. **2.** to depart on a journey, begin. **3.** to escape. *tr. v. SN* **1.** to set out. **2.** to reveal externally. **3.** to confess, speak of. **4.** *suppl. v.* to go out and do (something). (*HI, HJ, MS, SN, TM*)

IZU-CHI いづち (何方・何処)   *pron.* somewhere, wherever, which way. *adv.* in which direction, which way. (*HM*)

izu-kata いづかた (何方)   *pron.* **1.** which direction, which thing. **2.** which person, who. (*GM, HJ*)

IZU-KO いづこ (何処)   *pron.* where. (*TZ*)

izu-ku いづく (何処)   *pron.* where, which. (*HJ, MY*)

izumi いづみ (泉)   *n.* spring, fountain. (*TZ*)

IZU-RE いづれ (何れ)   *pron.* **1.** which. **2.** when. **3.** where. (*TM*)

jaku-maku じやくまく (寂寞)   *n., tari adj. v.* (Buddhist) lonesome, secluded, still, hushed. (*OH*)

ja-shō じやしやう (邪正)   *n.* evil and good, wrong and right. (*TO*)

*JI じ   *aux. v.* (follows MZ) **1.** neg. spec. with regard to someone else's possible actions or intentions, usually in the third person: (they) probably will not. **2.** neg. intent. in the first person: I will not. (*US*)

ji-butsu ぢぶつ (持仏)   *n.* personal Buddhist statue, kept in one's room. (*GM*)

ji-gai じがい (自害)   *n.* suicide. (*HM*)

ji-goku ぢごく (地獄)   *n.* hell. (*HJ*)

ji-karo ぢくわろ (地火炉)   *n.* hearth, stove. (*MS*)

JI-MOKU ぢもく (除目)   *n.* [fr. *ji*, "removal of previous appointments," and *moku*, "recording of new appointments"] ceremony for announcing the appointments of provincial governors and officials other than ministers. (*MS*)

jō ぢやう (丈) *n.* unit of length: 10 *shaku*, or approx. 3.03 meters (approx. 10 feet). (*HJ*)

joku-aku ぢよくあく (濁悪) *n.* (Buddhist) the five pollutions and ten evils. (*HJ*)

jōri でうり (条理) *n.* [fr. *jō*, "east–west avenues," and *ri*, "north–south avenues"] city grid. (*HJ*)

jubutsu じゆぶつ (儒仏) *n.* Confucianism and Buddhism. (*TO*)

jū-monji じふもんじ (十文字) *n.* **1.** shape of the character *ju* 十, cross. **2.** moving one's body or weapon back and forth and right to left in a rapid motion. (*HM*)

*KA か *bound p.* **1.** interrogation, forming a question. **2.** rhet. question. **3.** (at end of a sentence) exclamation, emphasis.

ka か (彼) *pron.* (of things in the distance) that. (*HJ, TM*)

ka か (香) *n.* fragrance, odor. (*HJ*)

ka か (鹿) (also *shika*) *n.* deer. (*IM*)

ka-bakari かばかり *adv.* **1.** this much. **2.** only this much. (*GM*)

kaba-u かばふ (庇ふ) *tr. v. YD* **1.** to protect from external harm, defend. **2.** to store away carefully. (*HM*)

kado かど (門) *n.* **1.** gate, entrance. **2.** clan, lineage, family. (*HJ*)

kado-de かどで (門出) *n.* (lit., leaving the gate) departure on a journey, including the custom of moving to a nearby location to make the final travel preparations. (*SN, TN*)

kaede かへで (楓) *n.* maple tree, known for brightly colored autumn foliage. (*IM*)

kaera-ka-su かへらかす *tr. v. YD* (suffix *kasu*) to bring to a boil. (*US*)

kaeri-goto かへりごと (返事・返言) (also *kaeri-koto*) *n.* **1.** messenger's report. **2.** reply, return poem. **3.** note of thanks, return visit. (*TM*)

KAERI かへり (帰り・還り・返り) *n.* **1.** answer, reply. **2.** reply poem (abbrev. of *kaeri-goto*). **3.** return.

*KAE-RU かへる (帰る・還る・返る・反る) *intr. v. YD* **1.** to return to a former or an original place or situation. **2.** to turn around in the direction from which one came. **3.** (of a new season, year) to begin. **4.** (of a sleeve, etc.) to be turned inside out, reversed. **5.** (of colors) to fade. **6.** *suppl. v.* to do (something) thoroughly, do (something) almost entirely. (*HI, TM*)

kaeru-sa かへるさ (帰るさ) *n.* time to go home, on the way home. (*HJ, TM*)

KAESHI かへし (返し) *n.* **1.** answer, reply. **2.** return gift. **3.** return (of waves, wind, earthquake tremors).

*KAE-SU かへす (返す・帰す・還す・反す) *tr. v. YD* **1.** to make someone return (to his or her former place or position). **2.** to return something to a former owner or place. **3.** to reply (to a poem, letter). **4.** to vomit. **5.** to turn over (a sleeve). **6.** to hoe, plow a field, cultivate. (*GM, HJ*)

kagari-bi かがりび (篝火) *n.* **1.** flare or torch of pine branches or chips burned at night for security or illumination outdoors. **2.** metal basket (usually atop a pole) for such a flare; cresset. (*HJ*)

kagaya-ku *See* **kakaya-ku.**

*KAGE かげ (影・景) *n.* **1.** light (of the sun, moon, fire, etc.). **2.** shape or form made visible by light. **3.** reflected image (in a mirror, surface of water, etc.). **4.** image in one's mind. **5.** shadow. **6.** emaciated form. **7.** insubstantial figure. **8.** spirit of the dead. (*HJ, MY, TM, TZ, UM*)

kage かげ (陰・蔭) *n.* **1.** dark spot, place where light does not shine. **2.** place hidden from view. **3.** backing, favor, support.

*KAGIRI かぎり (限り) *n.* **1.** limit. **2.** utmost, extreme. **3.** between, while. **4.** all, entire. **5.** end, last. **6.** opportunity, time. (*TM*)

KAGIRI-NA-SHI かぎりなし (限り無し) *ku adj.* **1.** unlimited, endless. **2.** unusual, intense. **3.** unsurpassed, incomparable. (*IM, TM*)

kai かひ (貝) *n.* **1.** shellfish, mollusk. **2.** empty shell of a mollusk (clam, cowrie, etc.). **3.** conch shell used as a trumpet for signaling. (*TM*)

KAI かひ (甲斐・効)   *n.* **1.** effect, efficacy. **2.** value, worth. (*TM*)

kai かひ (匙)   *n.* [fr. n. *kai*, "shell"] spoon, ladle. (*TM*)

kaichō-su かいちやうす (開帳す)   *tr. v. SH* to open up (valued holdings, relics, etc.) for public viewing (at a Buddhist temple). (*OH*)

kai-hin かいひん (海浜)   *n.* seashore. (*OH*)

kai-jin くわいじん (灰燼)   *n.* ashes and embers. (*HJ*)

kaiko かひこ (蚕)   *n.* silkworm. (*HJ*)

KAIMA-MI かいまみ (垣間見)   *n.* peeping, peering (at someone) through a hole or gap in a fence, curtain, etc.

kai-ma-mi-ru かいまみる (垣間見る)   *tr. v. KI* [fr. v. *kaki-ma-miru*] to peep or peer (at someone) through a hole or gap in a fence, curtain, etc.

KAI-NA-SHI かひなし (甲斐無し)   *ku adj.* **1.** ineffective, fruitless, pointless. **2.** insignificant, trivial. (*HJ, TM, TN*)

kai-ya-ru かいやる (掻い遣る)   *tr. v. YD* [fr. YD v. *kakiyaru*, "to sweep away with the hand"] **1.** to brush aside, sweep away with the hand. **2.** to give, offer. (*GM*)

kaka-gu かかぐ (掲ぐ・挑ぐ)   *tr. v. SN* [fr. v. *kakiagu*, "to lift up"] **1.** to raise (a curtain, skirt, etc.). **2.** to increase the intensity of an oil lamp, trim a lamp.

kakaku くわかく (過客)   *n.* traveler(s), people who come and go. (*OH*)

KAKA-RI かかり (斯かり)   *intr. v. RH* [fr. adv. p. *kaku* and v. *ari*] to be this way. (*GM*)

KAKARU かかる (斯かる)   *attrib.* this kind of. (*GM, HJ, IM, TN*)

*KAKA-RU かかる (懸かる・掛かる)   *intr. v. YD* **1.** to hang down, dangle. **2.** to be involved with. **3.** to turn one's attention to, be concerned with. **4.** (of snow, rain) to fall. **5.** to lean on, depend on, cling to. **6.** to stop over, lodge. **7.** (of a spirit) to possess. **8.** to pass by, come near. **9.** to pounce on, attack. (*MY, TM*)

kakau かかふ (抱ふ)   *tr. v. SN* **1.** to hold, embrace, encircle. **2.** to protect. (*TM*)

kakaya-ku かかやく (輝く・赫く) (also *kagayaku*)   *intr. v. YD* **1.** to shine, glow, especially with radiant beauty. **2.** to blush with embarrassment. *tr. v. YD* to embarrass someone. (*NE*)

*KAKAZURA-U かかづらふ   *intr. v. YD* **1.** to be entangled with. **2.** to have a relationship with, be involved with. **3.** to live long, live without taking vows. **4.** to dwell on, be concerned with.

kake-au かけあふ (掛け合う)   *intr. v. YD* **1.** to match, be in accord with. **2.** to negotiate. *tr. v. YD* to do (something) mutually. (*UM*)

kake-dai かけだひ (掛鯛)   *n.* pair of dried, salted sea bream (*tai*) tied together with a rope and hung out at the New Year. (*NE*)

kake-gane かけがね (掛け金)   *n.* metal door latch. (*HJ*)

kake-hi かけひ (懸樋)   *n.* bamboo water pipe. (*HJ*)

kakei かけい (佳景)   *n.* scenic view, beautiful scene. (*OH*)

kake-mono かけもの (賭物)   *n.* prize offered at a competition. (*TZ*)

kake-wa-ru かけわる (駆け割る)   *tr. v. YD* to ride on horseback through enemy troops. (*HM*)

kaki かき (垣)   *n.* fence, hedge. (*HJ*)

kaki-tsu-bata かきつばた (杜若)   *n.* a type of iris, a perennial grass that grows in lakes and swamps. (*IM*)

kaki-tsu-ku かきつく (掻き付く)   *intr. v. YD* **1.** to cling to, grab hold of. **2.** to rely on. *tr. v. SN* to comb or stroke (the hair). (*TZ*)

kaki-tsu-ku かきつく (書きつく)   *tr. v. SN* to write down, record. (*TN, TZ*)

kaki-ya-ru かきやる (掻き遣る)   *tr. v. YD* to sweep away or brush back with the hand. (*GM*)

*KAKO-TSU かこつ (託つ)   *tr. v. YD* **1.** to complain, gripe about. **2.** to use as a pretext or an excuse, blame (something) on someone else or on circumstances. (*HJ, TZ, UM*)

*KAKU かく (斯く) *adv.* in this way, in this manner, in this fashion, thus. (*HJ, SN, TM, UM*)

ka-ku かく (掻く) *tr. v. YD* **1.** to scratch. **2.** to play (a stringed instrument). **3.** to clear away. **4.** to cut off. **5.** to comb. (*GM*)

ka-ku かく (駆く) *intr. v. SN* **1.** to ride swiftly on horseback, gallop. **2.** to attack enemy lines on horseback. (*HM*)

ka-ku かく (欠く・歉く) *intr. v. SN* to be lacking. (*HJ*)

*KAKU かく (掛く) *tr. v. YD, SN* **1.** to place an object so that it does not fall, hanging or fixing it or placing it on top of something. **2.** to think fondly of. **3.** to serve in two roles at once. **4.** to measure and compare. **5.** to deceive. **6.** to speak, address. (*HJ*)

KAKU-RU かくる (隠る) *intr. v. YD, SN* **1.** to hide, conceal oneself. **2.** to die, pass away. (*MY*)

KAKU-TE かくて (斯くて) *adv.* in this way, thus. *conj.* used to change the topic: and then, and so. (*TM*)

kamabisu-shi かまびすし (喧し・囂し) *shiku adj.* noisy, loud. (*HJ*)

*KAMA-U かまふ (構ふ) *tr. v. SN* **1.** to construct, put together. **2.** to prepare. **3.** to plan. *intr. v. YD* to be involved in. (*HJ, TM*)

kami かみ (髪) *n.* hair on the head. (*GM, SN, TM*)

*KAMI かみ (上) *n.* **1.** apex, highest place (of). **2.** source of a river, upstream. **3.** Kyoto, Kamigata. **4.** direction: toward the imperial palace, north. **5.** emperor, shogun, person of high rank. **6.** elderly person. **7.** seat of honor. **8.** beginning, especially the first phrase of a *waka*. **9.** a long time ago. **10.** first part of the month. **11.** (Edo) (another's) wife. **12.** (Edo) mistress, owner of a wineshop or teahouse (*hon.*). (*IM*)

*KAMI かみ (神) *n.* **1.** god(s), divine beings or spiritual forces. **2.** thunder, the god of thunder.

kami-age かみあげ (髪上げ) *n.* (lit., putting up the hair) girl's coming-of-age ceremony. (*TM*)

kami-naka-shimo かみなかしも (上中下) *n.* people of superior, equal, and lower rank. (*TN*)

kami-yo かみよ (神代) *n.* age of the gods. (*HI, NE*)

kami-zama かみざま (上様) *n.* **1.** top, upper part. **2.** high society, upper classes. (*US*)

*KAMO かも *final p.* (follows nominal, RT) (Nara) emphatic: marks an exclamation. (*MY*)

kamuna かむな (寄居虫) (also *kamina*) *n.* hermit crab. (*HJ*)

kamu-sabu かむさぶ (神さぶ) *intr. v. KN* to act like a god, manifest divine qualities, inspire awe, fear, and respect. (*MY*)

*KANA かな *final p.* [fr. final p. *kamo*] emphatic: marks an exclamation.

kanagu-ru かなぐる *tr. v. YD* to grab and pull, yank (hair, clothing, etc.). (*KM*)

kanarazu かならず (必ず) *adv.* **1.** for sure, without fail. **2.** (followed by neg. or by rhet. question) absolutely (not). (*MS, TM*)

*KANA-SHI かなし (愛し・悲し) *shiku adj.* (愛し) **1.** (mainly with regard to relatives, lovers) adorable, lovable. **2.** (of objects, scenes) charming, moving. (悲し) **3.** painful, sad, regrettable (to the point of tears). **4.** poor, indigent. (*TM*)

*KANA-U かなふ (適ふ・叶ふ) *intr. v. YD* **1.** to fit, match, be appropriate, be suitable. **2.** to accord with one's wishes. **3.** to be equal to, able (usually followed by neg.). *tr. v. SN* to cause (something) to accord with one's wishes. (*HJ, TM, TO, TZ*)

KANDACHI-ME かんだちめ (上達部) *n.* designation for nobles of the third rank and above (minister of the left, major counselor, etc.). (*MS, TM*)

KANE-TE かねて (予ねて) *adv.* from beforehand, in advance.

kan-gen くわんげん (管絃) *n.* (lit., pipes, strings) wind and string instruments, such as *fue* (flute) and *biwa* (lute). (*HJ*)

kan-ja くわんじや (冠者) *n.* boy who has undergone the *genpuku* (元服) coming-of-age ceremony, young man. (*HM*)

kan-kyo かんきよ (閑居) *n.* (living in) quiet reclusion. (*HJ*)

kan-nen くわんねん (観念) *n.* (Buddhist) contemplation (of the Pure Land, etc.). (*HJ*)

kan-nin くわんにん (官人) *n.* official. (*TM*)

KA-NO かの *attrib.* [fr. pron. *ka* and case p. *no*] refers to something at a distance: that. (*UM*)

kan-roku くわんろく (官禄) *n.* (official) position and emoluments. (*HJ*)

kan-seki かんせき (閑寂) (also *kanjaku*) *n., nari adj. v.* quiet retreat, the calmness of mind produced by such a retreat. (*HJ*)

kao かほ (顔) *n.* **1.** face. **2.** surface. **3.** bodily appearance. (*TM*)

*KARA から *case p.* (follows nominal or nominalized phrase) indicates **1.** point of origin (temporal, spatial): from, since. **2.** means, method: by, with. **3.** passage through: via. **4.** cause or origin of action: because. *conj. p.* (follows RT) indicates **1.** cause or origin: because, as a result of. **2.** (followed by bound p. *wa*) hypothetical situation: if it were the case that.

Kara から (唐・韓) *n.* China. (*IM*)

kara-bitsu からびつ (唐櫃) *n.* [fr. n. *kara-hitsu*] large Chinese chest or coffer with legs. (*TM*)

kara-koromo からころも (唐衣・韓衣) *n.* Chinese-style robe with long sleeves. (*IM*)

kara-kurenai からくれなゐ (韓紅・唐紅) *n.* bright crimson or scarlet. (*HI*)

*KARA-NI からに *comp. conj. p.* [fr. case p. *kara* and *ni*] indicates **1.** one action occurs immediately after another: no sooner (had X happened) than (Y). **2.** unexpectedly serious or adverse result from a seemingly trivial cause: on account of nothing more than. (*HI*)

*KARA-SHI からし (辛し) *ku adj.* **1.** salty (taste). **2.** cruel, brutal. **3.** bitter, hard, difficult, trying. **4.** dangerous. **5.** unpleasant. **6.** spicy, hot, peppery (taste).

karasu からす (烏) *n.* crow. (*MS*)

kare かれ (彼) *pron.* him, her, that. (*TM*)

kare-ii かれいひ (乾飯) *n.* cooked rice that has been dried (used as travel provisions). (*IM*)

kare-kore かれこれ (彼此) *pron.* this person and that person, this and that thing. (*TN*)

kari かり (仮) *n.* temporary, provisional. (*HJ*)

kari かり (雁) *n.* wild goose, wild geese. (*MS*)

kari-o かりほ (仮庵・仮廬) (also *kari-io* かりいほ) *n.* temporary shelter, temporary hut. (*HI*)

*KARI-SOME かりそめ (仮初) *n., nari adj. v.* **1.** temporary, ad hoc. **2.** ephemeral, transient. **3.** accidental.

kari-ya かりや (仮屋) *n.* temporary lodging. (*HJ*)

karo-mu かろむ (軽む) *intr. v. YD* to become light. *tr. v. SN* **1.** to make light of. **2.** to look down on, treat with disdain. (*HJ*)

karō-jite からうじて (辛うじて) *adv.* [fr. adv. *karaku-shite*] barely, with difficulty, narrowly. (*HJ, TM*)

KARO-SHI かろし (軽し) *ku adj.* **1.** light weight. **2.** fickle, frivolous, hasty. **3.** low-ranking. **4.** weak, insignificant. **5.** worthless. (*HJ*)

ka-ru かる (刈る) *tr. v. YD* to reap. (*HJ*)

*KA-RU かる (離る) *intr. v. SN* **1.** to be separated (spatially). **2.** to be separated (temporally). **3.** to grow distant (emotionally or psychologically).

KA-RU かる (枯る) *intr. v. SN* **1.** to dry up, wither. **2.** to grow hoarse. (*HJ*)

kasa かさ (笠) *n.* **1.** wide-brimmed hat to protect against snow, rain, sun. **2.** umbrella. (*HJ*)

kasana-ru かさなる (重なる) *intr. v. YD* **1.** to pile up. **2.** (for similar things) to happen at the same time or occur repeatedly. (*HJ, TM*)

kasa-nu かさぬ (重ぬ) *tr. v. SN* **1.** to pile up. **2.** to repeat the same action. **3.** to pass days and months. (*IM*)

kasasagi かささぎ *n.* magpie (*Pica pica*). (*HI*)

kasegi かせぎ (鹿) *n.* (alternative for *shika*) deer. (*HJ*)

*****KASHI** かし *final p.* **1**. emphatic: expresses strong emphasis. **2**. seeks confirmation (from someone) of or calls attention to (a situation, state of affairs, etc.). (*US*)

kashi-ko かしこ (彼処・彼所) *pron.* there. (*HJ*)

*****KASHIKOMA-RU** かしこまる (畏まる) *intr. v. YD* **1**. to respectfully take an order, obey a command. **2**. to show awe, respect. **3**. to apologize. **4**. to sit respectfully. (*NE, TM*)

*****KASHIKO-SHI** かしこし (畏し・恐し・賢し) *ku adj.* (畏し・恐し) **1**. frightening. **2**. awe-inspiring, exalted. (賢し) **3**. wise, sagacious, superior. **4**. lucky, fortunate. **5**. (in RY) very. (*HJ*)

kashi-ku かしく (炊く) (also *kashigu*) *tr. v. YD* to steam or boil rice, barley, etc. (*TM*)

kashira かしら (頭) *n.* **1**. person's head. **2**. hair on the head. **3**. top of something. **4**. head of a group, an organization. (*US*)

*****KASHIZU-KU** かしづく (傅く) *tr. v. YD* **1**. to raise carefully. **2**. to look after carefully.

kasumi かすみ (霞) *n.* mist, haze, especially of spring.

kasu-mu かすむ (霞む) *intr. v. YD* **1**. to be misty, hazy. **2**. to appear misty, hazy. (*GM*)

KATA かた (方) *n.* **1**. direction. **2**. place, location. **3**. aspect. **4**. means, method. **5**. time. **6**. person (*hon.*). (*HJ, KM, SN*)

kata かた (潟) *n.* **1**. flat, shoal. **2**. bay, inlet.

KATABU-KU かたぶく (傾く) *intr. v. YD* **1**. (of the sun, moon) to sink, set. **2**. to tilt, lean in one direction. **3**. to near the end, decline. **4**. to tilt one's head to the side and think. *tr. v. SN* **1**. to set something at an angle, tilt. **2**. to cause to decline, bring down. **3**. to criticize. (*HJ, TZ*)

*****KATACHI** かたち (形・容貌) *n.* **1**. form, shape, figure. **2**. countenance, visage, looks. **3**. beautiful person, beautiful face. **4**. physical appearance. (*HJ, SN, TM*)

KATA-E かたへ (片方) *n.* one side, one part. (*TN*)

kata-hashi かたはし (片端) *n.* part, portion. (*HJ*)

kata-i かたゐ (乞食) *n.* **1**. beggar. **2**. derogatory expletive. (*US*)

kata-inaka かたゐなか (片田舎) *n.* [fr. prefix *kata*, "half," and n. *inaka*] backwoods, remote countryside, remote village. (*TZ*)

KATAJIKENA-SHI かたじけなし (忝し・辱し) *ku adj.* **1**. embarrassing, shameful. **2**. gracious (enough to do something, to honor with one's presence, etc.). **3**. thankful, grateful. (*HM*)

KATAKI かたき (敵) *n.* **1**. enemy in war. **2**. opponent, competitor. **3**. object of revenge. **4**. spouse. (*HM*)

KATAKUNA かたくな (頑) *nari adj. v.* **1**. unrefined, uncultivated, uneducated. **2**. stubborn, obstinate. **3**. boorish, ugly. (*TZ*)

KATAMI かたみ (形見) *n.* keepsake, memento. (*TM*)

KATAMI-NI かたみに (互に) *adv.* mutually, alternatively, one after another.

kata-mu かたむ (固む) *tr. v. SN* **1**. to make something hard, firm. **2**. to tie or fasten securely. **3**. to make a firm promise. **4**. to guard or defend. **5**. to draw one's bow and aim. (*HM*)

*****KATARA-U** かたらふ (語らふ) *tr. v. YD* **1**. to talk to, ask. **2**. to be friendly with, on good terms. **3**. to talk with a member of the opposite sex. **4**. to persuade, tempt, convince. (*SN, TM*)

katari-tsu-gu かたりつぐ (語り継ぐ) *tr. v. YD* [fr. v. *kataru*, "to narrate," and v. *tsugu*, "to pass on"] to pass on orally. (*MY*)

KATA-RU かたる (語る) *intr. v. YD* **1**. to narrate, tell about an event. **2**. to recite (a story) to music. **3**. to speak intimately. (*SN*)

kata-tagae かたたがへ (方違へ) *n.* avoidance of directional taboo. (*MS*)

kata-toki かたとき (片時) *n.* (single) moment, very short time. (*TM*)

KATA-WARA かたはら (傍ら・側) *n.* **1.** one side. **2.** vicinity. **3.** person at one's side. (*HJ, TM*)

*KATAWARA-ITASHI かたはらいたし (傍ら痛し) *ku adj.* [fr. *katawara*, "side"] **1.** discomforting, causing one to feel uneasy, anxious (when witnessing another's predicament, behavior, etc.) **2.** (of another's actions or situation) embarrassing, shameful. **3.** pitiful, heartwrenching.

katawa-zu-ku かたはづく (片端付く) *intr. v. YD* to become disabled, crippled. (*HJ*)

kate かて (糧) *n.* provisions (for travel). (*HJ*)

KATSU かつ (且つ) *adv.* indicates **1.** two things occurring at the same time: while. **2.** two things occurring in succession. *conj.* as well as, furthermore, in addition. (*HJ, UM*)

katsura かつら (桂) *n.* **1.** species of tree (*Cercidiphyllum japonica*) noted for brightly colored autumn foliage. **2.** legendary Chinese tree thought to grow on the moon. (*HJ*)

katsura かつら (鬘) *n.* hairpiece, wig. (*KM*)

katte かつて (勝手) *n., nari adj. v.* **1.** usefulness, convenience. **2.** willfulness, doing as one pleases. **3.** circumstances, conditions. **4.** lifestyle, livelihood. **5.** kitchen. (*NE*)

ka-u かふ (換ふ) (also *ko-u*) *tr. v. SN* to trade, barter. (*HJ, TM*)

ka-u かふ (飼ふ) (also *ko-u*) *tr. v. YD* to raise, care for (animals). (*TZ*)

*KA-WA かは *bound p.* indicates **1.** doubt, skepticism. **2.** rhet. question, often ironic.

kawa かは (河・川) *n.* river. (*HJ*)

kawa-go かはご (皮籠) *n.* basket woven of bark. (*HJ*)

kawa-kujira かはくぢら (皮鯨) *n.* whale blubber (used for food). (*NE*)

ka-wara かはら (河原) *n.* **1.** riverbed. **2.** bed of the Kamo River, southern part of Kyoto. (*HJ*)

kawari かはり (代はり) *n.* **1.** replacement. **2.** substitute. **3.** cost. (*GM*)

KAWA-RU かはる (変る) *intr. v. YD* **1.** to change. **2.** to be different (from others). (*HJ*)

kawa-su かはす (交す) *tr. v. YD* to exchange. (*TM*)

kaya かや (茅) *n.* grasses, such as *susuki* (pampas grass), *chigaya*, and *suge*, used for thatching. (*HJ*)

kayoi-ji かよひぢ (通ひ路) *n.* commuting road, route. (*HI*)

*KAYO-U かよふ (通ふ) *intr. v. YD* **1.** to commute, go to and from a place. **2.** (for a man) to commute to a woman's residence; by extension, to maintain conjugal relations with a woman. **3.** to communicate (feelings, words, etc.). **4.** to understand intimately, be familiar with. **5.** to intersect, cross paths. **6.** to have points in common with, resemble. (*TM*)

kayuga-ru かゆがる *intr. v. YD* to feel itchy. (*US*)

kaze かぜ (風) *n.* wind. (*HJ, HI*)

kazo-u かぞふ (数ふ) *tr. v. SN* **1.** to count, calculate. **2.** to include, count on. **3.** to keep rhythm. (*MS*)

*KAZU-KU かづく (被く) *tr. v. YD* **1.** to wear on one's head. **2.** to receive, place (a gift) on one's shoulder. **3.** to take responsibility (for). *tr. v. SN* **1.** to place on one's head. **2.** to give a gift, place (a gift) on one's shoulder. **3.** to make someone take responsibility. (*TM*)

kazura かづら (蔓・葛) *n.* vine, creeper. (*HJ*)

ke け (毛) *n.* hair. (*TM*)

*KEBURI けぶり (煙・烟) *n.* **1.** smoke. **2.** smoke from cremation, act of cremation. **3.** (metaphor) death. **4.** smoke from fire for cooking, metaphor for livelihood. **5.** trailing of mist, steam, etc., like smoke. (*TM*)

kebu-ru けぶる (煙る・烟る) *intr. v. YD* **1.** (of smoke) to rise. **2.** to be hazy (due to mist or smoke). **3.** to appear faintly or softly beautiful. **4.** to be cremated and turn to smoke. (*GM*)

kega-su けがす (穢す・汚す) *tr. v. YD* to defile, tarnish, soil. (*HJ*)

ke-hai *See* **ke-wai**.

kei-ki けいき（景気） *n.* **1.** landscape, scene. **2.** appearance. **3.** (in poetry) image of landscape. (*HJ*)

***KEI-SU** けいす（啓す） *tr. v. SH* to say (used to address royalty) (*hum.*).

kejime けぢめ *n.* **1.** distinction, difference. **2.** separation, distance. **3.** change, transformation. (*TO*)

ke-katsu-su けかつす（飢渇す） *intr. v. SH* to starve, be hungry and thirsty. (*HJ*)

***KEMU** けむ *aux. v.* (follows RY) indicates **1.** speculation about the past. **2.** conjecture about the cause or origin of a past event. **3.** hearsay about a past event. **4.** circumlocution about the past.

ken-mon けんもん（権門） *n.* powerful and wealthy person, family, or institution. (*HJ*)

ke-nuki けぬき（毛ぬき） *n.* tweezer. (*US*)

ken-zoku けんぞく（眷属） *n.* **1.** family, immediate relatives. **2.** subordinate, follower. (*HJ*)

***KE-RASHI** けらし *comp. aux. v.* [fr. aux. v. *keri* and *rashi*] indicates **1.** speculation about the past, based on evidence. **2.** circumlocution about past events.

***KERI** けり *aux. v.* (follows RY) indicates **1.** hearsay past: so it is said. **2.** exclamatory recognition, discovery. **3.** direct past (third person or first person).

kesa けさ（袈裟） *n.* surplice worn by a priest on top of a robe. (*SN*)

***KESHI** けし（怪し・異し） *shiku adj.* **1.** strange. **2.** dishonest, cold-hearted.

***KE-SHIKI** けしき（気色） *n.* **1.** facial expression, attitude, tone of voice. **2.** intention. **3.** love, favor, kindness. **4.** symptom. **5.** landscape (of natural world). **6.** strange feeling. **7.** just a little.

***KESHIKI-BAMU** けしきばむ（気色ばむ） *intr. v. YD* **1.** (of season, flowers) to begin, emerge. **2.** to suggest (one's inner thoughts). (*GM*)

keta けた（桁） *n.* beam, crossbeam. (*HJ*)

KE-U けう（希有） *nari adj. v.* **1.** rare, unusual, strange. **2.** unbelievable, astonishing. (*TM, TZ*)

KE-WAI けはい（気配） *n.* **1.** appearance, air, mood. **2.** attitude, manner, demeanor. **3.** scent, fragrance. **4.** sound, voice. **5.** trace. **6.** connection, link.

kezu-ru けづる（梳る） *tr. v. YD* to comb (the hair). (*GM*)

***KI** き *aux. v.* (follows RY) expresses **1.** personal past, recollection. **2.** direct past.

ki き（騎） *n.* horseman, mounted soldier. (*HM*)

ki き（奇） *n., nari adj. v.* **1.** unusual, rare. **2.** surprising. **3.** odd (number). (*UM*)

ki-bi きび（気味） (also *kimi*) *n.* taste, flavor, feel, atmosphere. (*HJ*)

ki-chō きちやう（几帳） *n.* standing curtain, suspended on portable frames. (*SN*)

kiki-tsu-gu ききつぐ（聞き継ぐ） *tr. v. YD* to pass down (a story). (*KM*)

kiki-tsu-ku ききつく（聞き付く） *intr. v. YD* to listen intently. *tr. v. SN* to listen and understand, overhear. (*GM*)

***KIKOSHI-ME-SU** きこしめす（聞こしめす） *tr. v. YD* (*hon.*) **1.** to listen. **2.** to rule, govern. **3.** to eat, drink.

***KIKO-YU** きこゆ（聞こゆ） [fr. v. *kiku*, "to hear," and Nara aux. v. *yu*] *intr. v. SN* **1.** to hear a sound or voice. **2.** to be rumored, known. **3.** to understand. *tr. v. SN* **1.** to speak to a superior (*hum.*). **2.** to send a letter, message. **3.** to make a request. **4.** *hum. suppl. v.* (*GM, HM*)

***KI-KU** きく（聞く・聴く） *tr. v. YD* **1.** to grasp through sound, taste, smell, etc., to hear. **2.** to accept a request and follow the instructions. **3.** to ask, inquire about. **4.** (of wine, incense, etc.) to distinguish taste or smell, taste or sniff. (*HI, HJ, MS, TN*)

***KIMI** きみ（君） *n.* **1.** emperor. **2.** lord, master. **3.** person of high rank. **4.** *hon.* (following a name, rank). *pron.* (Edo) used by courtesans: you.

kimo-kokoro きもこころ（肝心） (also *kimo-gokoro*) *n.* spirit, heart, life, vitality. (*TZ*)

*KIN-DACHI きんだち (君達) *n.* **1.** sons and daughters of royal, regental, or ministerial houses. **2.** you (singular, plural). (*TM*)

kin-kai きんかい (禁戒) *n.* (Buddhist) precept, prohibition. (*HJ*)

*KINU きぬ (衣) *n.* **1.** dress, robe. **2.** (metaphor) skin, fur (of an animal). (*GM, MS, TM*)

kira-me-ku きらめく (煌めく) *intr. v. YD* to sparkle, shine, glisten. *tr. v. YD* **1.** to decorate ornately. **2.** to welcome or receive warmly. (*TZ*)

kira-u きらふ (嫌ふ) *tr. v. YD* to loathe, despise. (*TM*)

kiri-wata-ru きりわたる (霧り渡る) *intr. v. YD* [fr. n. *kiri* and v. *wataru*] to be covered in fog, mist. (*SN*)

ki-ru きる (着る) *tr. v. KI* to wear. (*IM*)

*KI-RU きる (切る) *tr. v. YD* **1.** to cut with an edged tool. **2.** to wound or kill with a knife or sword. **3.** to partition (time or space). *intr. v. YD* **1.** to be cut off. **2.** to be decided. **3.** to be exhausted, spent.

kisaki きさき (后) *n.* empress. (*SN*)

kise-naga きせなが (着背長) *n.* formal armor worn by a general. (*HM*)

kishi きし (岸) *n.* **1.** shoreline, coast, bank. **2.** rocky place, cliff. (*HI*)

ki-su きす (着す・著す) *tr. v. SN* **1.** to cause to wear, put on. **2.** to set on top of. (*TM*)

kitana-ge きたなげ (汚げ・穢げ) *nari adj. v.* dirty or disagreeable appearance. (*US*)

kitana-shi きたなし (汚し・穢し) *ku adj.* unclean, defiled. (*TM*)

kita-ru きたる (来たる) *intr. v. YD* [fr. v. *ku* and v. *itaru*] to come, arrive. (*HJ, MY, TM*)

kito きと *adv.* suddenly, quickly. (*TM*)

*KIWA きは (際) *n.* **1.** edge. **2.** side. **3.** divider, partition (between things). **4.** part. **5.** position, rank. **6.** limit. **7.** degree. **8.** time, occasion, case.

kiwamari-yu-ku きはまりゆく (極まり行く)

intr. v. YD to approach the end (i.e., death). (*HJ*)

*KIYO-GE きよげ (清げ) *nari adj. v.* **1.** trim and attractive, pretty, neat. **2.** neatly executed or finished. **3.** polished, refined. (*GM, SN*)

*KIYORA きよら (清ら) *nari adj. v.* pure and beautiful. (*TM*)

*KIYO-SHI きよし (清し) *ku adj.* **1.** unsullied and beautiful. **2.** innocent, pure. **3.** clear, fresh.

*KI-YU きゆ (消ゆ) *intr. v. SN* **1.** to disappear. **2.** to forget, lose one's senses. **3.** to die. (*HJ, TM*)

kizu きず (疵) *n.* **1.** shame, disgrace. **2.** wound, injury, damage. **3.** flaw, defect. (*HM*)

ko こ (子) *n.* **1.** child, fawn. **2.** egg. (*IM, MY, TM*)

ko こ (此・是) *pron.* these, this. (*GM, TM*)

ko こ (籠) *n.* bamboo container or box. (*TM*)

kō かう (剛) *n.* strength, ferocity, courage. (*HM*)

kō-bai こうばい (紅梅) *n.* **1.** plum (apricot) tree with pale crimson flowers. **2.** color of a dye: light red or lavender-tinted red. **3.** color in a *kasane* robe: outside is red (*beni*) and inside is lavender-tinted red (*sapang*) or lavender, worn in the spring until the Second Month. (*MS*)

kō-be かうべ (首) *n.* head. (*HJ*)

kobo-ru こぼる (零る・溢る) *intr. v. SN* **1.** to overflow, spill over. **2.** (of flowers, etc.) to scatter, fall. (*TN*)

kobo-su こぼす (零す・溢す) *tr. v. YD* (of liquid etc.) to spill.

KOBO-TSU こぼつ (毀つ) *tr. v. YD* [fr. v. *kohotsu*] to break up, destroy. (*HJ, TM*)

kōburi かうぶり (冠) *n.* **1.** hat worn with formal court costume. **2.** court rank. (*TM*)

ko-chi こち (此方) *pron.* here. (*GM*)

*KOCHITA-SHI こちたし (言痛し・事痛し) *ku adj.* [fr. n. *koto*, "things," and adj. *itashi*, "intense"] **1.** bothersome (due to gossip), annoying. **2.** excessive, numerous (to the point of annoyance). **3.** pompous, exaggerated, showy.

kodomo こども (子供) *n.* children. (*MY*)

koegoe こゑごゑ (声々) *n.* voices. (*MS*)

kōen かうえん (講演) *n.* sermon on sutras or Buddhist doctrine, teachings, etc. (*US*)

kogane こがね (黄金・金) *n.* **1.** gold, color of gold. **2.** money, coin. (*TM*)

kogi-i-zu こぎいづ (漕ぎ出づ) *intr. v. SN* to row out to sea. (*HI*)

ko-gu こぐ (漕ぐ) *tr. v. YD* to row. (*HJ*)

koho-tsu こほつ (毀つ) *tr. v. YD* [fr. v. *kobotsu*] **1.** to break up, destroy. **2.** to cut off. (*SN*)

koi こひ (恋) *n.* **1.** longing (for absent person). **2.** love, affection. (*HI*)

koi-ari-ku こひありく (乞ひ歩く) *intr. v. YD* to walk around and beg. (*HJ*)

koi-shi こひし (恋し) *shiku adj.* beloved, dear, missed, yearned for. (*TM, TZ*)

ko-jin こじん (故人) *n.* **1.** old friends. **2.** deceased person. (*HJ*)

ko-jin こじん (古人) *n.* **1.** ancients, people of a bygone era. **2.** elderly person. (*OH*)

kōjin くわうじん (荒神) *n.* **1.** fierce or angry god, demon. **2.** guardian deity of the Three Buddhist Treasures. **3.** guardian god of the kitchen or hearth. (*NE*)

koke こけ (苔) *n.* lichen, moss. (*HJ, OH*)

koke-musu こけむす (苔むす) *intr. v. YD* [fr. n. *koke*, "moss," and v. *musu*, "to grow"] **1.** to be covered with lichen or moss. **2.** to become old-fashioned. (*HJ*)

*KO-KO ここ (此処) *pron.* **1.** here, this place. **2.** first person: I. **3.** you. (*GM, IM, TM*)

*KOKO-CHI ここち (心地) *n.* mood, temper, feeling. (*TM, US*)

kokochi-a-shi ここちあし (心ちあし) *shiku adj.* ill, unwell. (*US*)

koko-da ここだ (幾許) *adv.* (Nara) many, this many. (*MY*)

koko-kashiko ここかしこ (此処彼処) *pron.* here and there, all over. (*UM*)

*KOKORA ここら *adv.* in large numbers, to a great degree, extremely. (*TO*)

*KOKORO こころ (心) *n.* **1.** mind, spirit. **2.** thought, judgment. **3.** will, intention. **4.** feeling, emotion. **5.** affection, sympathy. **6.** aesthetic discrimination, sensitivity. **7.** essence, nature of things. **8.** elegance (of a thing, an object, a scene). **9.** middle, deepest part (of a pond, etc.). (*HJ*)

*KOKORO-A-RI こころあり (心有り) *intr. v. RH* **1.** to understand things, be discerning. **2.** to be sympathetic. **3.** to appreciate refinement, have taste. **4.** to have hidden thoughts or motives. (*TZ*)

*KOKORO-BAE こころばへ (心延へ) *n.* **1.** disposition (of the heart), temperament. **2.** consideration, thoughtfulness. **3.** meaning, gist, purport. **4.** appearance, look. (*TM, TO*)

KOKORO-BASE こころばせ (心ばせ) *n.* temperament, disposition. (*TM*)

*KOKORO-BOSO-SHI こころぼそし (心細し) *ku adj.* **1.** uncertain, worrisome. **2.** forlorn, lonely. (*IM*)

kokoro fuka shi こころふかし (心深し) *ku adj.* **1.** thoughtful, profound, wise. **2.** sympathetic, loving. **3.** profoundly moving, tasteful, elegant. (*TZ*)

KOKORO-GURU-SHI こころぐるし (心苦し) *shiku adj.* **1.** painful, weighing on (one's own) heart. **2.** worrisome. **3.** pitiful, pathetic. (*SN*)

kokoro-madoi こころまどひ (心惑ひ) *n.* emotional confusion. (*TM*)

kokoromi-ru こころみる (試みる) *intr. v. KI* to attempt to do (something). (*KM*)

KOKORO-MOTO-NAGA-RU こころもとながる (心許ながる) *intr. v. YD* [fr. adj. *kokoromotonashi* and suffix *garu*] to feel uneasy, impatient, irritated. (*TM*)

*KOKORO-MOTO-NASHI こころもとなし (心許なし) *ku adj.* **1.** impatient, anxious. **2.** causing unease, anxiety. **3.** vague, indistinct. (*SN*)

*KOKORO-NA-SHI こころなし (心無し) *ku adj.* **1**. unkind, coldhearted. **2**. thoughtless, careless. **3**. unrefined. *n.* coldhearted or careless person. (*GM, TZ*)

*KOKORO-NIKU-SHI こころにくし (心憎し) *ku adj.* [originally: so wonderful as to cause envy] **1**. attractive, elegant, refined (usually with regard to depth of character, cultivation, taste, etc.). **2**. (so superior as) to seem intimidating, arousing caution. **3**. suspicious. (*HM*)

kokoro ni shi-mu こころにしむ (心に染む) *set phrase, intr. v. YD* to feel poignantly, be deeply impressed by. *tr. v. SN* to dwell on, be engrossed in. (*SN*)

KOKORO-SU こころす (心す) *intr. v. SH* to be careful, pay attention to. (*TZ*)

*KOKORO-U こころう (心得) *intr. v. SN* **1**. to understand, grasp. **2**. to be careful, on the lookout for. **3**. to have knowledge of. **4**. to give consent to, accept. (*TM, US*)

*KOKORO-U-SHI こころうし (心憂し) *ku adj.* **1**. painful, pitiful. **2**. unpleasant, distasteful. (*GM, HJ*)

*KOKORO-ZASHI こころざし (志) *n.* **1**. intention, direction of heart. **2**. affection, sincerity. **3**. offering a present (out of goodwill, gratitude). **4**. prayer to the dead. (*TM, TN*)

*KOKOROZUKI-NA-SHI こころづきなし (心付き無し) *ku adj.* (when the attitude or behavior of a person is not to one's liking) **1**. unattractive, uninteresting. **2**. disagreeable, unpleasant. (*GM*)

KOKORO-ZUKUSHI こころづくし (心尽くし) *n.* **1**. anxiety, distress, concern. **2**. thoughtfulness, consideration. (*TZ*)

kokoro-zuyo-shi こころづよし (心強し) *ku adj.* **1**. firm, determined, patient. **2**. coldhearted, unkind. (*TM*)

koku-ō こくわう (国王) *n.* king, sovereign, ruler. (*TM*)

koma-goma-to こまごまと (細細と) *adv.* **1**. finely. **2**. in detail. **3**. in a refined manner. (*TM*)

KOMAKA こまか (細か) *nari adj. v.* **1**. very fine, small. **2**. beautifully detailed and crafted. **3**. of great artistic or technical precision.

ko-matsu こまつ (小松) *n.* small pine tree. (*TN*)

KOMAYAKA こまやか (細やか) *nari adj. v.* **1**. finely wrought or finished, precise, delicate. **2**. attentive, considerate, kind-hearted. **3**. detailed, meticulous, elaborate.

*KOMO-RU こもる (籠る) *intr. v. YD* **1**. to be enclosed, inside. **2**. to be hidden. **3**. to remain in isolation. **4**. to stay at a temple or shrine for prayer. (*HJ, SN*)

KO-MU こむ (籠む・込む) *intr. v. YD* **1**. to be crowded, packed together. **2**. (following RY of main v.) to do (something) without cessation or interruption. *tr. v. YD* **1**. to stab (with a sword), pierce (with an arrow). **2**. to place inside. *intr. v. SN* (of mist, fog) to cover the ground entirely. *tr. v. SN* **1**. to keep indoors, place inside, store away. **2**. to keep in one's heart. (*GM, TM*)

kō-myō かうみやう (高名) *n.* fame, repute. (*HM*)

KONATA こなた (此方) *pron.* **1**. since then. **2**. before then. **3**. here, over here. (*GM*)

konokami このかみ (兄長) *n.* (lit., eldest child) **1**. eldest son, older brother or sister. **2**. one's senior. **3**. leader of a group, community. (*UM*)

ko-no-ma このま (木の間) *n.* gap or space between trees. (*TZ*)

kō-no-mono かうのもの (剛の者) *set phrase* brave warrior; exceptionally strong and courageous person. (*HM*)

kono-mu このむ (好む) *tr. v. YD* **1**. to like, love. **2**. to choose, order what one wants. (*HJ*)

konure こぬれ (木末) *n.* (Nara) tip of tree, tip of branch. (*MY*)

kō-shi かうし (格子) *n.* lattice. (*TM*)

kore-ra これら *pron.* **1**. these (people, things, etc.). **2**. this area, vicinity. (*TZ*)

kore ya kono これやこの (此れや此の) *emphatic comp.* used in poetry to express strong emotion at the sight of a place the speaker knows or has heard of in the past. (*HI*)

koro ころ (頃) *n.* **1.** general time: about. **2.** season. **3.** period of time (pronounced *goro* following time words like *toshi*, *tsuki*). (*MS*)

korobi-i-ru ころびいる (転び入る) *intr. v. YD* to fall, roll into. (*TZ*)

koromo ころも (衣) *n.* **1.** robe. **2.** priest's or nun's dress. (*IM*)

koromo-de ころもで (衣手) *n.* sleeve of a robe. (*HI*)

koro-su ころす (殺す) *tr. v. YD* to kill. (*TM*)

koshi こし (腰) *n.* hips, waist. (*TM*)

koshi こし (層) *n.* floor (of a building). (*KM*)

KOSHI こし (濃し) *ku adj.* **1.** (of color) deep, dark. **2.** dark lavender or crimson. **3.** rich, thick, dense.

ko-shiba-gaki こしばがき (小柴垣) *n.* low fence of woven brushwood. (*GM*)

***KOSO** こそ *bound p.* **1.** emphatic: indeed. **2.** concessive: granted, allowing (for certain exceptions, etc.).

kota-u こたふ (答ふ・応ふ) *intr. v. SN* to reply, answer. (*TM*)

***KOTO** こと (事) *n.* **1.** event, (immaterial) phenomenon. **2.** important event, incident. **3.** character, conduct, actions. **4.** job, work, position. **5.** ceremony, ritual. **6.** circumstances, reasons. **7.** (following RT) nominalizer. **8.** (at end of a sentence) emphatic: expresses emotional intensity.

***KOTO** こと (言) *n.* **1.** (spoken) words, language. **2.** rumor. **3.** poetry (*waka*).

***KOTO** こと (異) *nari adj. v.* **1.** different. **2.** special, exceptional. (*HJ, TM*)

koto こと (琴) *n.* zither. (*HJ*)

kotoba ことば (詞・言葉) *n.* word(s). (*UM*)

kotoba-gaki ことばがき (詞書) *n.* headnote to a poem, identifying the topic or noting the circumstances of composition. (*TZ*)

kotoba ni ka-ku ことばにかく (言葉に掛く) *set phrase, tr. v. SN* to put into words. (*HJ*)

koto-dokoro ことどころ (異所) *n.* another place, elsewhere. (*TM*)

koto-goto ことごと (異事) *n.* separate matter, something else. (*SN*)

kotogoto-ku ことごとく (悉く・事事く) *adv.* altogether, entirely, completely. (*HJ, UM*)

koto-hito ことひと (異人・他人) *n.* other people, different person. (*TM, US*)

koto-ni ことに (殊に) *adv.* **1.** especially, particularly. **2.** in addition, even more so. (*HJ, TZ*)

koto-ni-su ことにす (事にす) *intr. v. SH* to be satisfied with (doing something). (*US*)

koto-no-hoka-nari ことのほかなり (殊の外なり) *adj. v.* **1.** unexpected, surprising. **2.** special, extraordinary. (*HJ*)

KOTO-TO-U こととふ (言問ふ) *intr. v. YD* **1.** to speak to, address. **2.** to ask, inquire. **3.** to visit. (*IM*)

***KOTOWARI** ことわり (理) *n.* **1.** reason, logic behind things. **2.** judgment. **3.** explanation. **4.** apology. **5.** refusal. *nari adj. v.* reasonable, logical. (*HJ*)

***KOTOWA-RU** ことわる (理る) *intr. v. YD* **1.** to judge right or wrong based on a reasoned assessment. **2.** to explain the circumstances. **3.** to explain in advance, give prior notice.

kotsu-gai こつがい (乞丐) *n.* beggar, mendicant. (*HJ*)

kotsu-jiki こつじき (乞食) *n.* **1.** beggar. **2.** priest begging for alms. (*HJ*)

KO-U こふ (恋ふ) *tr. v. KN* **1.** to long for, think fondly of. **2.** to love. (*TZ*)

ko-wa こは (此は) *interj.* [fr. pron. *ko* and bound p. *wa*] expresses surprise, astonishment: what's this!? (*UM, US*)

kowa-daka こわだか (声高) *n.* high voice. (*TN*)

ko-warawa こわらは (小童) *n.* small child. (*HJ*)

kowa-shi こはし (強し) *ku adj.* **1.** strong,

powerful. **2.** stubborn, obstinate. **3.** coarse, rough. **4.** steep. (*TM*)

KOYO-NA-SHI こよなし *ku adj.* **1.** extreme, unsurpassed. **2.** especially superior, very good. **3.** especially inferior, very bad. (*GM, TO*)

KO-YU こゆ (越ゆ) *intr. v. SN* **1.** to cross over. **2.** to exceed. (*HJ*)

KOZO こぞ (去年) *n.* last year. (*HJ*)

kozo-ru こぞる (挙る) *intr. v. YD* to gather together, do together. (*IM*)

KŌ-ZU こうず (困ず) *intr. v. SH* **1.** to be troubled, find difficult. **2.** to be very tired.

ko-zue こずゑ (梢) *n.* tip of branch. (*TZ*)

kō-zui こうずい (洪水) *n.* flood. (*HJ*)

*KU く *suffix* (mainly follows MZ of YD) turns the preceding v. or adj. phrase into a nominalized phrase, as in *iwa-ku*: (someone) said.

KU く (句) *n.* one of the five phrases of a thirty-one-syllable (5/7/5/7/7) *waka*. (*IM*)

*KU く (来) *intr. v. KH* **1.** to come, return. **2.** to go. **3.** to visit. (*TM*)

kuboma-ru くぼまる (窪まる) *intr. v. YD* to be sunk low in the middle, caved in. (*TN*)

ku-bu くぶ (焼ぶ) *tr. v. SN* to burn. (*HJ*)

kuchi-ba くちば (朽ち葉) *n.* rotting leaves. (*HJ*)

*KUCHI-O-SHI くちをし (口惜し) *shiku adj.* **1.** regrettable, disappointing. **2.** dull, unsatisfying. **3.** lowly, base, pitiful. (*HM, TM, TN*)

*KUDA-RU くだる (下る・降る) *intr. v YD* **1.** to go downstream. **2.** (of rain, snow) to fall. **3.** to leave the capital for the provinces. **4.** to go south (within the capital). **5.** to give (from one of higher rank to one of lower rank). **6.** to be transmitted (from one of higher rank to one of lower rank). **7.** (of time) to pass. **8.** to fall in rank. **9.** to surrender.

*KUDA-SU くだす (下す・降す) *tr. v. YD* **1.** to let down, lower, let fall. **2.** to send down a river. **3.** to give an order or object to a person of lower rank. **4.** to dispatch someone from the capital to the provinces. **5.** to set brush to paper. **6.** to lower the sound or tone. (*TM*)

ku-doku くどく (功徳) *n.* good deeds. (*TM*)

ku-gō くごふ (口業) *n.* sins or karmic burdens arising from the (frivolous or deceitful) use of language. (*HJ*)

KU-GYŌ くぎやう (公卿) *n.* highest-ranking officials, nobles of third rank and above. (*HJ*)

kui くい (悔い) *n.* [fr. v. *kuyu,* "to regret"] regret, remorse. (*HJ*)

kuji-ru くじる (抉る) *tr. v. YD* to make a hole, hollow out, bore.

kukkyō くつきやう (究竟) *nari adj. v.* **1.** outstanding. **2.** suitable, convenient, useful. (*HM*)

kuku-ru くくる (括る) *tr. v. YD* **1.** to tie together. **2.** to tie-dye. (*HI*)

kūkyo くうきよ (空虚) *n.* emptiness, fruitlessness. (*OH*)

*KUMA くま (隈) *n.* **1.** bend, corner. **2.** hidden spot. **3.** countryside, periphery. **4.** shadow, cloudy spot. **5.** weakness. **6.** secret.

*KUMA-NA-SHI くまなし (隈無し) *ku adj.* **1.** unshaded, unclouded, undarkened. **2.** perfectly prepared, extremely well informed. **3.** unconcealed, in plain view. (*TZ*)

kumi-oto-su くみおとす (組み落とす) *comp. v., tr. v. YD* to engage in combat and strike down. (*HM*)

kumo くも (雲) *n.* cloud. (*HI*)

kumo-de くもで (蜘蛛手) *n.* (lit., spider legs) **1.** river or road forking in multiple directions. **2.** moving in opposite directions (often while brandishing a sword). **3.** mental confusion, distraction, emotional turmoil. (*HM, IM*)

*KUMO-I くもゐ (雲居・雲井) *n.* **1.** sky, distant, cloud-filled skies. **2.** clouds. **3.** imperial palace. **4.** the capital. **5.** distant place. (*TZ*)

ku-mu くむ (組む) *intr. v. YD* to engage in combat. *tr. v. YD* **1.** to weave together. **2.** to put together, assemble. (*HM*)

*KUNI くに (国) *n.* **1.** country, province, land. **2.** one's native region. (*TM*)

kuni-guni くにぐに (国々) *n.* provinces. (*MS*)

kura くら (鞍) *n.* saddle. (*HJ*)

kura-bu くらぶ (比ぶ・較ぶ) *tr. v. SN* **1.** to compare two or more things. **2.** to compete against. **3.** to have a close relationship with someone. (*TN*)

*KURAI くらゐ (位) *n.* **1.** position of emperor. **2.** rank at court. **3.** bureaucratic position. **4.** level of achievement in artistic profession or scholarship. (*HJ, SN*)

KURA-SHI くらし (暗し) *ku adj.* **1.** dark. **2.** unclear, obscure, unknown. **3.** undeveloped, uncivilized. **4.** confused, uncertain. **5.** ignorant, foolish. **6.** lacking, insufficient, flawed. (*IM, TM*)

kura-su くらす (暮らす) *tr. v. YD* **1.** to spend the day. **2.** to spend time. **3.** to live. **4.** *suppl. v.* to do all day, continuously.

kura-u くらふ (食ふ) *tr. v. YD* **1.** to eat, drink. **2.** to make a living. **3.** to bear (a burden) (*TZ*)

kure-nai くれなゐ (紅) *n.* crimson (*HJ*)

ku-ru くる (暮る・昏る・暗る・眩る) *intr. v. SN* (暮る・昏る) **1.** (of the sun) to set. **2.** (of a season) to end. (暗る・眩る) **3.** to have one's vision darkened, see darkness. **4.** to be blinded by tears. **5.** to become confused, disoriented, lose one's reason. (*HJ, IM, TM*)

kuruma くるま (車) *n.* aristocrat's ox-drawn carriage. (*HJ, TM*)

KURU-SHI くるし (苦し) *shiku adj.* **1.** painful, hard, trying. **2.** unpleasant. **3.** inconvenient. (*HJ, TM*)

kusa-mura くさむら (草叢・叢) *n.* clump of grass, grassy place. (*HJ*)

kusa no to くさのと (草の戸) *set phrase* thatched hut, simple hut. (*OH*)

kusa-shi くさし (臭し) *ku adj.* foul-smelling, malodorous. (*HJ*)

kusuri くすり (薬) *n.* medicine. (*TM*)

KUTA-SU くたす (腐す・朽たす) *tr. v. YD* **1.** to make perish, rot. **2.** to discourage by disparaging or scolding.

ku-u くふ (食ふ・喰ふ) *tr. v. YD* to eat. (*IM, MS*)

ku-u くふ (構ふ) *tr. v. YD* to build (a nest). (*TM*)

kuwa-u くはふ (加ふ) *tr. v. SN* **1.** to add, pile up. **2.** to increase. **3.** to give, provide. **4.** to make someone a partner, an acquaintance, etc. (*HJ*)

kuyu-ru くゆる (燻る・薫る) *intr. v. YD* **1.** (of smoke, fragrance) to smolder, rise up. **2.** to be tormented by love or erotic desire, burn with passion. (*US*)

kuzu-ru くづる (崩る) *intr. v. SN* **1.** to crumble, break up. **2.** to disband, separate. (*HJ*)

kyō きやう (経) *n.* sutra. (*GM*)

kyō きよう (興) *n.* interest, delight, stimulation. (*TM*)

kyō けふ (今日) *n.* today. (*HM*)

kyōdō きやうだう (経堂) *n.* sutra hall (in a Buddhist temple). (*OH*)

kyō-gai きやうがい (境界) *n.* **1.** bounds, realm, border. **2.** (Buddhist) one's situation or station in life as determined by karmic causality. **3.** range of one's powers or cognition. (*HJ*)

kyōra けうら (清ら) *nari adj. v.* pure and beautiful in appearance.

kyō-soku けふそく (脇息) *n.* armrest. (*GM*)

kyō-zu きようず (興ず) *intr. v. SH* to be amused (by), take pleasure (in). (*TZ*)

kyū きう (灸) *n.* moxa, herbal preparation made from mugwort (*yomogi*) leaves. (*OH*)

kyū-den きゆうでん (宮殿) *n.* **1.** palace. **2.** shrine. (*HJ*)

*MA ま (間・際) *n.* **1.** interval, moment. **2.** space between things. **3.** rooms, partitioned areas. (*HI, MY*)

MABAYU-SHI まばゆし (目映し・眩し) *ku adj.* **1.** overwhelmingly bright, glaring, blinding. **2.** dazzlingly beautiful. **3.** (too much to watch) embarrassing, shameful. **4.** extreme (so much that one wants to turn one's eyes away).

machi-i-zu まちいづ (待ち出づ) *tr. v. SN* to wait for something (someone) to appear. (*HI, TZ*)

machi-ku-ru まちくる (待ち暮る) *comp. v.* [fr. v. *matsu*, "to wait," and v. *kuru*, " to grow dark"] to spend the whole day waiting for (someone). (*UM*)

madara まだら (斑) *n., nari adj. v.* spotted, dappled, something spotted. (*IM*)

MADE まで *adv. p.* **1.** expresses extent, scope, range, indicating a temporal, spatial, or quantitative limit: as far as, until, up to. **2.** unexpected degree, outcome, or state. (*TM*)

ma-dō まどほ (間遠) *n., nari adj. v.* (at) long intervals of space or time, few and far between. (*HJ*)

MADO-U まどふ (惑ふ) *intr. v. YD* **1.** to be emotionally or mentally confused, uncertain. **2.** to be lost, wander, stray. **3.** to panic, become upset, be flustered. **4.** *suppl. v.* to do (something) to an extreme. (*IM, TM*)

MADOWA-SU まどはす (惑はす) *tr. v. YD* **1.** to cause pain, emotional uncertainty. **2.** to confuse, perplex. **3.** to cause (someone) to lose track of (his or her bearings). **4.** to entrance, bewitch. (*HJ*)

MAE まへ (前) *n.* **1.** front. **2.** the past. **3.** front of a house, front garden. **4.** (usually preceded by hon. prefix such as *mi, o*) used in place of a proper name to refer to a god or high-ranking noble. **5.** (direct) attendance on a god or person of the nobility. **6.** (preceded by *no*) follows a woman's name, indicating respect. **7.** meal (served to a monk, etc.).

mae-wa まへわ (前輪) *n.* pommel, raised front of a saddle. (*HM*)

maga-maga-shi まがまがし (禍禍し) *shiku adj.* **1.** ill-omened, inauspicious. **2.** hateful, cursed, damned. (*US*)

MAGA-U まがふ (紛ふ) *intr. v. YD* **1.** to be mixed together so as to become indistinguishable, mingle. **2.** to resemble so closely as to be mistaken for another. **3.** to become unrecognizable. *tr. v. SN* **1.** to lose sight of. **2.** to confuse or mistake one thing for another. (*HJ*)

MAGI-RU まぎる (紛る) *intr. v. SN* **1.** to mix in with other things and become indistinguishable. **2.** to hide among other things. **3.** to be distracted by something. (*GM*)

ma-gu-ru まぐる (眩る) *intr. v. SN* **1.** to be dizzy, have vertigo. **2.** to faint, lose consciousness. (*HJ*)

MAHOSHI まほし *aux. v.* (follows MZ) **1.** first-person desiderative: I want to (do something). **2.** third-person desiderative: he or she wants to (do something). **3.** general desiderative: it is to be wished that (something be done).

mai-bito まひびと (舞人) *n. bugaku* dancer. (*HJ*)

MAIRA-SU まゐらす (参らす) *tr. v. SN* **1.** to give to a superior, offer (*hum.*). **2.** *hum. suppl. v.* (*TM, US*)

MAI-RU まゐる (参る) *intr. v. YD* **1.** to go to a place of a person of higher status (*hum.*). **2.** to enter the imperial court (*hum.*). **3.** to go to a temple or shrine (*hum.*). **4.** to go (*polite*). *tr. v. YD* **1.** to give, offer, serve (*hum.*). **2.** to eat, drink (*hon.*). (*MS, TM*)

maite まいて (況いて) *adv.* [fr. adv. *mashite*] **1.** all the more. **2.** needless to say. (*MS*)

MAJI まじ *aux. v.* (follows SS) expresses **1.** neg. spec. **2.** neg. expectation. **3.** neg. intent. **4.** neg. pot. **5.** prohibition.

majinai まじなひ (呪ひ) *n.* spell, incantation, especially prayer to the gods for protection from illness and disaster. (*GM*)

MAJI-RU まじる (交じる・混じる・雑じる) *tr. v. YD* **1.** to mix in with. **2.** to join, enter the company of. **3.** to leave civilization and enter the mountains or wilderness (seeking reclusion). (*SN, TM, TN*)

MAKA-RU まかる (罷る) *intr. v. YD* **1.** to leave a place or person of higher status (*hum.*).

2. to leave the capital for the provinces. **3.** to go, come (*hum.*) (*polite*). **4.** to die. (*TZ*)

maka-su まかす (任す) *tr. v. SN* to entrust, leave up to. (*TM*)

MAKA-ZU まかづ (罷づ) *intr. v. SN* [fr. v. *makaru*] **1.** to leave, depart (hum. form of *saru*). **2.** to go out, to go (polite form of *yuku*, *izu*).

maki まき (巻) *n.* book, volume, scroll, fascicle. (*SN*)

mak-kō まつかう (真甲) *n.* **1.** front of the helmet. **2.** center of the forehead. (*HM*)

MAKOTO まこと (真・誠・実) *n., nari adj. v.* **1.** truth, actuality, reality. **2.** sincerity. *adv.* truly. (*TM*)

ma-ku まく (負く) *intr. v. SN* **1.** to be defeated, lose. **2.** to be overwhelmed by. **3.** to give in to someone else's demands. (*TM*)

makura-gami まくらがみ (枕上) *n.* at or by the pillow. (*KM*)

makura-kotoba まくらことば (枕詞) *n.* (lit., pillow word or phrase) epithet used in poetry, usually of five syllables. (*HI*)

*MAMA まま (儘) *n.* (often followed by case p. *ni*) **1.** as is. **2.** as expected, as desired. **3.** as soon as, immediately. (*SN*)

mama-haha ままはは (継母) *n.* stepmother. (*SN*)

*MAME まめ (忠実・実) *nari adj. v.* **1.** serious, faithful, devoted. **2.** diligent, hardworking. **3.** healthy, strong. **4.** practical, pragmatic. (*HJ, TM*)

MAME-MAME-SHI まめまめし *shiku adj.* **1.** sincere, honest, earnest, serious. **2.** practical. (*SN*)

*MAME-YAKA まめやか (忠実やか・実やか) *nari adj. v.* **1.** serious, honest, earnest. **2.** practical. **3.** true to a promise, faithful.

mami まみ (目見) *n.* **1.** one's gaze or manner of viewing (something). **2.** eye(s). (*GM*)

*MAMO-RU まもる (守る・護る) *tr. v. YD* **1.** to stare at, fix one's gaze on. **2.** to size up, ascertain, verify (a state or condition). **3.** to be

cautious, be on guard. **4.** to protect, defend. (*GM, TM, TZ*)

ma-na-kai まなかひ (目交ひ・眼間) *n.* (lit., the area between the eyes) (Nara) before one's eyes. (*MY*)

*MANA-BU まなぶ (学ぶ) *tr. v. YD* **1.** to imitate, do as one has learned. **2.** to study.

*MANE-BU まねぶ (学ぶ) *tr. v. YD* **1.** to imitate, mimic. **2.** to pass on by word of mouth, transmit verbally. **3.** to study, learn.

manima-ni まにまに (随に) *adv.* following, in accordance with. (*HI*)

ma-no-atari まのあたり (目のあたり) *n., nari adj. v.* **1.** before one's eyes. **2.** directly before or facing one. **3.** clear, obvious. (*HJ*)

mare まれ (稀) *nari adj. v.* rare, scarce, unusual. (*HJ*)

marobi-iru まろびいる (転び入る) *intr. v. YD* to roll into. (*HJ*)

maru まる (放る) *tr. v. YD* to defecate, urinate. (*TM*)

masa-ki まさき (柾・正木) *n.* spindle tree. (*HJ*)

MASA-NA-SHI まさなし (正無し) *ku adj.* [fr. adj. *masashi*, "correct," and adj. *nashi*, "without"] **1.** inappropriate. **2.** unexpected. (*SN*)

masa-ni まさに (正に) *adv.* **1.** truly, without question. **2.** actually, indeed. **3.** (followed by rhet. question p.) why? (*TM*)

masa-ru まさる (増さる・勝る・優る) *intr. v. YD* **1.** (増さる) to increase in number, length, or degree, grow strong. **2.** (勝る・優る) to be superior to, surpass, outdo. (*HJ, MY, SN, TM, US*)

masa-zama まさざま (勝様・増様) *nari adj. v.* **1.** (勝様) far superior in appearance. **2.** (増様) extreme in appearance, extreme. (*HJ*)

*MASHI まし *aux. v.* (follows MZ) indicates **1.** counterfactual speculation: if it were the case that. **2.** desire for a hypothetical state: if only. **3.** hesitation, often with explicit indication of doubt: should I . . . ?

MASHI-MASU まします (坐します) *intr. v. YD* **1.** to be, exist (*hon.* of *ari*). **2.** (following v. or aux. v. *su* and *sasu*) *hon. suppl. v.*

mashite まして (況して) *adv.* **1.** all the more. **2.** needless to say, not to mention. (*HJ, MS, MY, TM*)

*MASU ます (坐す・座す) *intr. v. YD* **1.** to be (*hon.* of *ari, ori*). **2.** to go, come (*hon.* of *ku, yuku*).

*MATA また (又・復・亦) *adv.* **1.** again, once more. **2.** in the same way, same fashion. **3.** separately. *conj.* **1.** and. **2.** furthermore, in addition. **3.** used to change the topic of conversation. (*GM, HJ, TM*)

MATA-NA-SHI またなし (又無し) *ku adj.* incomparable. (*TZ*)

MATA-SHI またし (全し) *ku adj.* perfect, complete. (*HJ*)

MA-TSU まつ (待つ) *tr. v. YD* **1.** to wait (for something or someone). **2.** to halt, postpone, delay. (*MY*)

matsu まつ (松) *n.* **1.** pine tree. **2.** pine branches or chips rich in resin burned for illumination, torch of such pine. **3.** pine tree decorations placed at entrance to home in celebration of the New Year. (*HI, TM, TZ*)

matsu-bara まつばら (松原) *n.* pine forest. (*HM*)

mayu まゆ (繭) *n.* cocoon. (*HJ*)

ma-zu まづ (先づ) *adv.* **1.** first. **2.** one way or another, in any event. **3.** truly. **4.** (followed by neg.) not even a little, not at all. (*SN*)

MAZU-SHI まづし (貧し) *shiku adj.* **1.** poor. **2.** weak, lacking. (*HJ*)

ME め (妻) *n.* **1.** woman. **2.** wife. **3.** female. (*HJ, TM*)

*ME め (目) *n.* eye. (*TZ*)

*MEDETA-SHI めでたし *ku adj.* **1.** wonderful, splendid. **2.** felicitous, auspicious, blessed. (*TM*)

me-gimi めぎみ (女君) *n.* (same as *onnagimi*) **1.** daughter of a noble (*hon.*). **2.** wife or lover of noble (*hon.*). (*SN*)

megu-mu めぐむ (恵む) *tr. v. YD* to bless, show mercy or kindness to. (*HJ*)

megu-ru めぐる (廻る・回る・巡る) *intr. v. YD* to go around, turn or move in a circle, walk a circuit. (*TM*)

MEKU めく *suffix* to have the appearance of. (*TN*)

me-no-to めのと (乳母・傅) *n.* **1.** (乳母) wet nurse. **2.** (傅) guardian, man assigned to watch over a young lord. (*GM*)

menoto-go めのとご (乳母子・傅子) *n.* **1.** (乳母子) child of wet nurse, foster brother. **2.** (傅子) child who acts as guardian. (*HM*)

me-otoko めをとこ (女男・妻男) *n.* wife and husband. (*HJ*)

me o miru めをみる (目を見る) *set phrase* **1.** to experience, encounter. **2.** to read. (*IM*)

*MERI めり *aux. v.* (follows SS except after RH) indicates **1.** supposition based on visual evidence: it appears that. **2.** circumlocution, indirection: it would seem that.

me-shi-a-gu めしあぐ (召あぐ) *tr. v. SN* **1.** to summon, entrust with a position (*hon.*). **2.** to confiscate, requisition. (*US*)

*ME-SU めす (召す) *tr. v. YD* (*hon.*) **1.** to summon. **2.** to have someone bring something. **3.** to eat, drink, wear. **4.** to board a boat. **5.** *hon. suppl. v.*

me-toma-ru めとまる (目止まる) *intr. v. YD* [fr. n. *me*, "eye," and v. *tomaru*, "to stop"] to catch one's eye, be noticeable. (*GM*)

me-ya めや *comp.* [fr. aux. v. *mu* and final p. *ya*] interrogative: marks a rhet. question with an implied neg. answer. (*TZ*)

ME-YASU-SHI めやすし (目安し・目易し) *ku adj.* (lit., easy on the eyes) pleasant, agreeable. (*GM*)

*ME-ZAMASHI めざまし (目覚まし) *shiku adj.* [fr. n. *me*, "eye," and v. *samu*, "to awaken"] **1.** disagreeable, offensive (too much for the eye). **2.** unexpectedly (eye-poppingly) splendid.

*ME-ZU めづ (愛づ) *tr. v. SN* **1.** to praise,

admire. **2.** to care for, love. **3.** to take a liking to. *intr. v. SN* to be impressed by, drawn to. (*TM, TO, US*)

MEZURAKA めづらか *nari adj. v.* unusual, peculiar, surprising. (*HJ*)

MEZURA-SHI めづらし (珍し) *shiku adj.* [fr. v. *mezu*, "to praise"] **1.** praiseworthy, wonderful. **2.** lovely, adorable. **3.** new, fresh, startling. **4.** unusual, rare. (*SN*)

mi み (御) *prefix* indicates **1.** hon. **2.** beauty or enhances cadence (as in *mi-yuki*). (*MY*)

MI み *suffix* (follows adj. stem) because, since. (*HI*)

MI み (身) *n.* **1.** body. **2.** position, status. **3.** one's lot or circumstances. **4.** life. **5.** sword blade, sword. **6.** content. *pron.* first-person singular: I. (*HJ, HM, SN, TM*)

mi-agu みあぐ (見上ぐ) *tr. v. SN* to look up at. (*GM*)

MICHI みち (道) *n.* **1.** course, road, path. **2.** journey. **3.** whatever a given direction has to offer. **4.** method, way of doing something. **5.** reason, logic, order. **6.** ethics, customary practices. **7.** religious teachings. **8.** academic discipline. (*IM*)

midare-so-mu みだれそむ (乱れ初む) *intr. v. SN* to begin to be disturbed, agitated, upset. (*HI*)

MIDA-RU みだる (乱る) *intr. v. SN* **1.** to be confused mentally or emotionally, be upset. **2.** to be disordered, chaotic, unconstrained. (*HJ*)

mi-dokoro みどころ (見所) *n.* part or aspect of something most worth looking at. (*TZ*)

mi-gushi みぐし (御髪・御首・御頭) *n.* **1.** (御髪) hair (*hon.*). **2.** (御首・御頭) head, neck (*hon.*). (*HJ, TM*)

mi-ha-tsu みはつ (見果つ) *tr. v. SN* **1.** to see completely. **2.** to look after until the end. (*SN*)

MI-IDA-SU みいだす (見出す) *tr. v. YD* **1.** to look outside. **2.** to find, search out. **3.** to keep an eye on.

MIJIKA-SHI みじかし (短し) *ku adj.* **1.** short

(time, length, distance). **2.** insufficient, inferior. **3.** short-tempered, irritable. **4.** of low status. (*HI*)

MIKADO みかど (帝・御門) *n.* **1.** gate, especially to imperial palace (*hon.*). **2.** imperial court. **3.** emperor (*tennō*). **4.** country ruled by emperor. (*HJ, TM*)

mi-kari みかり (御狩) *n.* imperial hunt (*hon.*). (*TM*)

mi-kata みかた (御方) *n.* supporter, comrade, ally, friend. (*HM*)

MI-KO みこ (御子・皇子・親王) *n.* **1.** (御子) child of a noble (*hon.*). **2.** (皇子) child or grandchild of an emperor. **3.** (親王) officially recognized prince, princess.

mi-koshi みこし (御輿) *n.* palanquin (*hon.*). (*TM*)

mi-kurai みくらゐ (御位) *n.* status or position of the emperor. (*HJ*)

mime みめ (見目・眉見) *n.* **1.** appearance, looks. **2.** reputation, prestige. (*US*)

mimi みみ (耳) *n.* ear. (*MS*)

mimi-ta-tsu みみたつ (耳立つ) *intr. v. YD* to hear. *tr. v. SN* to listen to carefully. (*MS*)

mina みな (皆) *adv.* all, without exception. (*HJ, TN*)

mina-hito みなひと (皆人) *n.* everyone. (*IM*)

mi-na-moto みなもと (源) *n.* source, origin. (*HJ*)

MINA-ZUKI みなづき (六月・水無月) *n.* Sixth Month (lunar calendar). (*HJ*)

mine みね (峯・峰・嶺) *n.* **1.** mountain peak, summit. **2.** highest part. **3.** dull edge of a blade. (*HI, TM*)

mi ni shimu みにしむ (身にしむ) *set phrase, intr. v. YD* to make a deep impression, touch (one) deeply. (*TZ*)

mi-no-hodo みのほど (身の程) *n.* one's rank, status. (*HJ*)

mi-no-ue みのうへ (身の上) *n.* one's life, fate, fortune, circumstances. (*UM*)

mi-oko-su みおこす（見遣す）　*tr. v. SN* to look in this direction. (*TM*)

mi-oku-ru みおくる（見送る）　*tr. v. YD* to send off. (*TM*)

mio-tsu-kushi みをつくし（澪標）　*n.* channel marker, poles or buoys that mark the deep parts of an inlet. (*HI*)

mi-o-tsuku-su みをつくす（身を尽くす）　*set phrase* [fr. tr. YD v. *tsukusu*, "to exhaust"] to exhaust oneself, put all of one's efforts or vitality into. (*GM*)

*MIRU みる（見る）　*tr. v. KI* **1.** to see, look at. **2.** to look at and judge, understand. **3.** to deal with, handle. **4.** to attempt, try. **5.** to experience, have an experience. **6.** to meet, come face to face. **7.** to have an intimate (carnal) relationship with (a woman); in particular, to marry a woman (often informally). **8.** to take care of, watch over. (*MY, TM, TN, SN*)

misago みさご（鶚・雎鳩）　*n.* osprey, fish hawk. (*HJ*)

misao みさを（操）　*n.* **1.** purity of heart. **2.** faithfulness, chastity.

misao-tsuku-ru みさをつくる（操作る）　*intr. v. SN* to feign indifference, pretend as if nothing were out of the ordinary or at odds with social convention. (*HJ*)

mi-so みそ（御衣）(also *mizo*)　*n.* robe. (*TM*)

MISOGI みそぎ（禊）　*n.* lustration, ritual ablution of sins and pollutions (in a river or the sea).

MISOKA みそか（密）　*nari adj. v.* secret, covert, intimate. (*SN, TM*)

*MI-SU みす（見す）　*intr. v. YD* to see (*hon.*). *tr. v. SN* **1.** to show, make visible. **2.** to bring about a marriage. **3.** to cause (someone) to judge or make an augury. **4.** to cause (someone) to experience (something). (*TM, TO*)

mi-su-tsu みすつ（見捨つ）　*tr. v. SN* to abandon (a person), leave behind. (*TM*)

mita-su みたす（満たす）　*tr. v. YD* **1.** to complete, make full. **2.** to achieve. **3.** to satisfy. (*UM*)

mi-tō みとう（御灯）　*n.* lamp in front of a Buddhist altar. (*US*)

mi-tsu みつ（満つ・充つ）　*intr. v. YD* **1.** to become full. **2.** (of the moon) to become full. **3.** (of the sea) to reach high tide. **4.** (of wish, desire) to be fulfilled. **5.** to be renowned. *tr. v. SN* **1.** to fill up, make full. **2.** to satisfy, fulfill. (*HJ, TM, UM*)

mitsugi-mono みつぎもの（貢物）　*n.* tax, tribute. (*HJ*)

mi-tsu-ku みつく（見付く）　*intr. v. YD* to become familiar with. *tr. v. SN* to discover, seek out. (*GM, TM*)

*MIYABI みやび（雅び）　*n.* refinement, elegance, particularly that associated with the capital (*miya*).

MIYAKO みやこ（都・京）　*n.* capital, site of the imperial palace. (*HI, HJ, HM, TM*)

miyako-dori みやこどり（都鳥）　*n.* (lit., capital bird) type of water bird. (*IM*)

miyako-utsuri みやこうつり（都遷り）　*n.* relocation of the capital. (*HJ*)

MIYA-ZUKAE みやづかへ（宮仕）　*n.* court service. (*TM*)

MI-YO みよ（御世・御代）　*n.* imperial reign (*hon.*). (*HJ*)

*MI-YU みゆ（見ゆ）　*intr. v. SN* **1.** (spont.) to become visible to the eye. **2.** (passive) to be seen. **3.** to meet, face. **4.** to marry, become a wife. **5.** to be a familiar sight. **6.** to come, appear. **7.** to find oneself feeling or thinking. (*HM, MS*)

mi-yuki みゆき（御幸・行幸）　*n.* imperial progress, imperial procession (*hon.*). (*TM*)

mizo みぞ（御衣）(also *miso*)　*n.* robe (*hon.*). (*TM*)

mizu みづ（水）　*n.* water. (*HI*)

MIZUKARA みづから（自ら）　*n.* oneself, the person himself or herself. *pron.* first-person singular: I. *adv.* by oneself, directly.

mizu-tsu-ku みづつく（水漬く）　*intr. v. YD* to be soaked in or covered with water. (*TN*)

*MO も *bound p.* indicates **1.** listing of similar things: and such. **2.** inclusion or addition (of something): also. **3.** outer limit or range (of a set of things): even.

mo も (裳) *n.* **1.** (Nara) skirt worn by a female. **2.** skirt a girl wears upon coming of age. **3.** skirt worn by a priest. (*TM*)

mō まう (猛) *n., nari adj. v.* strong, fierce, rough, powerful. (*TM*)

mochi もち (十五日・望) *n.* full moon, day of the full moon, fifteenth of the lunar month. (*TM*)

MOCHI-IRU もちゐる (用ゐる) *tr. v. KI* **1.** to use, make use of, adopt. **2.** to appoint, employ.

MOCHI-ZUKI もちづき (望月) *n.* full moon, moon of the fifteenth night (lunar calendar). (*TZ, TM*)

moga もが *final p.* (Nara) desiderative: expresses a wish for a state of affairs impossible or unlikely to come about.

mogamo もがも *final p.* (Nara) desiderative: expresses a wish for a state of affairs impossible or unlikely to come about.

mogana もがな *final p.* desiderative: expresses a wish for a state of affairs or condition, especially for something unlikely to come about: if only . . .

mohara もはら *adv.* **1.** wholly, entirely. **2.** (followed by neg.) not at all, not a bit. (*TM*)

MŌKU まうく (設く・儲く) *tr. v. SN* **1.** to prepare. **2.** to construct, set up, furnish. **3.** to obtain. **4.** to catch (e.g., a disease).

momi-ji もみぢ (紅葉・黄葉) *n.* [fr. n. *momichi*] brightly colored autumn leaves, coloration (red, yellow) of the leaves in autumn. (*HI*)

momochi ももち (百千) *n.* (lit., hundred thousand) great number. (*US*)

momohiki ももひき (股引き) *n.* leggings wrapped around the thighs. (*OH*)

*MONO もの (者・物) *n.* **1.** (deliberately unspecified or identified by context) thing, object. **2.** food, furniture, clothing, medicine, etc. **3.** person (derogatory or *hum.*). **4.** (circumlo-cution) destination. **5.** supernatural being, spiritual force, deity. (*TM*)

mono-dō-shi ものどほし (物遠し) *ku adj.* **1.** distant, remote. **2.** remote, distant. (*TO*)

MONO-GATARI ものがたり (物語) *n.* **1.** rumor, gossip, story. **2.** tale, romance, genre of narrative fiction. (*SN*)

MONO-GURUO-SHI ものぐるほし (物狂ほし) *shiku adj.* crazed, mindless, silly. (*TZ*)

*MONO-IMI ものいみ (物忌み) *n.* **1.** period of purification (to serve a deity). **2.** voluntary confinement, seclusion. (*UM*)

*MONO-KARA ものから *conj. p.* (follows RT) **1.** concessive: though, but, in spite of. **2.** causal: therefore, since.

MONO-KAWA ものかは *final p.* **1.** used to form a rhet. question: is it (the case that)? no, it is not. **2.** emphatic confirmation: isn't it (so)? indeed (it is)!

mono-kiki ものきき (物聞き) *n.* discreet inquiry about affairs, those who make such inquiries. (*MS*)

mono-kokoro-boso-shi ものこころぼそし (物心細し) *ku adj.* **1.** vaguely forlorn, bereft **2.** arousing a sense of anxiety or helplessness. (*IM*)

mono-mō ものまう (物申) [fr. v. *monomō-su*, "to speak humbly"] excuse me! (used when entering a person's home). (*NE*)

mono-mōde ものまうで (物詣で) *n.* pilgrimage to a temple or shrine. (*MS*)

mono ni kan-zu ものにかんず (物に感ず) *set phrase* to be affected or (emotionally) moved by something. (*TO*)

mono ni tsu-ku ものにつく (物につく) *set phrase* (of a vengeful spirit) to possess (someone). (*OH*)

MONO-NO ものの *conj. p.* (follows RT) concessive: though, but.

*MONO-NO-AWARE もののあはれ (物のあはれ) *n.* **1.** deeply felt response to some thing, event or quality (in nature, society, poetry, etc.). **2.** refined aesthetic sensibility. (*TO*)

mono-no-fu もののふ (武士) *n.* warrior. (*HJ*)

mono-no-gu もののぐ (物の具) *n.* **1.** tools, furniture. **2.** materials. **3.** weapons, especially armor, helmet, etc. (*HJ, HM*)

mono-no-kokoro もののこころ (物の心) *set phrase* **1.** the true meaning of things (in general). **2.** (a grasp of) the sense or import of a situation or state of affairs, etc. (*HJ*)

mono-no-satoshi もののさとし (物の諭し) *set phrase* omen from the gods or buddhas. (*HJ*)

MONO-O ものを *conj. p.* (follows RT) indicates **1.** concessive connection: though, but. **2.** causal connection: because. *final p.* (follows RT) concessive exclamation: even though, but!

mono-omoi ものおもひ (物思ひ) *n.* troubled thoughts, worries. (*TM*)

*MONO-SU ものす (物す) *intr. v. SH* **1.** to be, have. **2.** to go, come. **3.** to be born. *tr. v. SH* to do.

mono-u-ge ものうげ (物憂げ) *nari adj. v.* [fr. adj. *mono-ushi*, "depressing," and suffix *ge*, "appearance"] appearing to be disconsolate, depressed, unenthusiastic. (*MS*)

*MONO-YUE ものゆゑ *conj. p.* (follows RT) concessive: though, but.

mora-su もらす (漏らす) *tr. v. YD* **1.** to spill. **2.** to quietly reveal a secret. **3.** to leave out. **4.** to allow to escape. (*HM*)

moro-moro もろもろ (諸々) *n.* many, various, all kinds of. (*HJ*)

moro-tomo-ni もろともに (諸共に) *adv.* (acting) together. (*TN*)

moru もる *tr. v. YD* to pick, pluck. (*HJ*)

moru もる (漏る・洩る) *intr. v. YD* **1.** (of light, water, sound, etc.) to seep through, leak out. **2.** (of a secret) to be divulged. **3.** to be excluded, be cut out.

moru もる (守る) *tr. v. YD* **1.** to protect, guard. **2.** to be careful, secretive, discreet.

moshi もし (若) *adv.* if by chance, in case (of), supposing that. (*HJ, KM, TM*)

mō-shin まうしん (妄心) *n.* (Buddhist) delusion caused by attachment. (*HJ*)

*MŌ-SU (MAUSU) まうす (申す) *tr. v. YD* **1.** to speak to a superior (*hum.*). **2.** to request, ask a favor (*hum.*). **3.** to say (*polite*). **4.** *hum. suppl. v.* (*HM, TM*)

mota-gu もたぐ (擡ぐ) *tr. v. SN* [fr. comp. v. *mochi-agu*, "to lift up"] to raise, lift up. (*TM*)

motari もたり (持たり) *tr. v. RH* [fr. comp. v. *mochi-ari*] to hold, be in possession of. (*TM*)

mote-a-gu もてあぐ (持て上ぐ) *tr. v. SN* [fr. comp. v. *mochite-agu*] to lift up. (*US*)

mote-iku もていく (もて行く) *intr. v. YD* (same as *mote-yuku*) to do gradually.

*MOTE-NASU もてなす (持て成す) *tr. v. YD* **1.** to carry out. **2.** to behave properly. **3.** to treat, take care of.

mote-wata-ru もてわたる (持て渡る) *intr. v. YD* to bring, carry. (*MS*)

*MOTO もと (本・元・原・許) *n.* **1.** root, base, foundation. **2.** origin, beginning. **3.** stem, base (of a tree, plant). **4.** vicinity, area next to. **5.** place, dwelling. **6.** first half (5/7/5) of a *waka*. **7.** capital, funds. **8.** past, earlier times. *adv.* previously, earlier. (*HJ, TM, TZ*)

motodori もとどり (髻) *n.* topknot. (*UM*)

MOTO-MU もとむ (求む) *tr. v. SN* **1.** to seek out, look for. **2.** to desire. **3.** to invite, summon. **4.** to buy. (*IM, UM*)

motona もとな *adv.* **1.** rashly, for no apparent reason. **2.** persistently, constantly. (*MY*)

moto-yori もとより (元より・固より) *adv.* **1.** from before. **2.** from the beginning. **3.** it goes without saying (that). (*HJ, IM*)

MO-TSU もつ (持つ) *tr. v. YD* **1.** to hold, take in hand. **2.** to possess. **3.** to use, employ. **4.** to hold (a thought or feeling in one's heart). **5.** to keep, maintain. (*TM*)

mot-te もつて (以て) *comp.* [fr. *mochi-te*] **1.** with, by means of. **2.** for the reason that. **3.** used to add emphasis to the preceding: indeed. (*HJ*)

mottomo もつとも (最も・尤も) *nari adj. v.* **1.** truly, indeed, as claimed. **2.** very, especially.

3. (followed by neg.) (not) at all, (not) in the least. (*TM*)

moya-su もやす (燃やす) *tr. v. YD* to burn. (*TM*)

*MOYŌ-SU もよほす (催す) *tr. v. YD* **1.** to draw out, bring out. **2.** to urge. **3.** to perform, undertake, carry out. **4.** to cause (someone) to prepare (something). **5.** to summon, gather. **6.** to prepare in advance.

*MŌ-ZU まうづ (詣づ) *intr. v. SN* **1.** to go. **2.** to make a pilgrimage to a shrine or temple (*hum.*). (*HJ, TM*)

*MU む *aux. v.* (following MZ) indicates **1.** speculation, conjecture about the future: will probably. **2.** intention: (I, we) intend to. **3.** appropriateness: should. **4.** persuasion: how about? why don't you? **5.** circumlocution: it seems that. **6.** hypothesis: if.

mube むべ (宜) (also *ube*) *adv.* used to express approval or affirmation: truly, indeed. (*HI*)

*MUGE むげ (無下) *n., nari adj. v.* [fr. n. *mu*, "nothing," and n. *ge*, "lower"] **1.** terrible, inferior, extremely bad. **2.** very vulgar, uncouth. **3.** tragic, pathetic. **4.** (*muge-ni* followed by neg.) absolutely (bad), indescribably (bad). (*TN*)

mu-gon むごん (無言) *n.* **1.** silence, muteness. **2.** (Buddhist) vow of silence. (*HJ*)

mugura むぐら (葎) *n.* creepers, trailing plants. (*TM*)

MU-JŌ むじやう (無常) *n.* **1.** impermanence, evanescence. **2.** fleeting nature of human life. (*HJ*)

mukae むかへ (迎へ) *n.* welcome, welcoming party. (*TM*)

mukashi むかし (昔) *n.* distant past. (*TM*)

MUKA-U むかふ (向かふ) *intr. v. YD* **1.** to face, sit facing each other. **2.** to go to meet (someone). **3.** to approach, come close. **4.** to be equal to, match. **5.** to defy, resist. *tr. v. SN* **1.** to make (something) face a particular direction. **2.** to send someone to meet. **3.** to cause someone to contend with another. (*TM, TZ*)

muka-u むかふ (迎ふ) *tr. v. SN* **1.** to welcome. **2.** to invite. (*TM*)

mukui むくい (報) *n.* **1.** revenge, retaliation. **2.** retribution, repayment for past action (reaping what one has sown). **3.** reward, compensation (for services). (*HJ*)

*MUKUTSUKE-SHI むくつけし *ku adj.* **1.** frightening, weird, unnatural, eerie. **2.** uncultivated, rough.

muku-u むくふ (報ふ) *tr. v. YD* [fr. v. *mukuyu*, "to repay"] **1.** to repay (an obligation, etc.). **2.** to retaliate (for an offense, etc.). **3.** to remunerate (for work done). (*HJ*)

muku-yu むくゆ (報ゆ) *tr. v. KN* to repay (an obligation, etc.), retaliate. (*HJ*)

muma むま (馬) *n.* (same as *uma*) horse. (*HM*)

muma-ru むまる (生まる) *intr. v. SN* (same as *umaru*) to be born. (*TM*)

*MUNA-SHI むなし (空し) *shiku adj.* **1.** empty, vacant. **2.** dead. **3.** untrue, unfounded. **4.** fleeting, transient. (*TM*)

mune むね (棟) *n.* ridge (of a roof), ridgepole. (*HJ, TM, UM*)

mune-to むねと *adv.* mainly, primarily. (*TO*)

mura-kumo むらくも (村雲) *n.* cluster of clouds, gathering of clouds. (*TZ*)

murasaki むらさき (紫) *n.* **1.** perennial flowering plant from the roots of which a purple dye can be extracted. **2.** shade of pale reddish purple, lavender. (*MS*)

murasaki-da-tsu むらさきだつ (紫だつ) *intr. v. YD* to appear lavender, reddish purple. (*MS*)

mu-ru むる (群る) *intr. v. SN* to gather in one spot. (*IM*)

muse-bu むせぶ (咽ぶ) *intr. v. YD* **1.** to choke (as from inhaled smoke), suffocate. **2.** to be choked with tears. **3.** to sob quietly, suppress tears. **4.** to be obstructed, get stuck. (*HJ*)

mu-sha むしや (武者) *n.* warrior. (*HM*)

mushi むし (虫) *n.* insects. (*MS*)

mushin むしん (無心) *nari adj. v.* (lit. lacking

heart) **1**. insensitive, thoughtless. **2**. inelegant, uncultivated. *n*. **1**. (abbrev. for *mushin renga*) popular linked verse (as opposed to orthodox or classical *renga*). **2**. (of *waka* or *renga*) humorous, heterodox.

mu-su むす (咽す・噎す) *intr. v. SN* to choke, to suffocate. (*HJ*)

*MUSU-BU むすぶ (結ぶ) *intr. v. YD* (of dew, frost, froth) to congeal, condense, take form (dew, frost, ice, froth). *tr. v. YD* **1**. to tie together (thread, rope). **2**. to build (a hut), weave (a net). **3**. to construct, make. **4**. to promise, pledge. (*HJ*)

*MUTSUKA-SHI むつかし (難し) *shiku adj*. **1**. dismal, dull, gloomy, unpleasant. **2**. troublesome, annoying, vexing. **3**. uncanny, creepy. **4**. shabby, squalid.

*MUZU むず *aux. v.* (follows MZ) [fr. aux. v. *mu* and v. *su*, "to do"] indicates **1**. intention, resolve: I will, let us. **2**. speculation about the future: will likely, most probably. **3**. appropriateness: should.

muzu-to むずと *adv.* with a jerk, swiftly and powerfully. (*HM*)

*NA な *final p.* indicates **1**. neg. imperative: expresses a prohibition. **2**. emphatic: marks an exclamation. **3**. confirmation.

NA な *final p.* indicates **1**. a wish or desire. **2**. a request. **3**. (Nara) a suggestion: how about?

NA な *adv.* **1**. (Nara) prohibition: don't . . . (do something). **2**. (followed by final p. *so*) prohibition: don't (do something, let something happen).

*NA な (名) *n*. **1**. name. **2**. rumor, reputation, fame. **3**. something that exists in name only, groundless reputation. (*HI, TM*)

na な (汝) *pron.* you. (*MY*)

NABE-TE なべて (並べて) *adv.* **1**. all, generally. **2**. common, ordinary. (*HJ*)

nadaraka なだらか *nari adj. v.* **1**. smooth, soft. **2**. tranquil, uneventful. **3**. calm, gentle. **4**. safe. **5**. fluent, eloquent. (*TO*)

nadefu *See* **najō**.

*NADO など *adv. p.* indicates **1**. example, implying a group of similar items: and such. **2**. circumlocution, to soften an expression: and such. **3**. citation, in conversation or internal monologue, indicating content of v. such as *iu* and *omou*: (to say) such things as, (to think) such things as. **4**. emphasis (in neg., rhet. question, doubt sentences). **5**. scorn, self-deprecation.

nado など *adv.* [fr. personal pron. *nani*, "what," and case p. *to*] (sentence ends with RT) indicates **1**. doubt: why. **2**. rhet. question.

nagae ながえ (轅) *n.* carriage pole, attached to the halter of an ox. (*MS*)

NAGAME ながめ (眺め) *n.* gazing off into the distance, lost in melancholy thought. (*HI*)

naga-me ながめ (長雨) *n.* [fr. n. *naga-ame*] prolonged or incessant rain. (*HI*)

NAGA-MU ながむ (眺む) *tr. v. SN* **1**. to gaze out across a distance, look off into the distance. **2**. to become lost in melancholy thoughts. (*TZ*)

*NAGA-MU ながむ (詠む) *tr. v. SN* **1**. to recite a poem aloud, often drawing out the vowels, chant a poem. **2**. to compose a poem. (*TZ*)

naganaga-shi ながながし (長々し) *shiku adj* extremely or tediously long. (*HI*)

*NAGARA ながら *conj. p.* indicates **1**. (following nominal, RY) continuation of the same state: as before, unchanged. **2**. (following RY) simultaneous action: while, as. **3**. (following nominal, RY, adj. stem) concession: though.

nagare ながれ (流れ) *n.* **1**. flow, current, stream. **2**. drops of saké left in a cup. **3**. lineage, bloodline. **4**. school, artistic tradition. (*HJ*)

NAGA-RU ながる (流る) *intr. v. SN* **1**. (of water, mist, etc.) to flow. **2**. (of the moon, sun) to pass through the sky. **3**. (of a stream, river) to be carried along, move with the current. **4**. (of rain, tears, blood) to fall. **5**. to spread gradually. **6**. to move from one place to the next. **7**. to live long, survive. **8**. to be exiled.

naga-shi ながし (長し) *ku adj.* long. (*GM, HM, SN*)

*NAGA-SU ながす (流す) *tr. v. YD* **1**. to let (something) float. **2**. to shed (tears, sweat). **3**. to wash (with water), flush. **4**. to exile, send to a distant island. **5**. to spread rumors. **6**. to ignore, let pass by. (*TM*)

nageka-shi なげかし (嘆かし・歎かし) *shiku adj.* lamentable, deplorable, pitiful, sad, wretched. (*MS, TM*)

*NAGEKI なげき (嘆き) *n.* **1**. sigh. **2**. grief, distress. (*HJ*)

*NAGE-KU なげく (嘆く・歎く) *intr. v. YD* **1**. to sigh. **2**. to grieve, lament. **3**. to plea, pray desperately. (*SN, TM*)

nagisa なぎさ (渚) *n.* beach, shore. (*HJ*)

*NAGORI なごり (名残) *n.* **1**. feeling or mood that remains after something has passed. **2**. regret at parting, lingering feelings after parting. **3**. orphan, memento of deceased, grandchildren. **4**. end, last sheet of the transcription of a linked verse.

nagori なごり (余波) *n.* **1**. seaweed, shells, etc., left after tide or waves recede. **2**. ripple, waves that continue after wind dies. (*HJ*)

nagusa-mu なぐさむ (慰む) *intr. v. YD* to feel refreshed, comforted, have one spirit's lifted. *tr. v. YD* **1** to comfort, cheer up, please. **2** to tease. *tr. v. SN* **1**. to comfort, cheer up, please. **2**. to console, soothe, show sympathy for. (*HJ, TM*)

nai なゐ (地震) *n.* earthquake. (*HJ*)

nai-ga-shiro ないがしろ (蔑) *nari adj. v.* **1**. condescending, disdainful, contemptuous. **2**. indifferent to (the feelings of) others, carelessly casual. (*HJ*)

naigu ないぐ (内供) *n.* [fr. n. *naigu-bu*] priest who serves at imperial court. (*US*)

naishi ないし (内侍) *n.* imperial handmaiden, female court official. (*TM*)

NAJŌ なでふ *attrib.* [fr. comp. *nani to iu*] **1**. indefinite reference: such and such. **2**. expresses doubt: what kind of? **3**. used to make a neg. or a rhet. question: why would . . . ? *adv.* **1**. expresses doubt: why? **2**. used to modify a neg. or a rhet. question: why would . . . ? (*TM*)

*NAKA なか (中・仲) *n.* **1**. inner part. **2**. center. **3**. middle rank, middle level. **4**. one among many. **5**. second brother or sister. **6**. middle of the month. **7**. relationship, especially between men and women. (*HJ*)

naka-gaki なかがき (中垣) *n.* fence surrounding a building or separating neighboring houses, etc. (*TN*)

naka-goro なかごろ (中比) *n.* **1**. middle age. **2**. recent past. (*HJ*)

*NAKA-NAKA なかなか (中々) *nari adj. v.* half-done, halfway, insufficient. *adv.* **1**. carelessly, by half measures. **2**. rather, instead, contrary to expectations. **3**. (followed by neg.) (not) easily, (not) by any means. **4**. considerably. *interj.* affirmation: yes, that's it! quite right. (*HJ*)

na-ku なく (泣く・鳴く) *intr. v. YD* **1**. to weep. **2**. (of birds, insects) to sing. (*HI, MY, TM*)

NAMA-MEKA-SHI なまめかし *shiku adj.* [fr. v. *namameku*, "to be alluring"] **1**. youthful, fresh. **2**. elegant, refined. **3**. sexy, alluring.

*NAMAME-KU なまめく *intr. v. YD* **1**. to appear fresh, youthful, pure. **2**. to be elegant, refined.

nama-nama-shi なまなまし (生々し) *shiku adj.* **1**. fresh, vivid, raw. **2**. inexperienced, immature. **3**. lively, active. (*UM*)

NAME-GE なめげ *nari adj. v.* (suffix *ge*) **1**. rude, insolent. **2**. heartless. (*TM*)

name-raka なめらか (滑か) *nari adj. v.* smooth, sleek. (*OH*)

*NAME-SHI なめし *ku adj.* rude, uncivil, bad-mannered. (*MS*)

nami なみ (波・浪) *n.* wave. (*HI, TM*)

namida なみだ (涙) *n.* tears. (*TM*)

namu なむ (嘗む) *tr. v. SN* to lick, taste. (*TM*)

*NAMU なむ *bound p.* (followed by RT) emphatic: (that) indeed, of all (things). *final p.* (follows MZ) used to express a wish or desire.

nan なん (難) *n.* **1**. fault, flaw, weak point. **2**. disaster, misfortune. **3**. trouble, difficulty. **4**. criticism. (*HJ*)

nando なんど *adv. p.* [fr. personal pron. *nani*, "what," and case p. *to*] See *adv. p.* **nado**. (*HM*)

***NANI** なに (何) *pron.* something unknown: what, which? *adv.* used to express doubt or make a rhet. question: what, why? *interj.* seeks confirmation from the listener: wasn't it? (*HM, MY, SN*)

nani-bito なにびと (何人) *n.* what person, what kind of person. (*GM, TM*)

***NANI-GASHI** なにがし (何某・某) *pron.* **1.** indefinite reference or cirumlocution: such and such, so and so. **2.** first-person singular (masculine): I.

na ni o-u なにおふ (名に負ふ) *set phrase* **1.** to bear a name, be known by a certain name. **2.** to be famous, renowned. (*HI*)

nani shi ni なにしに (何しに) *set phrase* [fr. pron. *nani*, v. *su*, and case p. *ni*] **1.** for what purpose? **2.** (in expressions of dismay, despair, etc.) why? (*TM*)

nanji なんぢ (汝) *pron.* (second person, for subordinates) you. (*HJ, HM, TM*)

nanjō なんでふ (何条) *attrib.* [fr. *nani to iu*] **1.** expresses doubt: what kind of. *adv.* **1.** makes a rhet. question: why? (exclamation) **2.** casts doubt on the addressee's words: what are you talking about! (*US*)

***NANOME** なのめ (斜め) *nari adj. v.* **1.** common, mediocre. **2.** careless, insufficient.

na-no-ru なのる (名告る・名乗る) *intr. v. YD* **1.** to announce one's full name, especially to the enemy in battle, identify oneself. **2.** to give as a name. **3.** (of birds, winged insects) to cry or make a sound (as if to announce their arrival). (*HM*)

nan-zo なんぞ (何ぞ) *adv.* indicates **1.** question: why? **2.** rhet. question. (*HJ*)

***NAO** なほ (尚・猶) *adv.* **1.** as before, as expected, still. **2.** all the more, even more. **3.** even so, nonetheless, still (affirming something that has been denied/questioned). (*HJ, IM, MS, SN, TM, TZ*)

NAOZARI なほざり (等閑) *n., nari adj. v.* **1.** halfhearted, negligent, remiss. **2.** measured, moderate, simple. (*TZ*)

nara-bu ならぶ (並ぶ) *intr. v. YD* **1.** to be in a line, row. **2.** to be equal to, a match for. *tr. v. SN* **1.** to line up, place in a row. **2.** to match, compare. (*HJ, HM, TM*)

***NARAI** ならひ (慣らひ・習ひ) *n.* **1.** custom. **2.** social norm. **3.** time-honored rite or action. (*HJ, TZ*)

NARA-NAKU-NI ならなくに *set phrase* [fr. copular *nari*, aux. v. *zu*, suffix *ku*, and case p. *ni*] though it is not the case that, because it is not the case that. (*HI*)

***NARA-U** ならふ (慣らふ・馴らふ) *intr. v. YD* **1.** to grow accustomed to. **2.** to become intimate or friendly with. *tr. v. YD* to learn, acquire a skill. (*TM*)

***NARI** なり *aux. v.* (follows SS except after RH, when it follows RT) indicates **1.** hearsay: they say that. **2.** supposition, to make a judgment or assumption based on sound (voice, conversation): it sounds as if. **3.** supposition based on surrounding circumstances: it seems that.

***NARI** なり *aux. v.* (follows RT, nominals, adv., particles) indicates **1.** declaration, copula: to be. **2.** location, place or direction of something: to be located in. **3.** (Edo) naming: whose name is

nari なり (形・態) *n.* **1.** shape, figure. **2.** dress. **3.** appearance. (*IM*)

nari-masa-ru なりまさる (成り増さる) *intr. v. YD* to become even more so, increase in degree. (*TM*)

***NA-RU** なる (慣る・馴る) *intr. v. SN* **1.** to be used to, familiar with, accustomed to. **2.** to become intimate with. (*GM, HJ*)

na-ru (萎る) *intr. v. SN* **1.** (of clothing) to become well-worn, wrinkled, or limp (with the starch gone). **2.** to wear out. (*GM, IM*)

***NA-RU** なる (成る) *intr. v. YD* to become, change (into), be realized. (*TM*)

***NASAKE** なさけ (情) *n.* **1.** human feeling, emotion, especially warmth, sympathy, affection. **2.** aesthetic sensibility, discernment. **3.** atmosphere, taste, charm, flavor, mood. **4.** romantic love. (*HJ, TZ*)

*NA-SHI なし (無し) *ku adj.* **1.** nonexistent. **2.** no longer living. **3.** absent, away (from home). **4.** unprecedented, incomparable. **5.** abandoned, neglected. (*HJ*)

na-su なす (寝す) *intr. v. YD* to sleep, rest (*hon.*). *tr. v. YD* to allow to sleep. (*MY*)

*NA-SU なす (成す・為す) *tr. v. YD* **1.** to form, make. **2.** to carry out, do. **3.** to use one thing in place of another. **4.** to make one thing into another. **5.** to appoint to a position. **6.** *suppl. v.* emphatic: calls attention to the deliberateness of the main v. (*GM, HJ, TM*)

na-tane なたね (菜種) *n.* rapeseed. (*TM*)

natsu なつ (夏) *n.* summer. (*HI*)

*NATSUKA-SHI なつかし (懐かし) *shiku adj.* **1.** attractive, difficult to part from or relinquish. **2.** inspiring fondness, charming. **3.** inducing nostalgia, arousing memories of or longing for the past.

NAYAMASHI-GE なやましげ (悩ましげ) *nari adj. v.* [fr. adj. *nayamashi*, "sick," and suffix *ge*] to appear sickly, in poor health, pitiable, wretched. (*GM*)

nayama-su なやます (悩ます) *tr. v. YD* to trouble, cause to worry. (*HJ*)

*NAYA-MU なやむ (悩む) *intr. v. YD* **1.** to fall ill, suffer from illness or pain. **2.** to suffer anguish, emotional distress. **3.** to complain loudly or persistently.

na-yu なゆ (萎ゆ) *intr. v. SN* **1.** to become limp, lose strength. **2.** (of clothing) to become worn out. **3.** (of plants) to wilt. (*TM*)

nazora-u なぞらふ (準ふ・擬ふ・准ふ) (also *nazurau* なずらふ) *intr. v. YD* to be similar (to). *tr. v. SN* to compare, liken (to). (*HJ*)

na-zu なづ (撫づ) *tr. v. SN* **1.** to stroke, caress with the hand. **2.** to look after, tend. (*GM*)

NAZU-MU なづむ (泥む) *intr. v. YD* **1.** to falter, fail to make progress, hesitate (in the face of obstacles), stagnate. **2.** to be troubled by, anguish over. **3.** to dwell on, worry about.

ne ね *final p.* (follows MZ) (Nara) used to express a request.

ne ね (子) *n.* **1.** rat (first sign in the Chinese zodiac). **2.** hour of the rat (11:00 P.M.–1:00 A.M.). (*TM*)

ne ね (嶺) *n.* mountain peak. (*IM*)

NE ね (音) *n.* **1.** (beautiful) voice, sound. **2.** cry or sound of a person, an animal, an inanimate object. (*GM*)

nebi-yu-ku ねびゆく (ねび行く) *intr. v. YD* to mature, become an adult. (*GM*)

ne-dokoro ねどころ (寝所) *n.* bed. (*MS*)

negai ねがひ (願ひ) *n.* wish, request. (*TM*)

neji-kiru ねぢきる (捻ぢ切る) *tr. v. YD* to twist and cut off. (*HM*)

neji-yo-ru ねぢよる (振ぢ寄る) *intr. v. YD* to sidle up to, draw near to. (*TZ*)

neko-mata ねこまた (猫股) *n.* cat monster. (*TZ*)

nemugoro *See* **nengoro**.

nen-butsu ねんぶつ (念仏) *n.* recitation of Amida's name. (*HJ*)

*NENGORO ねむごろ (懇ろ) *nari adj. v.* **1.** careful, considerate, kind. **2.** familiar, close, intimate. **3.** honest, truthful, straightforward. (*HJ*)

nenji-sugu-su ねんじすぐす (念じ過ぐす) *tr. v. YD* to endure the passing of days and months. (*HJ*)

nenji-wa-bu ねんじわぶ (念じわぶ) *intr. v. KN* to find unbearable. (*HJ*)

nen-nen ねんねん (念々) *n.* (Buddhist) **1.** each instant of time, (at) all times. **2.** various thoughts. (*HJ*)

*NEN-ZU ねんず (念ず) *tr. v. SH* **1.** to pray. **2.** to endure, persevere. (*TM*)

*NETA-SHI ねたし (妬し) *ku adj.* **1.** irritating, vexing, hateful. **2.** regrettable, disappointing.

neya ねや (閨) *n.* **1.** bedroom. **2.** inner room, especially women's quarters. (*TZ*)

ne-zame ねざめ (寝覚め) *n.* awakening from sleep, especially before dawn or at night. (*HJ*)

*NI に　*case p.* (follows nominal or RT) indicates **1**. place of action: at, on, in. **2**. time of action: in, at. **3**. destination or direction of action: at, to. **4**. target of action: on, at, to. **5**. purpose, cause, origin of action: from, result of. **6**. result of a change: turn into, become. **7**. means of action: with, by means of. **8**. causative or passive agent: by. **9**. standard of comparison: compared with, more than. **10**. position, qualification: as, in the capacity of. **11**. addition: on top of, besides.

*NI に　*conj. p.* (follows RT) indicates **1**. causation: since. because. **2**. concession: despite the fact that, even though. **3**. temporal sequence: and, when. **4**. addition: on top of that.

ni に (丹)　*n.* **1**. red earth or clay. **2**. red coloring, pigment. (*HJ*)

niga-su にがす (逃がす)　*tr. v. YD* to release a captive (often, by mistake). (*GM*)

nigi-ru にぎる (握る)　*tr. v. YD* to grasp. (*TM*)

nigori にごり (濁り)　*n.* (Buddhist) impurity. (*HJ*)

ni-gu にぐ (逃ぐ)　*intr. v. SN* to flee, escape, run away. (*TM*)

niki にき (日記) (also *nikki*)　*n.* diary, journal. (*TN*)

*NIKU-SHI にくし (憎し)　*ku adj.* **1**. disagreeable, hateful. **2**. disgraceful, ugly. **3**. admirably resourceful, unflappable, spirited. (*MS, TM*)

*NIOI にほひ (匂ひ)　*n.* **1**. (glowing, often reddish) color. **2**. (shining, lustrous) beauty, radiance. **3**. attraction. **4**. fragrance, scent.

*NIO-U にほふ (匂ふ)　*intr. v. YD* **1**. to be dyed a shade of red, dyed beautifully. **2**. to shine beautifully, have a luster. **3**. to receive favor, flourish. **4**. to be fragrant. *tr. v. YD* to scent. *tr. v. SN* to dye.

niru にる (似る)　*intr. v. KI* to resemble. (*GM, HJ, TM*)

nishiga にしが　*final p.* used to express a wish, desire.

nishigana にしがな　*final p.* used to express a wish, desire.

nishiki にしき (錦)　*n.* **1**. brocade made of silk with gold or silver embroidery. **2**. (metaphor) something gorgeous or rare. (*HI*)

nishi-omote にしおもて (西面)　*n.* **1**. the west. **2**. west side of a building, a room on that side. (*GM*)

*NI-TE にて　*case p.* (follows nominals, RT) indicates **1**. place, time, age: at. **2**. means, materials: with, by means of. **3**. cause, reason: because, as a result of. **4**. condition, qualification, status, role: as, in the capacity of.

niwa には (庭)　*n.* **1**. garden, courtyard, open space in a residence. **2**. (specified) place for the performance of something (rites, hunting, battle, etc.). **3**. surface of the sea. **4**. earthen floor (of a kitchen, etc.). (*TZ*)

NIWAKA にはか (俄か)　*nari adj. v.* sudden, abrupt. (*HJ*)

*NO の　*case p.* (follows nominals, RT) indicates **1**. subject marker. **2**. attributive modifier: at, of. **3**. nominal that follows: that of. **4**. apposition, identity of status: it is . . .

nō のう (能)　*n.* **1**. talent, ability. **2**. skill, technique. **3**. medieval dramatic forms of *sarugaku* and *dengaku*. **4**. nō drama. (*US*)

*NOBO-RU のぼる (昇る・上る・登る)　*intr. v. YD* **1**. to climb, ascend, go upstream. **2**. to make one's way onto land (from the sea, a river). **3**. to go to the capital from the provinces. **4**. to make an appearance at court, enter the imperial palace. **5**. to rise in rank. **6**. to get excited, become dizzy. (*HJ, SN, TM*)

nobosu のぼす (上す・登す)　*tr. v. YD, SN* **1**. to cause to ascend or climb. **2**. to make go up a river. **3**. to summon. (*TM*)

no-bu のぶ (伸ぶ・延ぶ)　*intr. v. KN* **1**. (of time, space) to lengthen, expand. **2**. to escape. **3**. to relax. *tr. v. SN* **1**. to lengthen, expand. **2**. to let relax. (*GM*)

*NOCHI のち (後)　*n.* **1**. after. **2**. the future. **3**. after death, next life. **4**. descendants. (*TO*)

*NODOKA のどか　*nari adj. v.* **1**. peaceful, calm (weather). **2**. relaxed, at peace, calm. **3**. unconcerned, nonchalant. (*TZ*)

nodoke-shi のどけし (長閑けし) *ku adj.* **1**. peaceful, calm (weather, conditions). **2**. calm, collected (emotional state, character). **3**. leisurely, slow-paced. (*HJ*)

noga-ru のがる (遁る・逃る) *intr. v. SN* **1**. to escape from a particular situation, avoid (danger). **2**. to refuse. (*HJ, HM*)

nogo-u のごふ (拭ふ) *tr. v. YD* to wipe (away with the hand, etc.). (*US*)

noke-zama のけざま (仰け様) *n.* lying face up. (*TM*)

noki のき (軒) *n.* eaves. (*HJ*)

nokori-o-ri のこりをり (残り居り) *comp. intr. v. RH* to reside. (*HJ*)

noko-ru のこる (残る) *intr. v. YD* **1**. to remain behind. **2**. to survive. (*HJ*)

NOMI のみ *adv. p.* indicates **1**. restriction: only. **2**. emphasis: particularly, especially. **3**. intensity and continuous nature of a state or an action: nothing but. (*HJ, TM*)

no-mu のむ (飲む) *tr. v. YD* to drink. (*TM, TZ*)

*NONOSHI-RU ののしる (罵る・喧る) *intr. v. YD* **1**. to shout and make a commotion, be raucous. **2**. to earn a reputation, become the subject of gossip. **3**. to wield great power or influence. (*GM, TM, TN*)

nori のり (法・則) *n.* **1**. standard, model. **2**. rule, law. **3**. teaching, doctrine. **4**. Buddhist law, dharma. (*TO*)

nori のり (糊) *n.* paste, glue. (*NE*)

NO-RU のる (乗る) *intr. v. YD* to board (a boat). (*IM*)

no-su のす (乗す) *tr. v. SN* to place in (a vehicle or conveyance). (*TM*)

*NOTAMA-U (NOTAMŌ) のたまふ (宣ふ) *tr. v. YD* to say, announce (*hon.*). (*HM, TM, US*).

no-yama のやま (野山) *comp.* fields and hills. (*TM*)

nozo-ku のぞく (臨く) *intr. v. YD* to face (another, each other). (*GM*)

nozo-ku のぞく (覗く) *tr. v. YD* **1**. to peep (through a hole or gap). **2**. to peer down on. **3**. to observe. (*GM, KM*)

nozo-mu のぞむ (臨む) *intr. v. YD* **1**. to face directly. **2**. to attend, be present. (*TZ*)

nozo-mu のぞむ (望む) *tr. v. YD* **1**. to look afar. **2**. to wish for, desire. (*TN*)

*NU ぬ *aux. v.* (follows RY, RH) indicates **1**. perfection, the completion or realization of an action: to end up. **2**. sense of certainty that a particular action will be realized or completed: certainly, no doubt. **3**. (in pattern *nu . . . nu*) parallel action, indecision, and shifting between two or more actions: doing this and doing that.

NU ぬ (寝) *intr. v. SN* to sleep. (*OH, TM*)

nu-gu ぬぐ (脱ぐ) *tr. v. YD* to remove (an article of clothing). (*TM*)

nuka ぬか (額) *n.* **1**. forehead. **2**. prostration (pressing the forehead to the ground or floor). (*SN*)

nuka-go ぬかご (零余子) *n.* small black bulblets found on the vine of a mountain yam. (*HJ*)

nuka-zuku ぬかづく (額突く) *intr. v. YD* to press one's forehead to the ground or floor in reverence or submission.

nuki-to-ru ぬきとる (抜き取る) *tr. v. YD* to pull out, extract, uproot. (*KM*)

*NU-KU ぬく (抜く) *intr. v. SN* **1**. (of a tightly packed place) to come out, fall out. **2**. to excel. **3**. to escape, run away. *tr. v. YD* **1**. to pull out, unsheathe. **2**. to deceive. **3**. to strike down in combat. (*HJ, HM*)

nu-ru ぬる (濡る) *intr. v. SN* to get moist or wet. (*HI, TZ*)

nuru-shi ぬるし (温し) *ku adj.* **1**. lukewarm. **2**. insensitive. **3**. cold, lacking passion. (*MS*)

nusa ぬさ (幣) *n.* **1**. offering for the gods, made from hemp or cotton. **2**. parting gift. (*HI*)

*NUSHI ぬし (主) *n.* **1**. master, lord. **2**. owner. **3**. husband. **4**. animal (e.g., snake, toad) believed to inhabit a certain place and possess supernatural powers. *pron.* second-person, indicating respect: you. (*TZ*)

nusu-mu ぬすむ (盗む) *tr. v. YD* **1**. to steal. **2**. to act in secret, deceive. **3**. to imitate. (*HJ*)

NYŌBŌ にようばう (女房) *n.* **1**. ladies-in-waiting at court. **2**. female attendants serving nobility or samurai families. **3**. (Edo) wife.

nyū-men にうめん (入麺・煮麺) *n.* miso soup prepared with fine *sōmen* noodles. (*NE*)

*O を *case p.* indicates **1**. object of action. **2**. point of transit: through. **3**. point of origin: from. **4**. object of causative action: to have (someone) do. **5**. assumption (*o* + *ni* or *o* + *nite*): assuming that . . .

*O を *conj. p.* (follows nominal, RT) indicates **1**. loose causal connection: and so. **2**. concessive connection: though, even though. **3**. loose connection between previous and following phrase: and. *interj.* indicates **1**. (in middle of a sentence) emphasis: you know. **2**. (at end of a sentence) exclamation, emotional reaction.

o を (尾) *n.* tail. (*HI, TM*)

o を (緒) *n.* strap, lace. (*OH*)

ō わう (王) *n.* king. (*TM*)

oba をば *comp. case p.* [fr. case p. *o* and bound p. *wa*] emphatic, foregrounds object of v. (*TM*)

ō-ba おほば (祖母) *n.* grandmother. (*HJ*)

ō-ban わうばん (往反) (also *ōhen* わうへん) *n.* coming and going. (*HJ*)

obitata-shi おびたたし (夥し) *shiku adj.* **1**. extremely numerous. **2**. severe, terrible (degree). **3**. noisy, tumultuous. **4**. thriving, prosperous, magnificent. (*HJ*)

*OBOE おぼえ (覚え) *n.* **1**. reputation, how a person is perceived or received by others. **2**. high repute, esteem. **3**. affection, confidence (bestowed by a person of higher rank). **4**. (aesthetic) sense, feeling. **5**. memory, experience. **6**. confidence (in one's own skills).

*OBOROKE おぼろけ *nari adj. v.* **1**. (often followed by neg. or by rhet. question) ordinary, usual, few in number. **2**. extraordinarily numerous, special, unusual. (*MS*)

obo-shi おぼし (思し・覚し) *shiku adj.* **1**. similar (in appearance), bearing a resemblance to. **2**. desirable. (*TM*)

oboshi-awa-su おぼしあはす (思し合はす) *tr. v. SN* to compare, consider together (*hon.*). (*TM*)

*OBOSHI-ME-SU おぼしめす (思しめす) *tr. v. YD* to think, feel (*hon.*). (*HM*)

*OBO-SU おぼす (思す) *tr. v. YD* to think, feel (*hon.*). (*TM*)

*OBOTSUKA-NA-SHI おぼつかなし *ku adj.* **1**. faint, blurred, indistinct. **2**. worrisome, uncertain. **3**. unknown, suspicious. **4**. impatient. (*HM*)

*OBO-YU おぼゆ (覚ゆ) *intr. v. SN* [fr. v. *omou* and aux. v. *yu*] **1**. to think or feel naturally. **2**. to come to mind, be recalled, remember. **3**. to resemble. *tr. v. SN* **1**. to recall. **2**. to memorize, commit to memory. **3**. to narrate one's memories. (*HJ, HM, TM, TZ*)

ō-chi おほち (大路) *n.* [fr. Muromachi-period n. *ō-ji* おほぢ] main street, wide road. (*US*)

ochi-a-u おちあふ (落ち合ふ) *intr. v. YD* **1**. to come together, meet in one place, come across one another. **2**. to agree in opinion. **3**. (of reinforcements in battle) to merge from the flanks, join ranks. (*HM*)

ochi-bo おちぼ (落穂) *n.* fallen ears of rice. (*HJ*)

ochi-tsuku おちつく (落ち着く) *intr. v. YD* **1**. to fall down and stay. **2**. to decide on a dwelling, arrive at a destination. **3**. to cease worrying, be convinced, come to a conclusion. *tr. v. SN* **1**. to calm down, settle. **2**. to decide, bring to a conclusion. (*NE*)

ODOROKA-SU おどろかす (驚かす) *tr. v. YD* **1**. to surprise (someone). **2**. to draw someone's attention. **3**. to wake someone up. (*GM*)

*ODORO-KU おどろく (驚く) *intr. v. YD* **1**. to be surprised. **2**. to notice or realize suddenly. **3**. to wake up suddenly. (*GM*)

*ODORO-ODORO-SHI おどろおどろし *shiku adj.* [fr. v. *odoroku*, "to be surprised"] **1.** frightening, eerie. **2.** pompous, exaggerated. **3.** extreme, terrible. (*TM*)

odo-su おどす (威す・嚇す) *tr. v. YD* to frighten, threaten. (*KM*)

oga-mu をがむ (拝む) *tr. v. YD* to worship, pray. (*HJ*)

ōgi あふぎ (扇) *n.* fan. (*GM, HJ*)

ohagi おはぎ (蕣蒿) *n.* aster, starwort. (*HJ*)

oi-izu おひいづ (生ひ出づ) *intr. v. SN* **1.** to be born. **2.** to grow, mature, become an adult. (*SN*)

oi-naru おひなる (生ひ成る) *intr. v. YD* to grow, mature, become an adult. (*SN*)

OI-SAKI おひさき (生ひ先) *n.* one's future, what one will become or grow up to be. (*GM*)

oi-ta-tsu おひたつ (生ひ立つ) *intr. v. YD* to grow, mature, develop. (*GM*)

oi-ta-tsu おひたつ (追ひ立つ) *tr. v. SN* to drive someone away, chase off. (*US*)

ōi-zukasa おほひづかさ (大炊寮) *n.* palace kitchen bureau. (*TM*)

*OKA-SIII をかし *shiku adj.* **1.** tasteful, charming, interesting. **2.** admirable, praiseworthy, outstanding. **3.** adorable. **4.** ridiculous, absurd. (*MS, TM, TZ*)

OKASHI-GE をかしげ *nari adj. v.* tasteful, charming, adorable.

*Ō-KATA おほかた (大方) *n.* **1.** greater part (of). **2.** usual, prevailing, or conventional (form, etc.). *nari adj. v.* normal, usual. *adv.* **1.** in general, on the whole. **2.** (followed by neg.) absolutely. *conj.* used to mark a change of topic: well, then. (*HJ, TN*)

ŌKI (OOKI) おほき (大き) *nari adj. v.* **1.** big, large. **2.** important. **3.** splendid. **4.** great (degree). (*HJ, TM*)

oki-aga-ru おきあがる (起き上がる) *intr. v. YD* to get up. (*TM*)

*OKINA おきな (翁) *n.* **1.** old man. **2.** type of nō drama featuring an actor wearing an old man's mask, mask for this role. *pron.* **1.** first-person singular: I (used by an old man) (*hum.*). **2.** second-person singular: used to show both familiarity and respect toward an elderly man. (*TM*)

OKI-TSU おきつ (掟つ) *tr. v. SN* **1.** to plan, decide in advance. **2.** to order, command. **3.** to manage.

*OKO をこ (痴) *adj. v.* stupid, ridiculous, silly. (*US*)

*OKO-GAMA-SHI をこがまし (痴がまし) *shiku adj.* stupid or silly in appearance, ridiculous looking.

ō-kōji おほかうじ (大柑子) *n.* large citrus fruit, similar to a tangerine. (*US*)

*OKONAI おこなひ (行ひ) *n.* **1.** action, procedure (carried out in a particular order, as in a ritual). **2.** (Buddhist) prayer, service.

*OKONA-U おこなふ (行ふ) *intr. v. YD* to follow the Buddhist path, pray, engage in religious devotions. *tr. v. YD* **1.** to carry out (a ceremony, ritual). **2.** to govern, rule, control. (*GM, US*)

OKO-RU おこる (起こる) *intr. v. YD* **1.** to begin, occur, arise. **2.** to come out in large numbers. **3.** (of illness) to break out, spread. **4.** to gain momentum, force. (*HJ*)

*OKO-SU おこす (起こす) *tr. v. YD* **1.** to set (something) upright. **2.** to wake (someone) up. **3.** to excite, stir up. **4.** to start again, begin with renewed resolve. **5.** to light, kindle. (*MS*)

*OKO-SU おこす (遣す) *tr. v. SN* **1.** to send here from another place. **2.** *suppl. v.* to (do something) in this direction (e.g., *mi-okosu*, "to look in this direction"). (*TM*)

*OKOTA-RU おこたる (怠る) *intr. v. YD* **1.** to be idle, lazy. **2.** to get better, recover from illness or pain. *tr. v. YD* to neglect, fail to do. (*HJ*)

*OKU おく (置く・措く) *intr. v. YD* (of dew, frost) to form (on leaves, on the ground). *tr. v. YD* **1.** to place, set up. **2.** to leave as is. **3.** to leave behind. **4.** to create a gap, distance (temporal, spatial, psychological). **5.** to add a design. **6.** *suppl. v.* to do (something) in advance.

OKU おく （奥）　*n.* **1**. remotest part (of a mountain, region). **2**. inner thoughts, heart. **3**. living quarters for wife of a noble, wife of a noble. **4**. end, colophon, appendix (of a book, letter, document, etc.). (*SN*)

oku-byō おくびやう （臆病）　*n.* timidity, nervousness, diffidence. (*HM*)

okuri おくり （送り）　*n.* **1**. seeing someone off (on a trip). **2**. funeral. **3**. banishment, exile. (*TN*)

OKU-RU おくる （送る）　*tr. v. YD* **1**. to accompany or guide to a certain place, show the way. **2**. to send off. **3**. to hold a funeral (to send off the dead). **4**. to divorce a wife and return her to her family. **5**. to pass time. **6**. to compensate, make up for something. **7**. to grant a rank or post posthumously. **8**. to send a gift. (*HJ*)

*OKU-RU おくる （遅る・後る）　*intr. v. SN* **1**. to be late, fall behind. **2**. to become separated from, remain behind. **3**. to survive the death of a beloved. **4**. to be inferior, meager, insufficient. (*HJ*)

oku-yama おくやま （奥山）　*n.* distant or remote mountain. (*HI*)

OMAE おまへ （御前）　*n.* **1**. place before a god or noble (*hon.*). **2**. emperor, noble (*hon.*). *pron.* **1**. you (*hon.*). **2**. that person (*hon.*). **3**. (Edo) you (derogatory).

ome-ku をめく （喚く，叫く）　*intr. v. YD* to yell, scream, shout. (*HM*)

*OMOI おもひ （思ひ）　*n.* **1**. thought. **2**. intention, wish. **3**. worry, concern. **4**. love, desire, longing. **5**. expectation. **6**. (dressed in) mourning, (in) a state of mourning.

omoi-i-zu おもひいづ （思ひ出づ）　*tr. v. SN* to remember, recall. (*TN*)

omoi-ka-ku おもひかく （思ひ掛く・思ひ懸く）　*tr. v. SN* **1**. to think of, take seriously. **2**. to fall in love with. **3**. to anticipate, hope for. (*SN*)

omoi-kun-zu おもひくんず （思ひ屈ず）　*intr. v. SH* to be dispirited, depressed. (*SN*)

omoi-na-su おもひなす　*tr. v. YD* to assume, take for granted, be convinced (that). (*IM*)

omoi-no-hoka おもひのほか （思ひの外）　*nari adj. v.* unexpected, surprising. (*GM, HJ*)

omoi o ka-ku おもひをかく （思ひを懸く）　*set phrase* **1**. to pin one's hopes on, be obsessed with. **2**. to fall in love with. (*HJ*)

omoi-oko-su おもひおこす （思ひ起こす）　*tr. v. YD* **1**. to renew one's resolve, arouse oneself to action. **2**. to recall.

omoi-shi-ru おもひしる （思ひ知る）　*tr. v. YD* to understand, become fully aware of. (*GM*)

omoi-todomu おもひとどむ （思ひ止む）　*tr. v. SN* **1**. to give up, resign oneself to. **2**. to keep in one's heart, persist in thinking of, remain attached to, dwell on.

*OMOI-YA-RU おもひやる （思ひ遣る）　*tr. v. YD* **1**. to think of something or someone far away. **2**. to imagine, see in the mind's eye. **3**. to dispel gloomy thoughts, seek relief from melancholy. (*IM, TZ*)

*OMO-KAGE おもかげ （面影）　*n.* **1**. image (of a face or scene) that floats in one's mind. **2**. illusion. **3**. (in poetry) image or scene that emerges through overtones or is evoked by suggestion, allusion, etc.

omoku-su おもくす （重くす）　*tr. v. SH* to place emphasis on, privilege. (*HJ*)

omomuki おもむき （趣）　*n.* **1**. condition, appearance. **2**. meaning, point, purport. **3**. charm, elegance, tastefulness. (*HJ, TO*)

*OMO-MU-KU おもむく （趣く・赴く）　*intr. v. YD* **1**. to face (in a particular direction) and go. **2**. to follow (the will of another), agree with, bend toward. **3**. to aim toward, concentrate on. *tr. v. SN* **1**. to make a person face in a particular direction. **2**. to make a person agree or follow.

OMO-NASHI おもなし （面無し）　*ku adj.* (lit., without face) **1**. disgraceful, shameful. **2**. impudent, shameless.

*OMOO-YU おもほゆ （思ほゆ）　*intr. v. SN* [fr. v. *omohu* and aux. v. *yu*] to think of naturally or spontaneously, often with regard to things far away. (*MY, TM*)

omo-shi おもし （重し）　*ku adj.* **1**. heavy.

2. important, high-ranking. **3.** calm, solemn. **4.** extreme. (*HM*)

OMOSHIRO-SHI おもしろし（面白し）*ku adj.* **1.** charming, wonderful, delightful, interesting. **2.** elegant, refined, tasteful. (*IM, TM*)

*OMOTE おもて（面・表）*n.* （面）**1.** face. **2.** surface. **3.** honor, reputation. **4.** mask (nō drama). （表）**5.** outside. **6.** front (of house), entrance. **7.** official stance. (*HM, TM, UM*)

*OMO-U おもふ（思ふ）*tr. v. YD* **1.** to think of, consider. **2.** to recall fondly, long for. **3.** to hope for, wish for. **4.** to love, cherish. **5.** to worry, lament. **6.** to speculate, anticipate. (*GM, HI, HJ, HM, IM, SN, TM, TN, TZ*)

ōmune おほむね（大むね）*n.* essentials, gist, key points (of a discourse, etc.). (*TO*)

ŌN おほん（大御・御）*prefix* [fr. *ōmi* おほみ] strong hon. preceding a n.

on-ai おんあい（恩愛）(also *on-nai*) *n.* deep affection between parent/child, siblings, husband/wife, etc., in Buddhist doctrine often considered the attachment most liable to obstruct the path to enlightenment. (*HJ*)

onaji おなじ（同じ）*shiku adj.* same, equivalent. (*HI*)

*ONI おに（鬼）*n.* **1.** demon, devil. **2.** (metaphor) (something) ferocious, strong, threatening. **3.** spirit of the dead.

on-inori おんいのり（御祈）*n.* prayer (*hon.*). (*HJ*)

on-ko おんこ（恩顧）*n.* obligation. (*HJ*)

on-mi おんみ（御身）*n.* **1.** (one's) body, self (*hon.*). **2.** personal status (*hon.*). **3.** (one's) life (*hon.*). *pron.* you (light *hon.*). (*HM*)

*ONNA をんな（女）*n.* **1.** woman. **2.** wife, female lover.

onna-go をんなご（女子）*n.* young girl. (*GM*)

ono おの *pron.* I, me. (*GM, TM*)

ono-ga おのが（己が）*comp.* [fr. pron. *ono*, "one's," and case p. *ga*] **1.** I, myself. **2.** one's own (belongings, etc.). (*GM*)

*O-NO-KO をのこ（男・男子）*n.* **1.** man, male.

2. boy, son. **3.** court official. **4.** manservant, low-ranking man. **5.** suffix to the name of a man of low status. (*TM*)

onono-ku をののく（戦く）*intr. v. YD* to quiver in fear. (*HJ*)

ONO-ONO おのおの（各々）*pron.* (used to address an audience) everyone, all present. *adv.* each and every. (*HJ, NE*)

*ONORE おのれ（己）*pron.* **1.** first-person singular: I (*hum.*). **2.** derogatory second-person: the likes of you. (*GM, HJ, HM, KM, TM*)

*ONO-ZU-KARA おのづから（自ら）*adv.* **1.** naturally, of its own accord, before one knows it. **2.** accidentally, by chance, on occasion. **3.** (followed by hypothesis) if by chance, maybe. (*HJ, SN, TO*)

on'yōji おんやうじ（陰陽師）(also *onmyōji* おんみゃうじ）*n.* yin-yang priest, diviner. (*UM*)

*O-RI をり（居り）*intr. v. RH* **1.** to be, exist. **2.** to sit. **3.** *suppl. v.* to continue doing (something), remain in a (certain) condition or state. (*MS*)

ori をり（折）*n.* **1.** moment, occasion, opportunity. **2.** time, season. (*IM, TM, US*)

*ORI-FUSHI をりふし（折節）*n.* **1.** each moment, time, occasion. **2.** season. *adv.* **1.** occasionally, from time to time. **2.** just at that time, by coincidence. (*NE, US*)

ori-iru おりゐる（降り居る）*intr. v. KI* **1.** to dismount (from a horse) and sit. **2.** to abdicate, step down. (*IM*)

ori-goto をりごと（折り琴）*n.* folding zither. (*HJ*)

ori-ori をりをり（折々）*n.* times, moments. *adv.* **1.** sometimes, occasionally. **2.** gradually, little by little. (*HJ, TM*)

ori-ta-tsu おりたつ（降り立つ・下り立つ）*intr. v. YD* **1.** to step or get down (from a horse, boat, etc.) and stand. **2.** to do by oneself, become directly involved. (*TZ*)

ori-to-ru をりとる（折り取る）*tr. v. YD* to break off (e.g., a branch) and take away. (*TZ*)

*ORO-KA おろか（愚か・疎か）*nari adj. v.* **1.** irresponsible, remiss. **2.** indescribable, beyond words. **3.** stupid, foolish, ignorant. **4.** immature, unskilled, inexperienced. (*HJ, TM*)

oro-soka おろそか (疎か)   *nari adj. v.* **1.** scattered, sparse. **2.** insignificant, of no gravity. **3.** humble, simple. **4.** poor, inferior. (*HJ, TM*)

*ORO-SU おろす (下す)   *tr. v. YD* **1.** to lower, let down, unload. **2.** to drop. **3.** (of the wind, a storm) to blow down (from the mountains). (*TM*)

*O-RU をる (折る)   *tr. v. YD* **1.** to bend. **2.** to break off. **3.** to fold. *intr. v. YD* (of waves) to break, rush in and then recede. *intr. v. SN* **1.** to bend, curve. **2.** to bend and break. **3.** to lose heart, be defeated. **4.** (of *waka*) fault of composition in which the fourth phrase does not syntactically or semantically follow the third phrase. (*HJ, MS, TM*)

o-ru おる (降る)   *intr. v. KN* **1.** to get down from a high position. **2.** to leave (a noble's presence). **3.** to retire, resign from a position. (*IM*)

osama-ru をさまる (治まる・収まる・納まる) *intr. v. YD* (治まる) **1.** (of the state or land) to become peaceful. **2.** (of the body or mind) to be cured, recover (from illness, agitation, etc.). (収まる・納まる) **3.** to be stored properly. **4.** to be organized. **5.** (of an image, light etc.) to fade, grow dim or faint. (*HJ*)

*OSA-MU をさむ (治む・修む・収む・納る) *tr. v. SN* (治む・修む) **1.** to rule, govern, maintain peace. **2.** to cause to settle down, ameliorate. **3.** to cure, treat medically. (収む・納む) **4.** to store properly, put away. **5.** to harvest. **6.** to bury the dead, inter. (*HJ*)

OSANA-SHI をさなし (幼し)   *ku adj.* **1.** young, infant, small. **2.** childish, infantile, juvenile. (*TM*)

ōse-goto おほせごと (仰言)   *n.* **1.** order, command. **2.** words, speech (*hon.*). (*TM*)

*O-SHI をし (愛し・惜し)   *shiku adj.* **1.** (愛し) adorable, cute. **2.** (惜し) difficult to leave behind, causing lingering attachment. (*TM*)

ō-shi おほし (多し)   *ku adj.* many, numerous. (*HJ, SN*)

oshi-heda-tsu おしへだつ (押し隔つ)   *tr. v. SN* to separate by force. (*HM*)

oshiki をしき (折敷)   *n.* [fr. n. をりしき] square tray. (*US*)

oshi-mu をしむ (愛しむ・惜しむ)   *tr. v. YD* (愛しむ) **1.** to love deeply. (惜しむ) **2.** to begrudge, be stingy. **3.** to feel regret. (*US*)

oshi-narabu おしならぶ (押し並ぶ)   *tr. v. SN* to force into a line. (*HM*)

ōshi-ta-tsu おほしたつ (生し立つ)   *tr. v. SN* to raise (a child). (*TM*)

oshi-u をしふ (教ふ)   *tr. v. SN* to instruct. (*HJ, TM*)

OSORO-SHI おそろし (恐ろし)   *shiku adj.* **1.** frightening, unsettling. **2.** shocking.

oso-shi おそし (遅し)   *ku adj.* **1.** late, tardy. **2.** (of cognitive ability or sensitivity) slow, dull. (*TM*)

oso-u おそふ (襲ふ)   *tr. v. YD* **1.** to attack suddenly. **2.** to pressure, hold down. (*TM*)

*Ō-SU (OHO-SU) おほす (仰す)   *intr. v. SN* **1.** to give an order. **2.** to say (*hon.*). (*TM*)

*OTO おと (音)   *n.* **1.** sound. **2.** rumor, reputation. **3.** communication (letter, visit, etc.). (*HM, TM*)

otogai おとがひ   *n.* jaw, chin. (*US*)

*OTODO おとど (大殿・大臣)   *n.* **1.** residence of a person of high rank, room in such a residence. **2.** minister, high-ranking noble (*hon.*). **3.** mistress of the house (*hon.*). **4.** wet nurse, female attendant (*hon.*).

*OTOKO をとこ (男)   *n.* **1.** man, male. **2.** adult male, male youth. **3.** husband, male lover. **4.** son. **5.** man who has not taken religious vows. **6.** manservant.

oto-me をとめ (乙女・少女)   *n.* **1.** maiden, young daughter, unmarried woman. **2.** courtly dancer at Gosechi Festival. (*HI*)

*OTONA おとな (大人)   *n.* adult. (*GM*)

*OTONA-SHI おとなし (大人し)   *shiku adj.* [fr. n. *otona*, "adult"] **1.** grown-up, mature. **2.** elderly and wise. **3.** gentle, compliant.

OTONA-U おとなふ (音なふ・訪ふ) *intr. v.* YD **1**. to make a sound. **2**. to visit, pay a call.

oto ni ki-ku おとにきく (音に聞く) *set phrase* **1**. to hear rumors, hear from someone. **2**. to be famous, well known. (*HM*)

ŌTONO-GOMO-RU おほとのごもる (大殿ごもる) *intr. v.* YD to sleep (*hon.*). (*GM*)

otoro-u おとろふ (衰ふ) *intr. v.* SN **1**. to decline, weaken. **2**. to age and lose one's beauty or charm. (*HJ*)

oto-ru おとる (劣る) *intr. v.* YD **1**. to be inferior, compare unfavorably (with). **2**. to suffer a loss. (*TZ, US*)

*OTO-SU おとす (落とす) *tr. v.* YD **1**. to drop, let fall. **2**. to lose. **3**. to overlook, lose sight of. **4**. to let go, allow to escape. **5**. to lower (speed, volume, sound). **6**. to depreciate, weaken, downgrade. **7**. to look down on, scorn. **8**. to attack and defeat. (*HM, IM*)

*O-TSU おつ (落つ) *intr. v.* KN **1**. (of humans, animals) to fall down. **2**. (of leaves, petals) to scatter. **3**. (of water, rain) to fall intensely. **4**. (of light) to shine. **5**. (of the sun, moon) to set, sink to or below the horizon. **6**. to decline (in social status). **7**. to escape or flee (after being defeated in battle). **8**. to recover (from illness). **9**. (of a stronghold, fortress) to fall into enemy hands. **10**. to confess. (*HI, HJ, TM*)

o-u おふ (生ふ) *intr. v.* KN to grow, sprout, flourish. (*HI, SN, TN*)

O-U おふ (負ふ) *intr. v.* YD to match, be appropriate, suitable. *tr. v.* YD **1**. to carry on one's back, shoulder. **2**. to bear a name or reputation. **3**. to bear, sustain. **4**. to borrow. (*HM, IM*)

O-U おふ (追ふ) *tr. v.* YD **1**. to chase, follow. **2**. to set out for a destination. **3**. to drive out, expel. **4**. to clear the way for a high-ranking person.

*OWA-SU おはす (御座す) *intr. v.* SH **1**. to be, exist (*hon.* of *ari, ori*). **2**. to go, come (*hon.* of *yuku, ku*). **3**. *hon. suppl. v.* (*TM, US*)

*OWASHI-MA-SU おはします (御座します) *intr. v.* YD **1**. to be, exist (*hon.* of *ari, ori*). **2**. to go, come (*hon.* of *yuku, ku*). **3**. *hon. suppl. v.* (*IM, TM*)

*Ō-YAKE おほやけ (公) *n.* [fr. pref. *ō,* "large," and n. *yake,* "residence"] **1**. imperial residence. **2**. emperor, empress, high imperial consort. **3**. court, government. **4**. public, society. (*TM*)

oyo-bu およぶ (及ぶ) *intr. v.* YD **1**. to reach, extend to. **2**. to stretch (legs, hands) or lean forward to reach. **3**. to become (a certain situation). **4**. (often followed by neg.) to be equal to, comparable to. **5**. (after case p. *ni,* followed by neg. or by rhet. question) to be necessary. (*HJ*)

OYOSU-GU およすぐ (also *oyosu-ku*) *intr. v.* SN **1**. (of a child) to become an adult. **2**. (of a young person) to act like an adult, be precocious. **3**. to appear plain, subdued.

o-yu おゆ (老ゆ) *intr. v.* KN to grow old, become elderly. (*HJ*)

o-zu おづ (怖づ・懼づ) *intr. v.* KN to be afraid, recoil in fear. (*HJ, KM, TM*)

ra ら (等) *suffix* **1**. (following nominal) indicates plural. **2**. (following name or pron.) indicates affection, humility: dear. **3**. (following adj. v. stem) creates a n. or an adj. v. describing a particular condition (e.g., *kiyo-ra*). (*MY*)

ra-gai らがい (羅蓋) *n.* large silk sunshade (for nobility). (*TM*)

rai-nen らいねん (来年) *n.* next year. (*MS*)

*RAMU らむ *aux. v.* (follows SS, but RT after RH) indicates **1**. conjecture about a current situation not visible to the speaker: now probably doing (something). **2**. speculation about cause: probably as a result of . . . **3**. hearsay statement: it is said that. **4**. circumlocution: it would seem that . . .

*RARU らる *aux. v.* SN (follows MZ of conjugations other than YD, NH, RH) indicates **1**. spontaneity: to find oneself doing (something). **2**. potential: can. **3**. passive, with agent usually marked by case p. *ni.* **4**. respect toward the subject of main v. (*hon.*).

*RASHI らし *aux. v.* (follows SS, except after

RH) indicates evidential supposition: it appears that . . .

RAYU らゆ *aux. v. SN* (follows MZ of SN) (Nara) expresses potential.

*****REI** れい (例) *n.* **1**. precedent. **2**. custom, convention. **3**. what is usual, ordinary, the norm.

ren-ga れんが (連歌) *n.* linked verse. (*TZ*)

ren-ji れんじ (連子) *n.* lattice, lattice window. (*KM*)

ri り (里) *n.* unit of length: league, approx. 3.9 kilometers (2.5 miles). (*OH*)

RI り *aux. v. RH* (follows IZ of YD, MZ of SH) indicates **1**. resultative, indicating that the action has taken place and the result of that action continues: has been. **2**. continuative or durative, indicating continuing action or state: . . . ing. **3**. perfective, indicating the completion of an action or a process: to end up.

rō-dō らうどう (郎等) *n.* retainer, vassal. (*HM*)

RŌGAWASHI らうがはし (乱がはし) *shiku adj.* **1**. disordered, messy, untidy. **2**. noisy, loud.

ROKU ろく (禄) *n.* **1**. remuneration, payment. **2**. reward, present.

rōrō ろうろう (朧々) *tari adj. v.* hazy, blurred, dim, misty. (*UM*)

RŌRŌJI らうらうじ *shiku adj.* **1**. refined, sophisticated, skillful. **2**. elegant, graceful.

RŌTA-GE らうたげ *nari adj. v.* [fr. adj. *rōtashi*, "adorable," and suffix *ge*] appearing to be charming, adorable. (*GM*)

*****RŌ-TA-SHI** らうたし *ku adj.* adorable, charming.

RU る *aux. v. SN* (follows MZ of YD, NH, RH) indicates **1**. spontaneity: to find oneself doing (something). **2**. potential: can. **3**. passive, with agent often marked by case p. *ni*: was . . . by. **4**. respect for the subject of the main v. (*hon.*).

ryō りやう (両) *suffix* counter for things in pairs and for carriages, etc. (*HJ, HM*)

ryō りやう (領) *suffix* counter for suits of clothes, armor.

ryō れう (料) *n.* **1**. something prepared for a specific purpose, material. **2**. cost, necessary expense. **3**. objective, purpose, reason. (*TM, TO*)

ryō-sho りやうしよ (領所) *n.* territory, fief. (*HJ*)

ryū りゆう (竜) *n.* dragon. (*HJ*)

SA さ (然) *adv.* **1**. in that way. **2**. to that extent.

SA-BAKARI さばかり (然許り) *adv.* [fr. adv. *sa* and adv. p. *bakari*] **1**. to that extent, that much. **2**. very. (*HM*)

*****SABURA-U (SABURŌ)** さぶらふ (候ふ・侍ふ) *intr. v. YD* **1**. to serve a person of high status (*hum.*). **2**. to come, go (*hum.*). **3**. to exist, be (*polite*). **4**. *polite suppl. v.* (*SN*)

sadama-ru さだまる (定まる) *intr. v. YD* **1**. to be determined, decided. **2**. to become customary. **3**. to become stabilized, settled. (*HJ*)

*****SADA-MU** さだむ (定む) *tr. v. SN* **1**. to decide. **2**. to promise. **3**. to exchange opinions, consult. **4**. to stabilize, fix, set. (*TM*)

*****SAE** さへ *adv. p.* indicates **1**. addition: on top of that. **2**. minimal example, giving a lesser example to suggest something comparatively greater: even X, not to mention Y. (*HJ, TM*)

*****SAGA** さが (性・相) *n.* **1**. nature, innate character, personality. **2**. fate, destiny. **3**. custom, practice, way of the world.

saga さが (祥) *n.* **1**. portent, omen. **2**. augury, auspicious sign. (*UM*)

*****SAGA-NA-SHI** さがなし (性無し) *ku adj.* [fr. n. *saga*, "character," and adj. *nashi*] **1**. cruel, mean-spirited. **2**. long-winded, garrulous. **3**. mischievous.

sage-oro-su さげおろす (さげ下す) *tr. v. YD* to lower. (*TM*)

sagu-ru さぐる (探る) *tr. v. YD* **1**. to search or investigate with one's fingertips, etc. **2**. to visit, seek out. (*TM*)

sai-gen さいげん (際限) *n.* limit, end. (*HJ*)

sai-go さいご (最後・最期) *n.* **1.** end of something. **2.** end of life, death. (*HM*)

saina-mu さいなむ (苛む・嘖む) *tr. v. YD* to blame, scold, criticize, persecute. (*GM*)

sai-shi さいし (妻子) *n.* wife and children. (*HJ*)

*SAKAI さかひ (境) *n.* **1.** border (village, province, etc). **2.** land, region. **3.** state, condition. **4.** climax (of a story, drama). (*HJ*)

sakari さかり (盛り) *n., nari adj. v.* **1.** full bloom, peak. **2.** youth, time of vigor and strength, prime of life. (*HJ, SN, TZ*)

saka-sama さかさま (逆様・倒様) *n., adj. v.* **1.** inverted order or direction, upside down, backward. **2.** unreasonable, irrational. (*HM*)

*SAKA-SHI さかし (賢し) *shiku adj.* **1.** brilliant, quick-witted. **2.** skillful, accomplished. **3.** tough-minded, stout-hearted. **4.** crafty, cunning. (*TM*)

sakashira-gokoro さかしらごころ (さかしら心) *n.* pretentiousness, arrogance, brashness. (*TZ*)

saka-u さかふ (逆ふ) *intr. v. YD, SN* **1.** to oppose, block. **2.** to be hostile toward, fight against. (*TZ*)

saké さけ (酒) *n.* rice wine. (*TZ*)

sake-bu さけぶ (叫ぶ) *intr. v. YD* to scream, shout. (*TZ, UM*)

SAKI さき (先) *n.* **1.** tip, point. **2.** lead, vanguard. **3.** highest rank. **4.** future. **5.** past. (*HM*)

saki-da-tsu さきだつ (先立つ) *intr. v. YD* **1.** to precede. **2.** to predecease. (*HJ*)

saki-o-u さきおふ (前駆追ふ・先追ふ) *intr. v. YD* to clear the way (for a person of high station). (*MS*)

saki-zaki さきざき (先々) *n.* before, in the (distant) past, a long time ago. (*TM*)

sa-ku さく (咲く) *intr. v. YD* **1.** to bloom, blossom. **2.** (of waves) to crest. (*IM, TZ*)

sa-ku さく (割く・裂く) *intr. v. SN* to break apart, crack. *tr. v. YD* to split, break, tear apart. (*HJ*)

*SAMA さま (様) *n.* **1.** appearance, form. **2.** looks, personal appearance. **3.** layout, plan, design. **4.** method, form (of a poem, etc.). *pron.* (Edo) third-person, showing respect or affection. (*TZ*)

samata-gu さまたぐ (妨ぐ) *tr. v. SN* to hinder, obstruct. (*HJ*)

*SA-MO さも (然も) *adv.* [fr. adv. *sa* and bound p. *mo*] thus, in this way. (*MS*)

sa-mu さむ (覚む・醒む) *intr. v. SN* **1.** to wake up (from a dream, sleep, intoxication). **2.** to recover from depression, grief. (*SN, UM*)

samu-shi さむし (寒し) *ku adj.* (subjectively) cold. (*MS*)

*SA-NAGARA さながら (然ながら) *adv.* **1.** just as it is, unchanged, thus. **2.** all, everything, in its entirety. **3.** (followed by neg.) (not) at all. **4.** (followed by comparison) just like. (*HJ, US*)

sane さね (札) *n.* small narrow plates of iron or leather strung together to make armor. (*HM*)

san-gai さんがい (三界) *n.* (Buddhist) **1.** the three worlds of desire, form, and formlessness in which all sentient beings are born and die. **2.** all things in this world. **3.** one's previous, present, and future lives. (*HJ*)

sankō さんかう (三更) *n.* third watch, hour of the rat (11:00 P.M.–1:00 A.M.). (*UM*)

*SA-NOMI さのみ (然のみ) *comp.* [fr. adv. *sa*, "that," and adv. p. *nomi*] **1.** in this way only. **2.** (followed by neg.) (not) that much. (*HJ, TZ*)

san-zan さんざん (散々) *nari adj. v.* **1.** violent, fierce. **2.** ugly, unsightly. **3.** scattered. (*HM*)

san-zon さんぞん (三尊) *n.* **1.** Buddha, Buddhist law, Buddhist priesthood. **2.** triad of three Buddhist statues in a temple (e.g., Amida Buddha, bodhisattvas Kannon and Seishi). (*OH*)

*SARA さら (更) *nari adj. v.* (usually following v. *iu*, "to say") needless to say, needs no repeating, obvious. (*MS*)

*SARA-BA さらば (然らば) *conj.* if that is so, in that case, (well) then. (*TM*)

sara-de-mo さらでも (然らでも) *comp.* [fr. v. *sari*, neg. conj. p. *de*, and bound p. *mo*] even should it not be so. (*MS*)

sara-meka-su さらめかす *tr. v. YD* [fr. ono-matopoeia *sara* and suffix *mekasu*] to make a swishing, rustling sound. (*US*)

*****SARA-NI** さらに (更に) *adv.* **1.** again, anew, afresh. **2.** still more, more and more. **3.** (followed by neg.) (not) at all. (*HJ, TM*)

*****SARE-BA** されば (然れば) *conj.* [fr. v. *sari* and conj. p. *ba*] **1.** therefore, for that reason, that being the case. **2.** expresses surprise, disbelief: what on earth (is this)? **3.** used to introduce or change a topic: so, then. (*US*)

*****SARE-DO** されど (然れど) *conj.* [fr. v. *sari* and conj. p. *do*] although, nevertheless, however. (*HJ, TM, UM*)

*****SA-RI** さり (然り) *intr. v. RH* [fr. adv. *sa*, "that," and v. *ari*, "to be"] to be so, be thus. (*GM, TM*)

sari-tote さりとて (然りとて) *conj.* [fr. v. *sari*, case p. *to*, and conj. p. *te*] be that as it may, even so, nevertheless. (*TO, TZ*)

*****SA-RU** さる (去る) *intr. v. YD* **1.** to leave, go away from. **2.** (of time, season) to approach. **3.** to change, fade. **4.** to abdicate, retreat, withdraw. **5.** to die. *tr. v. YD* **1.** to keep at a distance. **2.** to break off a relationship. (*HJ*)

SARU さる (然る) *attrib.* [fr. v. *sari*] **1.** that, that kind of. **2.** appropriate, fitting, commendable. **3.** a certain (situation, etc.). (*HM, IM, TZ*)

SA-RU さる (避る) *tr. v. YD* **1.** to avoid. **2.** to refuse, decline an offer. (*TM*)

SARU-BEKI さるべき (然るべき) *attrib.* [fr. v. *sari* and aux. v. *beshi*] **1.** appropriate, suitable. **2.** natural, fated, destined. **3.** considerable, magnificent, great. (*HJ*)

SARU-HODO-NI さるほどに (然る程に) *conj.* **1.** meanwhile, as (that) was happening. **2.** (used to introduce or change a topic) so then.

SARU-KATA さるかた (然る方) *comp.* [fr. RT of v. *sari* and n. *kata*] **1.** in that direction, in that way. **2.** as fitting the circumstances, in its own way, after its own fashion.

saru-ni-te-mo さるにても (然るにても) *conj.* [fr. v. *sari*, copular *nari*, conj. p. *te*, and bound p. *mo*] even so.

saru-o さるを (然るを) *conj.* [fr. RT of RH v. *sari* and conj. p. *o*] **1.** be that as it may, even so. **2.** (used to introduce a shift in topic) that being the case, that said. (*TZ*)

*****SARU-WA** さるは (然るは) *conj.* **1.** even so. **2.** but. **3.** moreover, furthermore. **4.** (elaboration on what precedes) as for that. (*GM, TN*)

sasa-gu ささぐ (捧ぐ) *tr. v. SN* **1.** to lift high with one's hands. **2.** to raise aloft. (*TM*)

sasa-u ささふ (支ふ) (also *saso-u*) *tr. v. SN* **1.** to support, hold up. **2.** to block, guard against. (*HM*)

sa-se-ru させる *attrib.* (usually followed by neg.) considerable, notable, worth mentioning. (*US*)

sashi-iru さしいる (差し入る) *intr. v. YD* to enter. *tr. v. SN* to place in. (*TM*)

SASHI-I-ZU さしいづ (差し出づ) *intr. v. SN* **1.** to shine through. **2.** to protrude, appear, emerge. **3.** to meddle, intrude. *tr. v. SN* to hold out (to), offer (to). (*US*)

sashikata-mu さしかたむ (さし堅む) *tr. v. SN* **1.** to shut tight (a door, gate, etc.). **2.** to guard carefully. **3.** to take pains over one's appearance. (*OH*)

*****SA-SHIMO** さしも (然しも) *adv.* [fr. adv. *sa*, adv. p. *shi*, and bound p. *mo*] **1.** that much, to that extent. **2.** (followed by neg. or by rhet. question) that much, that far, that way, like that. (*HJ, TZ*)

sashitsume-hikitsume さしつめひきつめ (差し詰め引き詰め) *set phrase* [fr. v. *sashitsumu* and v. *hikitsumu*] shooting arrows in rapid succession. (*HM*)

*****SASU** さす *aux. v. SN* (follows MZ of KI, KN, SI, SN, KH, SH) **1.** causative: to cause, allow. **2.** (used with hon. suppl. v. such as *tamau*) maximum honorific.

*****SA-SU** さす (射す・差す・指す) *intr. v. YD* **1.** to shine. **2.** (of plants, trees) to bud. **3.** to reach full tide. **4.** (of clouds) to appear, rise. *tr. v. YD* **1.** to point to. **2.** to raise (an umbrella).

3. to set up, put in place. **4**. to stab, pierce. **5**. to pour, mix (liquids). (*MS, TM*)

*SASUGA さすが (流石) *nari adj. v.* while affirming what was said before, this asserts a seemingly opposite opinion, causing a sense that what was said may be true but cannot be left at that: though that may be the case, yet even so, nevertheless. *adv.* even so, nevertheless. (*GM, TM*)

*SASUGA-NI さすがに (流石に) *adv.* **1**. though that was the case, in the end . . . , contrary to expectations. **2**. after all.

sasura-u さすらふ (流離ふ) *intr. v. SN, YD* **1**. to drift along, wander aimlessly. **2**. to fall into decline, become down-and-out. (*OH*)

*SATA さた (沙汰) *n.* **1**. talk, consultation, conference, counsel, judgment. **2**. measure, action, means of accomplishing (something). **3**. order. **4**. message, letter. **5**. rumor. **6**. preparations, procedures for an undertaking.

*SATE さて (然て) *adv.* **1**. under those conditions, that being so . . . **2**. in addition. *conj.* **1**. then, next, as a result. **2**. but, however, having said that. *interj.* expresses surprise, frustration, exasperation. (*KM, UM*)

SATE-MO さても (然ても) *adv.* **1**. even under those circumstances. **2**. even so. *conj.* but, even then. *interj.* expresses pleasant surprise: my! (*GM*)

sate-wa さては (然ては) *adv.* [fr. adv. *sate* and bound p. *wa*] as it stands, in that state. *conj. p.* and then, in addition. (*GM, HM, TM*)

sato さと *adv.* **1**. suddenly, quickly. **2**. all together, in unison (when a large group laughs, cheers, etc., at the same time). (*UM*)

*SATO さと (里) *n.* **1**. village. **2**. hometown. **3**. home (dwelling). **4**. real family. **5**. province (as opposed to capital or court).

sato-ru さとる (悟る・覚る) *tr. v. YD* to realize, awaken, come to a higher understanding. (*HJ*)

satoshi さとし (諭し) *n.* omen, sign. (*HJ*)

sau-su *See* **sō-su**.

sawa さは (沢) *n.* swamp or marsh. (*IM*)

sawaga-shi さわがし (騒がし) *shiku adj.* **1**. noisy, disorderly, boisterous. **2**. busy. **3**. unsettled, seething, turbulent. (*HJ*)

*SAWA-GU さわぐ (騒ぐ) *intr. v. YD* [fr. v. *sawaku*] **1**. to be noisy. **2**. to panic, be upset, shocked. **3**. to become busy, rush about. **4**. to complain loudly. **5**. to become a widespread rumor. (*MY, TM*)

sawari さはり (障り) *n.* **1**. hindrance, impediment. **2**. menstruation. (*HJ, TM*)

SAWA-RU さはる (障る) *intr. v. YD* **1**. to be blocked, hindered. **2**. to become inconvenient. (*TZ*)

sawaru さはる (触る) *tr. v. YD* to touch. (*TM*)

SAYA-KA さやか (清か・明か) *nari adj. v.* **1**. clearly visible, distinct. **2**. clearly audible. **3**. very bright.

sa-yō さやう (然様) *n., nari adj. v.* that kind, that way. (*TM*)

SEBA-SHI せばし (狭し) *ku adj.* narrow, small, confined. (*HJ*)

*SECHI せち (切) *nari adj. v.* **1**. deeply felt, keen. **2**. (in RY) intense. **3**. eager, zealous. **4**. important, urgent, pressing. (*HJ, TZ*)

sechi-bun せちぶん (節分) (also *setsubun*) *n.* time of seasonal change, particularly the day before the beginning of spring, summer, autumn, and winter. (*MS*)

sei せい (勢) *n.* **1**. military strength, troops. **2**. power, momentum. (*HM*)

sei-byō せいびやう (精兵) *n.* outstanding warrior, especially a skilled archer. (*HM*)

seikan せいかん (清閑) *n., nari adj. v.* pure and still, removed from mundane affairs. (*OH*)

SE-KAI せかい (世界) *n.* **1**. human world, earth. **2**. human society. **3**. region, province. **4**. general area or vicinity. (*TM*)

*SEKEN せけん (世間) *n.* **1**. (Buddhist) world of sentient beings, secular world. **2**. human society. **3**. surroundings, environment.

seki-to-mu せきとむ (堰き止む) *tr. v. SN* to contain, check, dam up. (*TM*)

sema-ru せまる (迫る・逼る)　*intr. v. YD* **1.** to approach. **2.** to become narrow. **3.** to have difficulty surviving, become impoverished.

*SEMETE せめて　*adv.* **1.** forcibly, by any means. **2.** keen, deep, poignant. **3.** extreme, very. **4.** at the very least.

*SE-MU せむ (責む)　*tr. v. SN* **1.** to blame, chastise (for a fault, crime, sin). **2.** to pester, nag, press, remind. **3.** to trouble, bother. **4.** to seek out the truth. (*TM*)

se-mu せむ (迫む・逼む)　*intr. v. SN* to approach, draw near. *tr. v. SN* to keep close to one's body. (*US*)

se-ni せに (狭に)　*comp.* [fr. stem of *ku* adj. *seshi* and case p. *ni*] narrow, in narrow quarters. (*HJ*)

seri せり (芹)　*n.* Japanese parsley (*Oenanthe javanica*). (*HJ*)

seshi せし (狭し)　*ku adj.* narrow or confined (room, space, etc.). (*HJ*)

setsu-bun　*See* **sechibun.**

shaku しやく (尺)　*n.* unit of length: equivalent of 10 *sun*, or one-tenth of a *jō* (approx. 1 foot). (*HJ, TM, US*)

*SHI し　*adv. p.* **1.** singles out one item of a group for emphasis: this in particular. **2.** delimits conditions under which something can occur: only if (then . . .). **3.** (followed by neg.) strong negation: (not) at all, absolutely (not).

shiba しば (柴)　*n.* firewood, brushwood. (*HJ*)

shibashi しばし (暫し)　*adv.* for a (little) while. (*HJ, TM*)

shibo-mu しぼむ (萎む)　*intr. v. YD* **1.** to wilt, fade, lose vitality. **2.** to shrivel. (*HJ, US*)

shichi-dō しちだう (七道)　*n.* the seven major thoroughfares in areas outside the Kinai area. (*HJ*)

shichi-hō　*See* **shippō.**

shi-chiku しちく (絲竹)　*n.* (lit., strings, bamboo) musical instruments, music. (*HJ*)

shidai-shu しだいしゆ (四大種)　*n.* (Buddhist) four elements that constitute all matter: earth, water, fire, and wind. (*HJ*)

shidari-o しだりを (し垂り尾)　*n.* drooping tail (of a bird). (*HI*)

shi-de no yama-ji しでのやまぢ (死出の山路) *set phrase* mountain path of death. (*HJ*)

shige-ru しげる (茂る)　*intr. v. YD* to grow abundantly, flourish. (*IM*)

*SHIGE-SHI しげし (茂し・繁し)　*ku adj.* **1.** (of grass, shrubs, etc.) overgrown, lush. **2.** many. **3.** incessant, frequent. **4.** plentiful, abundant. **5.** complicated, troublesome. (*HJ, KM*)

shigi しぎ (鴫)　*n.* Japanese snipe (*Gallinago hardwickii*). (*IM*)

shigura-u (shigurō) しぐらふ (時雨らふ)　*intr. v. YD* [fr. v. *shiguru*, "to shower"] **1.** to grow dark or overcast as if about to rain. **2.** to gather, form a crowd. (*HM*)

SHIGURE しぐれ (時雨)　*n.* **1.** sudden intermittent showers in late autumn and early winter. **2.** (metaphor) weeping.

shiguru しぐる (時雨る)　*intr. v. SN* **1.** (of rain) to shower. **2.** (metaphor) to weep.

shii-shiba しひしば (椎柴)　*n.* type of oak tree, stand of such trees. (*TZ*)

shii-te しひて (強ひて)　*adv.* forcibly. (*TM*)

*SHIKA しか (然)　*adv.* in this way, thus. (*HI*)

shika しか (鹿)　*n.* deer. (*HI*)

SHIKA-MO しかも (然も)　*conj.* besides, moreover. (*HJ*)

shikiri-ni しきりに (頻りに)　*adv.* **1.** incessantly, repeatedly, constantly. **2.** extremely. (*TN*)

SHI-KU しく (及く・若く・如く)　*intr. v. YD* **1.** to catch up to, reach, attain. **2.** to be equal to, a match for. (*HJ, MY*)

shi-ku しく (敷く)　*tr. v. YD* to spread (something) out. (*HJ*)

shimatsu しまつ (始末)　*n.* **1.** situation or event from beginning to end. **2.** thrift, frugality. (*NE*)

*SHIMO しも *adv. p.* **1**. singles out a single item from a group for emphasis: this in particular. **2**. delimits conditions: only then. **3**. (followed by neg.) emphatic negation: (not) at all, absolutely (not).

shimo しも (霜) *n.* **1**. frost. **2**. (metaphor) white hair. (*HI, MS*)

shimo-ya しもや (下屋) (also *shimonoya*) *n.* room off the main living quarters (*moya*), usually used by people of low status such as servants. (*UM*)

SHI-MU しむ (占む) *intr. v. SN* **1**. to occupy, possess. **2**. to make a place one's home. **3**. to equip oneself with. (*HJ*)

*SHI-MU しむ (染む・浸む) *intr. v. YD* **1**. to be felt keenly, pierce one's heart. **2**. to be soaked in, permeated (with a color, scent, etc.). **3**. to become passionate about something. *tr. v. SN* **1**. to soak in a dye, perfume. **2**. to hold deeply in one's heart. (*HJ, SN*)

*SHIMU しむ *aux. v. SN* (follows MZ) indicates **1**. deliberate human action imposed on someone: to cause. **2**. respect toward the subject of main v. (*hon.*).

*SHINA しな (品) *n.* **1**. rank, class, lineage. **2**. character. (*GM*)

shi-nan しなん (指南) *n.* **1**. guidance, instruction. **2**. standard, criterion (for judgment). (*NE*)

shin-gon しんごん (真言) *n.* spell, charm, mantra. (*US*)

shini-i-ru しにいる (死に入る) *intr. v. YD* **1**. to faint, lose consciousness. **2**. to die. (*UM*)

shin-jitsu しんじつ (親眤) *n.* intimacy, intimate person. (*HJ*)

*SHINO-BU しのぶ (忍ぶ) *tr. v. KN, YD* **1**. to bear, endure, tolerate. **2**. to repress (an impulse, emotion), hide one's feelings. *intr. v. KN, YD* **1**. to bear, endure, hold back one's emotions. **2**. to hide, avoid the eyes of others. (*GM, TO*)

*SHINO-BU しのぶ (偲ぶ) *tr. v. YD, KN* [fr. v. *shinofu*] **1**. to think of fondly, long for, be nostalgic about, yearn for. **2**. to admire, praise for beauty. (*GM, HJ, TZ*)

shino-gu しのぐ (凌ぐ) *tr. v. YD* **1**. to press, hold down. **2**. to endure or overcome hardship. **3**. to surpass one's competition. **4**. to hold in disdain, look down on. (*OH*)

shino-ni しのに *adv.* somberly, dejectedly. (*MY*)

shin-tai しんたい (進退) (also *shindai*) *n.* (lit., advancing, retreating) **1**. movement, behavior. **2**. retreat and advance. (*HJ*)

SHI-NU しぬ (死ぬ) *intr. v. NH* to die. (*HJ, TM*)

shinu-bu しぬぶ (偲ぶ) *tr. v. YD* [fr. v. *shinufu*] (same as *shinobu*) to long for. (*MY*)

shio-jiri しほじり (塩尻) *n.* salt mound (seawater is poured on a sand mound and left to dry in the sun to produce salt). (*IM*)

shio-kaze しほかぜ (潮風・塩風) *n.* sea breeze, briny air. (*HJ*)

shiora-shi しをらし *shiku adj.* **1**. graceful, elegant, refined (words, manner). **2**. pretty, lovely. **3**. modest, reserved. **4**. praiseworthy. (*NE*)

SHIO-RU しをる (萎る) *intr. v. SN* **1**. (of vegetation) to wither, wilt. **2**. to feel dejected, miserable. **3**. (of clothing) to be drenched. *tr. v. YD* to cause to wilt, warp. (*HI, TZ*)

SHIO-TARU しほたる (潮垂る) *intr. v. SN* **1**. to fall in drops. **2**. to be soaked. **3**. to drench one's sleeves with tears.

shio-umi しほうみ (潮海) *n.* sea. (*TN*)

shi-ppō しつぽう (七宝) *n.* (Buddhist) seven jewels, variously identified; by one account: gold, silver, lapis lazuli, crystal, *shako* (giant clam), agate, and coral. (*OH*)

shira-bu しらぶ (調ぶ) *tr. v. SN* **1**. to tune. **2**. to play a musical instrument. **3**. to be in harmony with. (*HJ*)

shira-ga しらが (白髪・白毛) *n.* white hair. (*KM*)

shira-gu しらぐ (精ぐ・白ぐ) *tr. v. SN* **1**. to polish whole grain rice into white rice, make white. **2**. to polish and refine. (*NE*)

shira-kashi しらかし (白樫) *n.* white oak. (*TZ*)

shira-me しらめ (白目) (also *shirome*) *n.* white-eyed, with eyes rolled back into the head. (*TM*)

shira-nami しらなみ (白波) *n.* **1.** white waves. **2.** (euphemism) bandits, thieves. (*HJ*)

shire-mono しれもの (痴れ者) *n.* fool, idiot. (*US*)

shiri-i しりゐ (尻居) *n.* falling back on one's behind. (*UM*)

shirizo-ku しりぞく (退く) *intr. v. YD* to draw back, retreat. (*TM*)

shiro-shi しろし (白し) *ku adj.* **1.** white. **2.** un-dyed (fabric). (*GM, HI*)

SHIROSHI-ME-SU しろしめす (知ろしめす) *tr. v. YD* [fr. v. *shirashimesu*] **1.** to know, be aware of (hon.). **2.** to govern, rule (hon.). (*HM*)

shiro-tae-no しろたへの (白妙の) *pillow word* [fr. n. *shirotae*, "white fabric," and case p. *no*] modifying words associated with undyed clothing, like *koromo* (robe), or with whiteness, like *kumo* (clouds) and *nami* (waves). (*HI*)

shi-ru しる (痴る) *intr. v. SN* to be in a daze, lose one's senses. (*TM*)

*SHI-RU しる (知る・領る・治る) *tr. v. YD* (領る・治る) **1.** to govern, rule, occupy. (知る) **2.** to understand, recognize. **3.** to experience. **4.** to take care of, look after. **5.** to have a relationship with, be intimate with. *intr. v. YD* to understand. *intr. v. SN* to be known (by all the world). *tr. v. SN* to make known. (*HJ, IM, TM*)

*SHIRUSHI しるし (験・標・印・証・徴) *n.* (験) **1.** omen, prelude. **2.** efficacy, effectiveness. (標・印) **3.** distinguishing mark. (証) **4.** evidence. (徴) **5.** sign, symptom. (*HJ*)

*SHIRU-SHI しるし (著し) *ku adj.* **1.** clear, self-evident. **2.** expected, anticipated. (*HJ*)

shi-shō ししやう (死生) *n.* life and death. (*HM*)

shi-shō ししやう (師匠) *n.* master, teacher. (*HJ*)

shi-soku しそく (紙燭) *n.* torch. (*TM*)

*SHITA した (下) *n.* **1.** below. **2.** protection, aegis. **3.** interior, inside. **4.** thoughts, emotions. **5.** secret. **6.** low in degree, lacking in talent, such a person. **7.** young.

*SHITAGA-U したがふ (従ふ・随ふ) *intr. v. YD* **1.** to submit to, obey, surrender to. **2.** to follow after. **3.** to respond to. *tr. v. SN* **1.** to make someone obey, submit. **2.** to lead to, take to. (*HJ*)

shitataka したたか *nari adj. v.* **1.** strong, sturdy-looking, well-built. **2.** solemn-looking, serious, dependable. **3.** extreme-looking, pompous, exaggerated. **4.** large, sufficient, plentiful. (*TO*)

*SHITATA-MU したたむ (認む) *tr. v. SN* **1.** to organize, arrange, order. **2.** to prepare. **3.** to carry out. **4.** to eat. **5.** to write, record.

shita-u したふ (慕ふ) *tr. v. YD* **1.** to think fondly of, long for. **2.** to follow the traces of. **3.** to learn from a master, want to be like such a master. (*GM, TZ*)

shitchin-manpō しつちんまんぽう (七珍万宝) *n.* seven precious gems and myriad treasures, treasures, valuables. (*HJ*)

*SHITE して *case p.* (follows nominal, RT) indicates **1.** object of causative action: ordering, causing (some result). **2.** means, method, material: with, by means of, having. **3.** engagement in the same action: together with. *conj. p.* (follows RY) indicates that the previous phrase describes an existing condition: and, thus. *adv. p.* (follows case p. *wo, ni, yori, kara*) emphasizes the meaning of the previous case p.

shi-un しうん (紫雲) *n.* purple or lavender clouds. Amida Buddha was believed to ride on purple clouds to welcome the spirits of the dead to the Pure Land. (*HJ*)

shi-zai しざい (資材) *n.* property, possessions. (*HJ*)

shizu しづ (賤) *n.* people of humble origins or status. (*HJ*)

shizuka しづか (静か) *nari adj. v.* **1.** calm, peaceful. **2.** quiet. (*HJ*)

shō-batsu しやうばつ (賞罰) *n.* reward and punishment. (*HJ*)

shō-chi しようち (勝地) *n.* superior location, place with a superior view. (*HJ*)

shō-en しやうゑん (庄園・荘園) *n.* private estates owned by the nobility and temples. (*HJ*)

shōgai しやうがい (生涯) *n.* (one's) life, lifetime. (*OH*)

shō-gatsu しやうぐわつ (正月) *n.* First Month of the New Year (lunar calendar). (*HM*)

shō-haku しようはく (松柏) *n.* evergreen trees such as pines. (*OH*)

shō-ji しやうじ (障子) (also *sōji* さうじ) *n.* sliding screen used to divide rooms (in Heian aristocratic residences). (*HJ*)

shō-motsu せうもつ (抄物) *n.* copied text, excerpted text, textual commentary. (*HJ*)

shō-nagon せうなごん (少納言) *n.* lesser counselor. (*GM*)

shō-nen しやうねん (生年) *n.* age (counting from year of birth). (*HM*)

***SHŌ-SOKO** せうそこ (消息) *n.* [fr. n. *shōsoku*] **1.** letter, missive. **2.** visit, report, request for mediation or guidance. (*GM*)

shōtoku せうとく (所得) *n.* profit, gain. (*US*)

shō-zoku しやうぞく (装束) (also *sōzoku* さうぞく) *n.* **1.** clothing, dress, attire. **2.** preparations. **3.** decorations. (*TM*)

shō-zu しやうず (請ず) *tr. v. SH* to invite, request the presence of. (*TM*)

shū しふ (執) *n.* attachment (to a person, an object of desire, etc.). (*HJ*)

shu-gyō-ja しゆぎやうじや (修行者) (also *su-gyōza*) *n.* ascetic traveling monk. (*IM*)

shu-jū しゆじゆう (主従) *n.* lord and retainer(s). (*HM*)

shu-kun しゆくん (主君) *n.* lord, superior. (*HJ*)

shū-shin しふしん (執心) *n.* (Buddhist) deep attachment, adherence, fixation. (*HJ*)

***SO** そ *final p.* indicates **1.** mild prohibition: please don't . . . **2.** prohibition: do not . . .

sō そう (僧) *n.* priest. (*SN*)

sobada-tsu そばだつ (峙つ) *intr. v. YD* **1.** to rise up, stand tall, tower over something. **2.** (of hair) to stand up out of fear. *tr. v. SN* **1.** to prop up, set upright. **2.** to prick up (one's ears). (*UM*)

soba-zama そばざま *n.* beside, on the side. (*US*)

sō-bō そうばう (僧坊) *n.* monks' quarters, attached to a temple. (*US*)

sode そで (袖) *n.* sleeve. (*HJ, TM*)

so-gu そぐ (削ぐ) *tr. v. YD* **1.** to cut or trim (the hair). **2.** to abbreviate. (*GM*)

***SOKO** そこ (其所・其処) *pron.* **1.** (place or object) near the speaker, nearby. **2.** topic or place that has already been mentioned: that place, that topic. **3.** unspecified place: somewhere. **4.** you (for familiar addressee or subordinate).

***SOKOHAKATO-NA-SHI** そこはかとなし *ku adj.* without any particular reason or order, random. (*TZ*)

sokona-u そこなふ (害ふ) *tr. v. YD* to injure. (*HJ*)

***SOKO-RA** そこら *adv.* **1.** many. **2.** extremely. (*TM*)

sō-mon さうもん (桑門) *n.* monk, person who has taken Buddhist vows. (*IIJ*)

***SOMO-SOMO** そもそも (抑々) *conj.* used to start a new topic: well, now, as it turns out. (*HJ*)

***SOMU-KU** そむく (背く) *intr. v. YD* **1.** to turn one's back on. **2.** to rebel, resist. **3.** to part from, separate. **4.** to abandon the world, take religious vows. *tr. v. SN* **1.** to cause to turn away. **2.** to leave. (*HJ, TM, TO*)

sonmō-su そんまうす (損亡す) *intr. v. SH* to break down, be destroyed. (*HJ*)

***SO-NO** その (其の) *comp. pron.* [fr. pron. *so* and case p. *no*] **1.** something close to the listener: that. **2.** something already discussed: the aforementioned. **3.** indirect reference to a person or thing. **4.** something or someone whose identity or presence is uncertain. (*HJ, MY*)

***SORA** そら (空) *n.* **1.** sky, heavens. **2.** weather. **3.** uncertain destination, place. **4.** (often followed by neg.) state of mind, feelings. **5.** top (of tree, mountain, etc.). *nari adj. v.* **1.** distracted. **2.** lacking foundation, halfhearted. **3.** empty, vacant, ephemeral. **4.** (in RY form) (recalled) from memory, (learned) by heart. (*GM, SN, TM*)

sora-goto そらごと (空言・虚言) *n.* lie, fabrication. (*TM*)

*SORE それ (其れ・夫れ) *pron.* **1.** person, place, thing at a slight remove from the speaker or already mentioned: that, that person, that place, that thing. **2.** something unclear: such and such, so and so, a certain. **3.** second-person: you. *conj.* introduces a new topic: well. (*HM, MY, TM*)

sore-gashi それがし (某) *pron.* **1.** personal, used when the name of one referred to is not clear or is deliberately left vague: so and so, someone. **2.** first-person singular (masculine): I, myself. (*HM*)

sore-ni それに *conj.* [fr. pron. *sore* and case p. *ni*] **1.** however, in spite of that, even though. **2.** because of that. **3.** on top of that, in addition. (*US*)

*SŌRŌ さうらふ (候ふ) *intr. v. YD* **1.** to wait on a person of high status, be in service (*hum.*). **2.** to be, exist (*polite*). **3.** polite suppl. v. (*HM*)

soso-ku そそく (注く・灌く) (also *sosogu*) *intr. v. YD* **1.** (of water) to flow, run. **2.** (of snow, rain) to fall. **3.** to weep profusely. *tr. v. YD* to let flow, shed (tears). (*UM*)

sō-su さうす (左右す) *tr. v. SH* to make arrangements for doing (something). (*TM*)

*SŌ-SU そうす (奏す) *tr. v. SH* **1.** to speak to an emperor, a retired emperor, etc. (*hum.*). **2.** to perform, play music.

SO-U そふ (添ふ・副ふ) *intr. v. YD* **1.** to be added. **2.** to accompany. **3.** to live as a couple. **4.** to follow a particular shape. *intr. v. SN* to follow (with passage of time). *tr. v. SN* **1.** to add, supplement. **2.** to make someone accompany someone. **3.** to compare, liken one thing to another. (*HJ, TM*)

sō-zen そうぜん (僧膳) *n.* meals prepared for Buddhist monks. (*US*)

*SOZORO そぞろ (漫ろ) *nari adj. v.* **1.** somehow or another, for no discernible reason. **2.** at random, incidentally, by serendipity.

sozoro-gami そぞろがみ (漫ろ神) *n.* god who mysteriously induces people to leave home and wander. (*OH*)

*SŌZŌ-SHI さうざうし *shiku adj.* lacking something that should exist: insufficient, bereft, unsatisfactory.

sō-zu そうづ (僧都) *n.* (Buddhist) bishop. (*GM*)

*SU す *aux. v. SN* (follows MZ of YD, NH, RH) indicates **1.** causative, a deliberate, human action imposed on someone: to cause. **2.** *hon.*

*SU す (為) *intr. v. SH* **1.** to be in a given state, feel a certain way. **2.** (used as a substitute for a wide variety of intr. v.) to occur, take place, happen. *tr. v. SH* **1.** (used as a substitute for a wide variety of tr. v.) to carry out an action, do (something). **2.** to have an effect. **3.** (often following RY of adj. or case p. *to* or *ni*) to treat or view something in a given way.

su す (巣) *n.* nest. (*TM*)

suberi-i-zu すべりいづ (滑り出づ) *intr. v. SN* [fr. v. *suberu* and v. *izu*] to slip out, slip away. (*MS*)

sube-ru すべる (滑る・辷る) *intr. v. YD* **1.** to slide, move smoothly. **2.** to leave quietly, retire, slip away. **3.** to step down from the throne, cede the throne. (*MS*)

sube-te すべて (全て) *adv.* **1.** all, altogether. **2.** generally, on the whole. **3.** (followed by neg.) (not) at all. (*HJ*)

su-bitsu すびつ (炭櫃) *n.* large brazier. (*MS*)

subo-shi すぼし (窄し) *ku adj.* **1.** contracted, narrow, thin. **2.** shabby, poor-looking. (*HJ*)

su-dare すだれ (簾) *n.* hanging blinds. (*GM*)

SUDE-NI すでに (既に・已に) *adv.* already. (*HJ*)

*SUE すゑ (末) *n.* **1.** tip, end. **2.** the future. **3.** youngest child. **4.** descendants. **5.** second (concluding) part of a *waka*. **6.** insignificant. **7.** age of decline. (*GM*)

sue-ba すゑば (末葉) *n.* **1**. leaves on the tip of a branch. **2**. descendants. (*HJ*)

sue-hiro すゑひろ (末広) *n.* **1**. fan shape. **2**. another name for a fan (from the way a handheld fan opens). (*HJ*)

SUGATA すがた (姿) *n.* **1**. physical appearance, figure, shape. **2**. clothing, dress. **3**. aura, atmosphere. **4**. (in poetry) rhythm, tone of words. (*HI*)

sugi すぎ (杉) *n.* Japanese cedar (*Cryptomeria japonica*). (*TZ*)

***SUGO-SHI** すごし (凄し) *ku adj.* **1**. desolate, frightening. **2**. very lonely. **3**. outstanding. (*SN*)

sugo-su すごす (過ごす) (also *sugusu*) *tr. v. YD* **1**. to let time pass, pass the months and days. **2**. to make a living. **3**. to bring to an end. (*TM*)

***SU-GU** すぐ (過ぐ) *intr. v. KN* **1**. to exceed. **2**. to pass. **3**. to live. **4**. to be past prime. **5**. to die. (*HJ, TM*)

sugure-te すぐれて *adv.* especially, terribly. (*HJ*)

***SUGU-SU** すぐす (過ぐす) (also *sogosu*) *tr. v. YD* **1**. to let time pass. **2**. to leave as is. **3**. to bring to an end. **4**. to be elderly, grow old. **5**. to be excessive, abnormal. **6**. *suppl. v.* to do (something) to excess. (*HI, HJ, TM*)

sui-mono すひもの (吸物) *n.* soup. (*NE*)

sui-su すいす (推す) *tr. v. SH* to guess, speculate. (*NE*)

***SUJI** すぢ (筋) *n.* **1**. long, narrow object, counter for such objects. **2**. bloodline, lineage. **3**. inborn personality, character. **4**. logic behind an argument, reasoning. **5**. direction. **6**. artistic style or technique. (*HM, TM*)

SUKI すき (好き・数奇・数寄) *n.* [fr. v. *suku*] **1**. deep interest in the opposite sex, amorousness. **2**. one who is devoted to amorous or erotic pursuits. **3**. artistic pursuit (poetry, music, tea ceremony, etc.). **4**. one who is devoted to such pursuits.

suki-mono すきもの (好き者) *n.* **1**. person of taste, devotee. **2**. person of amorous disposition. (*GM*)

***SUKIZUKI-SHI** すきずきし (好き好きし) *shiku adj.* **1**. flirtatious, amorous. **2**. elegant, obsessed with taste and elegance.

sukoshi すこし (少し) *adv.* a little, slightly. (*GM, TM*)

SU-KU すく (好く) *intr. v. YD* **1**. to apply oneself to the pursuit of elegance and refinement, have such tastes. **2**. to be amorous, passionate. *tr. v. YD* to enjoy, have a taste for, like. (*TZ*)

suku-to すくと *adv.* jumping up suddenly, rising with force. (*TM*)

suku-u すくふ (救ふ) *tr. v. YD* to save. (*TM*)

suku-u すくふ (掬ふ) *tr. v. YD* to scoop up. (*TM*)

sumai すまひ (住居) *n.* house, dwelling. (*HJ*)

SUMA-SU すます (澄ます・清ます) *tr. v. YD* **1**. to purify (water, sound), quiet. **2**. to wash, clean. **3**. to pacify. **4**. to listen carefully.

sumi すみ (炭) *n.* charcoal. (*MS*)

sumi-ka すみか (住み処・栖) *n.* dwelling. (*HJ*)

SU MU すむ (住む) *intr. v. YD* **1**. to live, dwell. **2**. to go live with one's wife. (*HI, IM*)

SU-MU すむ (澄む) *intr. v. YD* **1**. to become clear, unclouded, unsoiled, pure. **2**. to sound or echo clearly. **3**. to attain a clear, unsoiled, detached heart. **4**. (of handwriting, character) to be calm, composed, settled. (*OH*)

sun すん (寸) *n.* **1**. unit of length: one-tenth of a *shaku*, or approx. 3 centimeters (1.193 inches). **2**. small amount. (*TM, US*)

su-nao すなほ (素直) *adj. v.* **1**. simple, unaffected. **2**. honest, straightforward. **3**. moderate, mild. (*HJ*)

***SUNAWACHI** すなはち (即ち・乃ち・則ち) *adv.* **1**. right away, immediately. **2**. then, at that time. *conj.* **1**. that is, in other words. **2**. therefore. (*HJ, TM*)

su-no-ko すのこ (簀子) *n.* **1**. porch or veranda. **2**. mat of rough-woven reeds or bamboo. (*HJ*)

*SURA すら   *adv. p.* indicates **1.** analogy, takes a special or a lesser example to point out the difficulty or gravity of a more common or extreme matter: if true for X, then all the more for Y; even X, not to mention Y. **2.** minimal desiderata: at least.

suri-bachi すりばち（摺鉢） *n.* mortar, used with a pestle for grinding sesame seeds, etc. (*NE*)

suri-na-su すりなす（擦りなす）   *tr. v. YD* to rub deliberately. (*GM*)

suru する（摺る・摩る）   *tr. v. YD* **1.** to grind in a mortar, mash. **2.** to rub together. **3.** to use up, use completely. **4.** to pick someone's pocket. (*KM, NE*)

*SUSAMA-JI すさまじ（凄じ）(also *susamashi*) *shiku adj.* **1.** depressing, dreary. **2.** desolate, bleak. **3.** cold, chilly, damp. **4.** extreme. **5.** (Edo) absurd, outrageous. (*MS, UM*)

*SUSAMU すさむ（荒む・進む・遊む） *intr. v. YD* (same as *susabu*) **1.** to become intense, fierce. **2.** to do as one pleases. *tr. v. SN* **1.** to be attracted to and love. **2.** to abandon, dislike and avoid.

suso-wa すそわ（裾廻）   *n.* area at the foot of a mountain. (*HJ*)

susu-ru すする   *tr. v. YD* to slurp, sip, suck up. (*US*)

SU-TSU すつ（捨つ・棄つ）   *tr. v. SN* **1.** to discard, abandon. **2.** to neglect, disregard. **3.** to take religious vows, forsake the world. **4.** to do casually. **5.** (following RY and conj. p. *te*) to end up doing (something). (*GM, HJ, SN*)

su-u すふ（吸ふ）   *tr. v. YD* to suck, suckle. (*HJ*)

*SU-U すう（据う）   *tr. v. SN* **1.** to place, leave as offering. **2.** to plant, sow seeds. **3.** to keep (animals, birds, etc.). **4.** to seat a person. **5.** to appoint to a position. **6.** to set up, build. **7.** to place a stamp (signature) on. **8.** to burn moxa. (*GM, HJ, OH, TM*)

suzoro   *See* **suzuro**.

suzume すずめ（雀）   *n.* sparrow. (*HJ*)

suzuri すずり（硯）   *n.* **1.** inkstone. **2.** case for inkstone and brush. (*TZ*)

*SUZURO すずろ（漫ろ）(also *suzoro*)   *nari adj. v.* **1.** appearance of things or thoughts occurring without reason or aim: somehow or another. **2.** unrelated, random. **3.** unexpected. (*GM, IM*)

ta た（誰）   *pron.* used to refer to an indefinite or unknown person: who. (*HJ, TM*)

TA-BAKA-RU たばかる（謀る）   *tr. v. YD* **1.** to plan, devise a way, strategize. **2.** to consult. **3.** to deceive, dupe. (*TM*)

tabi たび（度）   *n.* **1.** each time. **2.** frequency. (*HI, HJ*)

tabi たび（旅）   *n.* trip, journey. (*HI*)

tabi-tabi たびたび（度々）   *nari adj. v.* frequent, repeated. (*HJ*)

*TA-BU たぶ（賜ぶ・給ぶ）   *tr. v. YD* **1.** to give, bestow (*hon.*). **2.** *hon. suppl. v.* (*TM*)

tachi たち（太刀）   *n.* **1.** (Nara) sword. **2.** large sword. (*HM*)

tachi たち（館）   *n.* **1.** residence of an official. **2.** home of an aristocrat. **3.** well-fortified mansion, small castle. (*TN*)

tachi-aga-ru たちあがる（立ち上がる）   *intr. v. YD* to stand up. (*HM*)

tachi-do たちど（立ち所・立ち処）   *n.* footing, foothold. (*HJ*)

tachi-i たちゐ（起居）   *n.* **1.** standing and sitting, everyday activities. **2.** floating (clouds, etc.). (*HJ*)

tachi-i-zu たちいづ（立ち出づ）   *intr. v. SN* **1.** to stand and leave, depart. **2.** to go out to. **3.** to emerge. (*GM*)

tachi-machi-ni たちまちに（忽ちに）   *adv.* **1.** suddenly. **2.** actually. **3.** immediately, instantly. (*HJ*)

tachi-nao-ru たちなほる（立ち直る）   *intr. v. YD* to recover. (*HJ*)

tachi-nara-bu たちならぶ（立ちならぶ）   *intr. v. YD* **1.** to line up together, stand in a row. **2.** to be the same size, height, etc. *tr. v. SN* to treat equally. (*TM*)

tachi-nobo-ru たちのぼる (立ち上る) *intr. v.* YD to rise, ascend. (*TM*)

tachi-sa-ru たちさる (立ち去る) *intr. v.* YD to leave, get up and go. (*TZ*)

tachi-sawa-gu たちさわぐ (立ち騒ぐ) *intr. v.* YD **1.** to make a commotion. **2.** (of waves, wind) to make a loud sound. (*SN*)

tachi-tsura-nu たちつらぬ (立ち連ぬ) *intr. v.* SN to stand in a line. (*TM*)

tachi-waka-ru たちわかる (立ち別る) *intr. v.* SN to part ways, separate. (*HI, TM*)

tachi-yo-ru たちよる (立ち寄る) *intr. v.* YD **1.** to approach, draw near. **2.** to visit. **3.** (of waves) to come in. (*TM, TZ*)

*****TADA** ただ (直・徒) *adv.* **1.** directly. **2.** closely. **3.** recently, immediately. **4.** just like, similarly. *nari adj. v.* **1.** normal, usual. **2.** empty-handed, without doing or achieving anything. (*GM, HM*)

*****TADA** ただ (唯・只) *adv.* **1.** only, merely, just. **2.** truly. **3.** simply. (*HJ*)

*****TADA-BITO** ただびと (徒人・直人) *n.* **1.** ordinary person. **2.** human being (as opposed to *kami* or buddha). **3.** subject (as opposed to ruler). **4.** ordinary nobility (as opposed to *sesshō, kanpaku,* etc.), person of lower office. (*GM, TM*)

tada-goto ただごと (ただ事) *n.* normal, everyday matter. (*HJ*)

tada-koto ただこと (直言・徒言) *n.* plain, unadorned or nonrhetorical language. (*HJ*)

tadashi ただし (但し) *conj.* however. (*TM*)

tadayo-u ただよふ (漂ふ) *intr. v.* YD **1.** to float and sway. **2.** to wander aimlessly, uncertainly. **3.** to stagger, wobble. (*HJ*)

tae-i-ru たえいる (絶え入る) *intr. v.* YD **1.** to faint. **2.** to die. (*TM*)

TAE-TE たえて (絶えて) *adv.* **1.** (followed by neg.) (not) at all, (not) a bit. **2.** completely, totally. **3.** especially, extremely. (*HJ, TM, UM*)

tae-zu たえず (絶えず) *adv.* constantly, ceaselessly. (*TN*)

ta-ga たが (誰が) *set phrase* [fr. pron. *ta,* "who," and case p. *ga*] **1.** whose? **2.** who? (*TM*)

tagai-me たがひめ (違ひ目) *n.* disappointment, setback. (*HJ*)

*****TAGA-U** たがふ (違ふ) *intr. v.* YD **1.** to differ, disagree. **2.** to resist, oppose. **3.** to change, alter. *tr. v.* SN **1.** to oppose. **2.** to make a mistake. **3.** to change course because of a directional taboo. (*TZ, TM*)

TAGUI たぐひ (類・比) *n.* **1.** things of a similar kind, sort, type. **2.** colleague, companion, company. **3.** people in the same circumstances. (*HJ, TM, TO, TZ*)

*****TAGU-U** たぐふ (比ふ・類ふ) *intr. v.* YD **1.** to be together, come together, nestle together, act together. **2.** to resemble, match. *tr. v.* SN **1.** to bring together, place side by side, make accompany. **2.** to imitate, mimic. (*HJ*)

ta-i たゐ (田居) *n.* rice paddy, place with rice paddy. (*HJ*)

TAIDAI-SHI たいだいし (怠怠し) *shiku adj.* inconvenient, disadvantageous, unfavorable, troubling. (*TM*)

tai-hai たいはい (頹廢) *n.* deterioration, decline. (*OH*)

tai-men-su たいめんす (対面す) *intr. v.* SH to meet face to face. (*TM*)

taira-ka たひらか (平らか) *nari adj. v.* **1.** calm, safe, peaceful. **2.** flat, level. (*TN*)

taka たか (鷹) *n.* falcon, hawk. (*HJ*)

taka-ne たかね (高嶺) *n.* tall, lofty peak. (*HI*)

takara たから (宝) *n.* **1.** treasure. **2.** fortune, estate, material possessions. (*MY*)

taka-ru たかる *intr. v.* YD, SN to gather together. (*TN*)

*****TAKA-SHI** たかし (高し) *ku adj.* **1.** high, tall, lofty. **2.** high in the sky. **3.** high-ranking. **4.** superior, outstanding, self-respecting. **5.** loud. **6.** popular, well known. **7.** aged, old. (*HJ*)

take たけ (竹) *n.* bamboo. (*TM*)

take たけ (丈・長) *n.* **1.** height. **2.** length. **3.** depth, extent. **4.** military strength. (*KM, TM*)

TAKE-SHI たけし (猛し) *ku adj.* **1.** fierce, powerful. **2.** bold, brave. **3.** outstanding, superior, considerable. **4.** with all one's might, as much as possible. (*TM*)

taki-gi たきぎ (薪) *n.* firewood. (*HJ*)

takuwa-u たくはふ (蓄はふ・貯はふ) *tr. v. SN* to store, accumulate. (*TO*)

*TAMA たま (玉) *n.* **1.** jewel, beautiful stone. **2.** shell, particularly pearl. **3.** beautiful or valuable thing (as attributive modifier). **4.** (metaphor) dew. **5.** (metaphor) tears. *n. prefix* beautiful. (*TM*)

tama-saka たまさか (偶) *nari adj. v.* **1.** unexpected. **2.** by chance, happenstance. (*GM*)

tamashii たましひ (魂) *n.* spirit, soul. (*TM*)

tama-shiki たましき (玉敷き) *n.* (lit., strewn with jewels) beautiful object, beautiful place. (*HJ*)

tama-tama たまたま (偶・適) *adv.* occasionally, once in a while, rarely. (*HJ*)

*TAMA-U (TAMŌ) たまふ (給ふ・賜ふ) *tr. v. YD* **1.** to grant, bestow (fr. superior to inferior) (*hon.*). **2.** *hon. suppl. v.; tr. v. SN* **1.** to receive, drink, eat (*hum.*). **2.** *hum. suppl. v.* (*HM, TM*)

*TAMAWA-RU たまはる (賜る・給る) *tr. v. YD* **1.** to receive (*hum.*). **2.** to give, grant (*hon.*). **3.** *hum. suppl. v.* **4.** *hon. suppl. v.*

tama-yura たまゆら (玉響) *adv.* for even a moment. (*HJ*)

TAME ため (為) *n.* **1.** for the sake of. **2.** reason, cause, result. **3.** positive outcome, favorable result (on behalf of someone). **4.** as far as one is concerned. (*HI, HJ*)

TAMESHI ためし (例・試し) *n.* **1.** example, precedent. **2.** topic, subject. **3.** model. (*HJ*)

tami たみ (民) *n.* people, subjects. (*HJ*)

tamo-tsu たもつ (保つ) *tr. v. YD* to preserve, maintain, support. *intr. v. YD* to last, endure. (*HJ*)

ta-mu たむ (溜む) *tr. v. SN* to accumulate or collect in one place. (*HJ*)

tana-bi-ku たなびく (棚引く) *intr. v. YD* (of clouds, haze, mist) to trail. (*MS*)

TANOMO-SHI たのもし (頼もし) *shiku adj.* **1.** reliable, dependable, trustworthy. **2.** encouraging, reassuring, heartening. **3.** promising, eagerly anticipated. **4.** prosperous, affluent. (*TZ*)

*TANO-MU たのむ (頼む) *tr. v. YD* **1.** to depend on. **2.** to trust. *tr. v. SN* to make dependable.

taore-fusu たふれふす (倒れ伏す・倒れ臥す) *intr. v. YD* to fall and lie prone. (*HJ*)

tao-ru たふる (倒る) *intr. v. SN* **1.** to fall over, collapse. **2.** to submit, give in. (*HJ*)

tare たれ (誰) *pron.* who, whom. (*HI, HM*)

tare-ko-mu たれこむ (垂れ籠む) *intr. v. SN* to draw the blinds (shut the doors, etc.) and stay inside. (*TZ*)

*TARI たり *aux. v.* (follows RY) indicates **1.** resultative, that a certain action has already taken place and the result of that action continues: has been. **2.** continuative, durative: is in the course of (doing . . .). **3.** perfective: to end up (in a certain state, condition). **4.** parallel action: (doing) this and that. **5.** future realization.

*TARI たり *aux. v.* (follows nominals) declaration, copula: to be, have the qualities of.

*TASHI たし *aux. v.* (follows RY) **1.** first-person desiderative: I want. **2.** third-person desiderative: he or she wants. **3.** situational wish with regard to someone or something else: if only X were.

tasu-ku たすく (助く) *tr. v. SN* to help. (*HJ*)

tataka-u たたかふ (戦ふ) *intr., tr. v. YD* to fight. (*TM*)

*TATEMATSU-RU たてまつる (奉る) *tr. v. YD* **1.** to give, offer (*hum.*). **2.** to send a person (*hum.*). **3.** to eat, drink (*hon.*). **4.** to wear (*hon.*). *intr. v. YD* **1.** to ride, board (*hon.*). **2.** *hum. suppl. v.; tr. v. SN* **1.** to give (*hum.*). **2.** to send (a person) (*hum.*). **3.** *hum. suppl. v.* (*GM, HJ, HM, US*)

tate-sama たてさま (縦さま) *n., nari adj. v.* vertical direction, vertical. (*HM*)

tatoe たとへ (譬へ・喩へ) *n.* [fr. v. *tatou*] example, illustration, comparison, metaphor. (*HJ*)

tato-u たとふ (譬ふ・喩ふ) *tr. v. SN* to compare, liken to. (*IM*)

*TA-TSU たつ (立つ・起つ・建つ・発つ) *intr. v. YD* **1.** to stand. **2.** to get up and stand. **3.** (of plants) to grow, be growing. **4.** (of a horse, carriage, etc.) to stop, park. **5.** to reach a position or rank. **6.** to occupy a position. **7.** (of wind, waves, mist, etc.) to occur. **8.** (of a rainbow, the moon) to appear. **9.** to resound. **10.** to spread (rumor), be widely known. **11.** to get angry, get in a fight. **12.** (of a season, new year) to begin. **13.** (of time) to pass. **14.** to withdraw, leave. **15.** to depart on a journey. **16.** (of birds, etc.) to fly. **17.** to be useful. **18.** (of a sword) to be sharp, cut well. **19.** *suppl. v.* to do (something) to an extreme degree. *tr. v. YD* **1.** to erect, set up. **2.** to make known. *tr. v. SN* **1.** to make stand. **2.** to make someone sitting stand up. **3.** to place (in a vehicle), leave (something). **4.** to place in an official position or office. **5.** to stab, pierce (with a sword, knife). **6.** to close a door or gate. **7.** to erect a building. **8.** to cause waves, wind, etc. **9.** to make ring out. **10.** to make well known. **11.** to make (a pledge, request). **12.** to boil (water for tea). **13.** to anger (someone). **14.** to make (someone) pass the time. **15.** to cause to depart, send off on a trip. **16.** to make (a bird) fly. **17.** to support, protect (a reputation, life). **18.** to make an organ of the senses move (e.g., to open the eyes). **19.** to make one's thoughts come true. **20.** *suppl. v.* to do intensely. (*GM, HJ, MS*)

tatsu-mi たつみ (辰巳・巽) *n.* southeast (direction between dragon and snake in the Chinese zodiac). (*HI, HJ*)

ta-u たふ (堪ふ・耐ふ) *intr. v. SN* **1.** to endure, bear. **2.** to hold out, last. **3.** to be capable, talented. (*HJ, TM, TN*)

tawayasu-shi たはやすし *ku adj.* easy, simple. (*TM*)

tayasu-shi たやすし (容易し) *ku adj.* **1.** easy. **2.** careless, thoughtless. (*HJ*)

*TAYORI たより (便り) *n.* [fr. v. *tayoru*, "to depend"] **1.** reliable person, reliable support. **2.** source of livelihood. **3.** connection, relationship. **4.** letter, message, rumor. **5.** convenience, expedience. **6.** good opportunity. **7.** combination, composition. (*HJ, TN*)

TA-YU たゆ (絶ゆ) *intr. v. SN* **1.** to be exhausted, run out. **2.** to stop breathing, die. **3.** to break off a relationship. **4.** to be remote. (*HJ, TM, TN*)

TAYU-MU たゆむ (弛む) *intr. YD* to be lax, careless, negligent, inattentive. *tr. v. SN* to cause to be lax, off guard.

tayu-shi たゆし (弛し・懈し) *ku adj.* **1.** tired and lacking energy, slow, lethargic. **2.** dull, tiresome. (*HJ*)

TA-ZUKI たづき (方便) *n.* **1.** means, methods. **2.** appearance, condition. (*HJ*)

tazu-nu たづぬ (尋ぬ) *tr. v. SN* **1.** to inquire about the whereabouts. **2.** to investigate. **3.** to ask questions. **4.** to visit. (*HJ*)

*TE て *conj. p.* (follows RY) indicates **1.** temporal or sequential connection: and then. **2.** parallel connection: at the same time. **3.** causal link: therefore. **4.** existing condition: being. **5.** con- cessive: but, though, despite.

*TE て (手) *n.* **1.** hand. **2.** finger. **3.** handle, hilt, shaft. **4.** subordinate, one's men. **5.** letters, handwriting. **6.** artistic form, gesture, performance. **7.** skill, proficiency. **8.** means, method. **9.** tone, pitch. **10.** trouble, bother, effort. **11.** direction. **12.** wound. (*HM, MS*)

te-arai てあらひ (手洗ひ) *n.* washing of the hands. (*SN*)

te-buri てぶり (手振り) *n.* manners, custom, habit. (*HJ*)

temadoi てまどひ (手迷ひ) *n.* state of confusion, panic, fear. (*KM*)

ten-ga てんが (天下) (also *tenka*) *n.* **1.** world, earth. **2.** entire country. **3.** rule over the entire land. **4.** society, people of the world. (*TM*)

ten-geri てんげり *comp. aux. v.* [fr. RY of aux. v. *tsu* and aux. v. *keri*] (common in medieval military tales, *setsuwa*) ended up doing (something). (*HM*)

*TENJŌBITO てんじやうびと (殿上人) *n.* nobility of the fourth, fifth, and sixth ranks, who are allowed into the imperial palace.

ten-nin てんにん (天人)   *n.* heavenly beings (creatures). (*TM*)

ten-zu てんず (転ず)   *intr. v. SH* **1**. to turn, rotate. **2**. to go in a different direction, change. **3**. to fall over, tumble. (*TO*)

TE-SHIGA てしが   *final p.* expresses a desire to (do something).

TE-SHIGA-NA てしがな   *final p.* expresses a desire to (do something).

***TO** と   *conj. p.* (follows SS, RY of adj.) indicates **1**. hypothetical concessive: for example, even if. **2**. emphatic function, treating a given fact as a hypothetical situation in order to stress a certain point: though it may be the case that.

***TO** と   *case p.* indicates **1**. action taken with another: together with. **2**. parallel items: and. **3**. citational indicating the object of the following verb such as *omou, iu, kiku, miru*. **4**. (followed by v. *naru*) result of change: to become. **5**. metaphor or simile: like. **6**. standard of a comparison: compared with. **7**. object of an action: with the aim of, thinking to.

TO と   *adv.* that way, like that. (*TM*)

to と (外)   *n.* outside. (*TM*)

to-bashi-ru とばしる   *intr. v. YD* to splatter, splash. (*US*)

tobi-chiga-u とびちがふ (飛び違ふ)   *intr. v. YD* to crisscross in flight. (*MS*)

tobi-iso-gu とびいそぐ (飛び急ぐ)   *intr. v. YD* to fly hurriedly. (*MS*)

tobi-o-ru とびおる (飛び降る)   *intr. v. KN* to jump down. (*HM*)

to-bu とぶ (飛ぶ)   *intr. v. YD* **1**. to fly, float in the air. **2**. to run, jump. (*HJ*)

***TŌBU (TAUBU)** たうぶ (賜ぶ・給ぶ)   *tr. v. YD* **1**. to give, bestow (hon.). **2**. hon. suppl. v.

toburai とぶらひ (訪ひ)   *n.* visit, call (to show sympathy for or look after an ill person). (*GM, TM*)

***TOBURA-U** とぶらふ (訪ふ・弔ふ)   *tr. v. YD* (訪ふ) **1**. to visit. **2**. to investigate, inquire into.

3. to pay a visit to an ill person. **4**. to look after, care for. (弔ふ) **5**. to pay condolences. (*HJ, US*)

TODOMA-RU とどまる (留まる・止まる・停まる)   *intr. v. YD* **1**. to stay in one place. **2**. to be canceled, called off. **3**. to stay, spend the night. **4**. to remain behind. (*HJ*)

***TODO-MU** とどむ (留む・止む・停む)   *tr. v. SN* **1**. to stop, keep back, restrain. **2**. to suspend, discontinue. **3**. to attract (interest or concern). **4**. to leave behind. **5**. to finish off, kill. (*HJ*)

toga とが (咎・科)   *n.* **1**. fault, mistake. **2**. sin, offense. (*HJ*)

***TOGA-MU** とがむ (咎む)   *tr. v. SN* [fr. n. *toga,* "fault"] **1**. to criticize, find fault with. **2**. to be suspicious and pay attention to.

tō-jin とうじん (等身) (also *tōshin*)   *n.* equivalent to human height. (*SN*)

***TO-KAKU** とかく   *adv.* **1**. this and that, here and there, variously. **2**. in any event, in any case, regardless. **3**. apt to, prone to. (*HJ, TN*)

***TOKI** とき (時)   *n.* **1**. time, passage of time (months, days). **2**. one of the twelve units of daily time. **3**. age, reign. **4**. season. **5**. flourishing time. **6**. good chance, opportunity. **7**. that time. **8**. occasion. (*HJ, IM*)

toki-ji ときじ (時じ)   *shiku adj.* (Nara) unceasing, timeless. (*MY*)

toki-to-shite ときとして (時として)   *adv.* [fr. n. *toki,* copular *tari,* and conj. p. *shite*] **1**. (usually followed by neg.) (not) even for a moment. **2**. on occasion, depending on the situation and time. (*HJ*)

***TOKORO** ところ (所・処)   *n.* **1**. place, region, area. **2**. home, estate. **3**. point, item. **4**. location. **5**. situation, time. **6**. office, post. (*HJ, MS*)

tokoro-dokoro ところどころ (所々・処々)   *n.* **1**. here and there. **2**. people (multiple nobles). (*HM*)

to-ku とく (疾く)   *adv.* [fr. adj. *toshi,* "swift"] **1**. swiftly, quickly. **2**. already. (*SN, TN*)

toku とく (徳)   *n.* **1**. morality, moral sense. **2**. natural talent, strength. **3**. good reputation, personal virtue. **4**. blessing, favor, benefit. **5**. owing to, by the grace of, thanks to. **6.** wealth, possession, property. (*US*)

toku-toku とくとく（疾く疾く） *adv.* [fr. adj. *toshi*, "quick"] quickly, right away. (*HM*)

toma とま（苫） *n.* thatch (made from sedge or straw) used for roofing. (*HI*)

tomare-kakumare とまれかくまれ *set phrase* in any case, regardless. (*TN*)

tomare-kōmare とまれかうまれ *set phrase* [fr. *tomare-kakumare*] in any case, regardless. (*TN*)

*TOMA-RU とまる（止まる・留まる・泊まる） *intr. v. YD* **1.** to come to a stop. **2.** to be halted, discontinued. **3.** to be stationary. **4.** to stay, remain behind. **5.** to leave an impression (in the heart, memory). （泊まる）**6.** to anchor, moor (a boat). **7.** to lodge. (*TM*)

*TOMO とも *conj. p.* (follows SS, RY of adj.) indicates **1.** hypothetical concessive: even supposing, even if. **2.** emphatic, treats a given fact as a hypothetical situation in order to stress a certain point: though it may be the case that.

tomo とも（供） *n.* **1.** attendance upon a master. **2.** attendant. (*MS*)

tomo とも（友） *n.* **1.** friend. **2.** travel companion. (*TZ*)

*TOMO-SHI ともし（乏し・羨し） *shiku adj.* [fr. v. *tomu*, "to seek out"] （乏）**1.** insufficient, scarce. **2.** poor, impoverished. （羨し）**3.** fascinating, interesting. **4.** envious. (*HJ*)

tomoshi-bi ともしび（灯し火） *n.* lamp, lantern. (*NE, UM*)

tomo-su ともす（点す・灯す） *tr. v. YD* to light (a lamp, lantern), burn, set on fire. (*KM, SN, TM, TZ*)

to-mu とむ（富む） *intr. v. YD* to be wealthy, affluent. (*HJ*)

to-mu とむ（尋む・求む） *tr. v. SN* to follow traces, to seek out.

*TONO との（殿） *n.* **1.** residence of a person of high rank. **2.** person of high rank, especially

of *sesshō* or *kanpaku* (*hon.*). **3.** lord, master, ruler. **4.** husband (as referred to by wife). (*GM, HJ, MS, TM*)

tono-bara とのばら（殿原） *n.* (followed by plural suffix *bara*) used to address a group of high-ranking men: my lords, gentlemen (*hon.*). (*HM*)

ton-yoku とんよく（貪欲）(also *don'yoku*) *n.* (Buddhist) one of the three evil attachments: seeking to satisfy one's desire, greed, or avarice. (*HJ*)

tora-u とらふ（捕らふ・捉ふ） *tr. v. SN* to catch, seize, grab. (*TM*)

TORI-AE-ZU とりあへず（取り敢へず） *adv.* for now, soon, right away. (*HI*)

tori-a-u とりあふ（取り敢ふ） *tr. v. SN* **1.** to prepare. **2.** to make due. **3.** to bear, endure. (*HI*)

tori-i-ru とりいる（取り入る） *tr. v. SN* **1.** to receive (a letter, present, etc.). **2.** to place inside, store. **3.** (of a vengeful spirit) to possess and torment a person. (*SN*)

tori-iru とりゐる（取り率る） *tr. v. KI* to take away or escort forcefully. (*TM*)

tori-i-zu とりいづ（取り出づ） *tr. v. SN* to take out, select. (*HJ*)

tori-ko-mu とりこむ（取り籠む） *tr. v. SN* to surround, enclose. (*HM*)

tori-tatsu とりたつ（取り立つ） *tr. v. SN* **1.** to take up, use, handle. **2.** to select for special attention, look after especially. **3.** to prepare. **4.** to build. **5.** to appoint to a high position. (*TM*)

tori-tsu-ku とりつく（取り付く） *intr. v. YD* **1.** to grab hold of, cling to. **2.** (of a spirit or *mono-no-ke*) to possess. **3.** to begin work. *tr. v. SN* **1.** to make adhere. **2.** to cause (a spirit) to possess (a person). (*HM*)

tori-tsukuro-u とりつくろふ（取り繕ふ） *tr. v. YD* **1.** to repair, mend, fix. **2.** to dress up, treat in a dignified manner. (*HJ*)

TO-RU とる（取る・採る・執る・捕る） *tr. v. YD* **1.** to hold, grab, pick up, take. **2.** to catch, capture. **3**. to take something in hand, handle, operate. **4**. to harvest, gather, collect. **5**. to make one's own, rule, possess. **6**. to take from, steal, confiscate. **7**. to select. **8**. to speculate. **9**. to take in connection with something else. (*HM, TM*)

to-shi とし (疾し) *ku adj.* **1**. early. **2**. fast, quick. (*HJ, SN, TM*)

to-shi とし (敏し) *ku adj.* **1**. mentally agile, smart. **2**. sensitive, alert.

tō-shi とほし (遠し) *ku adj.* **1**. far (distance, time). **2**. estranged, unfamiliar. **3**. uninteresting, uninspiring. **4**. unconnected, irrelevant. (*TN, TZ*)

*TOSHI-GORO としごろ (年来・年頃) *n.* (for) many years. (*HM, SN*)

tōshin とうしん (灯心) *n.* wick (of a lamp). (*NE*)

TO-TE とて *comp.* [fr. citational case p. *to* and conj. p. *te*] thinking that, saying that. (*TM*)

tō-tō とうとう (疾う疾う) *adv.* [fr. adv. *tokutoku*] quickly, right away. (*HM*)

tōto-mu たふとむ (尊む・貴む) *tr. v. YD* (same as v. *tōtobu*) to respect, esteem. *tr. v. KN* to respect, esteem. (*HJ*)

*TOTONO-U ととのふ (整ふ・調ふ・斉ふ) *intr. v. YD* **1**. to be fully prepared, well supplied, without deficiencies. **2**. to be balanced, in harmony. **3**. to be in tune. *tr. v. SN* **1**. to put in order, regulate. **2**. to prepare, supply. **3**. to tune a musical instrument. **4**. to arrange a marriage. (*HJ*)

tōto-shi たふとし (貴とし) *ku adj.* **1**. noble, worthy of respect. **2**. excellent, of great quality. **3**. valuable, magnificent. (*US*)

totte-kae-su とつてかへす (とつて返す) *intr. v. YD* to turn back immediately upon arriving at a destination. (*HM, OH*)

*TO-U とふ (問ふ・訪ふ) *tr. v. YD* **1**. to inquire, ask. **2**. to show concern. **3**. to investigate. **4**. to visit, pay a sick visit. **5**. to pray for the soul of the dead. (*IM, MS, TM*)

TOYOMU とよむ (響む・動む) (also *doyomu*) *intr. v. YD* **1**. to reverberate, resound. **2**. to make a commotion. *tr. v. SN* to cause to ring out. (*HJ*)

tō-zoku たうぞく (盗賊) *n.* robber, thief. (*HJ*)

*TSU つ *case p.* attributive or modifying case p., indicating that what follows belongs to or is part of what comes above.

*TSU つ *aux. v. SN* (follows RY) indicates **1**. perfective, the completion or realization of an action: to end up. **2**. sense of certainty that a particular action will be realized or completed: certainly, definitely. **3**. (in pattern *tsu . . . tsu*) parallel action, indecision, and shifting between two or more actions: doing this and that.

tsubakura-me つばくらめ (燕) *n.* (kind of bird) swallow. (*TM*)

tsubo つぼ (壺) *n.* jar. (*TM*)

*TSUBONE つぼね (局) *n.* **1**. room (in the residence of a noble or in the imperial palace). **2**. female attendant at court housed in such a room (*hon.*).

tsubu-ta-tsu つぶたつ (粒立つ) *intr. v. YD* to be lumpy, granular. (*US*)

tsubutsubu-to つぶつぶと *adv.* [fr. n. *tsubu*, "grain"] **1**. (of round breasts, etc.) plump, full, ripe, attractive. **2**. in detail, carefully. **3**. (of water, blood, tears) dribbling, dripping, trickling down. **4**. excitedly. **5**. writing with each letter separated from the next.

tsubuya-ku つぶやく (呟く) *intr. v. YD* to mutter, murmur, grumble. (*UM*)

tsuchi-i つちゐ (土居) *n.* **1**. base for pillars of a house. **2**. base for bed and portable curtain (*kichō*) in Heian aristocratic residences. (*HJ*)

tsudo-u つどふ (集ふ) *tr. v. SN* to gather, assemble, collect. *intr. v. YD* to accumulate, gather. (*TM*)

tsugi-me つぎめ (継ぎ目) *n.* joint. (*HJ*)

TSU-GOMORI つごもり (晦日) *n.* **1**. last day of the month (lunar calendar). **2**. around the end of the month. (*HJ, IM*)

tsu-gu つぐ (告ぐ) *tr. v. SN* to report, inform. (*HI, TM*)

tsugu つぐ (継ぐ・続ぐ) *intr. v. YD* to continue. *tr. v. YD* **1.** to cause to continue, maintain, keep something up. **2.** to link, join. (*HJ*)

TSUIDE ついで (序) *n.* **1.** order (of things). **2.** occasion, opportunity.

tsuie つひえ (費え・弊え・潰え) *n.* **1.** (費え) cost, expense, waste, loss. **2.** (弊え) deterioration, fatigue, wear and tear, attrition. (*HJ*)

tsui-iru ついゐる (突い居る) *intr. v. KI* **1.** to kneel. **2.** to sit down, squat. (*GM*)

tsui-hiji ついひぢ (築地) *n.* (same as *tsuiji*) earthen wall, earthen wall with tile roof. (*HJ*)

TSUI-NI つひに (終に・遂に) *adv.* **1.** finally, in the end. **2.** (followed by neg.) (not) even once. (*HJ, HM*)

tsuiya-su つひやす (費やす・弊やす) *tr. v. YD* **1.** (費やす) to spend, use up, squander. **2.** (弊やす) to wear down, tire out. (*HJ*)

tsuji-kaze つじかぜ (辻風) *n.* whirlwind. (*HJ*)

tsukai つかひ (使ひ・遣ひ) *n.* messenger. (*TM*)

*TSUKAMATSU-RU つかまつる (仕る) *intr. v. YD* to serve, wait on (*hum.*). *tr. v. YD* to do, make, carry out (*hum.*). (*HM*)

tsuka-ru つかる (疲る) *intr. v. SN* to be tired, exhausted. (*HM*)

tsukasa つかさ (司・官・寮) *n.* **1.** office, ministry. **2.** official rank, position. (*HJ, MS, TM*)

tsuka-u つかふ (仕ふ) *intr. v. SN* **1.** to serve by the side of a noble. **2.** to serve as an official. (*HJ*)

TSUKA-U つかふ (使ふ・遣ふ) *tr. v. YD* **1.** to use (an object). **2.** to employ (a person). **3.** to consume (the heart). **4.** to manipulate. (*TM*)

*TSUKAWA-SU つかはす (遣はす) *tr. v. YD* **1.** to send (a messenger), dispatch (*hon.*). **2.** to give, send (a letter, etc.) (*hon.*). (*TM*)

TSUKI つき (月) *n.* **1.** moon, especially clear autumn moon. **2.** month. (*HI, TM, TZ*)

*TSUKI-NA-SHI つきなし (付き無し) *ku adj.* **1.** clueless, without means, at a loss. **2.** inappropriate, unsuitable.

tsuki-su つきす (尽きす) *intr. v. SH* to be exhausted, disappear. (*HJ*)

*TSUKI-ZUKI-SHI つきづきし (付き付きし) *shiku adj.* fitting, appropriate, harmonious, matching perfectly. (*MS*)

*TSUKŌ-MATSU-RU つかうまつる (仕うまつる) *intr. v. YD* to serve (*hum.*). *tr. v. YD* **1.** to do, make, carry out (*hum.*). **2.** *hum. suppl. v.* (*MS*)

*TSU-KU つく (付く・着く・就く・即く) *intr. v. YD* **1.** to stick to. **2.** (in *kokoro ni . . .* form) to take a liking to, get along with. **3.** to follow, become a wife. **4.** to become an ally, join. **5.** to be decisive. **6.** to be added to. **7.** (of a god or spirit) to possess. **8.** to attain (skill, knowledge). **9.** to burn, catch fire. **10.** to arrive at. **11.** to take on an official post, ascend the throne. *tr. v. YD* **1.** to learn, acquire (a skill, knowledge). **2.** to name. *tr. v. SN* **1.** to bring into contact, make stick. **2.** to make follow. **3.** to add, supplement. **4.** to entrust to someone. **5.** to light a fire. **6.** to name. **7.** to pay attention to. **8.** to make a record of, write down. **9.** to add a verse to the previous verse. **10.** to link two different things. (*IM, TM, US*)

tsu-ku つく (尽く) *intr. v. KN* **1.** to run out, be used up. **2.** to end. (*HJ*)

tsu-ku つく (突く・衝く・撞く) *tr. v. YD* **1.** to prod, pierce, stab (with sword, spear, stick, hand, etc.). **2.** to ring a bell. **3.** to prostrate oneself in prayer, touching one's head to the floor. **4.** to place an elbow, a hand, etc., on something. (*SN, TZ*)

tsukuro-u つくろふ (繕ふ) *tr. v. YD* **1.** to repair, mend. **2.** to decorate. **3.** to make excuses, keep up appearances. **4.** to treat an illness. (*HJ*)

*TSUKU-RU つくる (作る・造る) *tr. v. YD* **1.** to construct, build, put together. **2.** to do, create. **3.** to plow, cultivate a field. **4.** to raise, grow. **5.** to cook. **6.** to write, compose. **7.** to pretend. (*HJ, TM*)

tsuku-su つくす (尽くす) *tr. v. YD* **1.** to run out of. **2.** to exhaust, use up. **3.** to take to the extreme, push to the limit. (*GM, HI, HJ, TN*)

tsuma つま (夫・妻) *n.* wife. (*IM*)

tsuma つま (褄) *n.* hem (of a robe). (*IM*)

TSUMA つま (端) *n.* **1.** edge, side, end. **2.** eave. **3.** beginning, start, opportunity.

tsuma-gi つまぎ (爪木) *n.* twigs for fuel, brushwood. (*HJ*)

TSUMI つみ (罪) *n.* **1.** sin, transgression. **2.** punishment for a transgression. **3.** flaw, shortcoming. (*GM, TM*)

tsumo-ru つもる (積もる) *intr. v. YD* **1.** to pile up, accumulate. **2.** to increase. *tr. v. YD* **1.** (Edo) to estimate. **2.** to cheat someone, deceive. (*HI*)

tsu-mu つむ (摘む・抓む) *tr. v. YD* **1.** to pluck. **2.** to pinch. (*HI, HJ*)

tsu-mu つむ (積む) *intr. v. YD* to pile up, accumulate. *tr. v. YD* **1.** to pile up on top of. **2.** to load (a ship, carriage). (*HJ, HM*)

tsu-mu つむ (詰む) *intr. v. SN* to wait in a given place. *tr. v. SN* **1.** to contain and not allow to move. **2.** to corner a person. **3.** (Edo) to conserve, be frugal.

tsuna つな (綱) *n.* rope. (*TM*)

*TSUNE つね (常) *nari adj. v.* **1.** normal, ordinary. **2.** eternal, unchanging.

tsura つら (面・頬) *n.* **1.** side, edge (of a street). **2.** face. **3.** surface. (*HJ, US*)

tsura-nu つらぬ (連ぬ・列ぬ) *intr. v. SN* **1.** to line up in a row. **2.** to go together. *tr. v. SN* to take with one. (*MS*)

tsuranu-ku つらぬく (貫く) *tr. v. YD* to pierce, run through. (*HM, UM*)

*TSURA-SHI つらし (辛し) *ku adj.* **1.** coldhearted, icy, indifferent. **2.** unbearable, painful.

tsura-tsuki つらつき (面つき・頬つき) *n.* facial appearance. (*GM*)

*TSURE-NASHI つれなし *ku adj.* [fr. n. *tsure*, "connection," and adj. *nashi*, "without"] **1.** cold, icy, distant. **2.** feigning ignorance. **3.** indifferent, unconcerned. **4.** unchanging.

*TSURE-ZURE つれづれ (徒然) *n., nari adj. v.* **1.** idle, with time to spare, boredom, ennui. **2.** hopelessly depressed or troubled. (*GM, HJ, SN, TZ*)

tsuri-a-gu つりあぐ (釣り上ぐ・吊り上ぐ) *tr. v. SN* to hoist. (*TM*)

tsuri-bune つりぶね (釣船) *n.* fishing boat. (*HI*)

tsuri-dana つりだな (吊り棚) *n.* hanging shelf. (*HJ*)

tsuta つた (蔦) *n.* Japanese ivy. (*IM*)

tsutae-kiku つたへきく (伝へ聞く) *tr. v. YD* to be told about, learn secondhand. (*HJ*)

tsutana-shi つたなし (拙し) *ku adj.* **1.** inferior. **2.** unskilled, clumsy, inexperienced, green. **3.** cowardly. **4.** unlucky, unfortunate. (*HJ*)

tsuta-u つたふ (伝ふ) *intr. v. YD* to move from one place to another, transmit. *tr. v. SN* **1.** to teach, grant. **2.** to receive. **3.** to entrust with a message. (*TM, UM*)

tsu-tto つつと *adv.* swiftly, hurriedly, in a flash. (*HM*)

*TSUTOMETE つとめて *n.* **1.** early morning. **2.** next morning. (*MS*)

*TSUTSU つつ *conj. p.* (follows RY) **1.** repetitive or continuous action: repeatedly, continuously. **2.** simultaneous, parallel action: while.

tsutsu つつ (筒) *n.* tube, cylinder. (*TM*)

*TSUTSUMA-SHI つつまし (慎まし) *shiku adj.* **1.** reserved, restrained. **2.** awkward, embarrassed, bashful.

tsutsumu つつむ (包む) *tr. v. YD* to wrap. (*TM*)

*TSUTSU-MU つつむ (慎む) *tr. v. YD* to show restraint toward. *intr. v. YD* to be diffident, lose one's nerve. (*TM*)

tsutsushi-mu つつしむ (慎む) *tr. v. YD* **1.** to be very cautious, be careful with. **2.** to be abstinent or restrained (for the purpose of serving the gods or buddhas, avoiding pollution, etc.). (*UM*)

tsuwa-mono つはもの (兵) *n.* warrior. (*TM*)

tsuya-tsuya つやつや *adv.* (followed by neg.) absolutely, not at all. (*TZ*)

tsuya-tsuya-to つやつやと (艶々と) *adv.* lustrously. (*GM*)

*TSUYU つゆ (露) *n.* **1.** dew. **2.** something small in number or quantity. **3.** something trifling, insubstantial, fleeting. **4.** (metaphor) teardrops. *adv.* (followed by neg.) (not) at all, (not) in the least. (*GM, HJ*)

tsuzu-ku つづく (続く) *intr. v. YD* **1.** to follow, line up behind. **2.** to continue. (*HM*)

*U う (得) *tr. v. SN* **1.** to acquire, possess. **2.** to master, excel. **3.** to realize, understand, awaken (often in *kokoro o u* form). **4.** (following *o* or *koto o*) to be able. **5.** *suppl. v.* to be able to. (*HJ, SN*)

ubai-to-ru うばひとる (奪ひ取る) *tr. v. YD* to steal, snatch away. (*KM*)

ubu-ge うぶげ (生毛) *n.* downy hair (on cheek, back of neck). (*UM*)

ubu-ya うぶや (産屋) *n.* lying-in room, room set aside for childbirth. (*MS*)

uchi- うち～ *prefix* (precedes v.) **1.** strengthens meaning, emphasizes v. **2.** indicates brevity or lightness of the action. **3.** enhances phonic quality. (*MS, SN, TM*)

*UCHI うち (内) *n.* **1.** inside (a room, building). **2.** house, inside a home. **3.** inside one's heart, mind. **4.** inside (the capital, province). **5.** part (of a larger amount). **6.** within (a certain period of time). **7.** imperial court. **8.** emperor. **9.** Buddhism (in contrast to Confucianism). **10.** personal matter. **11.** one's spouse (husband or wife). (*TZ*)

uchi-a-gu うちあぐ (打ち上ぐ) *tr. v. SN* **1.** to clap (hands) and raise (voices). **2.** to hold a banquet.

uchi-fu-su うちふす (打ち臥す) *intr. v. YD* [fr. prefix *uchi* and v. *fusu*] to lie down, go to sleep. (*SN*)

*UCHI-I-ZU うちいづ (打ち出づ) *intr. v. SN* [fr. prefix *uchi* and v. *izu*] **1.** to come out, appear. **2.** to set out, (of soldiers) depart for the front. **3.** to obtrude, meddle. *tr. v. SN* **1.** to make a sound or fire by hitting a drum, stone, etc. **2.** to reveal a little (of a robe). **3.** to speak of, say or recite out loud. (*HI, MY, TM*)

uchi-jini うちじに (討死) *n.* death in battle. (*HM*)

uchi-mamo-ru うちまもる (打ち守る) *tr. v. YD* to gaze intently at. (*GM*)

uchi-mi-yaru うちみやる (打見やる) *tr. v. YD* (prefix *uchi*) to look at from a distance. (*SN*)

uchi-mono うちもの (打物) *n.* **1.** forged iron weapon (sword, pike, etc.). **2.** percussive instrument (bell, drum, etc.). **3.** cloth beaten to bring out a sheen. (*HM*)

uchi-na-su うちなす (打ち成す) *tr. v. YD* to strike and reduce (the enemy) to a small number. (*HM*)

uchi-ōi うちおほひ (打ち覆ひ) *n.* covering, makeshift roof. (*HJ*)

uchi-shigu-ru うちしぐる (打ち時雨る) *intr. v. SN* **1.** to rain suddenly. **2.** (metaphor) to be moved to tears. (*TZ*)

uchi-so-u うちそふ (打ち添う) *intr. v. YD* [fr. prefix *uchi* and v. *sou*, "to add"] **1.** to accompany, go along with. **2.** to be added, join. *tr. v. SN* to add. (*HJ, HM*)

uchi-to うちと (内外) *n.* **1.** inside and outside (of a building). **2.** self and other, inside and outside one's heart. **3.** (from Buddhist perspective) inside religion (Buddhism) and outside the religion (e.g., Confucianism). (*TM*)

*UCHI-TSUKE うちつけ *nari adj. v.* **1.** abrupt, sudden. **2.** careless, thoughtless, rash, imprudent. **3.** impolite, rude.

*UE うへ (上) *n.* **1.** surface. **2.** upper part. **3.** edge, border. **4.** emperor, retired emperor. **5.** principal wife of a noble. **6.** room for emperor and other royalty. **7.** room in the Seiryōden for courtiers (*tenjōbito*) allowed in the imperial palace. **8.** lord, shogun. **9.** addition, on top of. **10.** added to an aristocratic lady's name as a sign of respect (e.g., Murasaki no ue).

ugo-ku うごく (動く) *tr. v. YD* to move. (*TM*)

UKA-BU うかぶ (浮かぶ) *intr. v. YD* **1.** to float to the surface of the water. **2.** to be uncertain, unsettled. **3.** to come to mind, recollect. **4.** to be groundless. **5.** to succeed in the world (making one's way out of a difficult circumstances). **6**. to achieve buddhahood. *tr. v.* *SN* **1**. to set something afloat. **2**. to make someone succeed or rise in the world. **3**. to memorize, recite from memory. (*HJ, SN*)

*UKAGA-U うかがふ (窺ふ) *tr. v. YD* **1**. to look at (furtively), peek in. **2**. to wait quietly for an opportunity. **3**. to inquire. (*TM*)

UKAGA-U うかがふ (伺ふ) *tr. v. YD* to ask, inquire (*hum.*). (*HM*)

*UKE-TAMAWA-RU うけたまはる (承る) *tr. v. YD* [fr. RY v. *uku* and suppl. v. *tamawaru*] (*hum.*). **1**. to receive. **2**. to hear. **3**. to agree to, accept. **4**. to see. (*TM*)

uki-gumo うきぐも (浮き雲) *n.* floating cloud. (*HJ*)

uki-ta-tsu うきたつ (浮き立つ) *intr. v. YD* **1**. to float up into the sky, ascend. **2**. (of the heart) to flutter, float about. **3**. to be agitated, restless. (*HJ*)

*UKIYO うきよ (憂き世・浮き世) *n.* **1**. world of suffering and pain, this world. **2**. male–female relations filled with troubles. **3**. (Edo) the floating world, human life (as unpredictable, uncertain). **4**. (Edo) the world of pleasure, particularly erotic love in the licensed quarters.

*U-KU うく (受く・承く・請く) *tr. v. SN* **1**. to receive. **2**. to agree to (a vow, request, etc.), assent to. **3**. to acknowledge. **4**. to take (an examination). (*TM*)

*U-KU うく (浮く) *intr. v. YD* **1**. to float on water or air. **2**. to be unsettled. **3**. to be unreliable. *tr. v. SN* to cause to float. (*TM*)

uma-ru うまる (生る) *intr. v. SN* to be born. (*HJ, TM*)

umi-oto-su うみおとす (産み落とす) *tr. v. YD* to lay eggs or bear a child. (*TM*)

u-mu うむ (生む) *tr. v. YD* to lay eggs or bear a child. (*TM*)

un うん (運) *n.* luck, fortune, fate. (*HJ*)

unazuku うなづく (頷く) *intr. v. YD* to nod, especially in agreement or understanding.

UN-ZU うんず (倦んず) *intr. v. SH* **1**. to be-

come disgusted with. **2**. to be disappointed. (*TM*)

ura うら (占) *n.* augury, divination, omen. (*UM*)

urami うらみ (恨み・怨み) *n.* **1**. resentment, bitterness. **2**. regret. **3**. lament. (*HJ*)

*URAMU うらむ (恨む・怨む) *tr. v. KN* **1**. to resent, be dissatisfied with. **2**. to complain, express resentment. **3**. to take revenge. **4**. to find sorrowful. **5**. (used like an intransitive v.) (of insects, the wind, etc.) to sound sorrowful.

urara-ka うららか (麗か) *nari adj. v.* (suffix *ka*) **1**. warm, bright, sunlit appearance (often of a spring day). **2**. bright, radiant (voice). **3**. clear, without hiding anything. (*HJ*)

ura-ya-mu うらやむ (羨む) *tr. v. YD* **1**. to be envious, feel jealous of (someone). **2**. to be resentful, dissatisfied. (*HJ*)

uree うれへ (憂へ) *n.* **1**. sorrow, sadness. **2**. complaint. **3**. worry, concern. (*GM*)

ure-shi うれし (嬉し) *shiku adj.* **1**. satisfied, delighted, pleased. **2**. grateful. (*SN, TM*)

*URE-U うれふ (憂ふ・愁ふ) *tr. v. SN* **1**. to express dissatisfaction or distress, complain. **2**. to grieve, lament. **3**. to worry about, be concerned. **4**. to became sick. (*IIJ, TZ*)

uri うり (瓜) *n.* melon. (*MY*)

uruo-su うるほす (潤す) *tr. v. YD* to moisten, make wet. (*HJ*)

*URUSA-SHI うるさし *ku adj.* **1**. bothersome, troubling, annoying. **2**. intentionally unpleasant, sarcastic. **3**. outstanding. **4**. careful, meticulous. (*GM*)

*URUWA-SHI うるはし (麗し・美し) *shiku adj.* **1**. magnificent, grand, splendid (nature, land, buildings). **2**. graceful and beautiful (human figure). **3**. neat, flawless (human appearance, behavior, character). **4**. neat, well-ordered (garden, landscape, etc.). **5**. friendly, intimate (relationship, human interaction). **6**. formal, ceremonial, proper. **7**. correct. (*US*)

u-sa うさ (憂さ) *n.* [fr. adj. *ushi*, "painful," and suffix *sa*] sorrow, grief, distress. (*TZ, UM*)

*U-SHI うし (憂し) *ku adj.* **1**. hard to bear,

depressing, painful. **2.** unwilling. **3.** unfeeling, unkind, cruel.

ushi-kai うしかひ (牛飼) *n.* oxherd. (*MS*)

ushina-u うしなふ (失ふ) *tr. v. YD* **1.** to lose suddenly. **2.** to lose a loved one. **3.** to absolve someone of a crime, expunge a criminal charge. **4.** to kill. (*HJ*)

*USHIRO-META-SHI うしろめたし (後ろめたし) *ku adj.* **1.** worrisome, anxiety-producing. **2.** making one feel guilty. (*GM*)

ushiromi うしろみ (後ろ見) *n.* **1.** someone who looks after a child or person. **2.** support, backing. **3.** (public) supporter, backer, patron. (*GM*)

*U-SU うす (失す) *intr. v. SN* **1.** to die. **2.** to disappear. (*HM, KM, TM*)

usu-gōri うすごほり (薄氷) *n.* thin ice. (*HM*)

usura-gu うすらぐ (薄らぐ) *intr. v. YD* **1.** to lessen or abate, diminish in number. **2.** to fade, grow weak. (*HJ*)

USU-SHI うすし (薄し) *ku adj.* **1.** thin. **2.** light (in color, smell, taste, density). **3.** superficial, emotionally shallow, cold-hearted. **4.** poor, lacking, disadvantaged.

uta うた (歌・唄) *n.* **1.** thirty-one-syllable Japanese poem. **2.** poetry in general. **3.** song. (*TZ*)

utaga-u うたがふ (疑ふ) *tr. v. YD* to doubt, suspect. (*HJ*)

utakata うたかた (泡沫) *n.* froth, bubbles on the surface of the water. (*HJ*)

*UTATE うたて *adv.* **1.** intensifying, uncontrolled, inexplicable situation: worse and worse, severely, badly. **2.** strangely, mysteriously. **3.** disagreeably, terribly. *adj. stem* woeful, disgusting. *nari adj. v.* inexplicable, terrible, woeful. (*TM, US*)

UTATE-SHI うたてし *ku adj.* **1.** disappointing, **2.** pitiful, heart-wrenching.

utena うてな (台) *n.* tower, pedestal, dais. (*TM*)

*UTOSHI うとし (疎し) *ku adj.* **1.** remote, unfamiliar. **2.** troublesome, annoying, offensive. **3.** unknown. **4.** indifferent. **5.** insensitive.

U-TSU うつ (打つ) *tr. v. YD* **1.** to hit, strike, whip. **2.** to beat cloth with a fulling block to bring out its gloss. **3.** to pound (a stake, pole, etc.) into the ground, set up a tent or temporary shelter. **4.** to use a hammer to shape metal. **5.** to scatter, strew. **6.** to cultivate land, plow. **7.** to draw a line, affix a mark. **8.** to compete or perform. (*HM*)

utsu-bu-shi うつぶし (俯し) *n.* prone position, lying face down. (*TM*)

utsu-bu-su うつぶす (俯す) *intr. v. YD* **1.** to face down, look down. **2.** to be prone, lie down. (*GM*)

*UTSUKU-SHI うつくし (美し・愛し) *shiku adj.* **1.** lovable, adorable. **2.** cute, cuddly. **3.** beautiful, impressive. (*SN, TM*)

UTSUKUSHI-GE うつくしげ (愛しげ・美しげ) *nari adj. v.* [fr. adj. *utsukushi* and suffix *ge*] adorable-looking, cute-looking. (*GM*)

UTSUKUSHI-MU うつくしむ (愛しむ・慈しむ) *tr. v. YD* to care for dearly, adore, love.

utsuri-yu-ku うつりゆく (移り行く) *intr. v. YD* to shift from one place to another. (*HJ*)

*UTSURO-U うつろふ (移ろふ) *intr. v. YD* [fr. v. *utsuru*, "to transfer," and aux. v. *fu*] **1.** to transfer, move to another place, relocate. **2.** to change to a beautiful color, turn crimson. **3.** to fade in color. **4.** to have a change of heart. **5.** (of flowers) to scatter. **6.** to pass the peak and decline. (*HI*)

*UTSURO-U うつろふ (映ろふ) *intr. v. YD* [fr. v. *utsuru*, "to reflect," and aux. v. *fu*] to glow, be lit up, reflect (light). (*HJ*)

*UTSU-RU うつる (移る) *intr. v. YD* **1.** to move, shift to another place. **2.** (of rank, office) to change positions. **3.** (of a vengeful spirit) to possess (someone). **4.** (of time) to pass. **5.** (of color, fragrance) to permeate. **6.** (of color) to fade, to scatter. **7.** to have a change of heart. (*HI, HJ*)

*UTSU-RU うつる (映る・写る) *intr. v. YD* to reflect (light, shade, etc.) on water, a mirror, etc.

UTSU-SEMI うつせみ (現身・空蝉) *n.* (現身) **1.** person living in this world. **2.** this world, society. (空蝉) 3. cicada shell, cicada (symbol of the ephemerality of life). (*HJ*)

UTSU-SHI うつし (現し・顕し) *shiku adj.* 1. actually living (being). 2. actual, real. 3. sane, in firm grip of one's senses. (*HJ*)

utsushi-gokoro うつしごころ (現し心) *n.* sense of sanity, feeling of reality (*utsushi*). (*HJ*)

UTSU-SU うつす (移す) *tr. v. YD* 1. to move, shift. 2. to place in exile. 3. to have a change of heart. 4. (of scent, etc.) to make penetrate. 5. to pass time.

UTSU-SU うつす (映す・写す) *tr. v. YD* 1. to copy. 2. to imitate. 3. to depict, represent. 4. to reflect.

*UTSUTSU うつつ (現) *n.* 1. life, living state (as opposed to death). 2. reality, awakened state (as opposed to dream). 3. sanity, sane state. 4. dreamlike state. (*IM*)

u-u うう (植う) *tr. v. SN* to plant (a seed, seedling). (*HJ, TO*)

U-ZUKI うづき (四月・卯月) *n.* Fourth Month (lunar calendar). (*HJ*)

uzumi-bi うづみび (埋み火) *n.* burning charcoal, buried in ashes. (*HJ*)

uzu-mu うづむ (埋む) *tr. v. YD* [fr. Muro. SN] 1. to place or bury in dirt or ash. 2. to cause melancholy, depression (in someone). (*HJ*)

*WA は *bound p.* indicates 1. topic marker: as for, when it comes to. 2. distinction and emphasis, singling out one item and distinguishing it from other items: in particular. 3. parallel comparison, with *wa* appearing twice, in parallel phrases: as for this, as for that.

wa わ (我・吾) *pron.* I, me, my. (*TM*)

*WABI-SHI わびし (侘びし) *shiku adj.* 1. painful. 2. lonely. 3. impoverished. 4. uninteresting. (*IM*)

wabi-shi-ru わびしる (侘び痴る) *intr. v. SN* to be at a loss or bewildered as a result of encountering difficulty. (*HJ*)

*WA-BU わぶ (侘ぶ) *intr. v. KN* 1. to find

difficult to bear, be troubled. 2. to feel lonely, powerless. 3. to fall into ruin, be impoverished. 4. to be confused, perplexed. 5. to complain. 6. (Kamakura) to savor tranquillity and loneliness in a modest dwelling. 7. *suppl. v.* to find (something) difficult to do or complete. (*HI, HJ, IM, TM*)

WA-GA わが (我が・吾が) *set phrase* [fr. pron. *wa* and attrib. case p. *ga*] 1. my. 2. that person himself or herself. (*HI*)

WA-KA わか (和歌) *n.* Japanese poem following a basic metrical pattern of 5/7/5/7/7 syllables. (*HJ*)

waka-kusa わかくさ (若草) *n.* 1. newly budding grass in spring. 2. (metaphor) young girl. (*GM*)

waka-na わかな (若菜) *n.* young herbs, greens. (*HI*)

wakare わかれ (別れ) *n.* parting. (*TN*)

*WAKA-RU わかる (分る・別る) *intr. v. SN* 1. to be divided, separated. 2. to be separated by a great distance, die. (*MY, HI*)

*WAKA-SHI わかし (若し) *ku adj.* 1. young in years. 2. fresh, youthful. 3. immature.

waka-su わかす (沸かす) *tr. v. YD* 1. to boil water. 2. to melt metal. (*US*)

waka-tō わかたう (若党) *n.* young samurai. (*HM*)

wakima-u わきまふ (弁ふ) *tr. v. SN* 1. to comprehend, understand. 2. to distinguish between things, make a distinction. 3. to atone for, make reparations, settle a dispute. (*TO*)

*WA-KU わく (分く・別く) *tr. v. YD* 1. to separate, distinguish. 2. to comprehend, understand. *tr. v. SN* 1. to separate, distinguish. 2. to push one's way through, particularly a large group of people.

wanana-ku わななく (戦慄く) *intr. v. YD* to shiver, quiver. (*MS*)

warabi わらび (蕨) *n.* bracken (type of fern). (*HJ*)

wara-u わらふ (笑ふ) *intr. v. YD* to laugh. (*TM*)

*WARAWA わらは (童) *n.* **1.** child. **2.** servant. **3.** dancing girl. **4.** child's hairstyle. **5.** child serving at a temple. (*TM, US*)

warawa-be わらはべ (童べ) *n.* **1.** child. **2.** child serving in a house of a noble or a temple. (*GM*)

warawa-gu わらはぐ (童ぐ) *intr. v. SN* to be childish, appear childish. (*TM*)

warawa-yami わらはやみ (瘧) *n.* ague, the shakes, a disease frequently caught by children, malarial fever. (*GM*)

*WARE われ (予・我・吾) *pron.* **1.** first-person singular: I, myself. **2.** that person. **3.** second-person: you. (*HJ, SN, TM*)

wari-kuda-ku わりくだく (割り砕く) *tr. v. YD* to smash, break up. (*HJ*)

*WARI-NA-SHI わりなし *ku adj.* [fr. n. *koto-wari*, "reason," and adj. *nashi*, "without"] **1.** indiscriminate, illogical. **2.** unbearable, intolerable, insufferable. **3.** unavoidable. **4.** extreme, excessive. (*GM, TZ*)

*WARO-SHI わろし (悪し) *ku adj.* **1.** bad. **2.** ugly. **3.** clumsy, unskilled. **4.** inappropriate, unsuitable. **5.** poor. **6.** stale, rotten. (*MS, SN*)

wa-ru わる (割る) *tr. v. YD* **1.** to break, smash, cleave. **2.** to split up, divide. **3.** to push one's way through. *intr. v. SN* **1.** to break up, shatter. **2.** to be separated. **3.** to become confused, disturbed. **4.** (of a secret) to be disclosed. (*HJ*)

washi-ru わしる (走る) *intr. v. YD* to run, run about. (*HJ*)

wasu-ru わする (忘る) *tr. v. YD, SN* to forget. (*GM*)

wata-no-hara わたのはら (海の原) *set phrase* wide-open sea. (*HI*)

WATARI わたり (辺り) *n.* **1.** vicinity, surroundings. **2.** (circumlocution) people. (*HJ, TM, UM*)

*WATA-RU わたる (渡る) *intr. v. YD* **1.** to cross a river, the sea, etc., and go to the other side. **2.** to pass by. **3.** to spend years and months. **4.** to span a wide area. **5.** *suppl. v.* to do (something) continuously. (*IM, TM*)

*WATA-SU わたす (渡す) *tr. v. YD* **1.** to make transfer from one place to the other. **2.** to make cross (a river, the sea). **3.** to lay down a bridge, make straddle both shores. **4.** to help to the far shore (enlightenment), save by divine aid. **5.** to give, hand over, provide. (*HI, IM, SN*)

wa-tō わたう (我党・和党) *pron.* [fr. prefix *wa*, "my," and n. *tō*, "colleague"] second-person, expressing affection or mild derision: you, the likes of you. (*US*)

*WAZA わざ (業・技・態) *n.* **1.** action, deed. **2.** job, occupation. **3.** technique, skill. **4.** Buddhist ritual, ceremony. **5.** state of affairs, situation. **6.** disaster, curse. (*HJ, TM, TZ*)

*WAZA-TO わざと (態と) *adv.* **1.** deliberately, intentionally. **2.** officially, formally. **3.** especially.

wazuka わづか (僅か) *nari adj. v.* **1.** small number, few. **2.** (in RY) barely, after great difficulty. **3.** scant, meager, poor. (*HJ*)

wazurai わづらひ (煩ひ) *n.* **1.** worry, anxiety. **2.** illness, sickness. (*HJ*)

*WAZURA-U わづらふ (煩ふ) *intr. v. YD* **1.** to be troubled, distressed. **2.** to be ill. **3.** to suffer pain doing (something) **4.** *suppl. v.* (*TM*)

*WAZURAWA-SHI わづらはし (煩はし) *shiku adj.* **1.** troublesome, vexing. **2.** awkward, ill at ease. **3.** very ill.

wiru *See* **iru**.

wokashi *See* **okashi**.

woko *See* **oko**.

wokogamashi *See* **okogamashi**.

wonna *See* **onna**.

wonoko *See* **onoko**.

worifushi *See* **ori-fushi**.

wosamu *See* **osa-mu**.

wosanashi *See* **osa-na-shi**.

wosawosa *See* **osa-osa**.

woshimu *See* **oshi-mu**.

wotoko *See* **otoko**.

*YA や   *bound p.* indicates **1.** question, doubt. **2.** rhet. question.

YA や   *interj.* **1.** address, summons. **2.** expression of surprise.

ya や (屋・家)   *n.* **1.** house, room. **2.** roof. (*TM*)

*YABU-RU やぶる (破る)   *intr. v. SN* **1.** to break down, be destroyed. **2.** to fall apart, cease to function. **3.** to be defeated. *tr. v. YD* **1.** to break, smash to pieces, rend. **2.** to injure, harm. **3.** to disrupt, violate. **4.** to defeat. (*HJ, TZ*)

*YA-DO やど (宿・屋戸)   *n.* **1.** dwelling, house. **2.** house entrance. **3.** garden. **4.** inn, temporary lodgings. (*TZ*)

yadori やどり (宿り)   *n.* dwelling, lodging. (*HJ*)

yado-su やどす (宿す)   *tr. v. YD* **1.** to put up for the night, lodge. **2.** to keep. **3.** to make pregnant. (*HJ*)

*YAGATE やがて (軈て)   *adv.* **1.** as is, just like that, in that very condition. **2.** immediately. **3.** namely, in other words. **4.** sooner or later, eventually. (*TM, TZ, UM*)

yagoto-na-shi やごとなし   *ku adj.* [fr. v. *yamu*, "to stop," and adj. *koto-nashi*, "without"] (*see* **yamugoto-na-shi**) **1.** unavoidable. **2.** precious, valuable, important. **3.** high-ranking, of a noted family. **4.** learned, well-respected. (*US*)

ya-ku やく (焼く)   *intr. v. SN* **1.** to burn, catch fire. **2.** to be distraught. *tr. v. YD* **1.** to set fire to. **2.** (of the heart) to trouble. (*HJ*)

*YAMA やま (山)   *n.* **1.** mountain. **2.** Mount Hiei, Enryaku-ji temple on Mount Hiei. **3.** small-scale artificial mountain in a garden. **4.** pile. **5.** imperial tomb. (*MS, TM*)

yama-be やまべ (山辺)   *n.* periphery of a mountain, vicinity of a mountain. (*IM*)

yama-buki やまぶき (山吹)   *n.* **1.** yellow flower (*Kerria japonica*) that blooms in late spring. **2.** color combination of a robe (yellowish brown on the outside, yellow on the inside) worn in the spring. (*GM*)

yama-dori やまどり (山鳥)   *n.* (lit., mountain bird) copper pheasant (*Syrmaticus soemmeringii*). (*HI, HJ*)

yama-gatsu やまがつ (山賤)   *n.* mountain dweller, woodcutter. (*HJ*)

yama-giwa やまぎは (山際)   *n.* **1.** mountain ridge, rim. **2.** foothills. (*MS*)

yamai やまひ (病)   *n.* illness. (*TM*)

yama-ji やまぢ (山路)   *n.* mountain path.

yama-mori やまもり (山守)   *n.* mountain watchman. (*HJ*)

yama-no-ha やまのは (山の端)   *n.* ridge or rim of a mountain (*MS*)

YAMI やみ (闇)   *n.* **1.** darkness, night. **2.** turmoil. **3.** (Buddhism) this world of ignorance and illusion. (*MS, TM*)

*YA-MU やむ (止む)   *intr. v. YD* **1.** to come to an end, stop. **2.** to be canceled. **3.** (of sickness, anger, pain) to be cured, overcome. **4.** to die. *tr. v. SN* **1.** to bring to an end, stop. **2.** to heal, improve. (*HJ, TM, TZ*)

ya-mu やむ (病む)   *intr. v. YD* to be sick, afflicted. (*TM*)

*YAMUGOTO-NA-SHI やむごとなし   *ku adj.* [fr. v *yamu*, "to stop," and adj. *koto-nashi*, "without"] **1.** unavoidable. **2.** precious. **3.** high-ranking, of a noted family. **4.** learned, well-respected. (*HJ*)

yaniwa-ni やにはに (矢庭に)   *adv.* (lit., place where arrows are shot) on the spot, immediately. (*HM*)

YA-RU やる (破る)   *intr. v. SN* to break down, be torn apart. *tr. v. YD* to tear, rip apart. (*TN*)

*YA-RU やる (遣る)   *tr. v. YD* **1.** to dispatch (a person). **2.** to deliver, send, give. **3.** to dispel an unpleasant feeling, console. **4.** *suppl. v.* to do (something) extensively, pervasively. **5.** *suppl. v.* (usually followed by neg.) to do (something) completely, thoroughly. (*GM, TM*)

*YASA-SHI やさし (恥し・優し)   *shiku adj.* [fr. v. *yasu*, "to grow thin"] (恥し) **1.** so unbearable or painful as if to make one grown thin. **2.** shameful, embarrassing. **3.** modest, reserved.

(優し) **4.** elegant, graceful. **5.** kind, sympathetic. **6.** simple, uncomplicated.

yashina-u やしなふ (養ふ) *tr. v. YD* **1.** to raise, care for. **2.** to preserve, take care of. (*TM*)

ya-so-shima やそしま (八十島) *n.* [fr. n. *yaso*, "eighty," and n. *shima*, "island"] countless islands. (*HI*)

yasu-i やすい (安寝・安眠) *n.* sound sleep. (*MY*)

YASURAU やすらふ (休らふ) *intr. v. YD* **1.** to hesitate. **2.** to stand, stop. **3.** to wait for a while. **4.** to rest, take it easy.

*YASU-SHI やすし (易し・安し) *ku adj.* (易し) **1.** easy, simple. **2.** casual. **3.** (following RY) readily tending to (attain a certain state or condition). (安し) **4.** at ease, untroubled. **5.** tawdry, cheap-looking, careless. **6.** inexpensive. (*HJ, TM*)

yato-u やとふ (雇ふ) *tr. v. YD* **1.** to employ, hire. **2.** to use as a temporary substitute. **3.** to make do with, use. (*HJ*)

ya-tsu-ko やつこ (奴) *n.* servant, lowly person. (*HJ*)

YATSUSU やつす (俏す・窶す) *tr. v. YD* **1.** to dress down, dress shabbily (to disguise one's identity or status), dress inconspicuously. **2.** to take holy vows, take on the appearance of one who has taken vows.

yauyau *See* **yōyō**.

*YAWA やは *bound p.* indicates **1.** interrogation, question, doubt. **2.** rhet. question. **3.** invitation, suggestion. *final p.* (follows SS, IZ at end of a sentence) rhet. question.

YAWARA やはら *adv.* stealthily, slowly, quietly, softly. (*KM*)

yawara-bu やはらぶ *intr. v. YD* to appear calm, be gentle, congenial. (*TO*)

YA-YA やや (稍) *adv.* **1.** gradually, eventually. **2.** (of extent, degree, size, etc.) somewhat. (*HJ, UM*)

YAYOI やよひ (弥生) *n.* Third Month (lunar calendar). (*HJ*)

*YO よ *interj. p.* **1.** exclamation. **2.** address, summons. **3.** prohibition. *case p.* (Nara) indicates **1.** starting point. **2.** point of transit. **3.** means. **4.** comparison.

*YO よ (世・代) *n.* **1.** world. **2.** society. **3.** (metaphor) imperial court. **4.** one's (whole) life. **5.** certain historical moment, (current) times. **6.** secular world, fashion, trends. **7.** desire for worldly things like power, fame, profit. **8.** relationship between a man and woman, husband and wife. (*GM, HJ, TM*)

yo よ (余) *n.* **1.** and others. **2.** (following a unit of measurement) somewhat more than, and a little. (*HM*)

yo よ (予・余) *pron.* first-person singular (masculine): I. (*OH*)

YO よ (夜) *n.* night. (*HI, TZ*)

yo よ (節) *n.* joints or hollow spaces between joints. (*TM*)

*YŌ やう (様) *n.* **1.** appearance, shape. **2.** form, style, pattern. **3.** reason, circumstance. **4.** means, method. **5.** (following RT) phrase nominalizer. (*GM, HJ, IM, TM, TZ*)

yō よう (用) *n.* **1.** need. **2.** business, engagement. (*TM*)

YŌ やう *nari adj. v.* **1.** like, as if (simile). **2.** (for example) if it were . . . **3.** to be in a condition in which . . . **4.** desiderative or intentional (in the form *yō-ni*). **5.** indirection: it seems that . . .

yoba-i よばひ (婚ひ) *n.* courtship, suit, marriage proposal.

yobe よべ (昨夜) *n.* last night, previous night. (*UM*)

yō-dō ようどう (用途) (also *yōtō, yōdo*) *n.* necessary expense. (*HJ*)

yodomi よどみ (淀み) *n.* still water, still place in a stream or river. (*HJ*)

yoi よひ (宵) *n.* dusk, early evening (from sundown to midnight). (*NE, TM*)

yō-i ようい (用意) *n.* **1.** attention, care, regard, consideration, concern. **2.** preparation. (*UM*)

yoi-i よひゐ (宵居) *n.* (staying up) late at night. (*SN*)

yoji-nobo-ru よぢのぼる (攀じ登る) *comp. v.* [fr. v. *yozu*, "to crawl up," and v. *noboru*] to crawl up. (*HJ*)

yoji-ru よぢる *intr. v. YD* to twist. (*US*)

yō-jō やうじやう (養生) *n.* maintaining or attending to one's health, recuperation. (*HJ*)

yoki-hito よきひと (よき人) *n.* person of good taste, connoisseur. (*TZ*)

yoko-sama よこさま (横さま) *n., nari adj. v.* **1.** horizontal direction, horizontal. **2.** unconventional, abnormal, irrational (behavior, appearance, etc.). (*HM*)

yo-ku よく (避く) *tr. v. YD, KN, SN* to avoid, evade. (*HI*)

yo-kyō よきよう (余興) *n.* lingering pleasure, added or unexpected interest. (*HJ*)

YOMO よも *adv.* (often followed by neg.) hardly, surely, definitely. (*US*)

*YO-MU よむ (読む・詠む) *tr. v. YD* (読む) **1.** to count. **2.** to read aloud poetry, text. (詠む) **3.** to compose a poem. (*IM*)

yō-na-shi えうなし (要なし) *ku adj.* worthless, unnecessary. (*IM*)

YO-NI よに (世に) *adv.* **1.** verily, truly. **2.** (followed by neg.) (not) at all, absolutely (not).

yo ni fu よにふ (世に経) *set phrase* [fr. intr. SN v. *fu*, "to live"] to live in this world.

YO-NO-NAKA よのなか (世の中) *n.* **1.** human society. **2.** secular world. **3.** social position. **4.** male–female relationship. (*HJ*)

yo no tsune よのつね (世の常) *set phrase* **1.** ordinary, commonplace. **2.** needless to say. (*HJ*)

*YORI より *case p.* indicates **1.** point of origin: from. **2.** standard of comparison: compared to. **3.** means, method: by. **4.** point of transit: through. **5.** two actions in rapid sequence: as soon as. **6.** restriction of scope: except for, outside of (X there was no one). **7.** cause or origin: because.

yoroi よろひ (鎧) *n.* armor. (*HM*)

YOROKOBI よろこび (喜び・悦び) *n.* **1.** happiness, joy. **2.** happy event, felicitation, celebration. **3.** congratulatory message or celebration on the occasion of a government promotion or appointment. **4.** gift, gratuity.

yoroko-bu よろこぶ (喜ぶ・悦ぶ) *intr. v. KN, YD* to rejoice, be delighted. (*HJ, TM*)

*YORO-SHI よろし (宜し) *shiku adj.* **1.** relatively good, satisfactory. **2.** common, matter of course. **3.** fitting, appropriate. **4.** conducive to recovery from illness, amelioration of difficulties, etc. (*HJ*)

*YOROZU よろづ (万) *n.* **1.** ten thousand, myriad things. **2.** all things. *adv.* in regard to all things, in every case. (*TM, TZ*)

yo-ru よる (因る・由る) *intr. v. YD* **1.** to be based on, due to, the result of. **2.** to follow, respond to. (*HJ, HM, TM*)

*YO-RU よる (寄る) *intr. v. YD* **1.** to approach. **2.** to gather together. **3.** to be inclined toward, favor. **4.** to rely on, depend on. **5.** to lean against. **6.** to be possessed by (evil spirits). **7.** to receive donations, contributions. (*HI, TM*)

yo-san よさん (余算) *n.* remainder, remaining years of one's life. (*HJ*)

yo-sari よさり (夜さり) *n.* evening, nighttime, tonight. (*TM*)

*YOSHI よし (由) *n.* **1.** way, means. **2.** origin, cause. **3.** reason, circumstance. **4.** elegance, atmosphere, taste. **5.** main point, gist (of). **6.** connection, bond. **7.** appearance, look, manner. (*HI, OH, TM, TN*)

*YO-SHI よし (良し・好し・善し・吉し) *ku adj.* **1.** valuable, excellent, superb. **2.** physically beautiful. **3.** of good character. **4.** healthy. **5.** high-ranking, of good lineage. **6.** flourishing, wealthy. **7.** elegant. **8.** skilled. **9.** lucky, auspicious. **10.** convenient, effective. **11.** sufficient. **12.** correct. (*TM*)

*YOSHI-NA-SHI よしなし (由無し) *ku adj.* **1.** groundless, unreasonable. **2.** without means or method. **3.** lacking taste. **4.** useless. **5.** uninteresting. (*HJ, TM*)

yoshinashi-goto よしなしごと (由無し事) *n.* [fr. adj. *yoshinashi*, "groundless"] trivial things, trivial thoughts. (*TN, TZ*)

YOSO よそ (余所) *n.* **1.** separate or remote place. **2.** other person or persons. *nari adj. v.* **1.** unrelated, foreign, irrelevant. **2.** distant.

yoso-ji よそぢ (四十) *n.* **1.** forty. **2.** forty years, forty years old. (*HJ*)

yoso-nagara よそながら (余所ながら) *adv.* **1.** while at a distance, at a remove. **2.** one way or another, by indirection. (*TZ*)

***YO-SU** よす (寄す) *intr. v. SN* **1.** to approach, draw close. **2.** to attack. *tr. v. YD* to make (someone) approach, send (someone) to go close. *tr. v. SN* **1.** to bring close, let come near. **2.** to entrust. **3.** to compare, connect. (*HJ, TM*)

yō-su ようす (用す) *tr. v. SH* to use, employ. (*HJ*)

***YOSUGA** よすが (便・縁・因) *n.* **1.** source or basis of support, something that can be relied on. **2.** one who can be relied on for support (husband, wife, child, etc.). **3.** means, method, convenience, connection. (*HJ*)

yowai よはひ (齢) *n.* **1.** age. **2.** lifetime, life span. (*GM, HJ*)

yowa-shi よわし (弱し) *ku adj.* **1.** inferior, lacking ability. **2.** physically enervated, weak. (*TM*)

yo-watari よわたり (世渡り) *n.* living or getting by in the world. (*NE*)

yo-yo よよ (世々) *n.* **1.** generation after generation, many years. **2.** man and woman living separately, each in his and her own world. **3.** (Buddhist) past, present, and future lives. (*HJ*)

***YŌ-YŌ** やうやう (漸う) *adv.* [fr. adv. *yōyaku*] **1.** gradually, little by little. **2.** barely. **3.** finally (*GM, MS, TM*)

YU ゆ *case p.* (Nara) indicates **1.** starting point (for some action). **2.** point of transit. **3.** means (of doing something).

YU ゆ *aux. v.* (Nara) indicates **1.** passive. **2.** potential. **3.** spontaneity.

yū いう (有) *n.* **1.** existence. **2.** possession, property. (*HJ*)

***YŪ** いう (優) *nari adj. v.* **1.** splendid. **2.** elegant, refined. (*HJ, TM*)

yū ゆふ (結ふ) *See* **yu-u.**

YŪBE ゆふべ (夕べ) *n.* evening, dusk. (*TM*)

***YUE** ゆゑ (故) *n.* **1.** reason, cause, circumstances. **2.** atmosphere, charm, elegance. **3.** origins, lineage, status. **4.** malfunction, obstacle, interference. **5.** connection, karmic bond. **6.** (following nominals or RT) due to, as a result, even though, in spite of. (*HI, HJ, TM*)

***YŪGEN** いうげん (幽玄) *n., nari adj. v.* **1.** mystery and depth. **2.** elegance, refinement. **3.** quiet, lonely beauty.

yū-gure ゆふぐれ (夕暮) *n.* evening, nightfall. (*MS*)

yu-gyō-su ゆぎやうす (遊行す) *intr. v. SH* **1.** (Buddhist) to travel (e.g., on a pilgrimage) for the purpose of worshipping, proselytizing, etc. **2.** to walk around, stroll. (*HJ*)

yū-hi ゆふひ (夕日) *n.* evening sun, setting sun. (*MS*)

YUKARI ゆかり (縁) *n.* bond, connection, affinity. (*SN*)

***YUKA-SHI** ゆかし *shiku adj.* **1.** intriguing, attractive (causing one to want to see, hear, or know). **2.** causing longing, nostalgia. (*GM, SN*)

yuka-shi-sa ゆかしさ *n.* [fr. adj. *yukashi* and suffix *sa*] **1.** attraction, desire to see, hear, or learn about. **2.** nostalgia. (*SN*)

yuki ゆき (雪) *n.* snow. (*HI*)

yuki-ka-u ゆきかふ (行き交ふ) *intr. v. YD* to come and go. (*HJ*)

***YU-KU** ゆく (行く) *intr. v. YD* **1.** to go, proceed toward. **2.** to pass by. **3.** to leave, depart. **4.** (of clouds, water, etc.) to flow by. **5.** to die, pass away. **6.** to be satisfied with. (*HI, HJ, MY*)

yuku-e ゆくへ (行方) *n.* **1.** direction, destination. **2.** future, outcome. (*HM, TZ*)

***YUKURI-NASHI** ゆくりなし *ku adj.* suddenly, unexpectedly.

*YUME ゆめ (夢) *n.* **1.** dream. **2.** (metaphor) dreamlike reality, ephemera. **3.** (followed by *bakari*) just a little. (*IM*)

yume ゆめ (努・勤) *adv.* (followed by prohibition) absolutely (not).

yume-yume ゆめゆめ (努努・勤勤) *adv.* **1.** strong prohibition: absolutely, never (followed by prohibition). **2.** strong negative: (not) in the least (followed by neg.). (*HM*)

yumiya-tori ゆみやとり (弓矢取り) *n.* warrior. (*HM*)

yu-mizu ゆみづ (湯水) *n.* hot water (for bathing). (*TM*)

yūnami-chidori ゆふなみちどり (夕波千鳥) *n.* (poetic phrase) plovers that fly above the waves in the evening. (*MY*)

yura-yura-to ゆらゆらと *adv.* **1.** waving or moving gently in the air or on top of the water. **2.** gradually, leisurely. (*GM*)

yuri ゆり *case p.* (Nara) indicates starting point, point of transit.

yuru-bu ゆるぶ (緩ぶ・弛ぶ) *intr. v. YD* [fr. ゆるふ] **1.** to ease or loosen up, subside. **2.** to become lax, negligent. **3.** to relax. (*MS*)

yuru-gu ゆるぐ (揺るぐ) *intr. v. YD* **1.** to totter, waver. **2.** to change one's mind. **3.** to relax, take it easy. (*MS*)

yururu-ka ゆるるか (緩るか) (also *yururaka*) *nari adj. v.* **1.** loose. **2.** relaxed, leisurely. **3.** slow, unhurried. (*GM*)

*YURU-SU ゆるす (許す) *tr. v. YD* **1.** to untie, loosen. **2.** to set free. **3.** to accept a request. **4.** to pardon. **5.** to recognize (excellence, value). (*HJ, TM*)

yutaka ゆたか (豊) *nari adj. v.* [fr. adj. v. *yuta*, "comfortable," and suffix *ka*] **1.** wealthy, prosperous. **2.** leisurely, easygoing, comfortable, at ease. (*TM*)

YU-U ゆふ (結ふ) *tr. v. YD* **1.** to tie, bind. **2.** to fix up one's hair. **3.** to construct, assemble, build. **4.** to sew. (*TM*)

yu-ya ゆや (湯屋) *n.* **1.** bathhouse. **2.** bath. (*US*)

*YU-YU-SHI ゆゆし (忌々し) *shiku adj.* **1.** godlike, awesome, frightening. **2.** inauspicious, unlucky. **3.** extreme. **4.** beautiful (so much so that it causes anxiety or dread).

yu-zu ゆづ (茹づ) *tr. v. SN* **1.** to cook in boiling water. **2.** to bathe a wound in hot water. (*US*)

yuzu-ru ゆづる (譲る) *tr. v. YD* to turn over, transfer, yield. (*HJ*)

*ZAE ざえ (才) *n.* **1.** education, knowledge (specifically, of Chinese.). **2.** talent, skill (in calligraphy, *waka*, music, etc.).

zai-gō ざいごふ (罪業) *n.* (Buddhist) sin, karmic burden. (*HJ*)

zai-hō ざいほう (財宝) *n.* treasure. (*HJ*)

zai-shō ざいしやう (罪障) *n.* sins, obstacles to rebirth. (*HJ*)

zai-zai-sho-sho ざいざいしよしよ (在々所々) *n.* everywhere, all over the place. (*HJ*)

za-shiki ざしき (座敷) *n.* **1.** place to sit, seat. **2.** dining room. **3.** waiting room. (*NE*)

za-tto ざつと *adv.* **1.** (onomatopoeia) plunging in (to water) suddenly, with a splash. **2.** approximately, roughly. (*HM*)

zek-kon ぜつこん (舌根) *n.* (Buddhist) tongue and its functions, sense of taste (one of the six senses). (*HJ, US*)

zen-ji ぜんじ (前司) *n.* (same as *senji*) former provincial official. (*MS*)

*ZO ぞ *bound p.* **1.** (sentence ends with RT) emphatic: calls attention to the subject of the sentence, object of a v., etc. **2.** (at end of a sentence) declarative: carries the force of a copula.

zoku ぞく (粟) *n.* **1.** grain, provisions. **2.** millet (*awa*). (*HJ*)

zoku-jin ぞくぢん (俗塵) *n.* (lit., dust of the world) worldly affairs. (*HJ*)

zō-me ざうめ (象馬) *n.* elephants and horses, metaphor for valuable property. (*HJ*)

zomeki ぞめき（騒き）　*n.* [fr. n. *someki*] merry-making, bustle, activity. (*HJ*)

zō-ni ざふに（雑煮）　*n.* soup prepared with rice cakes and vegetables to celebrate the New Year. (*NE*)

zō-sui ざふすい（雑炊）　*n.* porridge made with vegetables. (*NE*)

*ZU ず　*aux. v.* (follows MZ) negative: not.

zui-sō ずいさう（瑞相）　*n.* **1.** auspicious sign. **2.** omen, portent (positive or negative). (*HJ*)

Also by Haruo Shirane

The Bridge of Dreams: A Poetics of The Tale of Genji
Traces of Dreams: Landscape, Cultural Memory, and the Poetry of Bashō
Inventing the Classics: Modernity, National Identity, and Japanese Literature
Early Modern Japanese Literature: An Anthology, 1600–1900
Traditional Japanese Literature: An Anthology, Beginnings to 1600
Classical Japanese: A Grammar